Tales of Transmigration - Sisters

Tales of Transmigration - Sisters

Elena Clark

Cover design by Michelle Vymenetz

authorHOUSE®

AuthorHouse™
1663 Liberty Drive
Bloomington, IN 47403
www.authorhouse.com
Phone: 1-800-839-8640

Published by AuthorHouse 09/18/13

ISBN: 978-1-4918-0170-3 (sc)
ISBN: 978-1-4918-0169-7 (e)

Library of Congress Control Number: 2013913099

Cover design by Michelle Vymenetz

Table of Contents

Babi Yar

THEY MET WHILE waiting in line. It was a grim line, starting from
Artem Street and winding down the entire length of Lukyanovka,
the old part of Kiev. It extended all the way to a forested area with a
large ravine. The ravine was called Babi Yar. That was where the line
ended.

The year was 1941. The two five-year-old girls didn't know their
destination but they could feel the tension, even despair, emanating
from their grandmothers.

Manya was holding the hand of her grandmother Anna, a middle-
aged and still good-looking woman. The resemblance between
grandmother and granddaughter was astonishing - the same round
face, the same hazel eyes, and the same shade of red hair. Manya's uncle
Kolya was standing nearby. Mother and son were having a conversation
similar to the ones they had already had several times before on that
day.

"Kolenka," Manya's grandmother was pleading with her son, "I'm
scared. Can't you hide us somewhere? Can't you take us from here?"

"Mama, what are you talking about? The Germans have already
registered you. It's even dangerous for me to stay here and talk to you
right now."

"Kolya, can't you at least take Manya?"

"Mama, I can't. Just look at her. She looks exactly like you - so
Jewish! And you've read the posters that the Germans put up on almost
every wall: *Any person who illegally harbours Jews will be executed.* I have
two children of my own to worry about. Do you want anything
happen to them, eh? They're your grandchildren as well.

1

"Stop worrying so much. For some reason the Germans want all the Jews to live in the same place. It's not even certain that the place will be all that bad. And after all, Galina asked you to take care of Manya, didn't she? She'd be very cross if I were to take Manya from you. Now I must be going." Nikolai quickly kissed his mother on the cheek and withdrew from the line.

"Hey, you! Where are you going? Back in line!" shouted a German soldier in broken Ukrainian.

"No, no! I'm not a Jew! I was just saying goodbye to our neighbours, that's all. Here are my papers!" stammered Nikolai. "These people are my neighbours, just neighbours!"

The German summoned a Ukrainian gendarme who took the papers and read aloud, "Nikolai Fedorovich Karpenko. Born - April 17, 1915. Nationality - Ukrainian."

He looked carefully at the blond, blue-eyed Nikolai and said, "He's okay."

"Then get out of here! Now! Fast!" the German soldier commanded.

Manya wanted to say, *He is not our neighbour! He's my uncle! My mommy's twin brother!* But she didn't say anything; she just observed how her dear uncle scurried away into the crowd of onlookers.

"Is that your son?" a lady who stood nearby asked. The woman looked a bit older than Manya's grandma and was much heavier and dressed much fancier. She was holding a young girl about Manya's age by the hand. The girl was looking intently at Manya.

"Yes," grandma quietly answered, "he and my daughter Galina are twins. I have one more son, Phillip. My husband and Phillip are in Sverdlovsk. They were among the first to leave Kiev because they were helping to evacuate the machinery and equipment from their plant. We were supposed to go with them, but Manya had a terrible cold. It turned into pneumonia. She needed medication and had to stay in bed. She had such a high fever that I couldn't take her on the train. When she recovered we were supposed to evacuate with Kolya and his family, but he was hesitant to leave Kiev and then it was too late…"

"Where are Manya's parents?" the lady asked.

"They joined the army as soon as the war started. Galina's a nurse. Ivan, Manya's father, is a carpenter. I'm sure he'll be as good a soldier as he was a carpenter," Anna said proudly. "How about you? What's your name?" Anna asked.

"Mila Semenovna. It's actually Malka, but everybody calls me Mila. It's more Russian, you know. I have one grown daughter, Vera. My husband of blessed memory passed away when Vera was only five years old and I never remarried. Vera's an engineer now."

Mila Semenovna was evidently very proud of her daughter. "Vera married a military man. He's an officer; already a captain."

The woman quickly glanced at her granddaughter and then continued, almost in a whisper. "Or was a captain. Who knows if he's alive or dead? He was stationed in Latvia. They were attacked, one of the first... Anyway, Vera has two children: Dima, he's nine, and Raya," the lady nodded at the girl, "she's five. At the beginning of the summer Vera brought Raya to spend two months with me. I wanted to take both children but Dimochka wanted to go to summer camp. Vera was supposed to take Raya back in the middle of August, but now I don't know where Vera, Dima or Boris, my son-in-law, might be."

The line slowly inched forward. The girls became tired of listening to their grandmothers and started their own conversation. Within mere minutes they became good friends. They even managed to play some simple children's games.

Finally they reached the edge of the forest. They could hear screaming and crying, yelling and shooting. The girls became frightened and clutched their grandmothers. Their suitcases were taken from them and thrown into a huge pile.

They were ordered to strip naked. The girls did as they were told and looked around. Naked and frightened people surrounded them: old men, women, and many more children. Twelve of them were being formed into a separate line and led to the bottom of the ravine. Everyone was crying.

There were German soldiers milling about, but most of the guarding and rounding up of the Jews was being performed by Ukrainian gendarmes.

At the bottom of the ravine there were bodies everywhere. The floor of the ravine was crimson from all of the spilled blood. Some of the poor souls were still alive but badly wounded. Some were screaming, some moaning.

Terrified, Raya quietly whispered to Manya, "We're going to die now."

"I'm scared," Manya replied in a very subdued voice. She stumbled but was helped back on her feet by her grandmother.

"Faster, faster!" the gendarme closest to them shouted. Manya quickly glanced at her would-be executioner, and even in her frightened state she clearly noticed that he was a young man with a round, boyish face. He was close enough for Manya to notice that his eyes were somewhat wild, as if aflame with excitement and anticipation. He was smiling. For a brief moment the eyes of the victim and executioner met.

"Grandma, look at that man," Manya whispered. "He's going to kill me."

The Jews were ordered to lie face-down on the top of other bodies.

Anna shook her granddaughter and urgently whispered, "Manya, I will distract them. Bury yourself under these bodies. Try to hide. You must live, Manechka."

Mila Semenovna, upon hearing Anna's whisper, repeated the same instructions. "Raya, hide with Manechka."

A command was repeated and wailing people started to lie down, waiting to be shot in the back of the head. All of a sudden there was a commotion and instead of lying down, Anna attacked the closest soldier. She scratched and bit him. She was screaming like a banshee. Mila Semenovna hurled herself into another soldier.

For a few moments the order of the proceedings was interrupted, and during that chaos, the two little girls hid under other, still-warm bodies. They heard the screams of their grandmothers, but then they heard shots ringing out and their grandmothers fell.

Even in her last moments, Anna thought about her granddaughter. She stretched her hand out, so as not to fall directly onto the girl. "You live, Manechka, you must live," Anna whispered... and then she was quiet.

The rest of the group that came together with them to the bottom of the ravine were promptly killed. Nobody noticed the two girls who remained obscured from view.

The girls, terrified of being seen, crawled under the bodies of their grandmothers and lay completely still. They furtively looked up toward the top of the ravine. The soldiers had gone away, evidently to fetch the next group of victims. The Ukrainian gendarmes had gathered together above the ravine and the girls could see them lighting their cigarettes. The girls quickly looked at each other, nodded, and slithered away, ever so slowly away from their dead grandmothers.

The execution process was repeated with the next group. The girls again crawled under the dead, trying not to be smothered by the bodies and not to be noticed. In a lapse between the shootings the girls again crawled closer to the far side of the ravine.

Raya, all her senses heightened, had noticed a concrete pipe, almost completely covered over by bushes, protruding from the sidewall of the ravine. She didn't know if it was a sewer pipe or the remains of some unsuccessful construction project, nor did she care.

"Manya, let's run and hide in that pipe," Raya whispered.

"I'm scared, Raya. They'll see us."

"Give me your hand, Manya. Let's run together. Now!"

The girls locked their hands and sprinted. The pipe would have been too small for a grown person, but the five-year-old girls easily crawled into the open end and nestled inside as deep as they could.

"We need to cover the opening of the pipe," Manya whispered and Raya, being closer to the entrance, rearranged the undergrowth of bushes, thereby concealing the pipe opening more fully.

There, naked and covered in the blood of the Jewish people, the girls sat silently together and waited for darkness.

At dusk the ritual of mass executions ceased. However, instead of quietness, the girls could hear more shootings that were much closer to them. The gendarmes and soldiers had descended into the ravine. They were milling about, listening for moans and killing the wounded. Some pointed their rifles and began stabbing their victims with the sharp spikes mounted on the end of their rifles, making sure that all of the victims were dead. If they saw movement or heard a moan, they would stab again and again until that person fell quiet and still.

The girls were trembling from fright and cold. They were hugging one-another tightly and trying not to breathe when the murderers were closest to their hiding place.

Finally, the ghastly massacre was over for the day and the executioners left the ravine. Then the girls heard the rumble of heavy trucks as one after the other, each truck, loaded with earth, began dumping its contents over the dead bodies.

Eventually, an eerie silence fell over Babi Yar. The girls cautiously got out from their hiding place and quickly climbed towards the top of the ravine. The branches of the bushes growing on the slope of the ravine slashed at their naked bodies and their feet were cut by the small, sharp rocks. They didn't allow themselves to slow down, except once when Manya almost lost her footing, Raya stopped and pulled her friend forward. When they reached the crest, the girls could see flashlights and hear the sound of the voices of night guards. They ran in the opposite direction from the voices and continued to run for as long as they could. Finally they stopped under a large tree. The streets of Kiev were very quiet.

"Where are we going to go now?" Raya asked. "I don't know Kiev. I don't even live here."

"We could go to my grandma's apartment. It's not far from here," Manya responded. "I think I could figure out where it is. But I don't like her neighbour, Aunt Shura. She was always screaming at grandma, 'Hey, dirty Jew, get out of the kitchen when I'm cooking! I don't want my food to smell like yours'."

"We can't go there! She'll hand us right back to the Germans," Raya said, shaking her head.

"You're right!" Manya exclaimed. "There's a school nearby. My mother went there when she was a girl. We might even find some clothes there. Let's go!"

"Wait girls," implored a nearby, quiet male voice. The girls were terrified and started to sprint away but the man continued, "Don't go there. The Germans took over School Number Seventy. I think they turned it into some offices or a dormitory for soldiers. I know this because I was a teacher of history at that school and I tried to go there to get some of my books. Anyway, it's the last place you should go. You had better come with me instead. You'll have to trust somebody if you want to survive. My name is Michael Aleksandrovich. Here, take this." The man removed his jacket and wrapped it over the girls' shoulders.

"What are your names?" he asked.

"Manya."

"Raya."

"We had better hurry along," the teacher said and began leading the way. The girls obediently followed.

About fifteen minutes later they arrived at a small, private house. Michael Aleksandrovich didn't approach the front door but instead opened a gate leading to the backyard. The girls trailed after him to the back door and they all entered the house.

Later on they would learn that they had accessed the house via a summer kitchen that Michael Aleksandrovich and his son, Sasha, had built several years before. The teacher's late wife used to be an excellent cook and usually spent all summer cooking jams and preserves for the winter. She used to pickle barrels of tomatoes, cucumbers, and cabbage, and needed a place to store all of her preserves. And so, Michael Aleksandrovich and Sasha had built a large cellar under the summer kitchen.

The old teacher opened a trapdoor and the girls made their way down the stairs. They immediately felt the chill and the stagnant, musty air of the cellar. Michael Aleksandrovich followed after them. The small cellar was already occupied by a number of other frightened people.

"Okay, Yulya," the teacher said to a dark-haired girl sitting there, "I've brought you some new friends. Why don't you give them something to wear?"

"Uncle Misha," the girl whined, "they're my clothes, why should I...?"

"Yulya!" the teacher commanded in a stern voice.

"Okay." Reluctantly, the girl went to a corner of the cellar, opened her suitcase and took out some clothes for the new arrivals. She was a pretty girl, with curly long hair, a dark complexion, rosy cheeks and plumb red lips. But now her face had a sullen expression and her lips trembled with anger. She was not happy to share her clothes with these two strange girls. She chose two of her oldest and dullest dresses and passed them to Manya and Raya.

The girls accepted the clothes, grateful to have something to wear, but were accosted by an elderly Jewish woman. "Wait. You two are all covered in blood," she said. "Are you badly wounded, sisters?"

"No, it's the blood of our grandmothers and other people who were killed today in the ravine," Manya replied.

"We aren't sisters. We only met today," Raya added, and then suddenly both girls burst into tears.

"But I want to be your sister," Manya was crying.

"And I want to be yours," Raya responded.

Someone passed them a pail of water and somebody else found a clean rag. The old woman began gently sponging the trembling little bodies, cleaning them of the caked blood.

For the first time, Michael Aleksandrovich could take a good look at his new charges. Both girls had red hair and hazel eyes, but there the similarity ended. Manya was short and rotund and very pretty. Her wavy, strawberry-blond hair softly framed her round face and accentuated her beautiful large eyes. There were several freckles around her cute nose which added a final charming touch to an adorable small girl.

Raya was tall and skinny and looked large for her five years. Her vibrant red hair was frizzy and cut short. Her entire face was covered by freckles, but the most distinguishing feature of Raya's face was her large, prominent nose.

The girls were washed, dried and quickly dressed. The people around them knew how tired the girls must have been, but they wanted to hear their story. All of those people, with the exception of a young woman and her infant child, had been confined to this cellar since early morning and didn't have the slightest idea what was happening on the outside.

Michael Aleksandrovich wanted to spare the girls from reliving their horror, but he knew people had a right to know. He wanted to know too. He had seen the gathering of the Jews into a long line, their marches into the forest, and had heard the shooting and feared the worst. But now, listening to the girls recounting the horror of the events in the Babi Yar ravine, including the deaths of their grandmothers and their own harrowing escape, he was appalled by the magnitude of the slaughter.

The people gathered around Manya and Raya began weeping. Two other young girls, sisters of around fifteen and seventeen years old, hugged each other and started to wail uncontrollably. An old Jewish man began praying devoutly. Only the young woman with the infant didn't react. She was rocking her baby and trying to give him her breast. "Eat, little one. Please eat. Eat just a little bit, baby boy, please eat for mama."

The baby was silent and motionless. "What's wrong with that lady?" Raya asked. "Why is she repeating the same thing? Maybe the baby needs to sleep."

The old woman just hugged Raya more closely.

"Her baby is dead," Michael Aleksandrovich explained.

"How did it happen?" Manya asked.

"You have had enough for one day," the teacher replied cautiously.

"How did it happen?" Manya repeated stubbornly.

"This baby's mother was walking in the line with her family toward the forest. She spotted another woman at the side of the road and started to cry out, *You were my friend. We grew up together. Save my son!* Then she thrust her baby into the arms of the other woman and started to walk away. The woman yelled, *I'm not going to die because of your Jewish bastard,* and threw the baby aside. The baby struck the hard asphalt before his mother or anybody else could break his fall. The poor mother ran back and picked up the child. In the chaos I pushed them into the crowd and led them away. The baby was still whimpering. I had hoped something could be done but the infant died soon after we came here. His mother doesn't want to give him up."

"Michael Aleksandrovich, why are people so cruel? Why are they so bad?" Manya asked in despair.

"Manechka, not all people are bad. There are a lot of good people in Kiev. Even now as we speak, I'm sure there are a lot of Jews being hidden away by good Ukrainian people." The teacher was trying to reassure the girls but Manya began shaking her head.

"My uncle put my grandma and me in that line. He didn't try to hide us away. And that man who killed my grandma and wanted to kill me, he was laughing even when he was shooting!" Manya whispered and began to cry again.

Michael Aleksandrovich couldn't even begin to comprehend the magnitude of the ordeal that the two little girls had to endure. In one day they lost not only their grandmothers but also their trust in humankind. They had witnessed unthinkable horror and had been forced to suddenly grow up and face an adult world in all its brutality.

He was overwhelmed with feelings of sorrow, pity and protectiveness. He wanted to give them something, anything, to compensate for their loss. These girls had nobody else to turn to. Their parents were at the front and even if they survived, how would those parents ever find their daughters again? All that they had now was each other. He thought for a moment and said, "You know what I think, girls? You were covered in the blood of your grandmothers, in the blood of the Jewish people. It made you sisters - blood sisters."

The two young girls hugged and kissed one-another. The teacher's words somehow helped.

Eventually, the people in the cellar fell quiet and Manya and Raya dozed off. But the young mother was still trying to feed her dead son. "Eat, little one, please eat," she continued to implore. By the morning she too had stopped talking.

Manya and Raya awoke to the sobbing of the people around them. They heard one woman saying to another, "And I thought that the words *dying from grief* were simply an expression. Poor thing!"

"She willed herself to die," another woman sighed.

"How could she will anything? She lost her mind yesterday. She was mad," an old man whispered and then resumed his praying.

The girls looked in the left corner and saw that there was a white sheet covering the young woman and her infant child.

Michael Aleksandrovich was not in the cellar. Manya and Raya were offered bread, but they couldn't eat. They just hugged one-another and sat on the end of a wooden bench very quietly. Yulia came to them and said, "I'm scared." The girls moved a bit and Yulia sat down near them.

Michael Aleksandrovich returned to the cellar around noon. "We must take them outside. We must bury them," somebody said, gesturing towards the dead bodies.

"We will have to wait for darkness. The Germans are carrying on the massacre again today. It's much worse than yesterday in the streets. At least yesterday the Jews didn't know what to expect. Today, they do. Somehow, the story leaked out. We must wait until night-time."

The teenage girls were hugging and trying to comfort each other, but time from time they were starting to sob anew.

Throughout the day, Manya and Raya learned the stories of their cellar-mates.

The teenage girls had been students of Michael Aleksandrovich. The older one was in grade ten and her sister in grade eight. The prior morning, their mother had told them to go to their teacher and ask him for advice about the relocation procedures. He was the only person whom their mother trusted. The girls wanted their mother to go with them but she couldn't leave their infirm grandfather alone. The sisters had planned to just ask for advice and return home. Instead, their teacher urged them to stay put in his cellar. He then went to fetch their mother but she was already in the line with her father. All that Michael Aleksandrovich could do was to explain to her through gestures from a distance that her daughters were hidden away safely.

Next to the sisters there sat a fifteen-year-old boy with his mother. He was another student of Michael Aleksandrovich. Yesterday morning, he had persuaded his mother to go and ask his teacher for refuge. The teenage sisters were looking at their former schoolmate, feeling guilty for not having saved their own mother and grandfather as well.

The old woman who had washed Manya and Raya the night before was a school nurse. The old man was her husband and he used to work in the same school as a janitor. Their son and daughter were in the Red Army. When the posters, instructing all Jews to proceed to a designated gathering place on Artem Street, went up on the walls of Kiev, they immediately sought out their neighbour, Michael Aleksandrovich, for help.

There was also a young, pregnant woman who was taking care not to look in the corner at the sheet-covered bodies. She was patting her huge belly and quietly whispering, "You will live, my darling. Mommy will take care of you. And Daddy will come back soon with victory. We'll be okay, my love."

"Is she mad as well?" Raya asked the old woman quietly.

"No, she's fine. It's quite normal for pregnant women to talk to their unborn children."

Then there was Yulia, the girl who gave Manya and Raya their dresses. She referred to Michael Aleksandrovich as *Uncle Misha* and behaved as if she was right at home. She was the only one who had a suitcase stuffed with clothes.

"Why does she call you Uncle Misha? Can we call you Uncle Misha too?" Manya asked the teacher.

"Uncle Misha's my neighbour," Yulia explained. "My mama left me with him for the entire summer when she went to see my papa last May. My papa is an important engineer and he's building a new plant in the north of Russia," she said proudly, and then sadly added, "my mama was supposed to pick me up in August."

"Okay, girls," Michael Aleksandrovich agreed in a kind voice. "You can both call me Uncle Misha too."

The refugees gathered in the cellar were terrified of what they heard about the events taking place outside and of the dead bodies lying visibly so close to them; and so, to somehow suppress their fears, they were constantly talking amongst themselves. They were telling their cellar-mates, these people who were total strangers the day before, about their families and their life stories, and it seemed to them very natural to speak openly. In just one day, they had become a family amongst themselves. Eventually it was the turn for Manya and Raya to talk about their families.

"Manechka," the boy's mother asked, "you mentioned last night that your uncle put you in the line. Was he the son-in-law of your grandmother?"

"No, he was her son." Manya had to explain that her grandfather was Ukrainian; it was only her grandma Anna who was a Jew.

"And what's your father's name?" the woman asked.

"Ivan Stepanovich Matveev," Manya answered.

"So, you're only a quarter Jewish! Poor child! You shouldn't have been there in that hellish line at all!" the woman exclaimed.

Manya thought about that for a long while. Then she pursed her fingers before her, concentrated and tried to calculate something by bending and straightening out her fingers. Finally, she shook her head and said, "I don't think that I'm a quarter of a Jew. I think I'm completely a Jew."

The woman tried to explain to the young girl about the mix of her bloodline. "Your father is Russian, your mother's father is Ukrainian, and your mother's mama is Jewish. It means that you are only about one-quarter Jewish, one-quarter Ukrainian, and half-Russian. Do you understand this?"

Manya's eyes became very large and she looked at the woman directly with utmost attentiveness. Then she sighed and pronounced her verdict. "When the Germans put me in the line they didn't put only a quarter of me in, they wanted all of me to be in that line. And when that gendarme looked at me and raised his rifle, he didn't want to kill just a quarter of me, he wanted to kill all of *me* - Manya. All of me. It means that all of me is really Jewish."

The woman couldn't contradict such logic and simply nodded silently.

The girls also learned that Uncle Misha's wife had died two years earlier, and that Uncle Misha had one son, Aleksander (Sasha), who was in the army and away somewhere at the front.

When darkness descended over Kiev, Uncle Misha, the boy, and the old man took the dead bodies outside. They were absent for quite a while, then they returned and reported, "We have given them a proper burial."

And that night nobody wanted to claim the vacant corner which the young mother and her child had occupied.

Life In The Cellar

FOR THE NEXT week, Uncle Misha did his best to provide for the daily needs of his cellar-dwelling guests, but it soon became evident that something more had to be done. Winter was looming and the cellar was built to stay cold, even in the summer. Uncle Misha got a job as a gardener in the Kiev Botanical Gardens but the meagre food allowance that he received couldn't possibly suffice for eleven people. Even the food that was still preserved in the cellar couldn't help much. Michael Aleksandrovich had saved his charges from Babi Yar, not to have them die from starvation or freeze to death in his cellar.

The following week, Uncle Misha came to the cellar accompanied by a young Ukrainian woman. "This lady is one of my former students and she's a good woman. She has promised to help me," he explained.

The woman looked directly at the expectant mother and said, "I have a cousin in Ternopol. My neighbours know about her but have never seen her before. If I change your hairdo and give you some of my clothes, you'd look more or less Ukrainian... I'm sure that I can make it work. Let's go."

The pregnant woman quickly bade her cellar-mates goodbye and left with her new-found *cousin*.

The teenage sisters were the next to go. Uncle Misha had met an old female colleague, another teacher, in the market. The poor woman's only daughter had recently passed away. When Uncle Misha told her about the two beautiful sisters hidden in his cellar, she volunteered to take them in. "I have a large attic in my home," she assured Uncle Misha. "They can stay there. I'll treat them as my own daughters.

Please, let me do it, Michael Aleksandrovich; otherwise my life has no purpose."

Uncle Misha believed her and the very next night he escorted the two teenage sisters to their new home.

A further week passed and Uncle Misha then found a home for the boy and his mother. Another former student who was living just outside of Kiev, in the town of Vorzel, had promised to harbour and provide for the mother and her son.

The remaining tenants of the cellar started to prepare for the winter. Uncle Misha had located some plywood, some wooden planks, and some insulation material. Together with the old janitor, Chaim, they built new walls in the cellar and constructed bunk beds for the three girls. Uncle Misha gathered apples from his garden and Auntie Eva (as the girls called the old nurse) made apple preserves.

One day, Uncle Misha appeared with a huge, fifty kilo sack of potatoes. "It's good to have a lot of students who remember you," was all that Uncle Misha said.

With the immediate logistics resolved, Uncle Misha organized a schedule for his tenants so they all might get some fresh air. Every night, Uncle Chaim and Yulia went out for a half-hour. They would return, and then Auntie Eva would take the sisters (as everybody referred to Raya and Manya) outside. After half-an-hour, Uncle Misha would call them back inside.

In the evenings after work, Uncle Misha studied with the girls. He taught them to read, write, and to do arithmetic. At the end of the lessons, he always gave them a lot of homework to keep them occupied for the next day.

In the morning, the girls would get dressed in Uncle Misha's huge, warm sweaters and do their homework. It became apparent almost immediately that Raya was the smartest of the girls; Manya was the most diligent, while Yulia was astute enough to know that she needed to do her work or face the disapproval of her teacher. Uncle Misha never punished the girls and never raised his voice to them. One of his raised eyebrows was sufficient to make the girls realize when their work was not on a par with his expectations.

Manya and Raya loved their Uncle Misha very much. They eagerly waited for Sundays when he would teach them their favourite subject: history. Raya wanted to understand how wars started and why countries needed to fight each other. Manya's interest was more focused: she wanted to understand why the Germans wanted to kill the Jews, what made Jews different, and what it really meant to be a Jew.

And so, this Ukrainian man, Michael Aleksandrovich, spent untold hours telling the sisters the history of the Jewish people. He told them about the slavery in Egypt, the story of the Exodus, and about their unwavering belief in one G-d and the Torah given by Him to His prophet Moses. The most difficult part for Michael Aleksandrovich was in adapting the complex stories to the level of understanding of the five-year-olds. After all, despite their horrific experience, they were still only little girls. Uncle Misha didn't want to traumatize them further by introducing concepts that would be too difficult for them to comprehend, but from another side, he wanted them to truly appreciate the history of their people.

Uncle Misha told the girls about the persecution of the Jews in the Middle Ages during the Inquisition and about the Tsarist pogroms. He also told them about the involvement of the Jews in all aspects of human history, including their many contributions to science, the arts, and politics.

Raya and Yulia couldn't understand Manya's fascination with the subject. They knew that they were Jews and accepted the good and bad of being a Jew as something inevitable. For Manya, however, it was altogether different. She had never been exposed to Judaism or a Jewish way of life. No Jewish traditions had ever been observed in her family. Her father referred to her grand-aunt Rivkah and grand-uncle Baruch as 'Jews', but that designation never was applied to Manya herself. Now she was constantly thinking about her ancestors, asking Auntie Eva and Uncle Chaim about their traditions and their holidays, and without even realizing it, Manya was making a real commitment to being a Jew.

In the autumn of 1942, Uncle Misha found another place for Uncle Chaim and Auntie Eva to live. Food was becoming scarcer and he was exceedingly worried that there wouldn't be enough to feed six people.

One day he went to the local market to buy something for their next meal. He was standing near the vegetable stand contemplating the fact that the quality of the products was steadily going down while the prices were skyrocketing. All of a sudden, he heard someone calling out his name. Michael Aleksandrovich turned around and was pleasantly surprised to see that an old doctor who had been working before the war in a local clinic was walking towards him.

"Michael Aleksandrovich, how are you? So, you didn't evacuate. As you can see, we're stuck in Kiev as well. Do you remember my wife?" The doctor gestured towards the woman beside him.

"Of course I do," Michael Aleksandrovich replied and warmly shook hands with the doctor and his wife.

He noticed that they had aged a great deal, were dressed in ragged, simple clothes, and that the doctor held a walking cane in his hand. Michael Aleksandrovich had known this couple for ages. The doctor had been treating his family members ever since he was a teenage boy. The doctor's wife used to be an elegant brunette, admired for her style and beauty. But standing before him now was a gray-haired, wrinkled woman with a stooped back.

Michael Aleksandrovich was glad to see familiar faces and tried to conceal the pity he felt towards the old couple. The war was not easy on anyone.

"What brings you to this part of town?" he asked. "Isn't it a bit too far from your apartment? I thought you were living in the center of the city, near Khreschatik."

"We exchanged our apartment for a small house. Now we're your neighbours," the doctor explained in a weary, dejected voice.

"I still miss our apartment. I raised my children there. I loved it," his wife commented, "but we just couldn't stay there any longer." She sounded just as depressed as her husband.

"May I ask why?" Michael Aleksandrovich carefully inquired.

"Because of the shame! Shame and guilt," the doctor responded with surprising passion. "Do you really want to know why we had to leave the place where we had lived for over thirty years?"

They walked together to the nearby park, sat down on a bench and the doctor told Michael Aleksandrovich their story.

"There were three families living in our apartment, sharing the same kitchen and washroom. Each of the families had two rooms. Our flat was on the left, there were an engineer and his wife on the right, and a dentist in the middle flat. We were all good friends, raised our children together, celebrated family birthdays and the holidays together, and even sent our grown-up sons to the front at the same time," the doctor recounted.

"Do you remember, Misha, when you had that horrible toothache and came to my apartment almost at midnight?"

"Sure I do," Michael Aleksandrovich replied. "Your dentist neighbour, Arkady Issakovich, treated me right then and there. The pain was excruciating; I thought I would die that night!"

"He was a good man," the doctor's wife sighed.

The doctor looked at his wife sternly and then resumed his story. "When the Jews were instructed to gather in Artem Street, Arkady Issakovich and his wife gave us the keys for their apartment and asked us to take care of it for them. We promised that we would. We all gathered in the kitchen and there were tearful farewells. As soon as they left, Klava, the engineer's wife, suggested that we should take over their apartment *until their return*. Her logic was that if we didn't do it while we had an opportunity, some other total stranger would move into those quarters.

"Misha, I must confess that at that moment, the third room seemed like a godsend. And while Arkady Issakovich and Sofia Semenovna, his wife, were still being marched towards Babi Yar, we called a handyman who was instructed to close off the door from their flat to the hall and to construct new doorways between our flat and the dentist's flat. Then he was to make the same change between the dentist's second room and Klava's flat. As a result, instead of three flats, two rooms each, there would be two flats, each with three adjoining rooms.

"Then my wife," the doctor began as he glared again at the woman who was cringing sheepishly, "and Klava divided Sofia's clothes between themselves. The next day I found out about what was happening at Babi Yar and went home to tell everybody. The handyman was already working on the remodelling of our apartment and I found my wife dressed in Sofia Semenovna's dress and shoes."

The doctor's wife started to sob and then she stammered, "I don't know what came over me! I had always admired Sofia's clothes and her impeccable taste, but that doesn't excuse me. On that day, I was so happy to put on her best dress and to admire myself in the mirror. But when I found out what had become of her and her husband, I took off that dress and those shoes and gave all the clothes to Klava. She was jubilant to inherit all of Sofia's outfits and what's more, she was happy that nobody would ever take the third room from her."

"We simply couldn't live there any longer," the doctor said, "and it was easy to find an exchange. Misha, I'm asking you as one Ukrainian man to another Ukrainian man: how could this massacre happen in our homeland? Why didn't we do anything to protect those innocent people? We could say we didn't know, but on some level we knew. It is said that over thirty thousand Jews have perished and we were just glad to get an extra room!"

After a long silence, Michael Aleksandrovich carefully responded. "There may have been people who did do something. There were many more than thirty thousand Jews living in Kiev when the occupation began."

"What are you trying to say?" The doctor wanted to be sure that he understood correctly. He was whispering now. "Are there still some Jews in Kiev? Are there people who are actually hiding them?"

"If you know somebody who is caring for more than one family of Jews, Michael Aleksandrovich," the doctor's wife said, "please let us know. We would be happy to hide them and look after them. Maybe then I could regain my dignity and be able to look in the mirror again without seeing myself wearing poor Sofia's dress!"

The very next week, Auntie Eva and Uncle Chaim moved to the house of the doctor and his wife.

And so, during the winter of 1942-1943, Uncle Misha was looking after the three girls on his own. Their daily schooling routine was still carrying on, and by the following summer the girls had acquired enough knowledge to enter grade two. But there was no school that Manya, Raya or Yulia could attend.

Uncle Misha constantly worried about their health. All three girls were pale and thin because of their horrific living conditions and the lack of nourishing food. Raya was constantly coughing, while Manya developed chronic sinusitis and Yulia suffered from frequent stomach aches.

To make matters worse, Raya and Manya suffered recurring nightmares. At night, Raya often pushed her blanket aside and started to scream. Again and again she felt herself being buried under still-warm, dead bodies and felt her own grandmother falling over her, and so she was scrambling away so as not to be smothered by the heavy, collapsing body.

Manya dreamt time and again about the round-faced gendarme in the ravine. She was certain that he knew that he hadn't killed her and that one day he would come back to finish the job.

Apart from the school curriculum, Uncle Misha also spent time telling the girls stories about old Kiev, life in the Ukraine before the Revolution, and about the Revolution itself. More than anything else, the three girls liked to hear about his own glorious past. He told them how he had been a revolutionary, and then a soldier in the Red Army, fighting the enemies of the new Soviet state; and how he met a young girl whom he married, and how he and his young bride wanted to help build a new world where everyone would be considered equal and would be happy.

"Uncle Misha," Raya once asked, "why did you become a teacher instead of a general or a commissar?"

Uncle Misha was silent for a moment and then answered, "I've learned that it's impossible to change society without changing people's mentality, and the mentality of a person is formed during childhood. I decided to teach children to be honest, brave and knowledgeable. If children grow up to be good and responsible adults, then society will be better off. Don't you think so, girls?"

"What about that young Ukrainian man who killed my grandma and wanted to kill me?" the persistent Manya asked. "Didn't he go to a Soviet school? What was wrong with his mentality?"

"I don't know him, Manechka, so it's difficult for me to answer. However, there were many things that went wrong during the last twenty years. Many people were wronged and are now looking for revenge in one way or another," he replied.

"My grandma didn't wrong him!" Manya exclaimed.

"I know, dear. That's the worst thing that can happen to people. They become so angry and they concentrate so much on revenge that they become worse than their enemies. Quite possibly something really terrible happened in the life of that Ukrainian boy who shot your grandma and his thirst for revenge made him truly evil."

It was Yulia who asked the critical question and the compelling answer was something that Manya and Raya would remember for their entire lives.

"Uncle Misha, aren't you afraid that the Germans will find us here? Aren't you afraid that they'll arrest you and kill you?" Yulia asked.

"Of course I'm afraid. I'm very afraid. But there's something else, Yulia, which I'm afraid of much more than mere death."

"What can be worse than death?" Yulia wondered.

"To be afraid to look at yourself in the mirror; to be ashamed of yourself."

"I wonder if my Uncle Kolya is ashamed to look at himself in the mirror," Manya mused.

Uncle Misha hugged the little girl. He was concerned about Manya's preoccupation with her uncle and her own would-be executioner. He hoped that she would never encounter that evil man, but how best to prepare her for a meeting with her uncle, an eventuality that might very well come to pass in the future?

Evidently, Manya was worrying about the same thing. "Uncle Misha, what should I do if I ever meet my uncle again?"

"Whatever your heart tells you to do," Michael Aleksandrovich replied.

"But would you forgive him?" Manya asked.

Uncle Misha paused and was thinking of an appropriate answer, but then decided to say just what he felt. "No, Manya. I wouldn't forgive him. I know that it's a horrible thing to keep grudges, that we are all G-d's children and that we are expected to forgive. I'm all for forgiveness – I teach forgiveness to my students. But evil committed without bounds must be punished. There are some things that just cannot be forgotten or forgiven."

One day that fall, Uncle Misha entered the cellar and exuberantly announced, "Girls, we'll be free soon! It's only a matter of days now. I can hear the sounds of battle just outside the city. I'm sure that within a week the four of us will be freely walking the streets of Kiev and celebrating victory and freedom!"

Revenge And Betrayal

NOT EVERYONE WAS happy to hear the increasingly loud sound of artillery coming from the outskirts of Kiev. As a matter of fact, Taras was terrified by it. For him, the arrival of the liberating Red Army would mean almost certain death at the hands of vengeful Kiev residents. For over two years as a gendarme, Taras had held absolute power over their fates – a power that he had exercised with enthusiasm and cruel fervour. Now he feared that he would have to pay the ultimate price for it.

Taras had been born in 1920 in a village not far from Kiev. His father was one of the most successful farmers in that area. Taras lived in a large house with his parents, his older sister, and later on, her husband. He was a happy boy and had a good childhood. He loved helping his mother in the garden and his mother told him that he had a *green thumb*. He loved to work in the fields and in their orchard in the spring and to observe the awakening of the trees and the emergence of new flowers. He wanted to be a farmer like his father and make the plants and crops flourish. He loved his hard-working father but was especially close to his mother. Taras remembered for years afterwards the smell of freshly- baked bread and the flushed face of his mother when she was removing the warm bread from the oven. They had a simple but good life. Taras was liked by his many young friends and loved dearly by his parents.

Then everything changed. The collectivization process began and individual farms were taken away from the owners. Taras' folks were considered to be *kulaks*, or *kurkuls*, because they had a large acreage of land and had engaged hired help to work in the fields.

23

Later on, in the Kiev school, he was taught that labourers who hired themselves out to work for kulaks were defrauded by their oppressors because they were forced to sell their rightful possessions to these unscrupulous bloodsuckers. Taras remembered when their neighbour, Aunt Gannah, sold her farm to his father. Her daughter Mariyka and Taras were the best of friends and often played together. On that day they were close by and overheard the conversation between their parents.

Aunt Gannah was crying and telling Taras' father that she couldn't manage the farm on her own, that her good-for-nothing drunkard husband borrowed money from everyone before he disappeared and that now she was left to pay his debts.

So, Taras' father acquired the farm and Aunt Gannah paid off the debts. Aunt Gannah started to work for his father and Taras' mother was working beside her as well. The two families even ate together. Both children were helping on the farm and Taras didn't have any easier time of it with his chores than Mariyka.

But one day Mariyka's father unexpectedly returned, accompanied by a Jewish man clad in a leather jacket. They gathered the villagers together and the Jew gave an impassioned speech about equality and about the bright future when everyone would work together on common land and share the proceeds equally.

He told the villagers that all their troubles were because of the people like Taras' father, those *kulaks.*

It didn't matter that his father was one of the hardest-working people in the village. He had people working for him, and therefore, in the eyes of the Soviet Government he was a *kulak,* and *kulaks* were exploiters and bloodsuckers that had to be squished and destroyed.

Fortunately for Taras, his mother had sensed that trouble was coming and had sent him off to Kiev to live with his aunt. Soon after that, his family was banished to Siberia and Taras was not sure what had become of them. He didn't even know if they were still alive. But wouldn't they send him a letter or something if they were still alive?

His aunt Olesya was married to a fine man named Petro. They had no children of their own and were happy to welcome Taras into the family.

"Don't get too comfortable in Kiev," his mother told him before leaving the city to return to her village. "Your place is on the farm. But stay here with your aunt for a couple of months until this trouble blows over and then we'll take you back."

They never did.

"Why have they sent my parents away?" Taras was asking his aunt. "They did nothing wrong. Mariyka's father was shouting that my dad had stolen his farm and was forcing his wife to work hard seven days a week. It's not true! And dad didn't steal anything from anybody. He paid Aunt Gannah a fair price for the farm! I saw it! And my parents were working just as hard as Aunt Gannah was."

"Don't blame Mariyka's father. He was brainwashed by the Jews," Aunt Olesya explained. "It's a Jewish government so what good can we expect from it?"

And then the *great famine* struck Ukraine. People were dying in increasing numbers every day from starvation.

Taras didn't starve, at least not in the beginning. Petro was working in a meat factory and always managed to bring home something to feed his family and his parents. That was until one day when he was arrested for taking a piece of ham out of the factory and he was banished to a labour camp. The large ham, carefully rationed, would have fed all of them for many days. But before long, without sustenance support from Petro, his parents died of starvation.

If Petro had stolen that ham from some individual he would have been considered a thief, a common criminal, and he would have received a light sentence. But since he stole from the government (all the factories belonged to the State), his offence was deemed a political act against the State. The punishment, as far as Olesya was concerned, far outweighed the crime, but there was no appeal of the edicts and criminal convictions imposed by the government authorities. Five years after Petro's arrest, Olesya received an official notification of his death. There was no specific explanation of the cause of death, merely a vague statement indicating that his death occurred as a result of illness. What illness? Petro was a young and healthy man when he was taken away to the camps.

Olesya never married again and never dated anybody either. She despised the Soviet Government and everyone associated with it. She hated Jews too, considering them to be personally responsible for the Revolution and for the fate of her husband, her sister and her sister's family. Day after day, over the course of the next ten years, Olesya ingrained in her nephew that same hatred.

Taras had not been popular in his class at school. The girls were constantly teasing the short, round-faced, overweight boy with the heavy peasant accent. The other boys ignored him and didn't include him in any of their games and activities.

A peculiarity in the capital of Soviet Ukraine was that the city residents spoke only Russian. To speak native Ukrainian was to reveal oneself as a peasant, a village bumpkin. At home in his village, Taras spoke only Ukrainian and had to hastily learn to switch to Russian after his relocation to Kiev. The Russian and Ukrainian languages are similar but with their own unique identities. Taras' use of a mixture of Russian and Ukrainian words when he spoke sounded strange, and what was worse, amusing to his classmates.

Taras' worst tormentor was the beautiful Stella. This girl had huge black, sparkling eyes and it seemed to Taras that they bore deep inside his soul and could detect his anguish. Stella had everything – beauty, intelligence, smart-looking clothes, and the best lunches in school, including fresh fruits and vegetables, even in the winter months. In the Soviet Ukraine that was lacking of almost everything, those lunches rendered a strong statement about the wealth of her family.

Stella never received any mark other than 'A'; she was the captain of the girls' gymnastics team; she played beautifully on the piano and had a lovely voice. In all school concerts, Stella was the star performer.

This school-goddess singled out Taras as the prime victim of her witticism and mockery. She would stand during recess, surrounded by giggling girls, and call out to him using the words from a famous Ukrainian fairy tale, *"Tarasiku-Telesiku, sail to me, my dearest!"*

And Taras, who knew better, still eagerly turned his head toward his tormentor. This caused the girls to laugh even harder. Taras felt helpless; he couldn't resist looking at Stella. He was in love. Who wouldn't be? All the boys in his class were in love with the regal, dark-haired beauty.

Taras' rescuer was Aleksander, or as everyone was calling him, Sasha, the son of their history teacher. Sasha felt pity for the boy and started to include him in his own company of friends. The other boys in the class respected and listened to the tall and strong, always level-headed young Aleksander and so eventually the mockery stopped. Even Stella relented and left Taras alone.

When the war started Sasha joined the Red Army, whereas Taras hid in the attic of his aunt's house. He had no intention of fighting for the Soviet Union. When the Germans occupied Kiev, Taras was one of the first to sign up for the newly-formed gendarme unit.

One day he met Stella on the street. "What are you doing here?" Taras asked. "Why didn't you evacuate?"

"Taras, look at me," Stella answered confidently. "Who would want to harm me? Who would want to destroy such a beauty as mine? I have absolutely nothing to be afraid of."

But she was quite wrong.

When the official posters were hung throughout Kiev, directing all the Jews to gather in Artem Street, Stella and her parents decided to disobey the orders and stay put in their well-appointed apartment. Two days later, there was a raid carried out in that neighbourhood. Stella's parents were seized and executed on the spot. The frightened and distraught Stella managed to escape the raid and ran off to find Taras.

"Taras, please hide me! Save me! You are the only one in the city who can help me! I'll do anything for you!" Stella begged.

Taras could scarcely believe his good fortune - his first and only love, the girl whom he had dreamt about for so long, had now come to him in desperation, offering her body and indeed her life to him.

Taras obliged and hid Stella in his attic in spite of his aunt's protests. He knew the risks but he didn't care. He would show Stella how good, kind and generous he could be. He would earn her love. The war wouldn't last forever and then he would enjoy life-long happiness with his Stella. Besides, it was about time for him to experience the secrets and pleasures of manhood and what could be better than to be introduced to them by someone like Stella? Taras couldn't resist such a temptation. What man would?

For several months Stella lived in the attic of the house of Taras' aunt. She asked him to bring her some paper and paints and drew pictures to hang on the wall. She also crafted some paper flowers and arranged them in a vase on the table. Soon the small attic room was looking cozy and inviting.

Stella actually grew to care for her saviour and together they spent many evenings talking about their lives before the war and even about their future after the war would be over. They were both dreaming about victory, and although it had a quite different meaning to each of them, Taras didn't dissuade Stella when she was talking about the expected liberation by the Red Army.

The hours in the attic were passing by very slowly every day; Stella was lonely and always impatiently waiting for Taras to return. He was an eager and enthusiastic lover and his passion afforded Stella an illusion of safety.

Taras was a happy man indeed in those days.

He vividly remembered the day of the Babi Yar massacre. That morning he had been nervous. He had never killed another human being. Before the executions started he remembered the words of his aunt: *Jews caused the Revolution in Russia and Ukraine. Jews killed your family.* Through the years his aunt had been repeating those words again and again.

Before the war Taras didn't really think much about his feelings towards the Jews; he assured his aunt that he hated them, but this hatred was dormant and seemed unimportant to him.

After war started, that all changed.

When the first victims lay down at the bottom of the ravine beneath his feet, Taras looked at the naked old women and children and his only thought was that these were his enemies. They and their relatives were guilty of the deaths of his family. So he shot...again and again.

Towards the middle of that day, a feeling of absolute power and utter control over human life got into his head. Taras didn't need to drink vodka as the other gendarmes did. The sight and smell of spilt blood was intoxicating enough for him. He looked at all the shivering, naked people standing before him and thought, *this is the payback for my family!* He relished killing the Jews – man, woman and child alike.

There were so many victims to be killed that Taras couldn't even distinguish faces, genders or ages. That was the case except for two individuals: a middle-aged woman and a little girl. He specifically remembered them because they had looked so much alike. It was uncanny how much the little girl resembled the older woman, evidently her mother or grandmother. And then that woman attacked him and bit and scratched his face. In anger and shock, Taras pushed the witch away, raised his rifle and killed her on the spot. Then he looked around for the little girl; he wanted to kill her himself too, he was so angry! But someone else must have already done the deed. Taras couldn't spot the girl in the melee and then he became too engaged in killing other Jews to think any more about that red-haired little girl.

In the months that followed, Taras killed literally hundreds of people. He was an eager participant in the raids and loved to wield his power and authority over the terrified residents of the occupied city.

But the war and the daily killings were set aside as soon as he returned to the attic. There, in Stella's arms, Taras was an entirely different person: loving, tender and affectionate.

He enjoyed bringing presents for Stella. When he was placing a beautiful golden necklace around her neck, he neglected to mention that he had removed it from a woman whom he had killed. In fact, Taras didn't reveal anything about his activities to Stella. But even as she was kissing him affectionately in gratitude, he was thinking that perhaps that same day he might have killed some of her own friends, or even some relatives. Such thoughts aroused him even more.

Stella outwardly still seemed to be just as appreciative of Taras, yet in time their relationship slowly changed. Not a word was ever spoken, but Stella started to fear him; he could feel it. For his part, Taras stopped thinking about Stella as his companion-for-life, or about the true extent of their professed love. Sometimes when he was making love to her he would imagine seeing Stella lying naked on the bottom of the ravine. Then, just as he was reaching a heightened climax, he was shooting her just like all the others.

After several more months of listening to the constant objections of his aunt, Taras began to doubt if Stella was still worth the risk. And so, in March of 1942, after he heard talk in the local regiment headquarters about upcoming raids in his neighbourhood, he made up his mind to act.

Taras approached his superiors and informed them that a young Jewish woman had come to him the night before, seeking refuge. He explained that he knew the girl because she had been a school classmate. He said he had decided to let her stay in his attic only so he could then inform the authorities about her presence.

That same afternoon, two Germans and three other Ukrainian gendarmes accompanied Taras to his aunt's house to arrest one solitary, unarmed Jewish woman. It was only when they entered the attic that Taras realized his mistake. The attic looked much too feminine and comfortable; clearly the woman had occupied the place for more than a day.

"Yesterday you said?" the superior officer asked him with a sneer. "You should be shot yourself for harbouring this Jewess, but I can't say that I blame you for keeping her. As a matter of fact I may use her myself for a couple of hours!" All five men started to laugh cruelly.

Taras retreated downstairs to the kitchen.

"Finally!" his aunt exclaimed approvingly. "Here, eat!" and she placed before him a large bowl of red borsht and a plate of meat stew. She also set a bottle of vodka on the table for him.

While the five men in the attic viciously raped Stella, Taras slowly consumed his dinner and drank copious amount of vodka.

There were moments when he felt remorse and tremendously sorry for Stella. He even got up from the table a couple of times, momentarily thinking to go upstairs and rescue her from further abuse. Then he would take his seat again and quaff down yet-another shot.

When they escorted a dishevelled Stella away, she glared in silence at Taras. There was so much loathing and hatred in that momentary stare that Taras felt a shiver run down his spine.

It was more than a year-and-half ago, but Taras still remembered that look vividly. Now he was regretting that he betrayed her. Not because of the sex, oh no! He had no shortage of other willing bed-mates.

But the Red Army was approaching and he could easily foresee the fate of the gendarmes. If Stella had still been living in his attic he could claim that he was saving a Jewish woman and that he only pretended to serve the Germans in order to protect her. After all, Stella had been his true love, the only woman he had ever loved and if not for that constant nagging from his aunt, he would never have betrayed her. Taras was certain of it.

Stella could have been his ticket back into mainstream Soviet life. He would have been regarded as a hero instead of a villain! But his beautiful Stella was dead and gone a long time ago.

The thought persisted in Taras' head, however, and became an obsession that evolved into a plan. Some locals might still be harbouring Jews! All he had to do was find such persons, get rid of them, and then frighten the Jews into saying that it was he, Taras, who had been hiding and protecting them! That shouldn't be too difficult - what choice would they have? The question was where to find those hidden Jews?

During the nighttime hours, Taras started creeping around the neighbourhood. He walked slowly and quietly, and dressed in his dark uniform he looked like a shadow. He got lucky on his fourth outing. He detected the familiar low voice of his old history teacher and from a distance he observed the outline of two or three small girls who had emerged for some fresh air. This was even better than Taras could have hoped for! He promptly guessed where Michael Aleksandrovich was hiding those Jews. After all, ironically, he had helped Sasha build the cellar. Taras decided to act: there was no time to procrastinate. The Red Army was already on the outskirts of Kiev. His scheme would have to be executed quickly and very, very carefully.

Taras' plan was straightforward: he would come to his old teacher and inform him that he had overheard news of an upcoming raid in their neighbourhood. And it would not be just a random raid, but a specific raid of Michael Aleksandrovich's house. Then he would suggest that he, Taras, knew of a perfect place to hide the girls. Taras was confident that his former teacher would believe him. After all, wasn't he a former school buddy of Sasha, Michael Aleksandrovich's son?

Then he would escort the girls to his own attic and browbeat them until they would be ready to say that it was he, Taras, who had protected them all the while.

The next evening, the girls were studying with Uncle Misha in the cellar when they heard a loud knock at the door. Uncle Misha quickly climbed up the ladder and slid a rug over the top of the trapdoor.

A bit later, he returned to the cellar and told the girls, "An old friend of my son wants to talk to me. Please continue to study without me. I'll be back soon."

The girls didn't like this interruption. Any change in their routine made them nervous and anxious. But Uncle Misha seemed relaxed and confident when he left the house with that unexpected visitor.

Taras' plan went awry from the beginning. Michael Aleksandrovich was clearly not willing to believe him or to give up his protective care of the girls.

"Michael Aleksandrovich," Taras was pleading, "I'm doing this for your sake. You were like a father to me. I don't want anything bad to happen to you. Sasha would never forgive me. Please believe me. There was an alert in our precinct that you are harbouring Jews. By the morning they will come to raid your house. We have no time to lose."

"Taras, I'm well-aware of your activities and you're the last person I would entrust anybody to. There are far too many things that have happened as it is for Sasha to ever forgive you. There was no such alert either; otherwise your comrades wouldn't be waiting until the morning. It was you who was sneaking around here, wasn't it? You want the girls for your own purposes, isn't that so? Why, Taras? What do you want from them?"

Taras didn't respond and just stared at his old teacher with undisguised loathing.

"Let me give you some advice instead," Michael Aleksandrovich continued. "Run while it's still not too late. Hide somewhere and pray that the citizens of Kiev would never find you."

Taras was enraged. Without thinking, he lashed out and struck the father of his friend with all his might. The old man staggered.

An evening patrol was passing through the street and the gendarmes recognized their comrade. "Who is this person, Taras? What's going on?"

Taras didn't have a good answer and improvised. "I've heard this man boasting of harbouring Jews so I'm taking him in for questioning."

"Where does he live?" the suddenly eager men asked him.

"I don't know. He hasn't told me yet," Taras lied.

The gendarmes surrounded a stunned Michael Aleksandrovich and led him to the Gestapo station.

The girls listened intently but nothing broke the silence for a long time. They had been waiting for Uncle Misha with impatient concern. In the cellar they had a small table clock and were constantly watching it; hour after hour was passing and early evening became late-night. They were hungry too, but they were too fearful to move. Finally the trapdoor opened and a man started to descend the stairs, but this man was not their Uncle Misha. When the stranger turned to face the girls, Manya screamed. This was a man she would recognize anywhere; he was the man of her nightmares, the very same man who had killed her grandmother Anna.

Taras, already upset that the first part of his plan hadn't gone smoothly, was unnerved and even shocked by the girl's violent reaction.

Before Yulia and Raya had time to react, Manya started to pound the big man with her little fists, all the while yelling at him. Taras recovered from his shock and grabbed Manya by her throat. He slowly started to squeeze his hands about her neck and said to the other two girls, "I'll kill her and then I'll kill you two the same way unless you do as you are told."

Suddenly he felt sharp teeth biting into his shoulder and the sharp nails of little fingers scratching him about his face. Yelling from the pain, Taras released Manya from his grasp. He angrily shoved Raya aside and took hold of his rifle. "Now I'm going to kill both of you." The enraged Taras gestured at Yulia and said, "Then she will be more obedient."

"Don't!" Raya begged, "don't kill us! Please, just tell us what you want from us!"

Taras seized Manya by her neck again. Instead of squeezing it, he easily lifted her off her feet. He looked at the other two girls and considered his options. To save just one or even two girls was hardly enough; it would be much better to be able to claim to have saved three girls. They were three scared little girls and surely he could deal with all of them. He looked severely at them and said, "From now on you'll only be doing what I tell you to do and saying what I tell you to say. Is that understood?"

"Please, let my sister and me live and we'll behave ourselves and obey you. We just got scared when you came into the cellar. Please forgive us," an outwardly meek and obedient Raya pleaded.

"Promise?" Taras asked.

"Yes, we promise," Raya responded, vigorously nodding her head.

"How about you?" Taras regarded Manya intently. Manya couldn't believe her ears. How could Raya promise this terrible man anything at all? But at that moment she noticed that Raya, in a manner honoured by all little children who make promises they don't intent to keep, had crossed her fingers behind her back. Raya was looking intently at Manya with a fixed stare.

"Yes, I promise. I'm sorry," Manya said, innocently putting her hands behind her back and crossing her fingers too.

"I promise too! I promise!" the frightened Yulia said.

"Good!" Taras was satisfied with the degree of fear he had instilled in all three girls. All that he needed now was another week or two to complete his plan and then he'd find a way to be out of Kiev for good.

For the next half-hour, Taras was coaching the girls. He made each of them repeat how and where he had found them and how he had been looking after them for two years. When he was satisfied that they knew their lines, Taras forced Manya and Yulia to take the heavy waste pail and carry it up from the cellar to the backyard outhouse. He followed after the girls with his rifle poised. Taras allowed Raya to fetch clean water and then he hustled the three girls back into the cellar, tossed some stale bread on the cellar floor, climbed up the stairs and secured the trapdoor. The girls could hear him dragging something heavy over the top of the trapdoor, and then finally it became deathly quiet.

The girls started to cry. Manya looked at her friends and quietly said, "He's killed Uncle Misha. Our Uncle Misha is dead. I just know it."

"I think he moved the table into the middle of the room to cover the trapdoor. Now nobody will find us," Yulia whimpered.

Taras returned home in a much improved mood, whistling a merry tune. The first phase of his plan was accomplished. Now he had to talk to his Aunt Olesya and make her understand why it was necessary to keep the girls in their attic. He would ask her to prepare the attic and tomorrow night he would move the girls. He just hoped that the old teacher would keep his mouth shut and that the Nazis would quickly kill him before Kiev was liberated. *Maybe the man is already dead,* Taras thought hopefully.

But Uncle Misha was still alive. He was interrogated and he was tortured; he was repeatedly asked where he was living and where he was keeping the Jews. Michael Aleksandrovich didn't utter a word.

The next day, during the ongoing interrogation, Michael Aleksandrovich looked at his tormentors and asked, "What is wrong with you? The Red Army is going to be here tomorrow or the next day. Why, even now, just days before your own demise, do you still worry about the Jews? Run. You should run like rats while you still have time." These words infuriated the Germans. They struck him so hard that he fell to the floor. They continued to kick him relentlessly with their hard-soled boots until Michael Aleksandrovich stopped breathing.

Taras was immensely relieved when he learned that Michael Aleksandrovich had died without revealing anything. But the next night he was participating in quelling a local uprising and couldn't move the girls as he had planned.

For some reason he remained disturbed by the behaviour of that little round-faced girl. Where had he seen her before? Several times Taras considered abandoning the girls and simply disappearing from Kiev. It was easier said than done, though. Where would he go? In any village freed by the Red Army, a young man in civilian clothes would raise suspicion. As for the Germans? Well, the Germans didn't care in the slightest about the fate of their Ukrainian underlings, and Taras certainly didn't want to throw in his lot with the losing army. At that imminent moment of panic it would be every man for himself.

In the end, Taras concluded that his best alternative was to remain in Kiev and proceed with his plan.

He knew that the girls must be hungry and desperate. *Let them starve,* Taras decided. *One day won't kill them; it will just make them more obedient.* He would move them tomorrow night.

Daylight At Last

THE FRIGHTENED GIRLS sat huddled together in the cellar and waited. They had finished the water and bread long ago and were very hungry. Their waste pail was full and it smelled terribly. The air in the cellar became heavy and oppressive. Their little clock told them that they had been alone for almost two days when they suddenly could hear footsteps on the floor above the cellar. Somebody was walking there. The steps became faint, but then became more audible again. Eventually, someone moved the table and opened the trapdoor.

"Is anybody there?" a young male voice asked curiously.

"Aleksander?" a surprised Yulia asked cautiously.

"Yulka? What are you doing down there? Where's my father? Come up here."

Yulia eagerly climbed up the stairs out of the cellar. Raya and Manya guardedly followed after her. They closed their eyes momentarily. It was the first time in two years they had seen the actual bright daylight that was streaming in the windows. Yulia hugged her old neighbour and started to cry.

Raya and Manya were startled when they looked at the tall, young soldier whose appearance was so much like their Uncle Misha.

"Who are you?" Aleksander gently asked the two red-headed girls.

"We are sisters. Uncle Misha was hiding us here for more than two years. But then that horrible man came two days ago. He wanted to kill us," the taller girl explained.

"What horrible man? Where's your Uncle Misha now? Let's go into the living room and sit down." Aleksander led the way. The girls

37

noticed that he was limping on his left leg and that there was blood seeping through the fabric of his army trousers.

It took the sisters ten minutes to tell their story: how Uncle Misha had found them near Babi Yar, how he had been hiding them and others, how two days ago a despicable young man came to the cellar, and how it was that Manya recognized that man.

"What is his name?" Aleksander asked.

"Taras," Raya said. "He told us his name. He forced us to promise to say that it was he who had saved us. We promised but we kept our fingers crossed, so the promise doesn't count, right?"

"That's right, Raya. You said this man was round-faced and stocky? Taras?"

"Yes, and he's going to kill us," Yulia said and started sobbing.

"Don't worry, girls. My father kept you safe for two years. That means it's now my responsibility to see that nothing bad happens to you.

"Are you hungry?" Aleksander asked the girls. Then he looked into their eyes and promptly concluded that the question was not necessary. He took some bread and cans of meat from his knapsack and the girls ravenously attacked the food.

Aleksander waited patiently until the girls finished eating and said, "I have to go back. I only asked for several hours off duty to visit my father. However, I don't want to let you stay here alone so I'm going to take you with me. Let's go."

Yulia and Manya took Aleksander's hands into theirs; Raya took hold of Manya's hand and the small procession left the house.

There was chaos on the streets of Kiev. Soviet tanks were rumbling through the streets and there were soldiers everywhere, but the girls were smiling. They were outside! In the bright daylight! They could see the sun again, at last! And the soldiers were Soviet soldiers, not Germans. Aleksander stopped a military vehicle, instructed the girls to climb in, and eventually brought them to the temporary headquarters of the Red Army. There he explained the story to a uniformed officer with a lot of stars on his shoulders.

"Maybe your father is still alive," the officer said. "You have to look for him. And what about your leg, Aleksander?"

"Girls," the man commanded, "you stay here. Not a step from here! Understood?"

"Yes, Comrade," all three of them responded in unison.

Aleksander and the officer departed and the girls were left sitting alone in a sparsely furnished room.

"Where are we?" Raya asked.

"I don't know but I think somewhere close to Khreschatik. It's the main street of Kiev. I recognized it when we were driving here," Manya whispered.

After a long while, Aleksander returned with a cane under his left arm. "It seems that everything has been worked out. The doctor bandaged my leg. I'll be stationed in Kiev for the next several months until my leg heals. You will live with me. Let's hope that within that time one of your parents will show up. Let's get going now. I want to find my father."

"What about Taras?" the anxious Manya asked.

"I told the authorities about Taras. There are two soldiers waiting for us outside. They'll escort us back home," he assured them.

When night fell over Kiev, the girls were led to a bedroom where a large, comfortable bed was waiting. "Go to sleep," Aleksander instructed. But the girls couldn't sleep. They cuddled together and listened for every sound. Some while later they heard the sounds of steps, then the sounds of fighting, and then two shots rang out.

Several minutes later, a grim-looking Aleksander came into the room. "You can't sleep?" he asked. "Everything's okay. You can sleep well now. That man will never bother you again."

"Where are you going?" Raya asked when Aleksander turned around to leave. She didn't want to think about those two shots and their implication.

"I'm going to look for my father. I'm taking Vasily with me but Sergey will stay here. You have nothing to fear. Time to sleep," he reassured them.

In the morning the girls awoke to the rays of the bright sun streaming through their bedroom window. They got up and went to look for Aleksander. They found him outdoors with the two soldiers.

Under an apple tree there was a large, freshly-dug hole in the ground. Nearby, the girls saw a plain wooden coffin.

"Oh, there you are. We were waiting for you. I thought you would want to say goodbye to your Uncle Misha," Aleksander said quietly. His eyes were red from crying.

Yulia, who had never seen a dead body before, ran to Aleksander and hid behind him. She whispered, "I'm scared."

Manya and Raya approached the open coffin and looked down at the mutilated face of their saviour and teacher. They both felt an outpouring of grief unlike any emotion they had ever experienced before. They didn't cry when their grandmothers had been killed – they'd been too stunned by the events of that day, and later were too frightened to cry out loud. But this time they could allow their heartfelt grief to be released. They grasped the cold, stiff hands of Michael Aleksandrovich and wept for a long time.

Eventually, Sergey and Vasily took the grieving girls aside and Aleksander buried his father under his favourite apple tree.

Sergey and Vasily departed and Aleksander was then left alone with the three girls.

"So, girls," he gruffly asked, "what did you do for all those two years you spent in the cellar?"

"Mostly we were studying," Manya answered.

"Good. Please bring me all of your books and show me what you've learned," Aleksander instructed them.

"Are you a teacher too?" Raya asked.

"As a matter of fact, I am. I finished teacher's college just before the war. I wanted to be a teacher of geography. Don't think that now, even though your Uncle Misha isn't with you any longer, that you can stop your studies! It will be good for all of us to have something else to think about," Aleksander said, sadly but firmly.

The following week Aleksander asked Manya to take him to her parents' apartment. Before the war, Manya and her parents had lived in an apartment that they had been sharing with two other families. Manya's family lived in a large room that had been divided into two sections by curtains. Surprisingly, she remembered her street and the particular building. After stumbling into several wrong apartments she found her parents' place. They rang all the door-bells but nobody answered. The entire apartment was empty and locked up.

Aleksander left a large note on the door. *"The parents of Manya Matveeva, please inquire at Ovrutzkaya Street, 11."*

Manya carefully supervised the procedure, making sure that Aleksander's address was written in a large, bold font and that the note had been securely affixed to the door. After all, that note was probably her only hope of ever seeing her parents alive again.

Raya, however, couldn't remember where her grandmother's apartment was located. She'd been travelling so much with her military family that she had had no single place that she could call home.

They all returned to Aleksander's house and a new stage in the girls' lives began.

The three girls were often talking about their families and discussing their anticipated reunion with their parents, refusing to even consider the thought of the alternative. Aleksander didn't encourage this kind of talk, for he knew how cruel the war was and that the chances of the girls ever finding their parents were dismal, especially for Raya. He did his best to keep the girls' minds focussed on their studies. Over the next several months, Aleksander continued to perform the duties begun by his father - taking care of the girls and continuing to foster their education.

The End Of The War

A MOMENTOUS EVENT occurred shortly after they celebrated the beginning of the 1944 year. The door-bell rang and when Aleksander opened the door, he found Yulia's mother standing there on the doorstep.

"Yulenka, look who's here!" Aleksander happily exclaimed.

The woman ran inside, lifted her daughter off her feet and started to hug and kiss her passionately. Manya and Raya stayed aside, watching the happy reunion.

Eventually the woman let Yulia out of her grasp and hugged Aleksander. "You can't imagine how grateful I am to you and to your father for saving my Yulenka for me. Our neighbour told me the whole story. Poor Michael Aleksandrovich! To survive through the entire occupation and then to be killed one day before the liberation! It's so tragic. I'm so sorry! If there is anything I can do…if you need money…" she offered.

"No, I don't need anything, but thank you," Aleksander replied impassively.

"Then we will be going. I came here only to find Yulia. Tomorrow morning we'll be going back to Perm where my husband is waiting for us. There are still so many other things I have to do today. Here's my Perm address. Please write me, Aleksander. I'm in your debt forever! I'm sorry to be in such a rush but I'm sure you understand." The woman blurted out all of that very fast, doing her best not to look directly towards the corner where the sisters were standing.

She pecked Aleksander on the cheek, took hold of her daughter's hand, and in the next moment they were gone. Aleksander just shook his head.

"That woman didn't even look at us!" Raya exclaimed. "And Yulka didn't even say goodbye!"

"We spent over two years together. I thought she was our friend!" Manya added sadly.

Aleksander, trying to sound reassuring, said, "Never you mind, children. I'm your friend. For now, I'm also your father, your mother, and most importantly, your teacher! Remember that."

The girls started to giggle. They weren't the least bit scared of the big and strong Aleksander. By now they had him pegged for a softie and loved him as much as they had loved their Uncle Misha.

"Get the table ready; time for lunch. Let's see what I can find," Aleksander said and went off to the kitchen. He laid his hands on the counter and sought to compose himself. He didn't want the sisters to observe his anger and frustration. He could readily guess the reason for the hasty departure of Yulia's mother - she didn't want to become saddled with two additional charges.

Aleksander loved the girls as only an older brother can love his younger sisters. He felt an incredible tenderness and protectiveness towards them. He adored the short-tempered and inquisitive Raya. He decided that she would become a scientist when she grew up and he would do everything he could to stir her mind in that direction. He also loved the patient, soft-spoken, but stubborn Manya. Aleksander surmised that behind her soft exterior there was an iron will.

He especially enjoyed observing the dynamics between the two girls. He knew very well that they weren't real sisters, but that was how they'd introduced themselves, and that was how his father named them. For Aleksander, Raya and Manya were as much sisters as any other true siblings, so that was how he always thought about them... and that was how he treated them.

The girls truly complemented one-another. Raya was always ready to help Manya with her studies, while Manya always knew how to settle down the high-strung, emotional Raya.

The girls were content to live with Aleksander but he knew that his leg had healed sufficiently and that it was his responsibility to rejoin the war effort again.

In April they had a new visitor. Aleksander opened the door and the girls could hear a soft female voice. "Excuse me, please. I just returned to Kiev and I found a note on the door of my apartment..."

"Mama, Mamochka!" Manya exclaimed and ran towards the door.

"You're alive! Manechka, you're alive!" the woman cried out.

"This is my mama. Her name is Galina," Manya informed Aleksander and Raya, while continuing to hold tight to the hand of her mother. "Mama," Manya continued her introductions, "this is Aleksander. He's the son of Uncle Misha, the one who saved us. And this is Raya. She's my sister. My blood sister."

After these unusual introductions, Galina had innumerable questions but was choked with emotion and didn't even know where to begin. She carefully observed her daughter and felt proud of Manya, yet somewhat saddened by the changes in her daughter's outward appearance. She remembered a cute, roly-poly, smiley little girl who looked at the world with the innocence and trust of a five-year-old. That girl was clearly long gone. Galina could feel that Manya had matured way beyond her age. There was something in her daughter's eyes... a seriousness of her look, the deep sadness, even at this happy moment...and what else? Could it be wisdom? Can an eight-year-old actually be *wise*? *What did she have to endure to have such an ingrained expression?* Galina pondered as she hugged her daughter closely.

Galina then looked with curiosity at the tall, homely girl that her daughter had said was her *sister*. All of Raya's features seemed to be awkwardly out of place. Her nose was too large for her small face; her arms and legs were too long for her skinny body; she had freckles everywhere; and her frizzy hair had an offensively bright red hue. But still, the girl's eyes were beautiful - large, dark green and finely shaped, like almonds. Now those eyes were looking back at Galina with inquisitiveness, hope and even fear. *She's scared that I'll take Manya away,* Galina mused silently.

She was invited to sit down on the couch, and so she then drew Manya onto her left knee, looked towards Raya and said, "Come, Rayechka, sit here," and she pointed to her right knee.

Aleksander related for Galina the story of the two girls: their escape from Babi Yar, their life with his father, the betrayal by Taras, and the death of his father. "Since last fall the girls have been living here with me," he explained, concluding his lengthy narrative.

Galina was crying by now. She had just learned about the death of her mother and about the cowardly behaviour of her own twin brother.

"Manechka, please tell me again," Galina practically begged. "Maybe you don't remember everything correctly. It was such a horrible day. Are you sure that Uncle Kolya said that grandma Anna and you were his *neighbours?*"

"I'm sure, Mama," Manya said with unwavering conviction. "Grandma and Uncle Kolya were fighting all the time. Grandma was constantly telling Uncle that he had to go to the Army and that we had to evacuate with Aunt Nina and my cousins, Alla and Petya. But he was always saying that he had no intention to leave his city or to go and fight in the war to get killed.

"When the posters appeared in the city, Grandma asked him to hide us or help us get out of the city. Uncle said that there was a new order in the city and that it was his responsibility to obey the new law. That morning, he came to grandma's apartment and helped us pack and took us to Artem Street."

Manya fell silent for a moment and then continued with mounting anger. "He was actually happy when they took us away. I turned around and looked at his face. He looked relieved, because he knew that without grandma being around, nobody would ever suspect that my uncle had any Jewish blood."

Galina was astonished. In the summer of 1941 she left behind a girl who knew or cared very little about world affairs or about her heritage. Seated before her now there was an eight-year-old girl who was speaking so much like an intelligent adult. *She has suffered so much in her short lifetime! Poor child!* Galina tried to envision her daughter at the bottom of the ravine, hiding under the dead bodies, and eventually crawling out of that place of horror and gruesome death, but she just couldn't bring herself to do it. Her mind refused to conjure up such an image; it was too horrendous even to visualize.

After she composed herself, Galina rose from the couch and went to Aleksander and embraced him warmly. She said, "Today, I lost one brother but I found another."

Aleksander smiled in gratitude.

Galina again looked tenderly at the girls and informed them, "Okay, ladies, we're going home. You, Rayechka, are as much my daughter as Manechka. You two sisters should never be separated.

"Aleksander says he must go back to the war, so we will look forward to seeing him come back soon and with a great victory," she added.

It didn't take the girls much time at all to get ready and just ten minutes later, all four of them were marching away from the house where the girls had remained isolated for two-and-a-half years. Aleksander, predictably, had decided to escort Galina and the two girls. Despite their age differences, Galina and Aleksander felt comfortable and at ease in each other's presence, as though they'd known one-another very well for many years.

While the adults walked ahead and were engaged in talking about the ongoing war, the girls' education, and Galina's prospects of finding a job in Kiev, Raya discreetly observed Manya's mother. For the third time in less than three years, Raya's life was changing dramatically and she would have to depend on yet-another stranger for her well-being. She had been very fortunate on the first two occasions: being saved by Uncle Misha and later being cared-for by his son Aleksander.

Raya quite liked this pretty, petite woman with her short-cropped blonde hair and vibrant blue eyes. She didn't look at all like her beloved, red-headed Manechka, but ever-observant Raya had already noticed some common traits between mother and daughter. Manya was compulsively neat and hated to see anything out of place. Even in the cellar, she had made sure that her bed was neatly made every morning and that everything was clean and every book was neatly placed on a shelf. Galina was still dressed in her simple military uniform, yet it was spotless and freshly starched and her shoes were polished. *She's going to hate me because I'm so sloppy,* Raya pondered.

Raya also noticed how Galina could scarcely keep her hands away from Manya; frequently she would almost absentmindedly touch Manya's shoulder, or pat her hair, or flittingly kiss her forehead. Time from time, as if moved by some secondary thought, Galina would turn her head towards Raya and smile encouragingly. Raya understood; after all, Manya was Galina's daughter whereas she, Raya, was simply a stranger. *I'll behave and try to always be neat and clean. I'll do whatever it takes to make Manya's mama love me too,* Raya resolved.

Raya was somewhat disappointed by Galina's small flat in an apartment that was shared with two other families. In one corner of the apartment there was a small kitchen, and in another corner there was a bathroom, both of which had to be shared by all tenants of the apartment. But at least the flat did overlook a small park with some ancient ruins visible in the middle of the grounds.

"Manya, what's that?" Raya asked.

"That's my park. Before the war I was always playing there with my mama, papa and my grandparents," Manya explained.

"No, I mean those ruins?" Raya inquired.

"Oh, I don't know," replied Manya.

"It's the ruins of the *Golden Gate,*" Galina explained. "There was a time when Kiev ended here. Now, it's in the center of the city. Tomorrow we'll go to see the park and the ruins, okay?"

"Great!" the sisters responded in unison.

The next day at the park, Raya became very quiet at one point. She was walking and looking about quite deliberately. Finally she said, "I've been here before, with grandmother Mila. I remember this place."

'That's wonderful!" Galina exclaimed. "It means that your grandmother was living somewhere nearby. Maybe you'll remember where."

"No, I just can't seem to remember," Raya replied sadly.

Aleksander came to help the small family get settled and the next week he came to say goodbye; he was returning to the front.

That year, Galina, Manya and Raya were rushing every day to the mailbox in the hope of receiving letters from the front. They were waiting for letters from Ivan, Manya's father, and of course, from Aleksander.

In the summer of 1944, a letter arrived from Manya's Uncle Phillip. He was writing from the front. He wrote that he was serving in an artillery battalion. As a valuable worker in some important industrial plant, he had an exemption from regular army duty and didn't even have to go to the front, but he had felt that he just couldn't stay behind. He had left Sverdlovsk in the winter of 1942 and had been fighting the enemy ever since. Phillip was writing not knowing if his letter would even reach somebody.

"Galina," he wrote, "I lost touch with Mama and Kolya. I don't know where they are. I hope you and your family are well." Then Philip informed his sister of the death of their father. There had been a serious accident in the plant and he had died in the spring of 1943. Phillip knew about the accident because he was constantly receiving letters from Sverdlovsk. At the end of the letter, almost as an afterthought, Phillip mentioned about a girl whom he had met in Sverdlovsk. He added that if he survived the war he was planning to return there and marry her.

Galina cried for a long time after receiving his letter. Now she knew she had lost both parents. But she was relieved and happy to know that Phillip was still alive and well.

In September, Galina went to work as a nurse in a hospital and the girls began attending school. The principal of the school tested the girls and had a long talk with Galina. "Both girls have more than enough knowledge to qualify for grade three or even grade four. But I'm worried about their social life. They've never been in a public school before, and they haven't been among other children for a long time. To begin with I'll place them in grade two, according to their age, and give them a chance to get adjusted to school life."

Manya loved school, but Raya found it to be boring. Manya easily befriended other girls; Raya had a much harder time making friends and gaining acceptance. Even so, they still had each other and to the surprise of Galina and their teachers, they never got into so much as a minor scrap with each other.

Raya's concerns about how readily she might be accepted by Galina proved to be unfounded. Galina liked and cared about Raya very much, and so the little family became close-knit and got along together just fine.

During the winter, Nikolai came to visit. Galina had been waiting for this visit to resolve the issue of what really happened on that fateful day in September of 1941. She hoped that Manya had been mistaken... that she had misunderstood Nikolai and his intentions. After all, she had only been five years old and it had been a difficult and emotional time. Surely Kolya would never be the cause of any harm to her Manechka; after all, Kolya was her twin brother. He loved his niece and he would never harm their mother. Galina was trying to convince herself of that again and again.

Nikolai arrived to the flat and hugged his twin sister. "Galina, my Galenka! When did you come back? Why didn't you come to see me right away? I was so worried about you. I met mama's neighbour, Shura, and she told me that she had seen you in the street," he related enthusiastically.

The girls were sitting behind the curtain doing their homework when they first heard Nikolai's voice. Manya began to tremble. She knew that the day would inevitably come when she would see her uncle again, but now she felt totally unprepared to confront him.

"Manya, you have to see him. I'm going to be with you," Raya reassured her. "Let's go together." They took hold of each other's hand and bravely stepped out from behind the curtain.

When Nikolai saw Manya, he released Galina and looked dumbstruck at the girl as though he was seeing a ghost. Galina didn't need any further confirmation. She walked directly to the door, held it open and calmly said, "Just go, Kolya. You are not welcome here any longer."

Without uttering a word in protest, Nikolai walked out the door and was gone.

On May 9, 1945, the war was officially over. The Soviet Union was victorious in the war against Germany and was celebrating the great victory.

Throughout the rest of the world, the media proclaimed that the victory over Nazi Germany and its allies was achieved by the Western Allies, together with the Soviet Union which had led the advance on the eastern front. However, the contribution of the Western Allies was downplayed to a large degree within the Soviet Union.

The intense Soviet propaganda seized upon the bitter feelings of its armed forces and most of the rest of the citizenry. After all, the Allies had only joined the war in 1944, which was long-after the great victory in the Battle of Stalingrad. Furthermore, it was also after the homeland territory of the Soviet Union had already been liberated and the Soviet soldiers were in hot pursuit of the retreating enemy forces beyond its own borders. The bitter joke among the Soviet soldiers was that the greatest help that America had provided was the rations of canned wieners.

While the war effort against Germany's ally, Japan, was still ongoing, this was a trivial side-show from the Soviet perspective. The *real* war had been between the Soviet Union and Nazi Germany. It was very much a war on a personal level for each and every Soviet citizen. After all, it was their homes that were destroyed and their villages that were burned to the ground; it was their families that were murdered and it was their country that had finally been freed from the German menace, inch by inch, kilometer by kilometer. The entire country was celebrating that day and it was the happiest day of their lives for all the grateful survivors.

Galina and her two girls ventured outside to celebrate the victory with the rest of the city. Galina bought flowers and the three of them took the streetcar to Babi Yar. Galina had been there several times before but this was the first time she dared to take the girls with her.

They reached the place where the girls had been ordered to undress and suddenly they stopped walking. The sisters were holding onto each other and couldn't force themselves to take another step. Galina placed her flowers on the edge of the ravine. The girls noticed that the entire length of the precipice of Babi Yar was covered with memorial bouquets of flowers.

It was a mistake to bring them here, too painful, Galina reflected. *They need more time.* Galina and the girls then made their way back home.

For the rest of that day the girls were holding hands to comfort one-another and remained quiet and pensive.

At the end of May, Aleksander, thankfully alive and in one piece, returned home. It was a very joyful reunion. Phillip also came to visit them with his new young wife at the end of the summer. He listened intently to Manya's story, scarcely able to believe what he was hearing. He ventured off to confront Nikolai and eventually returned, shaking his head in disbelief.

"I asked him why he didn't join the army; why he stayed behind. I also asked him what he was doing during the occupation. He didn't have any satisfactory answers for me. He's my older brother but he's nothing more than a coward and a traitor. I don't want to ever hear his name again," Phillip asserted with unmistakeable conviction.

Galina invited Aleksander to her home and organized a small banquet to celebrate, not only the war victory and Aleksander's save return, but also Phillip's marriage, and of course the survival of their family. Phillip and Aleksander immediately connected with one-other and spent countless hours commiserating and relating their war stories.

Galina and Philip talked about their acquaintances, neighbours and friends - those who perished in the war and those who came back.

With despair and anxiety, Galina revealed her worst fear, that Ivan might not be alive. Many people were returning home from the war but her Ivan was as yet unaccounted for. The last letter from him had been at the end of April, 1945, and then – nothing.

Galina hadn't received a funeral notice from the army and that meant that there was still some hope. But what could have become of him? She had made numerous inquiries but hadn't received any answer. She knew that there were thousands of soldiers that had been killed and buried in common, unmarked graves. All that Galina could do was to pray that Ivan wasn't one of those cruel casualties of the war.

The day after the party, Philip and Aleksander subdivided Galina's flat into two rooms, fabricating an interior wall out of plywood. It wasn't much but it afforded Galina and the girls some privacy.

Desperately, Galina tried to convince Phillip and his bride to remain in Kiev, but after a week-long visit, they departed. She was sad to see her brother and his wife take their leave.

After their departure, Galina felt very lonely and with each passing day and no letters or messages from Ivan, she was becoming increasingly depressed. Yet she couldn't allow herself to reveal her distress openly to the girls. She had to convey outward strength for their sake. It was only at night when the girls were asleep that Galina allowed herself to cry.

$\mathcal{A}$ $\mathcal{M}$iracle

O NE NIGHT WHEN Galina was feeling especially sad, she was lying awake in the dark and thinking about Ivan, and about Kolya. She missed her husband very much and was still hoping against hope for his eventual return. Her twin brother was alive and only several street-car stops away but he simply didn't exist for her any longer - not after what he had despicably done to her mother and to Manya...yet in some strange way Galina missed him nonetheless.

Suddenly she heard the patter of small feet and saw a girl running to her bed.

"Aunt Galya, may I lie down with you?" In a trembling voice, Raya said, "I can't sleep. I had that nightmare again; you know, the one when grandma's falling on me in the ravine."

"Climb in, Rayechka," Galina answered warmly.

For a while both of them lay still. "I know why you're not sleeping," Raya finally whispered. "You're thinking about Uncle Vanya, Manya's father, right? I hear you crying sometimes at night."

"Oh, I'm sorry, sweetheart. I thought I was being quiet," Galina replied.

"You are quiet; it's just that I can't sleep at night either. I'm always thinking about my mama and papa and Dimka. Aunt Galya, do you think they're alive? I miss them so much!"

"Dima would be thirteen years old now. I wonder how he looks... but I'll never find out, will I?" she asked. "Even if Dima and my parents are alive, how would they ever find me? At least Manya could leave a note on the apartment door, but I don't even remember where grandma's apartment was! I'm sure that it's close, but where? Please, don't think I don't like it here! I love Manya and you very, very much! And I love Aleksander too. But I wish I could find out something about my own family!" Raya wistfully declared.

"Oh, you poor girl!" Galina exclaimed. "Please don't despair, dear. There are quite a few committees that have been formed to help find lost family members. Raya, I didn't want to tell you this because I didn't think it right to raise your hopes too high, but Aleksander has already made some inquiries. He was told that he may have a response in four to eight weeks. You know, it takes time."

"When did Aleksander do that?" Raya asked excitedly.

"Three weeks ago," Galina responded.

"Oh, this is great! This is so great!" Raya exclaimed, as she spontaneously began hugging and kissing Galina affectionately.

From that day onwards, Raya lived with rekindled hope, impatiently waiting for news, any news at all about her family. She was incessantly talking about them too. She told Manya and Galina all about her beautiful mama, her big and strong papa, and about her stubborn brother Dimka. She felt sorry now that she used to fight with him so much and decided to be a good sister to him when they would meet again.

The news came two weeks later. But it was not the news that Raya had been hoping for.

One evening, Aleksander came to visit them. Just by looking at his composure, Raya sensed what she was about to hear. "Rayechka, darling, please be strong," Aleksander pleaded, taking Raya's hand gently into his own.

Manya came close to Raya and hugged her sister.

"Actually, I have no news about your mother or your brother. But your father, Captain Boris Lvovich Kushnir, was killed on July 1st, 1941," Aleksander revealed in a strained voice.

Raya glanced at everyone gathered around her with a distressed expression of incomprehension. Finally she spoke, all the while shaking her head. "How can this be? I was thinking about papa every day, dreaming about reuniting with him soon. I was even talking to him in my head, and yet he's been dead all these years?"

Raya began to sob uncontrollably and Manya did her best to console her, until she started to cry herself. For a long while the girls were holding to each other closely and crying together for Raya's father.

Eventually, when their emotions had subsided somewhat, Aleksander said, "Rayechka, I have an idea. Do you know the Central Post Office on Khreschatik Street? People who are looking for their lost family members gather there on Sundays. There are a lot of postings on the walls and on the lampposts in the area. I can write a notice and place it there. I can go there on Sundays too, and if your mother does come to Kiev looking for you she may go there herself. When there's life, there's always hope." Having offered that suggestion, he smiled encouragingly at Raya.

"Great idea, Sasha!" Galina enthused. "Why don't we alternate each week? I go one Sunday and you go the next. When I'm there, you can take the girls out to some nice place." Aleksander immediately concurred.

Raya looked gratefully at these people who had become her family and thanked them profusely. She resolved that she wasn't going to despair any longer. Aleksander was right. *When there's life, there's hope.*

Galina and Aleksander arranged a schedule. Every Sunday from eleven in the morning until three in the afternoon, one of them would be at the entrance to the Central Post Office.

In September the girls went back to school. Aleksander always felt that the work of a teacher was important, but now it seemed that it was not sufficient to entirely satisfy him. Caring for the girls had clearly altered his outlook on life. He secured a job at an orphanage close to his house. During the day he was teaching geography and history at the orphanage, but in the evenings he performed the duties of a counsellor there too. His main responsibility was the grade seven students. For those poor children who had been orphaned by the war, Aleksander became much more than a teacher and counsellor; he became their advisor, their primary caregiver, and in many cases, he was destined to be the only *parent* that they would ever know and remember.

Meanwhile, every Sunday, Aleksander and Galina maintained the search for Raya's mother at the Central Post Office.

Autumn replaced summer and before long an early winter had set in. By this time Raya was resigned to the fact that it seemed useless to continue the weekly vigil. She felt guilty seeing Galina and Aleksander coming home on Sundays afternoons tired, wet and cold. Each week she resolved that she would ask them to stop their seemingly futile search, but when each successive Sunday approached, she would think, *One more week... just one more week.*

On the third Sunday of December, a day when Aleksander was taking his appointed turn at the Central Post Office, Galina, Manya and Raya were preparing a midday meal when they heard the chime of the door-bell. Before the girls could manage to open the door to the apartment they distinctly heard the gruff voice of their neighbour as he let the visitors in, and then the voice of Aleksander. "Careful please, there's a step. Okay, here we are."

Galina and the girls had remained frozen, afraid to hope and not knowing what to expect.

Aleksander opened the door to Galina flat's and ushered in a tall, stately, attractive-looking woman, whose dark hair was braided and carefully fixed like a crown around the top of her head. The woman was holding an extremely skinny boy by the hand. She looked silently at Raya before extending her arms and starting to move across the room towards the girl. It seemed that all her strength left her just before she reached Raya. She fell to her knees, grasping the girl's legs and started to sob.

Raya looked with sparkling eyes at the boy, and then at the woman hugging her as she spoke out softly, "Mama... Dima...."

The adults and Manya didn't make a move. They simply looked on in silence at the sobbing woman and the boy. There was something strange about him. He had remained standing near the doorway entrance, in the same spot where his mother had released his hand. His large, dark brown eyes were focussed on his sister and his mother, but he remained standing on that spot.

Eventually Vera regained her composure enough to be able to speak to her son. "Dimochka, come here, darling. Say hello to Rayechka. It's our Rayechka. You remember her, right dear?"

The boy did as he was asked. He moved closer to his mother's side and absent any notable emotion, he said, "Hello, Raya."

Vera was now holding the hands of both her children and through her tears she intoned, "I'm blessed, I'm blessed. G-d loves me! He truly loves me! He has performed miracles for me! Oh, thank you, G-d!"

Finally Vera became a bit more settled. She rose to her feet and came closer to Aleksander and Galina, saying, "There are no words to express my gratitude to you both. All my words are inadequate compared to my feelings. Thank you with all of my heart for saving my girl."

Galina and Vera hugged one-another and then they both embraced the broadly grinning Aleksander.

Vera looked at Manya, hugged her warmly too and said, "I've heard that you call my daughter your sister. It means that you're part of my family too, darling. May I kiss you, Manechka?"

Manya immediately liked Raya's mama. She gave her a warm kiss and then worriedly asked, "Are you going to take my sister Raya away? Where will you live?"

"Hush, Manya. Our guests must be hungry. Let's have lunch and we'll talk about everything during the meal," Galina suggested.

While Manya, Galina and Aleksander were setting the table, Raya sat on the couch between her mother and brother and felt truly happy for the first time since the start of the war. Her mother was warm and loving, exactly as she remembered her, but what was wrong with Dima? Why was he so quiet and reserved?

Eventually the lunch was ready and everyone took their seats around the table. Dima was staring at the enticing variety of food at the table with hungry eyes but didn't touch anything until Vera prompted him. "Eat, darling. Look how nice everything is."

Dima extended his hand for a piece of bread and at that moment the mystery of his strange behaviour was unveiled. Aleksander silently gestured with his eyes for Galina to take a look at the boy's hand; the girls noticed the visual communication too and discretely glanced at Dima's hand. There was a prominent, black number tattooed on it.

During the lunch Vera related her story. "We were at Boris's military base when the war started. The base was located in Latvia.

Boris was killed in one of the first attacks. Raya, I'm so sorry! Did you know that your father had passed away bravely defending our country?"

"Yes, Mama. Aleksander made some inquiries and told me about papa back in September," Raya said in a restrained tone of voice.

There was a difficult silence around the table for a moment or so, and then Vera continued. "We were in a horrible position. For the independent-minded Latvians, the Red Army and the Russian people that moved into Latvia in 1940 were occupiers and oppressors, just as much as the Germans; and actually, even more-so.

"When the war started, the families of the officers tried to escape but the Germans were advancing too fast. Before we knew it Latvia was occupied. We had no time to get away. But I knew one Latvian woman who had been working on the army base as a cook. She was much older than me but we were good friends. Raya, do you remember Aunt Daina? No? Anyway, she was living on the outskirts of a small town nearby. We went to her and asked her to give us refuge.

"Aunt Daina looked closely at our appearance and said, "*Vera, you don't look at all Jewish. More like Ukrainian. Let's tell the neighbours that you're a niece of my husband from Lvov. But we must still hide Dima. His nationality is written all over his face.*"

Manya unobtrusively scrutinized Dima's appearance; she knew what it meant to be judged by one's looks and facial features. Dima had his mother's dark eyes and dark hair, although his short hair was curly. His large nose was prominent on his drawn, skinny face and his large head looked wobbly above his long neck. *Actually*, Manya thought, *he is quite a homely Jewish boy.*

Vera resumed her chronicle. "Somehow we managed to survive together 'til the spring of 1942. Dima wasn't permitted to go outside where he might be seen. Never. Only in the middle of the night we would open the heavily curtained windows for a while so that he could get some fresh air. The neighbours readily accepted me as a relative and didn't give us a hard time. Everybody was much more concerned about their own affairs than ours. It was an unbearably difficult time for everyone.

"In the spring I took up gardening. Aunt Daina had a large garden space behind her house and we intended to plant vegetables and potatoes. The food was so scarce! That garden was meant to save us from starvation. Then one day while I was working there, a large lorry pulled up and stopped near the house. I could see German soldiers in the cabin and on the open rear platform of that vehicle. The soldiers in the rear were guarding some young girls and women. One of the soldiers asked, *"Russian?"*

"I answered, *"Ukrainian"*. What else could I say? The soldier ordered me to come closer but I stood motionless, frozen in fear. I thought of running, but then they might have entered the house and found Dima. Before I knew what was happening, two soldiers dismounted from the truck, came over to me, took me under the arms, and tossed me like a sack of potatoes onto the back of the lorry with the other girls and women. They brought us all to a building with a large courtyard. After a while some German officers and Latvian civilians started to arrive. I didn't understand what was going on until I and four of the other captured girls were ushered towards a middle-aged woman and an old man.

"We were told that from now on they were our masters and that we must do everything that they told us to do," Vera explained.

"We were taken to a large farm where I was working until October of 1944. What can I say about my life there? We were treated like slaves, working long days on the farm, but at least no man ever..." Vera stopped in mid-sentence as she glanced at the attentive two girls and then carried on in a different vein.

"The husband of our mistress was off at war. He was some sort of general, or whatever. Compared with what my children had to endure, my life during the war was not all that bad," Vera said, as she kindly smiled at her own children and at Manya.

Galina and Aleksander exchanged knowing glances. It was clear that her forced labor on the farm had not been an easy experience but Vera obviously wanted to insulate her children from any additional trauma.

"When we were freed," Vera continued, "we were placed in a camp for displaced persons. We were interrogated; after all, we had been living in an occupied territory and had worked for the enemy, even though it was against our wishes. I think what helped me was the fact that we were in Latvia and not in Germany, and that my husband was a Soviet officer. Actually, I don't really know what may have helped me the most, but eventually I was released. Right away I made my way to the town where Aunt Daina lived and went directly to her house. But instead of finding the house standing there as I knew it, I saw nothing other than a large crater carved out by a bomb.

"I stood there alone for a long time and cried. Eventually an elderly Latvian man came by and asked who I was looking for."

"Aunt Daina. She lived here. Did she die during a bomb attack?" I asked.

"Oh, no," the man replied, "much earlier. There was a raid and the Germans found a Jewish boy in her house. They shot her right then and there."

"And the boy?" I cried, "what happened to the boy? Did they kill him too?"

"Why do you ask?" the man inquired.

"He's my son," I explained.

"Are you a Jew then?" the man curiously asked.

"Yes, I am a Jew," I told him.

"They didn't kill him…a least not in front of us. They found one more Jewish family hidden in the town and took them all away. I don't know what happened to them after that," the man explained.

"The elderly man went on his way," Vera sobbed, "and I started to search for Dima. I found out that many of the Jews had been deported to the Kaiserwald Camp near Riga and so I went there, and then to other camps – Dundaga, Jungfernhof, Lenta, and Spilwe. I wasn't able to locate him or find out anything at all about what might have become of him.

"Finally I was told that there were some children that had been freed from the camps in one of the hospitals near Riga, so I went to that hospital. By this time, I had basically no hope at all, but of course I went there anyway. I entered a room where there were twelve boys. I hadn't taken more than five steps into the room when I heard, "*Mama!*" And there he was - my son, my dear and only son! But he was so weak and so skinny that he couldn't be moved. I stayed at the hospital and cared for him and helped with the care of the other boys too. Some of them were in dreadful condition and didn't make it..."

Vera momentarily fell silent again, and then shook her beautiful head, recovered her gentle smile and said, "But my Dima made it! He gained quite a lot of weight. Doesn't he look good, Raya?"

Raya and Manya were looking sceptically at Dima. If this exceptionally skinny and frail-looking boy had gained a lot of weight, how might he have looked at the time his mother found him?

"Wasn't it a miracle?" Vera exclaimed. "Nothing short of a miracle! Although I was disheartened when I couldn't find any trace of him in any of the camps, I found him in the first hospital I went to and in the first room I entered.

"And today there's been another miracle. I arrived in Kiev only yesterday. I went to mama's apartment and one of our old neighbours was there. She told me about Babi Yar. I cried all night, mourning for my mother and my daughter. But this morning, my neighbour advised me to go to the Central Post Office where people who were looking for lost relatives were gathering. Maybe I too could get some information, she suggested. So I went there. What else could I do? I was there for only a few minutes when this latest miracle unfolded before my eyes! I caught sight of Aleksander with his poster."

Vera had finished her tale, so again she hugged both of her children and Manya too, as she looked towards Aleksander and Galina with eyes filled with gratitude.

"What are you planning to do now?" Galina asked tentatively. "The girls are so attached to each other. It would be a shame to separate them. Can't you stay here in Kiev?"

"Yes indeed, I can," Vera responded affirmatively. "In fact, I have nowhere else to go anyway. My wise mother never removed my name from the book of tenants, so I'm still officially registered in her apartment. It's just across the park, on Proresnaya Street."

"That's great!" Raya exclaimed. "I knew it was somewhere close by! Manya and I can still go to our school together and Dimka can go to the same school. Oh, Mama, I'm so happy!"

Galina, Aleksander and Vera started to discuss Vera's chances for employment, about the logistics of settling in Kiev, and about Dima's schooling.

Meanwhile, Manya again looked closely at Raya's brother. There was something about him that caused her to stare at him as if she was transfixed. It was those mysterious eyes, Manya eventually realized – so dark, so deep, so penetrating. Dima was sitting quietly at the table displaying no outward emotion, but in his eyes there was so much sadness, and yet, seemingly so much maturity and wisdom too.

The eyes of the two children briefly engaged...and on the same day that Raya found her family, Manya lost her heart to this strange boy.

A Year Of Peace
And Happiness

1946 WAS THE best year of Manya's childhood, by far. She would always remember it with fondness and nostalgia. On weekdays she would walk through Golden Gate Park and there, at the corner of Proresnaya and Korolenko Streets, Raya and Dima would be waiting for her. Together, the children would then go to school. Manya and Raya always had so many things to discuss; after all, they hadn't seen each other since the previous evening!

Dima was placed in a special class for children who had had no opportunity to study during the war and now needed to catch up. There were ten children in that class, of different ages ranging from eleven to sixteen years. The teachers tried to provide as much personal attention as they could to each of those children.

Dima studied hard; he loved studying and it was soon apparent that he was as brilliant as his sister. He preferred the company of Manya and Raya to the company of other boys his own age, perhaps because he was so much smaller than the other boys. The girls gave him all the love, companionship and friendship that he needed. Slowly but surely, Dima's inwardly-focussed personality started to thaw. He talked a bit more and even, if only rarely, started to smile.

That year the children remained inseparable. After school they would go to either Vera's or Galina's apartment where they ate together and studied together. Their mothers didn't mind in the slightest. In fact, the two women had become close friends too, almost as close as their daughters. These two families, who had not even known each other before the war, had evolved into one closely-knit extended family.

Every Sunday morning Aleksander would come to join this family. He really liked Dima and before long felt that he knew the boy just as well as his sisters. The children always waited impatiently to hear Aleksander's stories about the latest events at the orphanage and then to tell him about their own school days and their other experiences of the past week.

Aleksander marvelled at how different the three children were individually and yet how close they were to each other.

Raya was typically all emotion, ready to explode at the smallest provocation, very sensitive and easily brought to tears.

Dima was a serious, contemplative boy. He liked to analyze everything, to find a deeper meaning in the simplest event, and then to discuss his thoughts with Aleksander.

Manya was the sunshine of the family. She had a calming effect on Raya and she was the only one who could cause Dima to smile. She loved to smile herself and had the prettiest grin, and her infectious laughter was like the sound of bells chiming.

Raya's favourite word that year was *stupid*. "Aleksander," she would say, "the children in our class are so stupid. Our teacher of math is stupid too!"

"Okay, Raya," Aleksander would respond indulgently, "please explain to me why you have such an unfavourable opinion of the students and teachers at the school."

"Well, for example, the teacher was explaining about fractions; you know, how to add and subtract them. It's soooo simple. But the other kids just couldn't get it! The teacher had to repeat the same thing over and over again! It was so stupid! And then the teacher gave us three pages full of the same stupid exercises!

"I came to the teacher and said, *"Maybe the other kids need to do this, but I understood all about fractions right away so I shouldn't have to be doing all these stupid exercises!"*

And then, according to Raya, the teacher said, *"Raya Kushnir, if you don't complete all three pages I'm going to fail you!"*

"It's so stupid!" Raya lamented again.

"Okay, Raya, you have two choices," Aleksander suggested. "And I'm not talking only about math. You evidently belong to that ten percent of the smartest people on this planet. So, choice number one: learn to deal with people who aren't as smart as you are; learn to be patient with them and even offer to help them.

"Choice number two: because it's not easy to find people with the same level of intelligence as yours, learn to be satisfied being alone most of the time. You can continue to despise other people because they're not as smart as you, but in turn they will despise you because you will be seen as arrogant, or because you are tall and big boned, or just because you have red hair. When people are looking for some excuse to despise or look down upon someone else they'll always find a reason, whether it's fair or not.

"Now, let's also remember with kindness that your sister Manya belongs to that other ninety percent of the people who aren't gifted with being as smart as you. What do you say? What's your choice, Raya?" Aleksander patiently waited for a response.

"I don't want to be alone and I want to have friends," the girl replied sulkily.

"That's fine, but in that case please restrain yourself in future from referring to the other kids in your class as *stupid*.

"Second problem: the teacher. Raya, how important is it for you not to do those three pages of homework? Is it important enough to alienate your teacher, or even to die for it?" Aleksander asked.

"What? Of course not!" Raya replied irritably.

"Is it important enough for you to try to prove your point and to fail math unnecessarily, and then to have your mother called to the school?" Aleksander persisted.

"Well, no…" Raya stuttered.

"Then do it, Raya. Learn to compromise and to give in on the things that aren't important enough to fight for. Learn to be flexible. Take it easy. There's going to be times in your life when you will face real and sometimes difficult challenges or temptations; times when you'll be asked to compromise your principles, the ones that define you as a person. By all means be prepared to be unyielding at those times, because to compromise on something that important to you is to destroy your soul.

"Trust me, Raya; homework isn't even worth this discussion. It'll take you less time to get done it than to complain about it. It's so much better that you can allow yourself the sense of satisfaction of answering every question perfectly, and as a bonus it will make your teacher happy too," Aleksander suggested in his encouraging manner.

Manya's questions to Aleksander were always prefixed with the word *why?*

"Aleksander, why does our neighbour Aunt Nina leave her children every evening with her mother, Aunt Miriam? Aunt Miriam doesn't like it. She cries every night; I've heard her myself! And they always have a fight when Aunt Nina comes back home the next morning. Why can't Aunt Nina just stay at home if she knows that it's so important to her mother? And what does the word *prostitute* mean?"

Aleksander would rather have tackled Raya's more emotional but less challenging questions. After a few moments of careful reflection, he would explain, "Manya, a prostitute is a woman who sells herself, her body that is, to men for money. Your Aunt Nina is definitely not a prostitute, I can assure you. It's just that it's hard for her to live without a husband. She wants to be loved which is completely normal. She wants to meet a good man who could be a good future husband to her and a good father to her children."

"So what's wrong with that?" Manya asked.

"Nothing, except that Miriam isn't Nina's real mother, but her mother-in-law – the mother of Nina's late husband. Nina may find a new husband someday, but Miriam will never have another son and it hurts her that Nina has apparently forgotten her son so easily. It's a difficult situation, Manya. There's no right or wrong in these situations and we shouldn't make harsh judgements. The war took the lives of many good people but the ones who survived want to start to live normally again. Do you understand what I'm saying, Manya?" Aleksander asked.

It seemed that Manya, already quite mature for her age, really did understand.

With Dima it was an entirely different situation. He liked to talk about the future. Having endured more than two years in the camps, he didn't think he even had a future. He still seemed surprised at times that he was actually still alive. He never talked about his past as a younger child or about his experiences in the camps.

But now Dima had emerged from his cocoon and was anxious to talk about the future all the time. He wanted to be a doctor. His father was an officer, a professional soldier, but soldiers take lives or get themselves killed. Dima had seen too much of that during the war. Doctors give and protect life, so he would be a doctor.

And so, 1946 was indeed a very good year. It was a year of family reunification, a year of friendship, and a year of children's love.

Family Marriages

1947 BROUGHT MANY changes, and it all started during the New Year's Eve festivities which the family had decided to hold in Galina's flat.

Both Galina and Vera were living in communal apartments in large, four-story buildings in which they were sharing the kitchen and bathroom facilities with other families. Galina's flat was smaller, but Vera's three neighbouring families were all staying at home for the night. Galina, however, had the entire apartment to herself for this New Year's evening and was in a position to host the celebration. Nina was going to some party where she was told there would be a lot of eligible, single men present, while Miriam was taking the grandchildren to her sister to celebrate.

There was another family living in the apartment too - a young officer named Sergey Sergeivich and his wife. They had recently moved in to occupy a flat that formerly belonged to some other family that had perished during the war. The flat had been sitting empty for some while until it was assigned to these new tenants. For New Year's Eve, the officer and his wife planned to welcome in the year at the Kiev House of Officers, a famous club for the military elite.

Raya, Manya and Dima spent the day decorating the New Year pine tree in Galina's flat with shiny ornamental balls, sparkling miniature bears and cuddly little rabbits. At the top of the tree they placed a large red star. They were Soviet children, so they had no idea that all over the world people celebrated Christmas and that their pine tree was called a *Christmas* tree. They had never heard about Christmas; not because they were Jews, but because Christmas was not celebrated in the Soviet Union. Soviet children still decorated pine and fir trees, but they were called New Year trees.

After the children finished with the tree, then they decorated the entire apartment beautifully with pine branches, snowflake cutouts, and bright paper ribbons.

Galina drew upon all her connections to obtain meat, chickens, and even fresh fish for the party. She prepared a real banquet for the festive celebration.

At ten o'clock that evening the first guests arrived, and with them came the first surprise of the evening. Vera arrived not alone but in the company of a man. She introduced him as "Semyon Mikhailovich, the head bookkeeper at our plant." Then she added sympathetically, "Semyon Mikhailovich's family sadly all perished during the war. I didn't want this fine gentleman to be left all alone on such an important night. Galina, I hope you don't mind?"

"Not at all! Semyon Mikhailovich, welcome and make yourself at home! Please take a seat."

He's not simply a colleague of Vera's, Galina promptly decided. *Otherwise, why would she be blushing and apologizing so profusely?*

The children also noticed Vera's uneasiness and curiously studied the surprise guest. He was tall, practically bald, wore thick glasses, and looked considerably older than Vera. But when he was introduced, he smiled shyly and kindly at the children. Dima liked his gentle smile and solemnly offered a welcoming hand.

"Girls," Dima commanded, "let's go into the kitchen and bring more dishes and chairs for our guests."

Once they were in the kitchen, Dima undertook to instruct Raya. "You had better behave yourself, sis! He must be very important to mama; otherwise she'd never have invited him."

"But he's so old! And he's not the least bit good looking! Our papa was so much more handsome!" Raya objected.

"Raya! Our papa has been dead for more than five years. Mama deserves to have somebody who cares for her and Semyon Mikhailovich seems like a very nice and kind man. Please promise to behave," Dima insisted.

"Okay, okay, I will," Raya agreed reticently.

The arrival of the next pair of guests rendered the appearance of Vera and her head bookkeeper friend a comparatively non-event. Aleksander showed up with a bottle of champagne and with a glamorous young lady on his arm. She had the gaudy appearance of an overly-decorated New Year tree.

"Hello everybody! This is my Lisa!" Aleksander proudly announced.

The family had never seen Aleksander quite as happy. His face was literally beaming like a shiny new kopeck! He made the introductions as Lisa smiled and nodded politely in acknowledgement of everyone gathered around.

The children immediately took a marked dislike to this Lisa woman. They had always imagined the future bride of Aleksander much differently. For sure she would be pretty, but hardly like this!

Lisa was strikingly beautiful, with large blue eyes, platinum-blonde curls, and bright red lips. She was wearing a colourful, flowery dress and high-heeled shoes. An abundant string of shiny beads hung around her neck and her large earrings matched the necklace.

After the greetings had been dutifully completed, Lisa ignored everyone else and concentrated all her charms on Aleksander. She constantly smiled at him and frequently whispered in his ear, causing Aleksander to grin sheepishly and blush profusely. She often touched his hand tenderly, as she continuously heaped more food onto his plate and refilled his wine glass.

Lisa's flagrant behavior caused everybody else to feel quite uncomfortable. At times the din of conversation abated, but Aleksander was virtually oblivious to the presence of the other guests. It was evident that he was thoroughly smitten by this bright doll and very proud to have her at his side.

Shortly after midnight, Aleksander and Lisa departed and the rest of the family sighed with relief.

"So, did you like her, Dima? Do you think she was attractive?" Raya hotly inquired.

"Sorry, Raya, I can't honestly answer your question because I didn't have an opportunity to actually see her," Dima replied caustically.

"What do you mean you didn't see her? You were sitting right beside her!" a startled Raya exclaimed.

"I mean, my dear sister, that there was so much make-up on her, or should I say *paint*, that I didn't see the real Lisa as such," Dima casually remarked without cracking a smile.

Everyone burst out laughing at this comment. That is, everybody except Vera's guest. He remained sitting quietly and listening to the banter around the table.

"But why doesn't Aleksander see that she's a phoney?" Manya asked.

"Because he's in love, darling," Galina said, "and love can be blind."

"Mama, do you think Lisa really loves Aleksander?" Dima asked, now with a genuinely concerned tone of voice.

"I'm sure that she really loves his house," Vera said sarcastically.

"We have to stop him from making a big mistake before it's too late!" Raya exclaimed.

"Hush, girls!" Galina admonished, putting an end to that line of conversation. "Aleksander is a grown man. We have no right to tell him how to live his life."

They heard a slight cough. In the excitement of the banter about Lisa's appearance, everybody had forgotten about the presence of Semyon Mikhailovich. He started to speak in a quiet, slow voice. "I hope I'll not be judged as harshly as that girl after I leave."

"Semyon Mikhailovich, dear man! Please don't think badly of us! We're not a bunch of flighty gossipers. It's just... Aleksander is a very dear friend of ours and we're truly concerned about his well-being." Galina smiled reassuringly to Semyon as she spoke.

"I understand," he responded. "I just want to make something clear from the onset." Semyon hesitated for a moment and then said, "My wife and children died in Babi Yar. My parents and her parents were also killed at that wretched place. When I returned home from the war I found out that not a single soul from my family had survived: my uncles, aunts, cousins, nieces - I lost them all. Even my apartment was occupied by some usurpers and I had no desire to fight to get it back. I didn't see any reason to continue living. Yet here I am alive. I work,

I eat, and I sleep. I rented a small room in a house on the outskirts of Kiev, but quite honestly I didn't much care where I was living.

"I have spent the last two years consumed in grieving for my family and I thought that I would continue a joyless existence until the end of my days. But then I met this beautiful, kind, wonderful woman and felt a rekindled desire to live once more. I'm eight years older than Vera Aaronovna but I love her with all my heart. "

Semyon Mikhailovich looked directly at the subdued children who were absorbing the implications of all that he was saying. "Dima, Raya, I can never be a substitute for your father of blessed memory. But if you would allow me to be your friend…"

Dima got up, strode over to the older man without any hesitation and extended his hand. "If my mama loves you and if you're going to make her happy, then I'll be your friend."

Vera and Semyon were married at the end of February and Semyon moved into her apartment.

In March, Aleksander and Lisa had their wedding ceremony. Aleksander was as happy as only a man unreservedly in love could be. He confessed to Galina and Vera, "I realize that Lisa didn't make the best first impression. But when you get to know her better you'll really like her. She has such a sunny disposition; she's such an optimist. I know that I tend to look at life way too seriously. I need her and her easy-going attitude. I truly believe that Lisa and I will be very happy together."

Homecoming

A BIG SURPRISE awaited Manya in the middle of April. It happened on a Saturday. It was a rainy, windy day, and Manya, who was recovering from a bad cold, had stayed home. She felt upset that Galina had not permitted her to go to Raya's house and was sitting morosely staring out the window. She noticed an invalid in a soldier's uniform trying to navigate his way along the street, battling against the gusty wind. The man was on crutches and there was something strange about the way he held his right crutch. Manya felt an inexplicable feeling of pity and compassion towards that unfortunate soul. He finally disappeared from her view and Manya resolved to stop sulking and do her homework. She found her school bag, took out a history textbook and started to read. Moments later she was interrupted by the sound of the doorbell.

"Mama, it must be Raya and Dima!" Manya shouted cheerfully as she ran to open the door. But instead of her friends, standing before her was the same invalid soldier whom she had been observing earlier. His uniform was soaking wet and his right sleeve was stitched together just below the elbow. Instead of a right shoe, there was a stump of a crude wooden prosthesis. He was holding one crutch in his healthy left hand and the other crutch was tucked under his right arm. There was a long, ugly-looking scar on the right side of his face too.

Manya assumed that the soldier must have come to see their neighbour, the army officer, and politely asked, "Do you want to see Sergey Sergeivich?"

The man shook his head and asked with a hesitant voice, "Manya? Manechka, is it really you?"

At that moment, Manya recognized the man whom she had not seen for almost six years. "Papa!"

"Mama," Manya screamed, "papa is home!"

Ivan tentatively entered the apartment and stood near the entrance. Galina took one look at the disfigured form of her husband and the intended exuberant cry of welcome died on her lips.

"I came back. Will you have me, Galya? A one-legged, one-armed invalid?" Ivan asked in a restrained but emotionally stressed voice.

"Vanya! Vanechka, darling, you're alive!" Galina regained her composure and rushed to her husband and embraced him and then helped him to a couch. She was kissing his scarred face and gently stroking the stump of his right arm.

"Manya, papa's all wet. Let's find some dry clothes for him," she implored.

Ivan was so relieved to see his wife and daughter alive and well, and so overwhelmed by the warm welcome and evident wholehearted acceptance of his condition, that he started to weep with emotion.

Galina had never seen her strong husband crying before and was touched to the core by his outburst of unrestrained emotion. How much this man must have suffered, and how much he must have been troubled by the fear of her rejection. She whispered sweet words of affection in his ear and held onto his good left hand, kissing it again and again.

Ivan embraced his wife with his good arm and gently kissed her. Then he motioned Manya to come closer. He looked with admiration at his eleven-year-old daughter for a very long while, and then he tenderly kissed her on her forehead and her cheeks.

When he was changed into fresh, dry clothes, Ivan took a seat at the table with a full plate of beef stew before him. He asked Galina to tell him about everything that had happened since the last letter that he had received from her in April of 1945.

Galina's story was really quite simple. She was working; Manya was in school and very close to a girl that had been rescued with her, so close that the girls referred to one-other and behaved as devoted sisters.

Galina went on to say, "I've befriended Raya's family. They're very nice people, Ivan. You'll really like them. And we're good friends with Aleksander. I wrote you all about him. He just got married last month," she added.

Ivan was listening attentively and nodding his head as Galina was talking and asked about the neighbours. Finally he finished eating and started to speak about himself and his experiences in the war.

"I was wounded in Germany, close to Berlin. I was running during an attack, there was an explosion, and I felt a horrible pain in my right leg. I fell down but I was still conscious. I looked at my right leg and saw that it was badly mangled. Then there was another nearby explosion and I felt a sharp pain in my right arm, and after that there was blackness.

"The next thing I remember was waking up in the hospital and seeing a nurse with a kind face sitting near me. *"Soldier,"* she said, *"you're very lucky to be alive. You're lucky to be in the hands of Dr. Galperin too. Aaron Davidovich is a genius; he has hands of gold! He saved your life and he saved your left leg,"* she explained.

Galina and Manya were sobbing quietly as they were listening to the compelling story of Ivan's horrific ordeal.

"I was unbearably aggrieved," Ivan went on, "when I realized that I had only one good leg and one good arm. But the worst thing was that I couldn't even remember who I was. My right hand, I was told, bled on my uniform so much that it was impossible to read my papers. From the field hospital I was sent to a stationary hospital somewhere in Russia. I remember the train-ride but I don't even know where I was taken. I remember very little from that time. Then it was another hospital, and then another...

"I didn't see the point of living as an invalid with no memory! I didn't want to eat and I just wanted that nightmare to be over with. But then I was taken to another doctor, a physiatrist named Riva Moiseevna Zak. She spent countless hours with me. If I owe Dr. Galperin my life then I owe my memory to Riva Moiseevna. She helped me to remember my name and my past, and she gave me the courage and the inspiration to come back home to look for my family and resume my life.

"Galina," Ivan started to say after a hesitant pause, all the while looking intently at his wife who could see in his eyes that this was going to be an awkward moment, but he pushed on and got to the point. "You hadn't heard from me for two years. I'm sure you must have given me up for dead before now, so if you've met someone else, Galya, I'd understand…"

"Vanya, please, don't say such a thing! I love nobody but you and I don't need anybody but you. You're home at last and that's the most important thing in the world. The worst is over. You're alive and we're together again!" an emotionally-charged Galina reassured her husband.

The weather the next morning was bright and cheerful, much like the mood of the reunited family. Galina announced that she wanted to make a nice welcome-home dinner and invite all of her friends. She was eager to introduce Ivan to Aleksander and to Vera and her children. Right after breakfast, Manya kissed her parents and set off to inform Raya and her family about the return of her father and to invite them over for the celebratory dinner.

"Tell them to be here by five!" Galina called after her daughter as Manya rushed out the door.

Galina and Ivan now found themselves alone together for the first time in six years and they had much to discuss. "Galya," he inquired, "why didn't you invite Kolya? He's your twin brother and he's my best friend."

"Vanya, dear, I wrote in my letter about the horrible deed he did on the day when the Jews were marched to Babi Yar. He was relieved to be rid of my mother and our daughter so as not to be implicated as having any Jewish blood. You should have seen the look on his face when he showed up here and saw that Manya was alive and well. Now he doesn't exist for me any longer…it's as simple as that," Galina explained with deep conviction.

"Galya, let's not be so hasty coming to conclusions. It was a horrible day for our precious little Manya and she might have misunderstood Kolya's involvement and his intentions. Let's not forget that she was only five years old at the time.

"I must see Kolya; I want to hear his side of the story. After all, he was the one who introduced us to each other. I want to give him the benefit of the doubt until I find out the truth for myself… it's something that I need to do. Please, my love, ask him to come over. I want to see him before I see all of your new friends. If Manya's story is true and he really wanted to rid himself of our Manechka, then I swear I'll kill him with my one good hand! But what if our frightened young child overreacted? Galya, I must meet face to face with Kolya," Ivan persisted.

For years afterwards, Galina would reflect on how different life for Ivan and her might have been if she hadn't acceded to his insistent demand. But on that particular morning, Galina couldn't say *no* to her husband.

Manya ran to Raya's apartment as fast as she could. "Guess what, guess what!" she shouted.

"Aliens have invaded the Earth," Dima calmly responded.

"Wrong, Dima! My papa is home! And you are all invited for dinner! At five! I'm on my way now to invite Aleksander." Manya could scarcely contain her happiness as she conveyed the good news.

Raya ran to her sister, grasped her by the hands, and together the girls did a silly, exuberant dance of joy. There was much more jumping and leaping and screaming than actual dancing, but Vera and Semyon didn't mind in the slightest. They were happy for Manya in a way that only close relatives and friends could be.

But their enthusiasm was tempered considerably when they learned of Ivan's condition. They looked at one-another with an unspoken thought of mutual concern. It would be exceptionally difficult for a carpenter by trade, a man who was used working with his hands and who depended on the strength of his body, to find some other kind of job, considering his disabilities.

The three children then went together to deliver the news to Aleksander and Lisa. They had to take a tram and then a bus to get to his house. Aleksander's immediate reaction was predictable - he was exceedingly happy for Manya. Lisa was less enthusiastic. She was pre-occupied with her spring cleaning and didn't seem to care for any interruptions.

It was absolutely not possible for Manya to have that all-important dinner without Aleksander being a part of it, and that probably meant that Lisa would accompany him, so the girls came up with a spontaneous solution to the dilemma. "Lisa, we'll help you finish the cleaning. Just tell us what needs to be done. Then we can all go to my place together," Manya volunteered.

At five o'clock, as the joyful group was approaching Galina's apartment, they met up with Vera and Semyon. He waved a bottle of wine high in the air. Together, with smiles of anticipation, the happy friends entered Galina's flat and stopped short near the entrance, momentarily paralyzed in shock by the unexpected sight before their eyes.

On the table there was some scattered food and two bottles of vodka: one empty, the other more than half-empty. Around the table were seated a morose-looking Galina, a drunken Ivan and her brother Nikolai.

"Papa, what's *he* doing here?" Manya asked in dismay.

"Oh, there you are," Ivan slurred, swaying on his chair. "Come and kiss your uncle. He's told me everything. Manechka, he loves you very much. It's entirely your grandma's fault for everything that happened. She didn't want to leave Kiev and it was because of her that he and his family didn't evacuate. Your uncle endured a horrible hardship during the occupation and all because of the stubbornness of your grandmother. On that day, in September of 1941, he begged her to put you in the care of your loving uncle. Stubborn old woman! Sweetheart, you almost died because of her. Your uncle would never let any harm come to you."

"That's not true! I was there! I heard him when he told the Germans that Grandma Anna and Manya were his neighbours!" Raya reacted loudly in defence of her friend.

"Who are you?" Ivan asked impatiently.

"Papa, this is my sister, my Raya," Manya said with pride. She avoided looking in her uncle's direction.

"Congratulations, Vanya!" Nikolai muttered in a mocking, drunken voice. "Now you have two daughters."

"No way! Manya, she can't be your sister because she isn't my daughter. I could never be the father of anyone who looks that ugly!" Ivan slurred and with that, both men burst into loud, raucous laughter.

Vera and Galina gasped and Dima clenched his fists. By now in tears, Raya turned to run away from those awful people and from the place that she had considered her home for such a long time.

Aleksander seized her hand to restrain her from leaving. "One second! Ivan Stepanovich, there's no need to insult this girl. She's a loyal friend of your daughter. They went through so much together," Aleksander reasoned.

"Oh, so you're that pedophile who kept my daughter in your house! Tell me, what did you do to her? I demand to know the truth!" Ivan shouted and slammed a heavy left fist on the table.

Aleksander turned away in disgust and taking Raya by the hand, guided her out of the room. All the other guests and Manya followed after them, leaving only the dumbfounded Ivan, a distraught Galina and the drunken Nikolai by themselves in the room.

"Manya, come back here! Come back and kiss your uncle! I'm ordering you to come back right this minute!" They heard Ivan's booming voice, but Manya was firmly grasping Aleksander's other hand and never once looked back as they all hastily got out of the flat.

When they reached Vera's apartment, the girls hugged each other and sobbed uncontrollably. The adults sat nearby, without speaking and looking gloomy, waiting until the sisters' crying eventually subsided.

Dima knelt before the girls and spoke compassionately to his sister. "Rayechka, you are not ugly in the slightest. Everybody grows differently, at his or her own pace. I'm not upset that I'm the shortest in my class. I'll just grow taller later on. You just grew up earlier, that's all. You have beautiful eyes and beautiful hair. I'm telling you as a man that you'll grow up to be a very attractive woman."

Diminutive in every respect for his age, sixteen-year-old Dima hardly looked like a man at all, and so the girls looked at him and promptly ceased crying. Instead they started to giggle. Dima had successfully broken the tension of the moment and eventually Maya and Raya fell asleep, holding close to one-another.

Some while later that disastrous evening, Galina came to Vera's apartment, intent on trying to diffuse the unpleasant situation.

"Please," she pleaded, "don't judge Vanya too harshly. He didn't mean those words. He didn't know what he was saying. He hadn't had any vodka for a long time. You know, in the hospitals they discourage any sort of drinking. He got drunk very quickly. Please, have it in your hearts to forgive him."

"Galya," Vera asked, "why did you even invite your brother over in the first place? I thought you two weren't on speaking terms."

"I didn't want to, but Vanya insisted. Before the war, Kolya had been his best friend. Vanya said that he wanted to understand for himself what really happened on the day of Babi Yar," Galina reluctantly explained.

"And so what did he understand?" Aleksander asked skeptically.

"Sasha, please! Give him a chance. Just look at him! He used to be so strong, so healthy, and so independent. We will try again, okay? Without Kolya hanging around I'm certain that when you get to know Vanya and he gets to know you better, you will become good friends."

There was so much anguish in Galina's voice that her friends didn't persist any further with the conversation. Aleksander took the soundly-sleeping Manya into his arms and helped to carry her back home, accompanied by Galina and Lisa.

When Lisa and Aleksander were on the tram riding through the half-destroyed city on their way back to their own house, Lisa commented, "This is the gratitude you get for all the good that you did. You should stop being such a Good Samaritan. It never pays. Let this be a lesson to you for the future, Sasha. You'd be better off worrying about your own family."

Aleksander didn't respond. He continued looking absently out the window. The next stop was Artem Street.

Manya left for school the next morning while her father was still asleep. But after school, father and daughter had a serious talk.

"Manechka," Ivan was saying, "I'm sorry that I offended your friends. I had a bit too much to drink. But you're a big girl now and you should understand that not everything is what it appears to be. That Aleksander of yours... I have a hard time believing that a grown man had two little girls in his house for half-a-year without... without..."

"Papa! What are you talking about? What possible reason did Uncle Misha have for saving us other than his own kindness? And what self-interest could Aleksander possibly have had in taking care of us after Uncle Misha was killed?" Manya protested.

"Manechka, you are naïve and innocent. Tell me, did he ever touch you?" Ivan persisted.

"Of course he touched me! He never let either one of us to cross the street without holding our hands," was the innocent reply. Manya hadn't grasped her father's line of questioning.

"That's not what I meant... anyway, that Raya, she looks a bit dumb, doesn't she? Does she copy your homework?"

"Papa, Raya is the smartest girl in our class. As a matter of fact, I sometimes copy *her* homework. She helps me a lot. And Dima..." Manya started to explain, but she was cut short.

"Stay away from him!" Ivan interrupted.

"Why would you say that, Papa? He's a good friend of mine," a bewildered Manya replied. She was totally taken aback by her father's surprisingly strong and negative reaction when he heard mention of Dima's name.

"I can't explain it to you, sweetheart, but he was in the camps and he survived. Do you know what they did to pretty boys there? And do you know what the boys who survived were willing to do?" Ivan quizzed his eleven-year-old daughter.

"Papa, I have no idea what you're talking about and I don't want to know. Dima suffered enough without me making his life worse by asking him prying questions," an upset Manya replied.

"Manya, your uncle told me yesterday ..." Ivan began in an attempt to change the subject, but this time it was he who was cut short.

"Papa, please explain one thing to me. Why do you make unkind accusations about the people who saved me, supported me, and helped me to become strong, and yet you defend the one person who would gladly have seen me dead?" Manya posed the question while looking directly into the eyes of her father. There was such an unexpected intensity in her expression that Ivan was taken aback and kept silent.

"That's enough, you two," Galina intervened. "Let's have supper."

Over the next two months Ivan tried without any success to find steady employment. He got a job in a wine factory where he had to sit on an assembly line and to repetitively take a bright yellow foil cap, place it on a bottle-top, squeeze it, and then take the next cap for the next bottle passing along the assembly line. By lunchtime, Ivan's back was hurting him and his left arm felt like a lead weight. But more than anything, it was the conversation around him that irritated him. He was the only man working on the assembly line. The women who were his co-workers flirted with him initially for about ten minutes, but after that they completely disregarded him. They were busily engaged in talking about their boyfriends and husbands, about their children, and even about their monthly periods! Ivan left for lunch and never returned.

Vera, feeling badly for Galina, helped Ivan to get another job as a mechanic in the boiler-room at her plant. The work was easy: check the levels of water in the boiler, and from time to time push some buttons to restart the boiler and to raise the water levels.

He lasted in that job barely a week. One night, the shift supervisor came into the boiler room and found Ivan asleep instead of monitoring the boiler. Nearby there was an empty bottle. Invalid or not, Ivan was immediately dismissed.

In the post-war Soviet Union there were no facilities or support networks to assist disabled veterans. There were no good wheelchairs and no special transit facilities to help them get around. These unfortunate souls were left to fend for themselves.

There were a few notable exceptions. All Soviet citizens had heard the story of the brave pilot, Aleksey Mereseev, who crawled out from the forest a week after his fighter jet crashed. Both of his legs were shattered and later had to be amputated. In spite of this affliction, Aleksey learned to use his prosthesis, to walk without crutches and even to fly a plane again. He eventually became a flight instructor.

Ivan Matveev was not Aleksey Mereseev. Ivan hated his first crude, wooden prosthesis and he hated his new, replacement chrome version even more. It hurt the stump of his leg and it was difficult to put it in place with one hand. Besides, Ivan irritably wondered what use there was in having his right-arm prosthesis since he couldn't hold a hammer or even lift a fork with it.

The government had granted Ivan the status of *Category One Invalid* and allotted him a small pension. The rest was up to him. After several more unsuccessful attempts, Ivan simply stopped looking for other employment. When his wife and daughter left for work and school, Ivan would sit near the window and stare absently outside for hour upon hour.

Galina and Manya didn't want to leave Ivan alone for long periods of time, so Galina managed to re-arrange her schedule to work night-shifts and dedicated her days to looking after her husband. In the evenings, Manya helped her father remove his prosthesis and to get ready for bed.

One day in early June when Galina had gone grocery shopping and Ivan was sitting home alone, Aleksander came by. He had brought with him a bag of books.

"Ivan," he said, "we started off on the wrong foot. Let's try it again. I do want to be your friend. I want to assure you that I never slept with your wife and I most certainly never touched your daughter or her friend inappropriately. So please stop being suspicious of me. Galina and Manya are my friends. More than friends, I consider them part of my family, and because of that I sincerely want to help you if you would permit me.

"A man can work with his hands or with his head, Ivan. The first option has unfortunately been taken away from you and I do sympathize with your situation, but you can learn to work with your head instead. The only other likely alternative is to become a useless drunkard and I'm sure that's not what you want. A man of your age should be keeping busy. It's not healthy to sit home alone and brood about your misfortune. I've brought you some books that I hope you would enjoy reading."

"Easy for you to say... I'm thirty-five years old and the last time I read a book I was seventeen," Ivan responded gloomily.

"I didn't say it was going to be easy, Ivan. But it sure beats the alternative, wouldn't you agree?" Aleksander persisted.

"Okay, let's just say that I go back to a school desk. How is that going to help?" Ivan mused skeptically.

"Ivan, I don't know your interests, so I brought you geography books, history books, and several good fiction books. You have to start somewhere and just reading any book on any subject is at least a good beginning.

"Do you like working with numbers? Are you good in math? In that case, you could become a bookkeeper," Aleksander suggested.

"I hate numbers!" Ivan replied hotly.

"Okay, how about working as a librarian? You could sit in a warm library, receive books and lend them out. You'd be surrounded by intelligent people and might even make some new friends," Aleksander offered.

"Well, librarian actually sounds kind of nice. But I would need a college education and what college would accept me?" Ivan asked hesitantly.

"What college wouldn't? You're a veteran who served his country with honour. Sure, there's some work to be done, but we have almost two months before college entrance exams. If you're seriously interested, then I'll help you to prepare."

For the first time since Ivan awoke in that military hospital room, he foresaw the potential for a better life ahead of him. He extended his left hand to shake Aleksander's, thereby sealing the deal.

Galina and Manya were excited about the proposition. They wanted to do anything they could to help Ivan get ready for the entrance exams. Even Dima forgave Ivan the insult to his sister and studied with him whenever Aleksander was unavailable.

Nikolai was the only one who considered the college idea folly and he made sure that Ivan knew his opinion, even though these days he was not a frequent visitor at Galina's place. He was only coming by when Manya was at school and he knew that Aleksander was not going to be around either. Nikolai always brought two bottles of vodka: one for them to drink together and the second one for Ivan to keep at home for later…just in case. Ivan would hide this second bottle under his bed, away from the watchful eyes of his wife and daughter.

Manya always knew when her dear uncle had been around, not only from the smell of alcohol, but also by her father's moods.

One evening Ivan said, "It's too bad about the leg but it's the loss of my arm that really bothers me. If I only had two good hands, I'd be able to work in my proper profession; I'd be able to live like a normal man! I wonder if the doctor *really* had to cut it off."

"Do you think he did it just for kicks?" Manya responded incredulously. "Papa, you said yourself that the surgeon was a brilliant doctor who saved your life."

"Well, maybe if he had been a Christian man..." Ivan pondered.

"Did my dear uncle suggest this crazy idea? That the evil Jewish doctor cut off your arm just to mutilate you?" an agitated Manya asked.

"We'll never know, will we?" Ivan retorted.

"But the nurse said...." Manya began, but Ivan interrupted her with a ready answer.

"Her name was Faina. Would a Faina ever say something against an Aaron, eh?"

"Papa, please stop it! Enough is enough! And please don't think that way anymore; you're making it harder for us and for yourself," Manya pleaded with her father.

"Manya, you're still awfully naïve."

At that point Manya retreated to her corner and the conversation was over.

The next time she saw Aleksander, Manya asked him, "Why is my uncle doing this? Why does he bring vodka for my papa? Why does he try to poison him against the Jews? He has Jewish blood himself."

"Manya, your uncle did something exceptionally evil during the war. He sent his own mother to her death. That incident couldn't possibly leave him unscathed. That evil deed has corroded his soul. And now, in order to live with himself, he has to somehow justify his actions. Try to stay away from him and I hope your father will learn to do the same," Aleksander advised.

Ivan's hard work paid off in spite of Nikolai's meddling and on September first he started college as a student. Just a few years of studious work and he'd be a qualified librarian. Galina, Manya and their friends finally had some basis to celebrate Ivan's return; not simply his return from the war but a return to a normal, purposeful life.

Manya Turns Thirteen

COLLEGE STUDIES PROVED to be considerably more difficult than Ivan had anticipated. The other students in his class were much younger than him, and what's more, all of them were much more knowledgeable. He felt frustrated when the teachers casually made reference to books that he had never even heard of. He had a difficult time remembering names and birthdates of famous authors. Ivan was also reading much more slowly than the other students. By November he was so frustrated that he was ready to give up. Only his family's encouragement and their professed belief in him motivated him sufficiently to persevere.

Then one day while Ivan was struggling to read a book by Dostoevsky and ponderously re-reading the same page for a third time, Nikolai made an appearance.

"Hey, school-boy! Aren't you tired of pretending to be what you are not?" Nikolai asked mockingly. "Let me tell you what you are not: you're not a scholar. But just for the sake of argument, let's say you finish college. Then what? Do you know how much librarians make? Kopecks! You'll be poor forever, counting every last kopeck. Well, at least you'll be around all those kiddies...you could even share them with your new friend, that pervert Aleksander."

"Kolya, stop it! I don't need you to be talking to me so crudely like that!" Ivan retorted angrily.

"Vanya, I do it only because I love you. You're my friend. You're the husband of my beloved twin sister. I worry about you and I want to help you. Please believe me and think about this: how can you be a scholar and how can you study all these books, after that Jewish woman-doctor played with your head for so long?" Nikolai confronted his brother-in-law.

"Before you say anything I want you to listen to me carefully," Nikolai persisted. "I just got a job as a steward on the train. My train is going to Tashkent every week. I can bring back goods from there that you could never hope to buy in Kiev! Melons, early spring flowers, tomatoes, out-of-season cucumbers, and so on. All you'd have to do is to take the goods to the market and sell them there."

"This is a joke, Kolya, right? How could I possibly get such heavy loads of fruits and vegetables to the market?" Ivan shook his head negatively.

"Galina will help you. She's a smart woman. As soon as she sees some real money, she'll know what's good for her and her family. Vanya, think about my offer for a bit. I leave tomorrow and I'll be back in a week. I'll talk to you then," Nikolai concluded. Then he poured a generous portion of vodka into two glasses. The two men lifted their glasses in a toast and emptied them in a flash.

After Nikolai left, Ivan cast his eyes on his books with rekindled loathing. He brushed them aside and retrieved his own bottle of vodka from its hiding place under the bed.

The following week, Nikolai returned from Tashkent with a large, heavy suitcase stuffed with famous Tashkent melons. In the early morning he came to pick up Ivan and together the two men headed off to the market. Nikolai paid for the rental of some space on a sales counter, helped Ivan to settle in, and then left the new merchant to tend to the sale of his melons.

Nikolai's scheme was actually quite astute. The exotic melons were selling like hot-cakes, and nobody dared to ask for a discount from an invalid. Ordinary people felt good about buying the much sought-after melons from this unfortunate man. They even felt proud to see him, a disadvantaged fellow citizen, working instead of standing on a corner begging for money. The entire suitcase of melons was sold out in a matter of a few hours. Soon, Nikolai returned to the market and the proud men went off to celebrate the success of their new business venture.

After he had counted his share of the money, Ivan knew that his college days were over.

Ivan was severely disappointed by the cool reaction of Galina and Manya towards his new venture with Nikolai. "You're fools!" he admonished the women. "In a week I can make more money than you, Galina, are making in a month! We'll be rich before you know it! Then we can start living the good life! And what do you mean, *money isn't everything*? Just wait until you see a lot more money, then you'll know for certain that I'm right!" he asserted.

The college books were put aside and left to collect dust. Who needed books when in only a few hours at the market, he could make more money than a librarian could make in a week?

Nikolai rapidly expanded the enterprise. He found suppliers of the best fresh produce and other merchandise in every city where the train took him. Some local vendors would come to the train station with their goods. Nikolai paid them a good price on the spot and everyone was happy. In post-war Kiev, everything was scarce, not just fruits and vegetables. The opportunities for the Nikolai and Ivan partnership seemed limitless.

Before long, Nikolai shifted his main focus to other types of high-demand goods: shoes, gloves, silk fabrics, knitted hats, scarves and costume jewellery – whatever he could find from his growing list of suppliers.

Early on Sunday mornings, Nikolai would come to pick up Ivan and together they would go to work at the flea-market. When Nikolai was on the road, it was Galina's responsibility to carry the goods to the market for Ivan. She detested the idea but couldn't say *no* to her husband.

Officially, the flea-market existed to help people sell their second-hand clothes, but in reality it was the only place in Kiev where the ordinary people could buy decent brands and new, better quality merchandise. Of course the prices were quite different from those established by the government. The local militiamen were always circulating in the market area, ready to arrest those merchants who were openly peddling scarce, brand new goods at inflated prices. But the militia never bothered Ivan, a disabled war veteran, which was the real reason Nikolai needed him there.

Four Sundays a month at the black market were enough for Ivan to quite adequately provide for his family. The rest of the time he played dominoes in the park if the weather was good, or he would sit in local *watering holes*, drinking with his new-found buddies.

The relationship between Vera's family, Aleksander and Galina's family predictably deteriorated and became quite tense. There were no more mutual dinners or picnics.

In any case, there was scarcely any time for socializing. Vera gave birth to a boy and named him Misha, in remembrance of Semyon's father and in remembrance of Uncle Misha who had saved the girls from certain death.

Lisa and Aleksander had a new baby daughter, Tatiana, or as she became affectionately known, Tanya.

Galina missed seeing Vera and Aleksander, but what could she do? She knew that Ivan didn't like her friends in the slightest, and (she had to be honest with herself) Vera and Aleksander were not too fond of her husband either.

At least she had Kolya back in her life. *Vanya was right. Kolya is a real friend. He helped Vanya through a difficult time. Now, when Vanya has money in his pockets he's more relaxed, more confident. Okay, so he's a black market peddler, but is that his fault? What else can he do? Study in college? That was completely unrealistic after all,* Galina managed to convince herself.

Galina still grieved for her mother, but could she really blame Kolya for her mother's death? She rationalized that there had been over thirty thousand Jews killed in Babi Yar and it hadn't been Kolya who had killed any of them.

She wished that Manya would soften her attitude towards her uncle, but Manya still completely ignored Kolya. Because of this, he never came over to visit with his family. Galina yearned to spend time with her sister-in-law, her niece and her nephew. Kolya's children were just a bit younger than Manya but the difference in age wasn't that significant. Before the war, Manya had been good friends with Kolya's son. Surely they could be good friends again; after all, they were first cousins.

But Manya was very stubborn. Every Sunday when Ivan and Galina returned from the market, Manya was not at home. She usually returned late in the evening and when Ivan would ask her where she had been, she responded openly and honestly that she had spent the entire day with Raya and Dima at Aleksander's house.

Every time this situation arose, Galina hoped that Manya would offer some vague answer, such as *"I've been with friends..." Manya surely must know how much her straightforward answer always aggravates her father,* Galina reflected.

Yet Manya would always look directly at Ivan and give the same answer, "I spent the day with my best friends, Raya and Dima, at Aleksander's house."

Ivan once asked, "What's a girl your age doing every Sunday with a man so much older than yourself?"

Manya patiently explained, "Papa, we're talking about school, life, history and other things. There are always a lot of people coming to see Aleksander; his friends and many of his students."

"I pity his poor wife! Every Sunday she has to entertain a horde of strangers!" Ivan exclaimed.

"Papa, we're always helping Lisa," Manya replied.

"Great! My daughter's a maid and a servant!" an irritated Ivan concluded.

"I'm not any such thing. It's just that it's always so interesting over there. Aleksander is so wise..."

"And I'm stupid, is that it?"

"I didn't say that, Papa. If one person is smart, it doesn't mean that another person isn't smart too," Manya replied sweetly as she kissed her father on the forehead and then discreetly withdrew to her corner of the flat.

Sometimes Ivan would alter the nature of his verbal rebukes. "Stop spending so much time with those Kushnirs! They're not good company for you, Manya! Find yourself some other friends!"

Unmoved, Manya would always answer consistently. "I have a lot of friends in school but none of them are as close to me as Raya and Dima."

Galina frequently tried to admonish Manya, "Manechka, please don't aggravate your father. Just look at him! Have some pity on him!" Manya would become quiet and say, "I do pity him, Mama, and I wish that I could help him. But I'm not going to abandon my Raya and you know it very well. She's my sister."

These confrontations in one form or another became a predictable weekly affair in the Matveev household. Galina felt helpless to resolve the subtle but growing conflict between father and daughter.

There were still some days when Ivan and Manya conversed with each other. Ivan told his daughter war stories, while Manya talked about school.

At such times, Manya would think, *I wish papa wouldn't listen to Uncle Kolya all the time. And I wish he would stop drinking so much.*

And Ivan would think, *I wish those Kushnirs left my Manechka alone. They're brainwashing her.*

And then there were other days when Ivan and Manya abandoned all pretence of civility and literally shouted at one-other. Ivan would insist that Manya must reconcile with her uncle and stop associating with the Kushnirs and with Aleksander. Manya would retort just as loudly that she would never trade the brave and wise Aleksander for her cowardly uncle and that she would never give up her dear sister Raya either.

Galina always found herself caught in the middle of this family division. Something had to be done. Eventually she decided to make one more attempt to reconcile her family with her friends. She discussed the idea with Ivan and somewhat surprisingly, gained his agreement. They would hold a large party for Manya's thirteenth birthday and Galina planned to invite Kolya and his family, along with Aleksander and Lisa and Tanya, and Vera with her troops.

Galina understood full-well that she was walking a fine line when she decided to keep it a secret from Manya that Kolya and his family were invited; not to mention keeping it secret from Kolya that Vera and Aleksander had also been invited. At the party, Galina intended to ask everybody to put aside the past and make a genuine effort to become good friends, for Manya's sake, and for the sake of the unity of her own family. Everybody loved her Manechka, and so in Galina's mind it was reasonable to expect that everybody would agree to reconcile and let bygones be bygones.

Planning the party became an obsession with Galina. She started to prepare well-before April 19th, Manya's birthday. Delicacies were procured and the apartment was stocked with fine wines and cognacs. Galina was cooking for several days to prepare a real celebratory feast for her daughter.

At last the big day arrived. Galina was incredibly apprehensive, thinking to herself with heightened trepidation, *I hope this works!*

Unfortunately, the beginning moments of the party were not too promising.

Ivan decided almost immediately that the party was nothing more than Galina's folly and was destined to fail. The guests began to irritate him right from the start of the gathering.

Just one look at that big, ugly cow his daughter was calling *sister* caused Ivan's mood to plunge. At the age of thirteen, Raya was as tall as an average man. Her shoulders seemed to be hunched under the weight of her already-developed large breasts. In Ivan's mind, there was something indecent about a young girl having such breasts at that age. Raya had not developed proportionally in other respects either; her arms and legs were unusually long for her body and she had a childish face that didn't come close to suiting her large frame. Her party dress seemed totally out of place. Her red mane of hair looked untidy and wild. And her nose! *There's enough flesh there to make at least two noses,* Ivan scornfully thought to himself. What could there possibly be in common between his pretty and petite daughter and that towering, unsightly creature?

And that brother of hers! He looks exactly like that whore, his mother, with those large, soulful, dark eyes, and pale skin. That's what really irked Ivan the most – Dima's budding good looks. Pretty boy! Pederast! And to think he believes he has the right to look at his Manya as if she belongs to him. Ivan would never allow that Jew-boy to be in any serious relationship with his daughter. Over his own dead body!

The unsuspecting children ran straight to Aleksander when he arrived and engaged him in some animated discussion. Meanwhile, Ivan poured himself a shot of vodka and promptly downed it.

And his Galina! She greeted this Vera woman like a long-lost sister and was cooing to Vera's little brat as if he were her own! Ivan took another shot to calm his nerves.

At one point he noticed that Nikolai was deeply engaged in a discussion with Lisa. What was that about? Ivan stumbled in their direction.

"Lisochka, you look like an intelligent woman," Nikolai was saying. "It must be hard for you to stay at home with a child and live on Aleksander's meagre teaching salary."

"Practically impossible!" Lisa agreed. "I'm counting every kopeck and still can't make ends meet. But what can I do? I don't want to put Tanya in a nursery. She'd be sick all the time and I would end up staying home with her anyway."

"Oh, no! Don't even think about a nursery," Nikolai proclaimed his agreement with Lisa. "I have a different and much more suitable proposition for you. You know that I've been bringing some high-demand goods to Kiev and Ivan has been helping me to sell them. However, I've found a new supplier who can provide a large quantity of make-up and skin care products for women. I don't mean our Russian-made garbage. I'm talking about quality, imported stuff. Can you imagine Ivan selling make-up and the like to the ladies? But you, Lisochka, you could do it. All you'd have to do is work several hours every Sunday at the market. You'll earn more money than Aleksander makes in a month. He can help by looking after the child on Sundays. Just think about it, sweetheart, okay?"

Ivan was impressed. A real businessman, that brother-in-law of his, always thinking about expanding his enterprise. Good for him.

The time came for Galina to invite everyone to sit down for the birthday meal. The table was appealingly set with at least ten different salads, home-made appetizers, small sandwiches with black caviar, and bottles of vodka, cognac and wine. *Let the guests know that we're doing everything for our beloved Manechka,* Galina thought.

Despite all the appetizing food and drink, the conversation around the table was subdued and strained. It was obvious that Galina's friends and her relatives were, for the most part, avoiding so much as looking at each other, never mind engaging in any polite conversation.

After several more drinks, Ivan announced that he wanted to make a toast. He lifted his full glass and said, "I want to toast my beloved daughter and the only man other than myself who truly loves her, her uncle Nikolai. Manya, look around you. This food, your clothes, and all our prosperity - we owe all of it to your dear uncle. He is my one and only true friend. When I was down and needy, he came to me, not with harebrained ideas, but with a realistic proposal. I listened to him and today I can proudly say that I can provide very well for my family. Thank you, Nikolai."

Ivan wasn't done yet and he pressed on. "I know, Manya, that there was a misunderstanding during the war. But that's all it was – an unfortunate misunderstanding. It happened during a very difficult time, but that was almost eight years ago. Now it's time to forgive and forget. Manechka, I want all of us to be friends. I want you to be good friends with your cousins. Please, come and kiss your uncle and aunt."

Manya remained unmoved in her spot. Under the table, she found Raya's hand and squeezed it as hard as she could. Raya could feel that Manya was trembling.

Ivan repeated his request more forcefully. "Come here now, Manya, and kiss your uncle!"

Still Manya didn't flinch or make a move. The day that she wanted so desperately to forget had been cruelly brought back to haunt her yet-again. She saw before her eyes the image of her petrified grandmother looking at her son with both hope and despair, and then hearing her uncle saying to the soldiers, *"They are my neighbours"*. Manya could still envisage the smile of relief on Nikolai's face as he melted away from the line-up into the crowd, as clearly as if it had happened only yesterday.

Manya paled visibly. Seeing her anguish, Vera pleaded, "Ivan, please leave Manya alone. Don't you see how she's suffering from those horrible memories? It's her birthday, after all."

"Stay out of this," Ivan shot back. "This is a family matter."

"Manya! Get up!" he commanded.

"Never," Manya uttered in a voice barely above a whisper. "I'll never talk to or come close to this man who renounced his own mother. And I'd rather be hungry than eat any food provided by this traitor and coward."

Nikolai shot out of his seat and briskly said to his family, "Let's get out of here. I'm not going to sit here and listen to these lies!"

"Manya, you'll be sorry for this!" He looked menacingly around the table and added, "You will all be sorry! Lies! Nothing but lies!" With that, Nikolai stormed towards the front door.

Raya couldn't take it any longer; she couldn't stand to see her sister in such distress. She jumped up from her chair and retorted loudly, "They're not lies! It's all true! I was there!"

Nikolai's bewildered and frightened family had already hastily left the apartment. Following after them, Nikolai paused in the doorway and said vindictively while glaring at Raya, Dima, Vera and Semyon, "It's just too bad that Hitler didn't finish all of you off."

Ivan turned to Manya with undisguised anger, pointed at Raya and her family and said furiously, "Look closely at these people, Manya, because you're seeing them for the very last time. I forbid you to see any of these people ever again.

"Do you want to know the truth? Here's the real truth. Do you know what women were doing on the farms in Germany? Sleeping with their masters! Your beloved Aunt Vera is nothing but a German whore! And that pretty Jew-boy is a pederast! And your so-called sister is a dumb, ugly freak! Tomorrow, you're going to another school. I'll never forgive you for insulting your uncle like that!"

Galina burst into tears, crying hysterically. Semyon, holding his small son in his hands, ushered his family out of the apartment. Aleksander picked up Tanya and motioned to Lisa to follow him and left the apartment shaking his head in disgust.

Galina approached her husband and tried to calm him down. Manya, still unmoving, looked at the ruined party table, then at her parents, and muttered, "Happy Birthday to me." Then she dropped her head on the table and began to cry.

The next day, Galina transferred Manya from School Fifty-Seven to School Forty-Eight. Ivan considered the entire matter closed.

How little he knew or understood his daughter! The two schools were not far apart. The girls were still furtively seeing each other every day. They did their homework after school in the nearest library together and they spent all of their free time together. Manya was as frequent a visitor at Raya's house as before, and Galina was well-aware of this. The only difference was that Raya and Dima never visited Manya any longer. When Ivan asked Manya where she was after school, Manya would simply reply, *"With friends."*

She didn't lie; she just didn't name her friends.

Every Sunday, the inseparable trio of Manya, Raya and Dima was still going to Aleksander's house too, unbeknownst to Ivan.

In a way, their Sunday visits became less tense and much more pleasurable. Lisa was never at home on those mornings. Despite Aleksander's objections, she had become one of Nikolai's distributors and spent every Sunday working at the flea-market.

By this time Aleksander had come to the stark realization that his marriage was not made in heaven after all. His naïve desire to educate Lisa, to interest her in his books, and to encourage her to appreciate his values and ideas had all proven futile. He finally admitted to himself that his wife was a shallow, small-minded and selfish woman.

Lisa was no less disappointed in her marriage. She had grown up in a small provincial town in Ukraine and had always dreamt of living in the capital city, in Kiev. Her family was large but their meagre apartment had been small and over-crowded. She had to share a bed with her sister and in their youth the girls often discussed how one day they would escape the dreary life in their small town.

When the war began, Lisa and her sister joined a military hospital as orderlies. They fantasized about meeting a wounded general (at least a major!) and taking care of him, nursing him back to health and having him fall in love with one or the other of them.

The dream came true for Lisa's sister. Almost. The officer in question was only a lieutenant and he was from Donetsk, not from Kiev, or Moscow, or Leningrad – not from one of the large, exciting or as Lisa called them, *prize* cities. Even so, Lisa's sister got married and moved to Donetsk with that officer.

Lisa had met a wounded officer too and had fallen in love with him. But when the time came for him to leave the hospital, he informed her that he was married, had two children, and that he had no intentions of leaving his family.

Disappointed, bitter and disillusioned, Lisa was left with only one way of moving to Kiev. She succeeded in getting recruited for work on a construction project and was assigned a bed in the women's dormitory. The work was hard and the salary pathetic, but at least she was finally in Kiev, a city that seemed to hold the promise of unlimited opportunities.

Fate eventually smiled upon Lisa in the guise of a tall, young and broad-shouldered teacher who was dispatched by the Komsomol to give a lecture in the dormitory about the current state of political affairs.

At the conclusion of the lecture, most of the girls crowded around the handsome lecturer, fawning over him. Lisa stayed aside. She could detect that their animated giggling made him feel distinctly uncomfortable.

Finally, after the bevy of girls had disbursed and left the man alone, Lisa came forward to ask him a question about his presentation.

That's how the siege of a *fortress* named Aleksander began. Lisa was careful and meticulous in her approach to the challenge of winning his heart. She read all the books he gave her. She listened to his political views, debated with him a bit and eventually, seemingly convinced by his logic, concurred with them. When Aleksander invited Lisa to his place for the first time and she realized that she had the opportunity to become the mistress of such a fine house, she redoubled her efforts. She was determined that Aleksander was going to be her ticket to the good life.

Lisa quit her dreadful job at the construction site as soon as they got married. She had assumed that marriage would afford her security and the ability to enjoy her life without having to worry over every kopeck. But she soon learned otherwise. The salary of a teacher didn't go far and her life in post-war Kiev as a housewife with a small child proved difficult and dull. Lisa felt that what remained of her youth was slipping away, never to return. She wanted to party, to go to fashionable restaurants, to dance! She wanted to possess beautiful clothes and be surrounded by beautiful people. What was wrong with wanting to live the good life?

Aleksander's idea of entertainment on the other hand, was being immersed in his books or discussing politics with his cronies. *What a waste of time!* Lisa thought.

After Manya's abortive birthday party, Aleksander strongly suggested that Lisa stay away from Nikolai, and it was then that the spouses had their first serious fight.

Lisa shrugged her shoulders, glared at Aleksander with open disdain and in no uncertain terms let him know her opinion of him and his misplaced values.

"What do you expect from me?" Lisa asked bitterly. "Do you want me to continue to live like a pauper? Do you expect me to wear the same dress every day of the year? Do you want me to just stay home and never go out? Do you think that I'm your personal slave who will just sit here and look after your kids? Forget it! I'm destined for a better life than this!"

Aleksander now wondered how he could have been so easily fooled by a pretty face and fawning words in those early days. Even the physical attraction was no longer there.

Every morning he awoke beside a plain-looking woman with a washed-out complexion and unremarkable features. By the time he got home after school every day, Lisa would have applied a heavy amount of make-up and would be looking sexy and beautiful. However, it had come to the point where Aleksander found her made-up looks to be cheap and tawdry.

But there was still his beloved Tanya to consider and Aleksander wouldn't even entertain the thought of breaking up his family

And so, every Sunday, Lisa left the house early in the morning for the market, while the three child protégés made their appearance soon afterward to spend several enjoyable hours in the company of Aleksander and young Tanya.

Family Turmoil

MANYA WAS FOURTEEN years old when she completed Junior High, at which time she made a significant future career decision: she would go to nursing school and become a nurse, just like her mother. She was attracted to the idea of working in the hospital and caring for people, but most importantly, the thought that in only four years she could become truly independent greatly appealed to her.

That same summer, Dima applied to medical college. When he announced that he wouldn't be applying to Kiev University, but instead would seek admission to the Yaroslavl State Medical Academy in Russia, the family was saddened.

"I have no chance of passing the exams in Kiev. Without connections and being a Jew, they'll fail me for sure. Yaroslavl has a good medical college and the anti-Semitism is not nearly as bad there as it is here in the Ukraine," Dima explained. He was absolutely right.

"But it's so far and train tickets are really expensive. How will I support you, Dima?" Vera was worrying. "I still have to take care of Raya and Misha. You know that our salaries aren't very substantial."

"Mama, I'll work all summer and earn money for the train ticket. I'll find a part-time job there too. I don't need much. I want to be a doctor more than anything else. Please, Mama, let me go."

Reluctantly, Vera agreed.

In late July, Raya and Manya were standing at the train station and waving goodbye to Dima.

He has become so handsome, Manya thought. *With all those smart female medical students, he won't even remember me. I'm just a kid to him.*

Does she realize how pretty she is? Dima thought. *She'll go to nursing school and forget all about me.*

Maria Ivanovna Matveeva had no trouble gaining admission to nursing school. With such a traditional Russian name as hers, she didn't have to travel far. In her passport, in the fifth paragraph beside the word 'Nationality' it was clearly written, 'Russian', not as in Dima's or Raya's passports. The fifth paragraph in their passports stated 'Jew', and accordingly they were subject to the government-mandated admission quotas. Those quotas were never publicized or even acknowledged, but they were official policy nevertheless and every Jewish family was well-aware of them.

Manya passed her admission exams quite adequately and Raya felt immensely proud of her sister's achievement. The long hours that they had spent together in preparation for Manya's exams had paid off.

In mid-August, a telegram arrived from Yaroslavl. *"I got in. See you next summer,"* Dima announced matter-of-factly.

Raya went to high school in September to continue her own education. Aleksander's words of guidance and encouragement that she had a scientific mind remained firmly ingrained in her head. She knew exactly what she wanted - university, then grad school, and then to earn her PhD and dedicate her life to research. That was to be her destiny.

In October of the same year, a disaster struck Aleksander's family. Lisa was arrested. By that time she had become overly confident and careless with her behaviour at the flea-market. Her greed had gotten the better of her and she had been stuffing her bags with make-up kits to sell by the hundreds.

One Sunday, a man dressed in plain-looking civilian clothes approached her and innocuously asked, "Nice kit; how much do you want for one?"

"You don't need my merchandise," Lisa replied impatiently as her experienced eyes quickly appraised and dismissed the man.

"You never know," the customer said, "so, how much?"

"Five rubles," Lisa haughtily replied.

"Whew! The same kit only costs one ruble in the government store," the man said in apparent astonishment.

"Then go and buy a kit like this one in the store if you can find one. Get out of here and don't be in the way of the real customers," an impatient Lisa instructed the man dismissively.

"Open up your bag. I want to see how many kits you have there," he demanded.

"Just give him the stupid kit," the woman standing at the stall to the left of Lisa whispered urgently.

But Lisa, failing to sense the imminent danger, continued to defy the man. "It's none of your business what I have in my bag. Get lost!"

The man then produced a red, official-looking identification badge.

"Where did you get that?" Lisa asked. "Maybe you bought it at another stall, eh? Just look at him, people!"

Lisa looked about, inviting the gathering of vendors and shoppers within earshot to laugh with her at this pretender. However, the other peddlers and even the crowd of customers promptly stepped away, keeping their distance and leaving Lisa to deal with the man on her own.

Observing their cautious retreat, Lisa suddenly felt a wave of fear come over her. The officer motioned to one of his counterparts standing nearby and then the two of them flanked Lisa from each side. The pretence *customer* whom Lisa had confronted then took hold of her large bag and prepared to inspect it. At that moment, Lisa committed her second and costliest mistake - she tried to run away. She tugged aggressively at the bag, trying to wrest it from his hands and inadvertently struck the second arresting officer in the face with her elbow. With one hand the aggrieved officer grasped Lisa's arm firmly, and with his other hand he covered his now-bloodied nose.

Lisa was arrested on three charges: black-marketeering, resisting arrest, and assaulting an arresting officer. She was convicted and received a sentence of five years in prison.

Coming back from the trial, Aleksander was thinking that it must be his destiny to look after young girls. He was somewhat ashamed of himself for not feeling any genuine sympathy towards Lisa. But he had to admit to himself that he felt a strong sense of relief - no more screaming, fighting, or petty demands. *And who knows,* he thought, *maybe after her term in prison Lisa will come to her senses.*

On the day of Lisa's arrest, Nikolai had shown up at Aleksander's doorstep and demanded the return of the remaining merchandise plus compensation for the lost goods that had been confiscated by the officers at the market. Nikolai was shorter than Aleksander, although stockier. Aleksander just glared at the older man, picked him up roughly by the shoulders and set him down none too gently outside the house. Then he searched the interior of his house and located two bags of make-up kits and other goods, all of which he tossed outside while suggesting to Nikolai in no uncertain terms that he ought never to come back.

Manya and Raya did their best to support their friend. They were coming on weekends not just to visit, but to assist Aleksander with the household chores and to play with Tanya.

That year, Aleksander decided to make some improvements to his house. The old summer kitchen, under which the girls had hidden for two years, was insulated better and converted into an office. Aleksander built some bookshelves and moved all of his books into this renovated room. He also built an extension that became a separate entrance from the backyard to the house and a new summer kitchen.

The girls wished they had more time to spend with Aleksander, but free time was always short. Nursing school was challenging and Manya again needed Raya's help. Academic subjects always came easier for Raya and she was able to manage her own school studies, while at the same time learning anatomy, biology and physiology with Manya.

The greatest source of excitement in the girls' lives in those days was Dima's frequent letters. They were always addressed to both sisters and were filled with news of his student life, along with detailed descriptions of Yaroslavl and the university. His letters were always cheerful and humorous.

On one occasion, Manya took one of Dima's letters home to show her mother but Ivan happened to find it. For years afterwards, Manya remembered the ensuing outburst of yelling and the banging of his heavy fist on the table, along with the cursing and the threats. Ivan had assumed that Manya's relationship with the Kushnirs had ceased for good a long time ago. His obsessive dislike for Manya's friends had evolved into an overwhelming hatred.

After that incident with the letter, Manya had to find excuses to study outside of the home. Fortunately, she now had more freedom than when she was attending school. The names of Dima, Raya, Vera, and Aleksander were now taboo in Ivan's household, and Dima's letters were never brought to the apartment again.

When summer came, Dima returned home for the holidays and the trio spent a wonderful, carefree time roaming the great forests surrounding Kiev and sun-tanning on the sandy beaches on the shores of the Dnieper. On Sundays, Aleksander and Tanya joined in their outings and they all had a fine time together.

"Aleksander," Manya once said, "Papa's attitude has really changed. When he came home from the war, he was telling everybody that Dr. Galperin had saved his life and that Dr. Zak had restored his memory. Now he tells everybody that Dr. Galperin mutilated him for no reason and that Dr. Zak played with his mind, and that was why he had to quit the librarian course at the college. I think that by now he actually believes this nonsense. If only my dear uncle would leave him alone! But oh no, Uncle Nikolai is constantly fuelling my papa's hatred for Jews. I think my father's becoming a real anti-Semite."

Dima and Raya glanced knowingly at each other. As far as they were concerned, Ivan Matveev had been an affirmed anti-Semite for years.

"Well," Aleksander said, searching for the right words, "in a way, unfortunately this is your and your mother's fault."

"How could you say such a thing? Manya retorted hotly. "We're doing everything we can to keep papa comfortable. Mama has given up all her own friends. She doesn't go anywhere anymore and she dedicates all her time to him whenever she's not at work. Granted, I'm not at home as much as I should be, but when I am around I'm always trying to help him too. If only he would stop drinking! When he's sober he's so kind to mama and me, and he tells us how much he loves us and how much he needs us. But when he's drunk he screams at mama and threatens her. I don't know what she did wrong or what else she can possibly do?"

"Sometimes, doing less is doing more," was Aleksander's cryptic reply. "Your mama feels sorry for your papa and that's why she never rebukes him. She never says *no* to him. That isn't healthy for any relationship. Your father, I'm sure, is taking your mother for granted. Please understand that sometimes people resent the very people whom they're completely dependent upon. Manya, your father's biggest problem is idleness. He has far too much free time on his hands. He has money but doesn't know what to do with it. He doesn't even read and he doesn't have any hobbies. With time, his own misery and negative attitude towards his own caregivers will only become worse."

"Your father," Dima intervened, "didn't just lose a couple of limbs during the war; worse still, he lost his purpose in life. He actually believes that it's somebody else's fault that he's so unhappy. He can't continue to hate the Germans; the memory of war is too abstract by now, so the old enemy is too-far removed from reality. He needs a more immediate, more tangible enemy. Jews are a much easier target to hate; they're the more convenient enemies now."

Manya couldn't take issue with Dima's logic.

Sad to say, Manya's friends had already been proven correct. Ivan's anti-Semitism had several sources. First, there was his persistent and growing belief that the Jewish doctors had maimed him and played with his mind purposely. Secondly, he believed that he had been horribly deceived by life. He thought he had married a blonde, blue-eyed Ukrainian girl with a *safe* name: Galina Fedorovna Karpenko. In truth, he had married a Jewish woman who delivered him a Jewish daughter.

Of course Ivan had always known that Galya's mother was a Jew, but the petite, quiet, and smiling woman had seemed unimportant to his relationship with Galina. In those days Ivan had simply ignored her mother's existence. He was young; he was in love. At that time the nationality of his wife's mother hardly mattered at all, but now it did. The Jews had destroyed his life, even though he owed his survival to one of them! As wise Aleksander had concluded, Ivan's resentment and hatred towards Galina, being a Jewish woman, was growing proportionally with her continued concern and care for him. That was the ironic but sad reality.

What irked Ivan more than anything else was the fact that his daughter considered herself a full-fledged member of that accursed race. He wanted Manya to have non-Jewish Russian and Ukrainian friends, and to forget about the war and her stark ordeal. Ivan wanted his daughter to be truly *Russian* like him, but how could she with those meddlesome Kushnirs constantly lurking around and brainwashing her?

In December of 1952, Ivan was seemingly vindicated in his distorted belief about the crimes of Jewish doctors. The infamous case of the *murderers in white coats*, also known as the *Doctors' Plot*, had begun.

It all started with the death of the Mongolian dictator, Khorloogiin Choibalsan, in Moscow in early 1952. The ageing and paranoid Stalin had commented, *"They die one after another. Shcherbakov, Zhdanov, Dimitrov, Choibalsan... they all die so quickly! We must change the old doctors for new ones."*

That pronouncement served as a trigger for the relentless persecution of Jewish doctors. Under torture, prisoners seized in the Soviet investigation of the alleged *Doctors' Plot* were compelled to render evidence to prove that Kremlin doctors, led by Stalin's own personal physician, had in fact effectively assassinated those highly-placed officials mentioned by Stalin.

In a December 1st, 1952, Politburo session, Stalin proclaimed, *"Every Jewish nationalist is an agent of the American intelligence service. Jewish nationalists think that their race was saved by the United States. There you can become rich, bourgeois, and so on. They think they're indebted to the Americans. Among doctors, there are many Jewish nationalists."*

The next month, on January 13, 1953, some of the most prestigious and prominent doctors in the USSR were unilaterally accused of taking part in a wide-ranging plot to poison members of the top Soviet political and military leadership. *Pravda*, the official newspaper of the *Communist Party of the Soviet Union*, reported the accusations under the headline '*Vicious Spies and Killers under the Mask of Academic Physicians*'. All Soviet papers were filled with accusations against the Jewish doctors who had worked in the Kremlin hospitals. It was asserted that they had been actively trying to poison and kill members of the Central Committee, even including the leader of the Soviet people, Stalin himself! Day after day the papers were publishing more and more new names of Jewish doctors who had been detained by the authorities. The shaping of public opinion for the great trial was well underway, not only as an excuse for initiating a mass deportation of Jews to distant lands in Eastern Russia, but also possibly as a prelude to a plot conceived by Stalin to conduct an extensive purge of party brass within the Soviet leadership.

One day, a triumphant Ivan arrived home and tossed a newspaper onto the table. "Here, look at this! I was right all along! Dr. Galperin has been arrested! Murderer! Mutilator!"

Manya read the article and said in an unimpressed voice, "Papa, you said that the name of your surgeon was Aaron Davidovich, isn't that right? This Galperin is Lev Efimovich. He's an entirely different person."

"Who cares?" Ivan shot back. "They're all the same! It's him! Just you wait and see! The trains are already being prepared. Everybody knows that all the Jews will be sent to Birobidjan. Do you know where that is, Manya? Let me tell you - it's in the Far East where the weather is the foulest. That's where all Jews belong. That's where they'll all be left to starve and freeze to death."

"In that case," Manya replied quietly, "I promise to write you letters from Birobidjan before I die from starvation and the cold." She turned away and left the room, leaving her father yelling at her mother with impotent fury.

Manya felt truly sorry for her mother. Galina was a changed woman; it seemed she was half the person she had been before her husband's return. She never smiled anymore. She was constantly trying to appease Ivan, yet always fearful of his outbursts. Galina had aged noticeably too. She looked thin and fragile; her complexion was sallow and pallid.

As Manya was closing her door she could still hear the ongoing acrimonious exchange between her father and mother in their part of the flat.

"Hey, you! Jewish nurse! Are you trying to kill me too? To finish what those other two murderers started?"

Then the voice of her mother, "Vanechka, darling, please don't say such things. You know we love you."

After Stalin's death on March 5th of 1953, the new Soviet leadership acknowledged that the charges brought against Jewish doctors had been entirely trumped up by government officials who had abused their power.

The case against the Jewish doctors was dismissed on March 31st, 1953, and soon thereafter on April 3rd of the same year, the Presidium of the Central Committee of the Communist Party officially acquitted all those who had been arrested. The chief prosecutor, Riumin, a Stalin protégé, was blamed for concocting the plot to rid the country of the Jewish doctors. He was summarily arrested and executed. The doctors who had been used as pawns for Stalin's purposes were all released and the concept of making Birobidjan a distant Jewish homeland never materialized.

Ivan Matveev was the one person who continued to nurture his misplaced conviction that among those arrested (and wrongly acquitted), Dr. Galperin was the one who had severed his arm for the sole purpose of maliciously humiliating a Russian man.

In that same year, Lisa was paroled from her prison sentence and returned home. Prison had certainly changed her, but not in the way that Aleksander might have hoped.

Lisa took a month to recover from her incarceration ordeal. She soon realized that nothing much had changed. Her loser husband was still working as a teacher in the same school and even his meagre salary was no better. She learned, however, that the nature of the school had changed. Instead of the prior status as an orphanage, it had been converted to an *Internat,* a boarding school for under-privileged children. In cases where parents couldn't cope, whether financially or mentally, with keeping their children at home, their offspring were placed in residence at this school. On weekends, parents were permitted to take their children home for a visit.

This re-orientation of the school had not affected Aleksander's position. He wasn't promoted to become a department head, but instead still worked as a regular teacher and counsellor. *With his stupid habit of saying whatever he thinks and his elevated sense of so-called honesty and integrity, he'll never get a promotion,* Lisa decided. *He just doesn't have any idea of how to 'play the game'.*

And so, Lisa concluded that it was up to her alone to fashion a new and better life for herself and her daughter.

Evidently Lisa had made some useful connections while in the prison, because only one month after her release, she secured a job in a shoe store. The store manager was a shrewd woman who quickly taught Lisa the secrets of their trade - no more than thirty percent of the supply of imported shoes should go on sale openly. The remainder were quietly distributed amongst friends and trustworthy people at considerably higher prices. Several pairs had to be put aside for local authorities too - militia, local government and party members, and of course their spouses.

Be nice to them and they will never touch you. That was the most important lesson that Lisa learned…and Lisa was a good learner.

She soon got back to her winning looks with dyed hair, heavy make-up, and bright clothes. Lisa didn't physically attract Aleksander any longer but there were plenty of male customers who took notice of the attractive new saleslady. And Lisa noticed them too.

"I have to get rid of that loser once and for all," Lisa was telling her old friend Nikolai. "I want to find a man who can appreciate me and take care of me while I'm still young and still have my good looks. Sure, I could divorce Aleksander. That's not a problem, but then where would I live? I really don't want to lose the house."

"Lisochka, dear, you can have it all - the house and your freedom. I'm the one who can help you," Nikolai assured her.

"How can you help?" Lisa asked. Nikolai had tweaked her attention.

"Present a couple of pairs of sandals to Tanya's babysitters. Promise them good winter boots too, and then ask them to file an official complaint that Aleksander had sexually assaulted Tanya."

"Wouldn't work. Those old ladies are all good friends of Aleksander's parents. They would never say a bad word against him," Lisa countered.

"Then find somebody else who's more willing and flexible. I'll testify that he assaulted my niece too. I have papers which state that I came back to Kiev after the evacuation in 1943. I'll say that I found my niece and wanted her to live with me and my family but Aleksander refused to release the girl to her closest relative."

"Kolya, how did you manage to get those papers? Don't you ever worry that some of the people who lived in Kiev during the occupation will recognize you?"

"Lisa, you are so naïve, my dear. I didn't move to another part of the city for nothing. Besides, the people who stayed in Kiev during the war have their own good reasons to keep quiet. You fail to perceive the most important part of my foolproof little scheme - there will never be a trial.

"All that you have to do is to concoct the case and threaten Aleksander with the negative publicity that it would cause. He's smart enough and he will understand perfectly well that it won't matter if he's acquitted or not. After such an accusation becomes public he'll never be permitted to work as a teacher or as a children's counsellor again.

"Tell him that you won't allow him to see Tanya unless he does precisely as you say. He will sign over the house to you and thank you for not starting an official investigation. And all that I'm asking for my sound advice, my dear Lisa, is several pairs of good imported shoes at good prices now and then."

"Kolya, you are such a sly one! Of course you'll have the shoes. I'd much rather deal with you than with anybody else. So, how's business? Ivan still works for you?" Lisa inquired.

"No, he doesn't any more. He's become nothing but a disreputable drunkard. My poor sister! After I found out how badly Ivan was treating the customers at the market and how careless he was with the merchandise, I immediately dismissed him. I have enough reliable distributors now, so who needs him anyway?" Nikolai responded smugly.

"How did Galina react?" Lisa wanted to know.

"Oh, I didn't tell her the real reason. I just said that I could no longer have any dealings with the family that has treated me so shabbily. Actually, I made out like it all Manya's fault," Nikolai laughed.

"I don't blame you. I never liked that brat. Anyway, Kolya, this is the deal: you help me get rid of Aleksander and you get VIP service in my store forever," Lisa asserted.

While the unsuspecting Aleksander was still wondering if it might be possible to rebuild his marriage, Lisa had already begun to prepare the *evidence* of his pedophilia.

Aleksander would never forget the evening when Lisa casually tossed the binder with the *documents* citing the accusations on the table and dispassionately said just one word, "Read."

With mounting disbelief, Aleksander scrutinized the filth invented by his wife. *How much energy she must have put into gathering all these papers and bribing these alleged witnesses,* he thought.

Finally, Aleksander asked, "What do you want, Lisa? You know that there's not a shred of truth in any of these papers. You know it and I know it. It's obviously not a concern for Tanya's welfare that drives you. So what do you really want?"

"Divorce and the house," Lisa replied hastily.

"You can have the divorce if you wish but this house was built by my grandfather. Leave Tanya with me and just go."

"If that's your position, these documents will be made public tomorrow morning and I'll make sure that you never see Tanya again," Lisa shot back.

Before Aleksander had any opportunity to respond, Lisa started to scream at him. He was accused of destroying her best years. It had been his fault that she had to suffer three years behind bars! Lisa went so far as to accuse him of pleasuring himself with the two young girls, Raya and Manya.

This is a monster of a woman I have married, Aleksander thought, *and now I have no choice but to pay for my stupidity. The most important thing is to protect my Tanya.*

When Lisa was done with her hysterics, Aleksander offered a compromise. "Very well then, Lisa; you win. You can have the main part of the house. I'll keep the back room where my office is now and the use of the backyard. I'll change the doorway to a solid wall so you'll have your privacy. You will have ninety percent of the house but you'll never enter the backyard. Do you hear me, Lisa? The backyard is mine. Tanya can come to my part of the house at any time she likes. You will not poison my daughter against me and you will do nothing to prevent her from seeing me as often as she wants," Aleksander said in a steadfast voice.

Victory! Lisa was thinking, *such an easy victory. Who needs that stupid backyard with the grave under the apple tree? Let him have his little room... for now.*

"Agreed!" Lisa promptly acknowledged.

And that was how Aleksander began his second bachelorhood. He built an out-house at the far end of the backyard, improved the summer kitchen, and settled into his new life. The limited amount of space didn't bother him in the slightest; he had a bed, a table, a chair and enough bookshelves. What else did a person really need?

What irritated Aleksander the most were Lisa's new lifestyle and her seemingly never-ending parade of short-term, male *tenants*. Each new *uncle* was generous to Tanya and the little girl naively viewed the new arrangement as one big party.

"Papa," she would happily exclaim, running into the backyard, "Uncle Petya bought me a new dress! He's better than Uncle Vasya who was only buying me candies!"

Aleksander tried on a few occasions to reason with his estranged wife about the steady stream of *uncles* and how it was influencing Tanya. But Lisa's unrelenting barrage of filthy words, screams and threats soon discouraged him from pursuing the matter any further. He felt utterly powerless to protect his daughter and to shield her from her mother's careless and carefree life.

Lisa had no problem finding new lovers. However, not one of them stayed with her for longer than two or three months. She became extremely frustrated with her inability to become gainfully remarried and her seething anger began spilling over onto Tanya.

Even so, the greatest reason for Lisa's mounting frustration was Aleksander's growing popularity.

Every weekend the backyard was crowded with visitors. There was a steady stream of guests, especially former students who were coming to Aleksander for advice. Sometimes these young people were bringing their fiancées for his approval and blessing. Aleksander always smiled, reflecting on the irony of his situation. He was definitely not cut out to act as an authority on the subject of marriage.

Nevertheless, his students (current and former), fellow teachers whom he had befriended, along with Raya and Manya of course, kept coming one Sunday after the next to visit and talk with him.

What are those two still doing here? an irritated Lisa thought. *They aren't children any longer. Why don't they have boyfriends their own age? It's hardly a surprise that Raya doesn't have anybody, but Manya's certainly pretty enough. Can't she find somebody to be with?*

As a matter of fact, Manya *did* have a boyfriend. His name was Dima. The change in their relationship occurred when Dima returned home for the summer after his third year of university.

The sisters had been at the train station waiting for his arrival. Dima jumped from the train, warmly kissed Raya, and then gave Manya a long, lingering kiss that left her quite flustered and dizzy.

"Oh, don't mind me. I'm only a statue," Raya said mockingly, putting one foot forward, spreading out her hands and fingers, and tilting her head to one side. She put on such a funny face that Dima and Manya burst out laughing. The trio then made their way in the direction of Vera's apartment, but stopping first at one of the city outdoors cafes for ice cream and lemonade.

"So, how are you doing, girls?" Dima asked. "How are your parents, Manya? You were quite vague in your letters on that subject."

The girls looked askance at one-other.

"Worse," Manya confided. "Papa is drinking more than ever and as a result he's becoming more aggressive all the time. Sometimes I see bruises on my mother's arms. I think he's beating her when I'm not around but she never complains. She just cries quietly to herself. Papa also has a new source of income... "

Manya fell silent.

"Is he back on the flea-market?" Dima inquired.

"You wish!" Raya said hotly.

"Okay, girls," Dima prompted, "spill it out."

Manya spoke up first. "Dima, you know how we suffer from a never-ending lack of luxury items, especially big-ticket items, here in Kiev, right?"

"You don't know what a *lack* of things really means. Go to Yaroslavl and you'll find out." Dima replied.

"Anyway," Manya continued, "when the luxury goods arrive, there's always a huge line-up. And the goods arrive in small quantities. You know how it is: only a hundred fur coats, or rugs or blankets, or whatever else is being offered for sale on any particular day. The store manager then announces, *"Only one item per person."* So, the war veteran-invalids are making the money on these items."

"How's that?" Dima asked.

"By law, the veteran-invalids have the right to purchase the merchandise without standing in the long line. So they make arrangements with somebody at the end of the line who is willing to pay extra. For a negotiated compensation, an invalid would go to the front of the line and buy the desired item on behalf of that person."

"Is that so bad? If the government did more for those people, they wouldn't have to resort to this sort of scheme," Dima asserted.

"Dima, listen to this. One day Manya and I followed Uncle Vanya. We made sure that he didn't see us," Raya explained. "He met with two other men and they went downtown looking for a large line-up. They found one in the *Passage* neighbourhood. Wool sweaters from Romania were on sale. The group separated and Uncle Vanya went to the left of the line and remained there without saying a word to anybody. After a minute or two, a woman approached him and they started a negotiation process. Then some money exchanged hands and Uncle Vanya went to the front of the line. He was very courteous and polite, acting as if he was sorry that he was allowed to butt in. Five minutes later he returned with a sweater and handed it over to the woman.

"A little while later, the same routine was repeated for another customer. But this time, some people who had already been waiting in the line for a long time, recognized Uncle Vanya and started to make a fuss. He was protesting that they were mistaking him for somebody else. But the third time he appeared at the front of the line, everyone else started screaming at him and calling him a scoundrel. Uncle Vanya started shouting back at the disgruntled crowd. He was waving his empty sleeve and yelling, "*I spilled my blood for you! You are ungrateful pigs! While you were sitting in Tashkent, I was fighting for you!*"

"So in the end they reluctantly let him buy a third sweater," Raya continued.

"The other men in his group did the same thing. Then the invalids stepped aside and we saw how Uncle Vanya divided the money into two piles, "This stash is for Galina," he was saying. "Let her see that I'm still a man! I can still provide for my family. And this pile is for our celebration." Then they headed off in the direction of the nearest liquor store."

"Dima," Manya said, "I know that papa was hurt badly and that the war will never be totally over for him, but to scam money off your own misery... You know, when the people in the line were screaming at him and calling him names, I felt utterly ashamed that he's my father."

"But that's not even the worst news," Manya continued. "He's found another victim to torment; somebody even weaker than himself. Do you remember our old neighbour, Aunt Miriam? Her daughter-in-law finally got married and moved away. Now Aunt Miriam is living alone and papa takes pleasure in tormenting her. She started to get absentminded and several times had forgotten to turn off the burner after she finished cooking. Papa began to look for these opportunities to scream at her, claiming that she was going to burn down the apartment and kill everybody. Aunt Miriam tried to be more careful. So papa deliberately started turning the burner back on, just to fabricate an excuse to yell at her even more.

"I still don't understand why he's doing it except out of spite. Just last week, Aunt Miriam was telling mama and me that she remembered moving the pot from the stove to the table. Ten minutes later there was a smell of a burning pot and of course papa was there waiting to yell at her. Aunt Miriam began to seriously doubt her own mental capacity to remember things. She became terrified of papa and was afraid to enter the kitchen whenever he was at home. And three days ago..." Manya started to choke up from the disgusting memory, "papa put a pig's foot in her soup. He thought it was funny. Now, Aunt Miriam has decided to cook only at night when there's nobody else around. In the daytime she just sits in her room, afraid to venture out. She often cries in desperation. Mama and I are making tea and preparing some food each day and taking it to her room."

"Why won't she go to live with her relatives? Wouldn't she be better off?" Dima inquired.

"Dima, you haven't lived in Kiev for a long time," Raya reminded him. "Her grandson is assigned to the apartment so that when she dies he'll have a flat in the center of the city. If she moves out her grandson will lose the right to that future opportunity. "

"Poor woman!" Dima shook his head in dismay. "Manechka, I wish that I could help you, but I really don't know how. Your father needs to go to a detoxification clinic. He obviously needs proper treatment."

"Mama already tried to talk about treatment with papa but he wouldn't hear of it.

"Enough about all that! Let's talk about something more cheerful," Manya suggested, putting on a brave face.

"Raya, how are you? Are you ready for the entrance exams? Have you decided where you'll apply?" Dima asked, to move to a different line of conversation.

"Yes, oh brother-of-mine! I've decided to become a biochemist. Biochemistry is the most fascinating field in the entire world. It's about the chemistry of all living things! I feel there are practically unlimited opportunities for research. Who knows, maybe one day I might create a totally new substance, something like a fountain of youth that would help people to stay young and healthy. Can you imagine? I'm applying to the Faculty of Biochemistry right here at Kiev University."

Dima was not too enthralled about Raya's pronouncement. He evidently didn't share her enthusiasm about applying to Kiev University and decided to caution her. "Raya, do you know how difficult it is to get into the university in Kiev? And especially in such a popular faculty? Have you found out how many students they will accept for the first year?"

"Dimochka, with my preparedness, I have nothing to worry about! I'll dazzle them with my knowledge," a confident Raya assured her brother. "Actually, I'm looking forward to the entrance exams. Two more months and I'm going to be a university student!"

As it turned out, Raya never had a fair opportunity to dazzle anybody. The entrance exams started, as always in the USSR, at the beginning of August. Raya's first exam was a written essay in Ukrainian. She felt confident that she had scored a high mark. She knew the subject matter very well, and she had never received less than a *five* ('A') grade in Ukrainian grammar and literature.

Two days after writing the exam and feeling self-assured, Raya went in a perfect mood to check the results which had been published and posted on the faculty bulletin board. A crowd of would-be students was swarming around to check their grades. Raya waited patiently until most of the crowd had dispersed, but when she finally had an opportunity to examine the list of successful candidates, she was startled to find that her name was not present.

Raya bravely went to the administrative office and politely spoke to the office secretary. "I'm sorry to bother you but there seems to have been some mistake. My name is not on the list."

"It means that you failed the essay and aren't permitted to continue the exams," the woman responded indifferently without lifting her head from the paperwork she was shuffling on her desk.

"That's impossible! I'm a straight 'A' student. I've never received less than 'A' on my essays. I'm sure that there has been some mistake. Would you please just check it again for me?" Raya pleaded.

Finally, the woman lifted her head and looked intently at Raya. "There is no mistake. Our university never makes mistakes. May I suggest that instead of wasting my time you go and do a better job of studying the language of the country you are living in? Perhaps we'll see you next year. And don't forget to leave your applicant paperwork on my desk. You won't be needing it any longer."

Raya left the office in a daze and hastily made her way into the hot Kiev summer sun. She couldn't fathom what had gone wrong, but right then she couldn't bear to be in that university building one extra minute. She stared blankly at the happy faces of the successful candidates without really seeing anyone in particular. She heard the sound of muted voices and laughter too, but none of this actually registered with her. Raya was in a state of absolute shock.

Dima and Manya had been waiting for her outside on the campus grounds. The expression on Raya's face as she approached them conveyed the bad news.

"Raya, you're only seventeen! Nothing is lost. Go to work for a year or two. Applicants with two years of work experience always have an advantage. They're judged differently, more preferentially," Manya was saying in an attempt to comfort her friend.

"There isn't going to be *two* years of work experience," Raya bravely asserted. "I'll get in next year!"

When Raya returned home, Vera saw her daughter's distress and immediately made several phone calls and then went to see several of her old friends. Eventually, Raya got a job as a lab technician in the Kiev Vitamin Factory.

In August of the following year, Raya failed her written Mathematics exam, again with no plausible explanation. "I did everything correctly," she cried. "I checked and rechecked all the answers. There's something totally wrong about this examination process!"

"You must leave Kiev," Dima was insisting. "You're never going to be admitted here."

"And leave Manya alone? I can't do that," a distraught Raya challenged him.

Dima had no ready response. He was exceedingly worried about Manya, as much as Raya, if not more-so. But September soon came and it was time for him to return to his own studies in Yaroslavl.

Ivan's Tragic Death And New Beginnings

THE YEAR 1955 was filled with a number of major events. Manya graduated from nursing school and landed a good job in one of the most prominent hospitals of the city.

In the winter, Aunt Miriam passed away and the tussle for her room began. Nina attempted to install her son there, since he was officially a tenant in the flat. But Sergey Sergeivich wouldn't have it. He held the rank of colonel and therefore had much more clout with the local authorities than a teenage boy and his mother. Needless to say, the struggle was short-lived and conclusive - it was the colonel who occupied the vacant room.

The brave colonel was now better-positioned to pursue a new, more daring ambition: to have a completely separate, three-room apartment all to himself in the center of the city. All he had to do was find a way to force Galina and her family to vacate their part of the premises.

He was too savvy to openly pick a fight with his neighbours. Instead, he concocted a *win-win* scheme. Sergey Sergeivich wrote a letter to the City Party Committee explaining how a brave soldier and an invalid-veteran of the war was living with a wife and a grown daughter in just one small room. *Don't our veterans, who spilled blood for our freedom and safety, deserve something better? he* concluded his letter.

The plan worked like a charm, and in the fall of 1955, Ivan's family was re-located to a new, two-room apartment in one of the expanding suburbs of Kiev.

Galina was pleased to have a separate kitchen of her own with no neighbours to share with. Manya would have her own room and some privacy too. There was hot water right in the apartment so they could take a shower whenever they wished. But most importantly, the apartment was far away from the downtown, so Galina hoped that this would keep Ivan away from his daily boozing sessions with his buddies.

Ivan was actually happy too, but for his own reasons. They would finally live far away from the Kushnirs and Manya would hopefully make some new friends.

Even Manya was satisfied because the new apartment was only several stops on the trolley-bus from Aleksander's house. She would no longer have to cross the entire city every time she wanted to see her friend. As a bonus, the apartment was much closer to the hospital where she was working. She wasn't overly concerned about living far from Raya. Her relationship with her sister and best friend would easily surmount the inconvenience of the extra distance between them.

The Matveev family started to get acquainted with their new neighbours in the apartment building. Before long, Ivan singled out a young man named Peter. This was the man that Ivan decided he wanted for his Manya: tall, athletic, good-looking, and with an open, kind face. Peter was always exceptionally polite towards Ivan and Galina and it didn't take long for the parents to deduce that Peter was smitten with Manya.

At the age of nineteen, Manya had become a real beauty. Her frame was petite, like that of her mother and grandmother. She had shoulder-length wavy, strawberry-blonde hair framing her slightly rounded pretty face, while the several freckles dotting her small, cute nose just added to the attraction. Her large, vivid green eyes made her look irresistible and even a touch bewitching.

For the New Year's celebration, Peter's parents invited the Matveev family to join them. The party was a great success and Ivan was on his best behavior. He didn't drink excessively, he joked with the other guests, and he proudly observed his beautiful daughter being eyed by everyone present.

Peter was sitting beside Manya and it was readily apparent that he was seeking her attention. He was telling humorous anecdotes and

Manya was reacting with unrestrained laughter. Eventually he invited Manya to go for a walk in the neighbourhood. They were gone for half-an-hour and by the time they returned to the party it was already time for her family to go home.

Once they were back to their own apartment, Ivan initiated an interrogation.

"Did you like him?" Ivan inquired.

"He's a nice guy," was the polite and reserved response from his daughter.

"What did you two talk about? Did he invite you to meet him again?" Ivan persisted.

"Papa, I told him that I already have a man in my life that I love and hope to marry one day. I saw no point in raising Peter's hopes," Manya replied evenly.

"And who is this secret admirer of yours whom you're planning to marry?" Ivan growled in a low voice.

"Manechka, please! Don't aggravate your father," Galina pleaded. She knew perfectly well what Manya's answer would be and dreaded an impending fight.

"Papa, mama's right. It's New Year's. Let's not have a quarrel and start the new year off on the wrong foot. We can talk about it some other time if you like. Good night," Manya said, as calmly as she could.

"How dare you to turn your back and walk out of this room when your parents are talking to you! What's his name?" Ivan demanded.

"Dima," was the response expected by Ivan and feared by Galina.

At that point, Ivan completely lost control of his temper. "Never! Do you hear me? Never will I allow you to marry that boy! You're stupid if you dare to think otherwise. You're a disgrace to me and my name. For the first time in your life, a real man has taken a genuine interest in you. Not some weird Jew-boy, but a good, solid Russian man. And what do you do? Reject him outright! You have just foolishly thrown away your only chance for a good, normal life. Do you think I'll ever allow my grandchildren to be Jews? I'm not as stupid as your grandfather Feodor! I won't permit you to dishonour the name of Matveev. You carry the beautiful and proud name of Maria, but you behave like... like a Miriam!"

Ivan desperately hoped that by comparing his daughter to the despised old neighbour, he might bring Manya to her senses and impress upon her how low her esteem had sunk in his eyes.

Manya's reaction was entirely unexpected. Her face lit up with a smile as she asked, "Which Miriam are we talking about, Papa? If you mean our old neighbour Miriam, I do hope to be like her: so generous, kind, loving and caring. Or do you mean the biblical Miriam, the prophetess and sister of Moses?"

"Sister of whom?" a bewildered Ivan stammered.

"Moses, the Jewish prophet who freed the Jews from slavery. Miriam was his sister and the leader of the women during their forty years of wanderings in the desert," a serene Manya explained.

"Where did you hear such nonsense?" Ivan was livid with anger. "I didn't realize that my daughter believed in old myths and legends. Who told you this fairy-tale?"

"It's not a fairy tale, Papa. Uncle Misha told us all about the Exodus when we were living in his cellar," Manya replied, still managing to maintain her equanimity.

Perhaps the vodka had finally gotten to Ivan, because he allowed his overpowering anger to take complete control over his emotions. Staring at Manya with undisguised loathing, he said, "Sometimes I think it would have been better if that Uncle Misha of yours had left you where he found you. Sometimes I think it would've been better if you had never crawled out of that ravine!"

Galina gasped and Manya turned away without saying a word and retreated to her room. It had finally come to the point where her father simply didn't exist for her any longer. His injury, his deformity – none of that mattered any longer. For over ten years Manya had steadfastly refused to talk to her uncle. And now her father had joined the ranks of her enemies from within her own family.

Galina knew very well how stubborn her daughter could be and cried in despair in a corner of the room. The new apartment hadn't brought the harmony that she had yearned for her family!

Ivan now seemed to be drinking more than ever, if that was possible. He would wake up in the morning and head straight to the kitchen to have a drink to clear his hangover from the night before.

By the middle of the day he was usually drunk again. Sometimes he would fall asleep for the entire afternoon and in the evening he would drink some more and renew his verbal assaults on Galina. Other days he would leave the apartment about mid-day and venture all the way downtown to meet his drinking buddies.

There were nights when Ivan didn't come home at all. The militia in Kiev usually patrolled the streets and when they found a drunken man sleeping on the street they would arrest him and take him to the detoxification center. Most people tried to avoid this place because on the following day, a report was sent to the individual's place of work and the immediate family was also notified. Ivan didn't care in the slightest about those ramifications. For him, the detoxification center was a convenient place to spend the night from time to time. In the morning, he would return home and head straight for his bottle yet-again.

Those evenings when a drunken Ivan actually returned home from downtown were the most traumatic of all for his wife and daughter. He would be excessively aggressive and violent, and often his wrath was totally uncontrollable. It came to the point that Galina and Manya would listen for the sound of his keys in the door and then hustle into Manya's room and barricade themselves there for the rest of the night.

In the spring, Galina moved outright into Manya's room. She was terrified to be in the same room with her husband any longer. The situation had become utterly hopeless. Even so, Galina never actually considered leaving her invalid husband for good. Manya was so worried for her mother's safety that she tried to be at home with her as much as possible.

In the summer, Dima returned home again. He had completed the fifth year of his studies and was now getting ready for his internship. He would be required to work in the hospital for half-a-year as an intern and then to study for one more term. And so, by the summer of the next year, Dima expected to be a fully-qualified doctor of medicine.

The bond of love between Manya and Dima had grown stronger than ever in spite of their separation during the academic year. They weren't children any longer. They wanted to make plans and to talk about their lifelong future, but they understood, realistically, that for the immediate future all their hopes and dreams of being together had to be kept on hold.

Dima didn't ask Raya any more why she wouldn't leave Kiev and go to study somewhere else. He knew the answer; Raya simply couldn't abandon her sister under the circumstances at home.

But now it was the summer holidays and they were all young and optimistic. They spent much of their free time at their favourite beaches and parks. Every Sunday, in accordance to their established tradition, they went to visit Aleksander. He was still living alone, and still working in the same boarding school. He was still their ever-reliable and trusted source of wisdom and advice.

In August, Raya made yet-another unsuccessful attempt to gain admission to Kiev University as a full-time student. This time she passed all her exams without any failing grades, but her written exams were graded low (without explanation, of course), and when the lists of successful applicants were posted, her name was once again not to be found. Raya stood near the posting wall and stared at the list over and over again. Here was the letter 'K'... here were Kiselev, Kovalenko, and then Lavrov, but alas, no Kushnir. Raya was not so naïve anymore as to go and fight again with the administration staff of the university, yet she remained transfixed there for the longest time, as if expecting that some miracle would occur and her name would magically appear on the list.

Finally, Dima and Manya, who had accompanied her to check the results, hugged her and led her away. Raya spoke in a low voice reflecting her profound disappointment. "I knew everything... and I already have two years of work experience. What more can I do? What should I do now?"

"You should leave Kiev," Dima responded, without hesitation.

"Go somewhere in the middle of Russia, just as I did. You'll have no problem getting into some good university. Next year, I'll be staying in Kiev, so then you'll be able to go."

"Another whole year of the same old high school books! I can't see them any longer. I'll lose my mind if I have to spend even one more day, never mind another whole year going over the same material again and again," Raya lamented.

"Then don't," Dima offered. "Go to the university here after work. They have classes every evening. The auditoriums are so large that nobody would even notice that you're sitting there amongst all the other students. Get the university books. You don't have to stay mired at the same place academically, Raya. Move forward with your education. Granted, you won't be able to receive any official credits or take any of the exams, but at least you'll acquire valuable knowledge. That's the most important thing, Raya dearest. When you finally do become a registered student in another city, and you will, I assure you, you'll be able to graduate with no problem in four or maybe even three years, instead of the usual five. Look at the bright side!"

Raya smiled gratefully and said, "Thank you, guys. I can't imagine what I would do without you. I'll study as hard as I can. I'll attend every lecture that I can discretely manage to attend and I'll learn the university material."

"And once a week, you should still go back over your high school textbooks, just to make sure you don't forget anything. Next year you will get in for sure!" Manya chimed in with her typical cheerful optimism.

Dima applied for his internship to every hospital in Kiev and in August he received a letter of acceptance. Fate seemed determined to bring Manya and Dima together. He obtained a position in the same hospital where she worked. The trio celebrated this good fortune – Dima would be staying in Kiev until January!

In September, Raya started to covertly attend Kiev university evening lectures. In the factory's laboratory, her skills and determination were recognized and often she was assigned tasks that were usually performed by certified biochemists.

Manya and Dima were seeing each other at every opportunity almost daily. Dima often escorted Manya home, but they always parted several blocks away from her apartment building. The atmosphere in her home remained tense and there was no need to make it any worse.

In the fall, an unprecedented socio-political event occurred: namely the 1956 Hungarian Revolution. The Soviet papers began condemning the *band of rebels* that was said to be operating against the will of the Hungarian people. In order to purportedly save Hungary from itself, Soviet tanks rumbled into Budapest.

Something didn't make sense. If there were only a few disorganized rebels, then why were tanks needed? Dima decided to pay an urgent visit to Aleksander to discuss this state of affairs. He convinced Raya to skip a university lecture and the trio met after work and went to see their friend. Under the circumstances, Aleksander was not at all surprised to see them. He didn't mince words and referred to the crisis in Hungary as a genuine revolution. A friendly debate ensued and the young people didn't notice the passage of time, even as the clock reached eleven PM. Finally, they said goodnight to Aleksander and left his house.

"Raya," Dima suggested, "let's take Manya home. It's much too late to allow her to go home alone."

"That's a given," was the response, "so let's go."

They waited quite a long while for the trolley-bus under a flimsy, plastic shelter. It was a rainy and windy night and the young people were happy to finally get inside the warm bus. Despite the late hour, the bus was practically filled with passengers. Raya spotted a single seat near the front and hastily moved to take it. She sat down, opened one of her books, and soon was oblivious to anything that was going on around her. Manya and Dima remained standing together closer to the back of the bus.

At the next stop, a new passenger entered from the front door. He was loud and abrasive. "Aren't there any courteous people on this bus?" he bellowed, before anyone even had an opportunity to stand up and offer him a seat. Several passengers simultaneously rose hastily from their seats and Ivan tumbled awkwardly into one of them.

The bus made a sudden sharp turn and Dima instinctively gripped Manya's shoulders to steady her. And that was the moment when Ivan caught sight of them. His eyes blazed with fury and he started to cuss at them with foul words from a distance at his seat. The ruckus disrupted Raya's concentration and she raised her head, noticed Manya's father, and uttered an involuntary, quite audible gasp of horror.

Ivan glanced to where the sound came from and saw Raya. Dima and Manya were far removed towards the back of the crowded bus, so they were well out of his reach; but nearby was that dreadful girl who had stolen his daughter from him. Ivan raised his crutch to strike her and at that very instant Raya sprinted from her seat with a shriek and ran past other startled passengers towards the rear of the bus. A split-second later, the crutch landed heavily on the seat that Raya had just vacated.

By now everyone on the bus was reacting to the commotion. Some women were screaming, while some of the men were trying to restrain Ivan. Manya, along with every other passenger, could hear her father's drunken outburst, "I'll kill you! I'll kill all three of you! I swear that I'll kill you!"

The bus came to a stop and Dima grabbed hold of the girls and pushed them out by the rear door. The doors closed and the bus moved on, but Manya had just enough time to look through the window-pane at the hate-distorted face of her father. She could readily see his violent and bloodshot eyes, lit eerily aglow by the muted interior lights of the bus.

Manya started to cry. "Calm down, my love," Dima was comforting her. "Please don't go home tonight. You just never know what he's capable of doing in his condition. Let's all go to our apartment and by tomorrow he will sober up."

"I can't," Manya sobbed, "he'll attack mama. I have to warn her. He's so drunk and disturbed that I'm scared for her. I must get home as soon as possible."

"He's not done with his drinking yet," Raya remarked. "There's still a half-full bottle of vodka I noticed sticking out of his pocket."

"Then we'll go with you," Dima said firmly. "We must get Aunt Galina away from the apartment before Ivan Stepanovich returns."

Miracles do sometimes occur, even in Kiev. A taxi with the green, roof-mounted light shining, indicating that it was available for hire, came into view at the end of the street. Dima jumped into the middle of the street and raised his arm to flag it down and the taxi came to a stop. A moment later, the trio piled into the taxi and the driver sped away towards Manya's apartment building.

Fortunately they arrived ahead of Ivan. Manya woke her mother and hastily related the incident on the bus.

"Let's go!" Dima urged.

Galina reacted calmly and replied, "I'm not going anywhere. I can't leave Ivan alone in such a condition, but all of you had better go before he gets back."

"No way!" Dima exclaimed. "It's not safe for you to be here alone with him, Aunt Galya."

"Okay," Galina advised, "then go to Manya's room and lock the door."

"Mama, please come to my room with us. Please!" Manya pleaded. "You didn't see him this evening. He's never been as bad as this."

A distraught Galina nodded her head in agreement. They all assembled in Manya's room and locked the bedroom door. Then the wait began…

It was all quiet and remained so. Eventually, Galina and Manya hugged one-another and fell asleep on Manya's narrow bed.

Dima and Raya remained seated on the couch, leaning on each other for support and in time they dozed off too.

Everyone awoke around five AM. Galina unlocked the bedroom door, cautiously stepped out of the room, looked about the apartment, and upon returning said, "He isn't here. It means that the militia must have taken him to the detoxification center again. He's a frequent guest of the downtown center but this would be the first time he's been detained in our own neighbourhood. The detoxification centers open their doors at six AM, so Ivan most likely will show up at home before six-thirty."

"Do I have time to take a shower?" Raya inquired with a hopeful look in her eyes. For a young girl who had to attend the public baths once a week and had to wash herself with cold water for the rest of the week, a hot shower in the morning was a rare and incredible treat not to be missed.

"Certainly, go right ahead," Galina prompted the girl. "Meanwhile, Manya will find you something else to wear."

The doorbell rang ten minutes later, while Raya was still enjoying her shower and Galina was making breakfast for everyone.

Manya looked at Dima and motioned him towards her room. Dima slipped into the bedroom and closed the door quietly while

Manya went to open the entrance door. But instead of seeing her father, standing before her was a militiaman with a grave expression painted on his face.

"Is this the apartment of Ivan Stepanovich Matveev?" he asked.

"Yes, come in. Where's papa?" a bewildered Manya asked.

"Is your mother at home?" the militiaman asked sternly.

"Yes. Mama!" Manya anxiously called out.

Galina came to the entrance-way from the kitchen. Dima, who had heard the conversation, opened the bedroom door and joined them.

"What's happened?" Galina asked with rising consternation in her voice upon seeing the dower look on the face of the militiaman.

"Are you the wife of Ivan Matveev?" the unexpected official visitor asked.

"Yes, I am," Galina replied meekly.

"Your husband was found dead early this morning, lying in a small pool of water in the gutter," the militiaman announced matter-of-factly, without any apparent empathy as he eyed Galina disapprovingly. "You will have to come with me now to identify the body and answer some questions."

The officer then asked reproachfully, "How could you allow your invalid husband to wander about the city alone late at night?"

By now Galina was sobbing uncontrollably and she just shook her head. What could she say in response to that? That she had tried for more than nine years to satisfy every whim and every desire of her husband? That she had always tried to be a good, loving, and caring wife, yet clearly had failed through no fault of her own?

At that moment she felt nothing but heartfelt sorrow and grief.

"Wait a minute, we'll all go with you," Dima said as he went to knock on the bathroom door. "Raya, that's enough! Get out! We have to go."

Feeling refreshed and happy, Raya emerged from the shower, but the expression on her face promptly changed when she observed sobbing Galina and her best friend Manya staring transfixed at the militiaman in an obvious state of shock.

They all left the apartment together and piled into the militiaman's official car. Before long they arrived at the district morgue. Galina was led inside and shown the body of her husband which was laid out in one of the holding vaults. She nodded her head weakly and then slumped over Ivan's lifeless body, crying bitterly.

"Galina Fedorovna," the officer said in a softer voice, clearly affected by her tremendous grief, "we have to perform an autopsy. It's the rule when a person dies suddenly and under such circumstances."

"I understand," she replied.

Galina and the young people were led to a separate room and asked numerous questions. When did they last see Ivan Matveev alive and in what condition? How often did he drink excessively? How often did he come home late at night, or not at all?

Manya gathered all her strength and related the story of the incident on the bus.

The officer carefully noted down the number of the bus and the time of the incident, amongst other details.

"Why did your father threaten to kill you?" the officer asked.

"He hated my friends," Manya replied, barely whispering the words.

"Why was that?" the officer inquired further.

After a long pause, it was Dima who provided an explanation. "Because we are Jews, that's why. You can ask the bus driver and he will confirm that we left the bus and Ivan Stepanovich was still on it. You can also ask the taxi driver who delivered us straight to Manya's building. We spent all night waiting for Ivan Stepanovich to return home. My sister and I weren't prepared to leave Galina Fedorovna and Manya alone. It might not have been safe for them."

"Why didn't you go looking for him?" the officer persisted.

"He often spent his nights in detoxification centers. We thought that he would come home in the morning after the center was open," Dima explained.

At that point the officer scrutinized Manya, Galina, Dima and Raya, seemingly concluding that they were being truthful and decided to release them. They signed some official papers and left the morgue together.

Once they were outside the building, Dima instructed everyone: "Raya, go and tell Mama what has happened. Ask her to come to

Manya's place right away. I'll go and get Aleksander. Manya, you go on home and be with your mother. Please, my love, be strong. Your mother needs you now."

Galina glanced at Dima. That was the first time she had heard him or anybody else for that matter address her daughter as *my love*.

As soon as they were home, Manya prepared some hot tea for Galina, and then sat near her mother and held her hand. Ironically, in a fashion, Manya envied Galina her tears and even her anguish. She felt truly sorry for her mother and distressed by the entire situation, yet she didn't feel anything of the sense of grief that her mother was undoubtedly feeling. Manya tried to recall her father as he had been when she was a little girl; and then his kindness and love when he eventually came home from the war. But in her mind, all she could visualize now was the puffy, drunken face with the bloodshot eyes. His last words, so filled with vile hatred and spite, were still ringing in her ears.

Before long, Aleksander, Vera, Semyon and eight-year-old Misha arrived at Galina's apartment. Then at five o'clock that afternoon the entire family returned to the morgue.

The medical examiner emerged from his office to inform them of the results of the autopsy. "Ivan Matveev drowned in a puddle of water. Evidently he slipped, fell face-down into the pool of water by the roadside and couldn't get up. He had an enormous amount of alcohol in his bloodstream."

"It's entirely my fault!" Galina exclaimed. "I tried to give him the best possible care but that only alienated him even more."

"Don't blame yourself, Mama," Manya said gloomily. "My constant quarrels with him didn't help the situation one bit. If it's anyone's fault, it's mine."

The doctor shook his head and spoke with a heartfelt sadness in his voice. "There was a much more serious reason for his drinking than any of your family strife. Ivan Matveev was a very sick man. His liver had completely disintegrated. He had a cancer that had spread throughout all of his internal organs. He drank to kill the pain. If not for this accident, he would have died in a month or two in any event. I'm so sorry."

"I'm a nurse; I should've realized what was going on," Galina was wailing, still unwilling to absolve herself of fault for Ivan's sad demise.

The body was finally released to the family and Aleksander and Dima assumed responsibility for organizing the funeral.

The next day, trailing behind Ivan's coffin as they walked to the gravesite, were his wife, his daughter, and those people whom he had detested to the last days of his life - Vera, her family, and Aleksander.

That evening, when everyone had gathered at Galina and Manya's apartment after the funeral, Nikolai happened to come by and heard the news for the first time.

"It's all your fault! Ivan was drinking so much because of your stubbornness and your disobedience. I hope you're happy now! You killed your father!" Nikolai raged, all the while pointing an accusing finger at Manya.

"Kolya, stop it! Please, just leave us alone," Galina said in a strained tone of voice.

"What? Are you taking her side? After all I did for you?" an outwardly offended Nikolai accosted his sister.

"Kolya, you are quite right about one thing. You did quite enough for our family. Now leave," Galina insisted.

Nikolai turned to leave the apartment and slammed the door behind him as he made his exit.

"If only I hadn't agreed to invite Kolya on that day when Vanya came back home, maybe everything would've been very different. We could have had a normal life and Vanya would still be alive today. It's my fault for acceding to his wishes," Galina lamented.

"Stop torturing yourself with this remorse, Galya," Aleksander gently interjected. "Don't try to assume the attributes of the Almighty. Don't think that it's you who can control, influence or change somebody's life or destiny, not even in the case of your own husband. We are all blessed with a free will and we're all responsible for our own deeds. Yes, you invited Nikolai over, but it was Ivan's decision to drink that first bottle of vodka with him. It was Ivan's decision to quit college and become a black marketeer instead. You were always a good wife to him, in fact more-so than anyone could have expected. You did everything you possibly could."

Aleksander then addressed her daughter. "Manya, don't blame yourself either. You certainly didn't do anything wrong. On the contrary, you fought rightfully for your beliefs and were faithful to your friends. Your father suffered a lot but it was his own decision to choose a path of hate, misery, and alcohol abuse."

With that, Aleksander poured himself a drink and lifted his glass. "I want us to drink for the soul of Ivan Matveev; for the unrealized potential, and for a sadly unfulfilled human life. May Ivan's soul rest in peace."

From that day forward, a new life began for Galina and Manya. It was hauntingly strange to enter a quiet home, not to be afraid of angry outbursts or fights, and not to feel guilty about the companionship of dear friends.

Galina tried to renew her friendship with Vera but found it difficult. Vera had her own established circle of friends and her own interests. She was polite with Galina and gladly invited her over for occasional visits, but the past closeness between them was simply not there anymore.

One month after Ivan's death, Dima and Raya came to visit Manya. They were all sitting around the table drinking tea when Galina cautiously broached the subject of her own future.

"Manya, I received a letter from your Uncle Phillip. He has invited me to come, not just for a week or two, but to live and work in Sverdlovsk. There's a position for a nurse that has opened up in his plant. I've been thinking that maybe I should accept it. What do you think, Manya? I wouldn't be gone forever; just for half-a-year, or maybe a year."

"Mama, I think it's a wonderful idea! I mean, I'll miss you of course. I'll miss you very much. But you need a change of scenery. It would be good for you to spend some time with Uncle Phillip. He's a very good man," Manya encouraged her mother.

"What about you? I don't want you to live alone," Galina objected, if only mildly.

"Aunt Galya, please, let me to stay with Manya. I promise to be a good chaperone," Raya volunteered. "My mama will be quite happy to have a quiet apartment for a while. "

Galina looked at the two girls, their faces brimming with excitement and anticipation, and agreed.

"Hurrah!" Raya was jubilant. "I'll have a hot shower every day... maybe even twice a day!"

At the beginning of January, Dima and Galina both left Kiev. Dima had completed his internship and was headed back to the university for his final half-year of study, while Galina was leaving to begin her new life in the Ural Mountains. The sisters of course were more than happy to have the opportunity now to live together.

Manya's diligence, patience, and genuine care for her patients' well-being were soon recognized in the hospital and before long she was transferred to more challenging duties in the intensive care ward.

Raya studied a great deal. She was attending the evening university lectures even more diligently than some of the registered students. She studied the books that were available in her laboratory, and she was performing the functions of a fully-qualified biochemist more and more often, even though officially she was still only classified as a lab technician.

On the weekends the sisters spent all their time together. Kiev had finally recovered after the war and was more beautiful than ever. They walked for hours in Vladimir Hills Park and the Botanical Gardens, or simply along the main Khreschatik Street. Sundays were spent according to tradition with their best friend, Aleksander.

This was their time to dream. They were both turning twenty that year and their entire lives were ahead of them. They felt in their hearts that everything would be perfect from then on.

In June, Dr. Kushnir (aka Dima) returned home and the preparations began right away for his and Manya's wedding.

Manya and Dima were wed in July. Galina came to Kiev for the wedding with Phillip and his wife. Galina was a completely changed person and much for the better. Her radiant smile had returned; she had gained a little bit of weight and didn't appear as fragile and pale as before. She looked younger, fresher and much happier than she had in years.

After the civil ceremony, Galina took her daughter aside and said, "Manechka, the apartment is yours and Dima's. I'll stay, at least for now, in Sverdlovsk. I really do like it there."

"Thank you so much, Mama. That's the best wedding present I could possibly have hoped for. However, whenever you're ready to return..." Manya started to say, but Galina quieted her.

"I don't think I will be coming back to stay, Manechka. I've met a man... a good, kind man. He likes me very much and has become a close friend to me. We'll see what the future holds."

Galina blushed like a young girl and added, "Please, don't think badly of me. After all, it's less than a year since your father passed away."

"Mama, I'm so happy for you! You deserve all the happiness in the world. Don't delay living!" Manya fondly embraced and kissed her mother.

Unattainable Dream

AFTER THE WEDDING, Dima renewed his attempts to persuade Raya to apply to some university outside of Kiev. "Raya, in two weeks the university entrance exams will start. Don't waste one more year; go somewhere else in Russia. They are much more tolerant of Jews than here in Kiev. Not only that, in the small cities the competition isn't as tough."

Raya shook her head and replied, "I don't think that I need to do that right now. I want to try it here in Kiev, just one more time. I love this city; I love the university. You're both here too. Dima, this year it'll be different, you'll see."

"You're a masochist! Why is this year so special? Why would they take you this year after rejecting you the past three times, in spite of your excellent knowledge?" Dima challenged.

"Because now they know me. All the teachers and professors know me. For example, Professor Sinitsin. He's teaching biochemistry. One time in his class I wanted to ask a question, but I couldn't because I had no right to even be there, so I whispered to a girl who was sitting nearby and she asked him the question for me. His answer made me think about something else and I whispered another question.

"The Professor looked directly at me and said, 'Why don't you ask the question yourself, young lady?'"

"*But I am not...*" I started to say, but he interrupted me, smiled kindly and said, "*I know. So, what is your question?*"

Raya smiled confidently at her brother and continued. "After the lecture, Professor Sinitsin told me to keep asking my probing questions because they made the other students think. This year we became good friends. He even allowed me to attend laboratory classes. He said that I was the smartest person in his class, even though I'm not officially a student. Do you really think he'd fail me now? The professors of Mathematics and Physics – they all know me now too. Dima, this year I'll get admitted. I'm sure of it!"

"I still think that you're making a mistake," Dima sadly acceded.

Raya's good mood and confidence remained steadfast with her all throughout her exams. The last verbal exam was Chemistry and Professor Sinitsin was the examiner. Raya answered all the questions with zeal and the professor benevolently nodded his head in approval. Finally, Raya's examination was concluded and the time came for him to enter the grade into her entrance book. The professor hesitated for a moment and then apologetically said, "I'm sorry, I have to leave right now. Please wait here."

A bewildered Raya sat alone in the examination room for several minutes until the door was opened and a female faculty member entered the room. Raya had previously noticed her in the university but was surprised to see her now. Was she expected to answer all of the exam questions again?

The woman sat down and said, "Professor Sinitsin had to leave suddenly. He asked me to finish testing you. He told me that you have answered well."

She took the entrance book in hand and wrote in it '4' ('B').

Astonished by this turn of events, Raya asked, "But why '4'? I answered all of the questions correctly and completely. Please, ask me anything."

"The Professor said that you answered *well*. He didn't say *excellent*. A '4' is a good grade. You may go now."

Utterly dejected, Raya left the examination room. She went to see Dima and Manya and told them about her exam experience. "I can't understand why he did that. I can't understand how that woman could give me a lower grade without even asking me a single question. Is this some kind of a game, just a farce, or what?"

"It seems that your professor still has a conscience. He couldn't bring himself to give you a grade less than you deserved. But he obviously had his instructions. A '5' would have given you a total over the minimum entrance score," Dima pointed out. But he didn't feel vindicated in the slightest about his previous insistence that Raya should leave Kiev; he felt only sadness and pity that she had been treated so unfairly, so shabbily.

"Dima, don't be so negative. Raya still has a good overall score. Let's see what happens," Manya said, trying her best to sound cheerful.

"Raya, when will the student lists be published? The day after tomorrow? We'll go together and check the postings."

On that fateful day, Raya rose very early and decided to go to the university on her own. She was one of the first prospective students to arrive. Eventually, the administrator emerged from an office with the sheets of papers which he silently posted on the bulletin board wall and then promptly walked away. Raya was the first to examine the list. Her name was not there.

Dima and Manya arrived ten minutes later. Raya was nowhere to be found. They quickly browsed the lists to confirm their worst fear and then promptly left the university building.

"Have you seen a tall, red-haired girl?" Dima asked a girl sitting on the stairs near the main entrance to the university building.

"Yes, she went that way," the girl gestured.

The newlyweds ran off in the direction the female student had indicated.

"Have you seen a tall, red-haired girl?" Dima asked an old man sitting at the tobacco kiosk which they had reached several minutes later.

"Yes. She seemed to be distracted and in a hurry. She crossed the street on a red light; almost caused an accident. That's why I noticed her," the man said.

Dima and Manya continued to make inquiries along the way while trying to catch up with Raya. Then they suddenly realized that they didn't have to make any more inquiries. Intuitively they now knew where Raya was heading, so they started to run and soon they approached the bridge over the Dnieper. The bridge led to their favourite beach and they had crossed it countless times together. But they were fearful that it was not for a picnic on the beach that Raya would have gone there on this occasion.

The day was cloudy, a light rain was drizzling, and from a distance the bridge appeared deserted. But as they came closer they caught sight of Raya standing in the middle of the bridge, grasping the guardrail and slowly swaying back and forth, as if in a trance. Dima and Manya sprinted the remaining distance to the bridge and a minute later, they were standing on either side of Raya to steady her.

Raya didn't seem at all surprised by the sudden appearance of her brother and sister. Quietly and dispassionately she said, "You didn't think that I would...nothing to worry about. I just wanted to get some fresh air." She was still gazing down at the dark waters of the river below.

Then she abruptly looked up toward Manya and Dima and her facial expression changed dramatically. She couldn't pretend, not before these two people with whom she was so close. She resumed speaking but this time with heightened passion and anxiety.

"Yes, I did think about ending my stupid life. Why not? I'm ugly and I know it. I'll never get married, never have children, and never be loved. I started to get used to the idea of spinsterhood ever since I was a small girl. I accepted it because I thought that my future lay in study, work, and science. That was all I ever wanted – to be a scientist and dedicate my life to innovative research. But I can't even get admitted to the university. It's a hopeless lost cause."

Manya and Dima listened sympathetically without interrupting and allowed Raya to continue venting her frustration.

"I've been denied my dream. I'll just be a lab technician, doing nothing but menial work all my life. Even when they allow me to perform the duties of a biochemist, they treat me like a lab technician. Some days I spend the entire time working as a biochemist, working as hard as the rest of them, maybe even harder. And then, near the end of the day the Head of the Laboratory would say to me, "*Raya, go and clean the place and wash all the dishes; don't neglect your direct duties.*" He would always embellish his instructions with a comment, such as, "*It's good for your soul. It will keep you humble.*" Can you believe that?"

Raya started to cry in desperation. "I just can't take it anymore. Tomorrow, I'll go to work and they'll ask, *failed again?*

"Why, why can't I get admitted? Thousands of people become students. Am I more stupid than all of them? What am I doing wrong?" Raya was wailing.

"You're trying to get into the one place that's determined not to admit you," Dima responded, hugging Raya in hopes of comforting her. It was hardly the first time he had told her this. "Next year, I'll put you on the train myself. No more attempts in Kiev."

"One more year, sister. Please keep the faith for just one more year," Manya pleaded.

"What would I do without you guys?" Raya exclaimed through her lingering tears.

"You'll never be without us," Manya assured her, and with that the trio started to slowly make their way back to the city.

The following June, Semyon suffered a stroke. He had always lived quietly and unobtrusively, so the family basically took his presence for granted. He would never offer advice unless asked. He never told Raya and Dima what to do or how they should do it, yet he was always there to help them. He was a good husband to Vera, a good father to Misha, and of course a good friend to Raya and Dima. His illness was unexpected and hit Vera really hard. Semyon was placed in the hospital and Vera spent virtually all of her time there.

Somebody needed to care for Misha and prepare the meals for the entire family, and to carry meals to the hospital. Somebody had to perform the myriad of other tasks to help Vera in this trying time.

Dima and Manya were not in a position to help, since in that same month, Manya gave birth to a baby girl, Anna. And so those tasks fell upon Raya's shoulders.

Since she was compelled to stay in Kiev anyway, Raya applied yet-again to the same faculty at the university. Again she fell one meagre point below the entrance threshold requirement. Nothing had changed.

After a month of recuperation, Semyon was permitted to return home from the hospital. His left side was paralyzed and he couldn't speak properly. All winter, Vera and Raya did their best to nurse him back to health. It was an exceedingly trying time for them. Their small two-room apartment was hardly the place for the convalescence of a paralyzed man. Vera slept on a small, fold-a-way bed so as not to disturb her husband. Dima came every weekend to visit them and provide whatever assistance and support that he could.

Despite all their care, Semyon passed away quietly the next July. Vera fell apart after his death and Raya stayed in Kiev to be with her.

The next summer, Misha contracted a severe case of scarlet fever and Vera was out of her mind with worry. Raya stayed in Kiev yet-again to help her mother. By the time Misha was out of danger, it was too late to leave and seek university admission somewhere else for the upcoming academic year.

So, for the seventh time Raya applied to the Kiev University. For the seventh time Raya took the same exams. And for the seventh time success eluded her.

After she determined that her name was not on the admission lists, Raya made her way to the boulevard across from the university, found an empty bench and just sat there, devoid of any emotion. She felt nothing other than total emptiness within. Tomorrow, she would go back to the laboratory; and again back to the unkind smirks of her co-workers. *Eternal applicant* – that's how they were referring to her behind her back.

It was only a short while later when another person took a seat on her bench. Raya didn't even turn her head to look at the individual who had unobtrusively joined her.

"It was done in May. Everything was finalized back in May," she heard a restrained male voice saying.

"What?" Raya turned her head sharply in reaction and found that it was none other than Professor Sinitsin sitting beside her. But he was not looking directly towards her and he spoke distantly, as if not talking to anyone in particular.

"Biochemistry is currently the most desirable and prestigious faculty. There are a lot of young people with important parents. The lists for admission here in Kiev were already finalized last May. Go to Kazan. They have a good university there and a very good faculty of biochemistry. Stop torturing yourself and go to Kazan," the professor whispered. With that, he rose from the bench and briskly strode off without uttering so much as a parting good luck or goodbye.

_Kazan

I N 1960, THE twenty-four-year old Raya finally left Kiev to go and
try her luck in Kazan. She was not seeking to become a fulltime
day-study student any longer. She couldn't imagine herself sitting day
in and day out for five years at a desk among students seven years
younger than herself. There were also two additional considerations:
Vera needed her help, and furthermore, she had established an excellent
reputation and a certain degree of seniority in the factory.

Raya was informed by her boss that if she was to become a student
at the university, then in a year or two she would receive a promotion
and the job title of a *Biochemist*. So, Raya decided to apply for the *extern*
(distance) stream, meaning that twice a year she would need to travel
to Kazan for a month to pass exams and attend overview lectures. The
rest of the time she could continue to live in Kiev, continue working
at the laboratory, study in the evenings and submit the required
assignments to the university by mail.

When the train began to depart from the station, Raya leaned
towards the window and waved goodbye to all the family members
gathered on the platform to wish her well.

Manya held her new baby Mila in her arms, while Dima raised their
three-year-old Anna high onto his shoulders. Raya's mother cried as
she waved goodbye and Manya's mother consoled her. Standing beside
Galina was her new husband with their two-years-old son, Vladimir.

Raya's younger brother Misha ran after the train shouting loudly,
"Good luck, sister! Come back with the victory!"

During the train-trip Raya did her best not to think about past
disappointments and not to make any definite plans for the future. But

141

sub-consciously her mind was focussed on the entrance exams that lay ahead of her and how different her life might be after that. She had decided that this was going to be her very last attempt to qualify to become a biochemist. She couldn't continue to torture herself and her family indefinitely. If she failed to gain admission in Kazan, then she would apply the next year to some local community college in Kiev, obtain some other form of education and move on with her life.

Raya was determined to be resolute in her decision, but just thinking about it caused her to shudder with uncertainty and self-doubt. On the other hand, if she succeeded in gaining admission, she resolved that she'd work so hard that she'd finish her studies in four years or less and become a qualified biochemist that much sooner. The trip from Kiev to Kazan was a long one and Raya's mood was alternately soaring into her dream-world of real science and then plunging back into the abyss of prospective failure.

Upon arrival at the Kazan train station, Raya headed straight to the university to apply. She was startled by the sheer size and architectural magnificence of the main old campus building. She had imagined Kazan as a small, provincial town, but the city impressed her with its beauty and restrained stateliness.

At the university Raya submitted her application documents and made inquiries about where she might find a place to live.

"You're lucky," the lady in the administrative office said with a warm smile. "You're one of the first to arrive. Go straightaway to Aunt Dasha's. She lives close-by and has a large house. She always rents out rooms in the summer for applicants and during the academic year to the students. She's a charming woman and a great cook. You'll like it there. Here's the address."

The administrator was quite right. Raya liked the bright house, the neat, small garden with abundant flowers, and most of all she really liked Aunt Dasha.

"During the year," the hostess was explaining, "each student has a room of their own. I prefer girls," she added. "They don't smoke and they're much neater. They usually take good care of their rooms."

Aunt Dasha looked meaningfully at Raya and continued. "During exams there are so many applicants coming here that I place two girls in one room. I hope you won't mind that. This year, however, I'm keeping one room vacant - my son is about to come back from the army. I haven't seen him for three years. Don't worry about him though, he's a good boy and used to having the students around the house. He won't bother you." Aunt Dasha carried on chatting in the same pleasant manner as she bustled from room to room with Raya following closely behind.

Raya was shown to an inviting, bright room with a large window over-looking the garden. There were two beds in the room and Raya promptly dropped her suitcase on the bed closest to the window.

"Smart girl," the older woman said approvingly. "It's the best spot in the entire house."

A mere two days later, the house was already jammed and there were so many student applicants that Aunt Dasha relented and even rented the spare bedroom. When her son returned, he would just have to manage temporarily in the living room.

The student hopefuls immediately started studying in earnest. The girls formed a study group and it soon became apparent that Raya, with her maturity and her superior knowledge, should be the natural leader of the group.

Three days before the first exam, a happy event occurred in the household. Aunt Dasha's son, Maxim, finally returned home from the army. While his overjoyed mother was preparing a celebration meal, the girls were fawning over the handsome ex-solider.

"Have you seen him?" Raya's roommate was asking with flighty excitement. "Isn't he a dream? He looks like that French actor, Alain Delon, only he's taller and better-built! Did you see his eyes? I've never seen such bright, blue eyes before. And I swear his hair is naturally gold-coloured! Since he's just back from army, he can't possibly have a girlfriend yet. Wish me luck!"

"Luck with passing the exams or conquering the heart of the ex-soldier boy?" Raya inquired with a subtle smile.

"Who can possibly think about studying today?" the girl exclaimed.

"I could," Raya replied, and she went back to her book.

When Raya was introduced to Maxim, she quite liked his smile and his unobtrusive, shy manner. She shook his hand and smiled warmly in return, but then immediately dismissed any further thought about him.

Maxim was pleased to be home again and the presence of so many strangers didn't bother him in the slightest. He was used to having his mother's house perpetually crammed with students.

Aunt Dasha's son liked to sit unobtrusively in a corner of the room during group study sessions and listen in on the discussions of the student applicants. He liked all the girls that his mother had housed this year; they seemed like an intelligent, friendly, and pretty bunch. But little did they know that he had already singled out the tall, stately girl who was leading the study group. He had never seen anyone as exotically good-looking in her own unique way. Maxim was attracted to every aspect of Raya's appearance: the strong features of her face, the vibrant red hair falling to her creamy shoulders like a lion's mane, her erect and confident posture, the outline of her large firm breasts, and the long sculptured legs.

Maxim decided that with the other girls all gathered around, Raya took on the appearance of a queen in the presence of her ladies-in-waiting. With considerable astonishment he listened to her knowledgeable explanations, her ready answer to any question, and how she resolved with such ease all the problems posed by the other students in the group. Raya knew everything about the subject matters of the impending exams, or so it seemed to Maxim.

Three days later, the entrance exams got underway. Raya received the highest grade on both the first and second exams. But she didn't allow herself to relax; this was her big opportunity and she was determined to remain focussed. But when two of the girls in their study group failed their second exam, Raya took time to commiserate with them. Nobody could appreciate how they felt in that situation better than Raya herself. Those two girls left Kazan the next day and Maxim moved from the living room to the now-available spare bedroom.

Three more exams transpired and Raya aced each one of them. When she returned to the rooming house after the last exam, she found a beautifully carved wooden figurine that had been set down with deliberate care on the pillow of her bed. Raya took the carving into her hands and examined it carefully.

Her roommate entered their room, took one look at the carving and exclaimed in a disappointed voice, "I knew it! I just knew it! He's smitten with you!"

"Who is?" a bewildered Raya asked.

"Oh, Raya, don't pretend that you didn't notice how Maxim looks at you! And he didn't carve a figurine for me, did he? Are you blind?" the girl responded in dismay.

"Apparently I am. Anyway, I'm not interested in him," Raya commented with notable indifference. "Still, the carving is certainly exquisite so I'd better go and thank him for it."

"Maxim, you have such a wonderful talent. This carving looks like museum quality; at least it does to me. Thank you so much for your thoughtfulness. I'll always keep it as my dearest treasure," Raya said to Maxim when she located him watering the flowers in the garden.

"Do you really like it?" Maxim's asked, all the while looking earnestly at Raya.

"Of course I do! When did you make it?" Raya inquired.

"I carved it just yesterday, Raya. I've seen a lot of student applicants over the years in this house but I've never come across anybody as committed as you are. I really admire that and I wanted to be the first to congratulate you," Maxim said as he offered a warm handshake. The clasp of his hand lingered just a little longer and just a little more firmly than would have been usual.

"Don't congratulate me yet!" Raya exclaimed superstitiously, as she quickly tucked her hands behind her back and crossed her fingers. "There's nothing to celebrate yet."

"But you got a perfect score. That's incredible! What can possibly go wrong?" Maxim asked.

"All kind of things!" Raya replied cautiously.

"Raya, don't worry. I'm sure it's going to be just fine. May I go with you tomorrow morning to the university? You might feel better if you have some company and I want to be the first to congratulate the new student," Maxim proposed.

"Thanks, Maxim. I really do appreciate it," Raya replied with sincere gratitude. She didn't want to be alone when checking the student acceptance lists. *And if I don't get in you want to be the first to console me, don't you,* Raya thought to herself.

When she got back to her room, Raya found that her roommate was visibly upset. She avoided talking to Raya for the rest of the day.

That night, Raya couldn't fall asleep. She tried to calm herself, but as soon as she would close her eyes she would imagine the crowds of happy, cheering, successful student candidates examining their names on the lists on the posting wall. Those imaginary lists didn't have her name on any of them.

The next morning after that fitful night, Raya and Maxim walked to the university together. The lists had just been published and posted and the impatient applicants were pushing and shoving each other in a scramble to get to the announcement board. Maxim took Raya firmly by the hand and they gradually worked their way through the crowd. Finally they got to the wall where the lists were posted. Raya quickly found a posting list under the title *Faculty of Biochemistry* and looked anxiously toward the middle of the alphabetical list. And there it was! Her name, *Raisa Kushnir.*

Raisa Kushnir — student of Kazan State University, Faculty of Biochemistry. Overcome with a combination of joy and relief, Raya mouthed those words quietly to herself, as if in some sort of trance, and then she repeated them again and again, as though it was some kind of mantra.

They left the crowd behind and got out of the building into the fresh air.

"May I congratulate you now?" Maxim asked, all the while grinning broadly. For some unexplained reason he had brought a large knapsack with him but Raya had been too nervous to notice it beforehand.

"Yes indeed!" a jubilant Raya exclaimed as she embraced Maxim warmly. He was practically a stranger but right now that didn't matter! Raya was elated that someone was with her to share her moment of ultimate triumph.

"Raya," Maxim volunteered, "you haven't really seen the city yet, have you? Have you walked down to the Volga? No? Amazing! So, let me show you around. You deserve to enjoy the rest of this day."

"I would be delighted, my dear guide, to see your spectacular city. But before we go I must call home. My family deserves to hear about this great news."

Maxim led Raya to the public telephone booths at the post office where they waited patiently for her long distance call to go through. Then Maxim listened to Raya's happy conversation with her mother and then with some other people by the names of Dima and Manya and Misha. After Raya's phone call was done, they headed onto the streets, observing the Kazan Kremlin and the famous Krestovodvizhensky Cathedral, and eventually they wandered towards the shores of the great Volga River.

Raya was feeling as comfortable and at ease with Maxim as with an old familiar friend. She enjoyed their conversation and seeing the sights of the city on their improvised tour. She was happy and relaxed as never before. It had been a very long and frustrating wait for this day.

Maxim related the simple story of his life to Raya. He had been born in Kazan in 1940. His father never returned from the war. His mother had decided that her son would never call another man *father* and so she never remarried. His father's old friend, Konstantin, was always helping and protecting the small family. He was the one who taught Maxim how to work with wood and wood-carving had become the boy's passion. Five years ago, Konstantin became a widower and eventually proposed to Maxim's mother. She regretfully declined. They still continued to see one-another as close family friends but his mother remained adamant that she wouldn't marry ever again.

"Do you like our dining room furniture set at the house?" Maxim asked at one point.

"It's actually really nice. I love the chairs. They have a unique style and they're very comfortable," Raya acknowledged.

"I made the entire set," Maxim announced proudly. "I want to be a furniture maker. I love antique furniture with its fine, intricate details. In one book about antiques I've seen pictures of amazingly beautiful Italian furniture with elaborate etchings and engravings. It's out of this world! I want to make something like that too but I don't have all the necessary tools yet. It's too bad that our modern Russian furniture is so simple and so starkly utilitarian."

Raya regarded Maxim with profound amazement and new-found respect. He was talking about furniture with the same kind of enthusiasm and passion as she would speak about biochemistry. She could really appreciate this trait in a person – a passionate devotion to a chosen vocation.

They hardly noticed how quickly the time passed by. They were sitting in a secluded area on the shores of the Volga, shielded from the outside world by the overhanging foliage of a cluster of the large trees. With her bare feet caressing the cool grass, Raya idly observed how a little ant crawled over her foot.

It seemed to her that nature itself was celebrating this day with her. She heard congratulations in the rustle of the leaves and in the splash of the gently rippling waves against the shoreline. There came a point when she thought that perhaps they should be heading back to the city but she felt no desire or motivation to move from these lovely and peaceful surroundings.

A short while later, Maxim opened his knapsack, took out a large blanket, and jauntily announced, "Picnic time!"

He spread the blanket on the grass and started to remove various food items from his knapsack. Raya watched with bemusement how the blanket became a tablecloth for a picnic banquet. Clearly Maxim wanted to celebrate Raya's university admittance in style. Soon there was a feast laid out on the blanket: salami, cheese, tomatoes, cucumbers, apples, boiled eggs and boiled potatoes. Lastly, Maxim produced a bottle of wine and two glasses.

They drank some wine, ate some of the food, talked, and laughed. After the meal, Maxim gathered up the dishes and made his way down to the shore of the river to wash them. Raya folded the blanket in half, collected the remains of their feast, and packed it away into the knapsack. Then she sat down again and admired the picture-perfect scenery before her. The Dnieper that she knew so well was a great river, but middle Volga, here near Kazan, seemed so much larger and so much more majestic. The sun was starting to set and Raya contently followed its progress as it sank slowly on the horizon.

Maxim's hushed voice interrupted her quiet reverie. "Raya, you are so beautiful, so incredibly beautiful."

Even in her contented frame of mind, Raya couldn't resist a smirk. "Maxim, I believe you need to have your eyes checked! I'm not beautiful by any stretch of the imagination."

"You're wrong about that, Raya, totally wrong, if I may say so. You look so regal, like a stately queen. I mean it! And your skin – it's so smooth, like silk," Maxim marvelled.

Raya felt Maxim's fingers gently touching her hand and then sliding slowly upward onto her forearm. This slight touch caused her to shiver with mixed emotions.

"May I kiss you?" Maxim whispered, and without waiting for a response he leaned his head toward Raya and their lips met. For the first time in her life, Raya was feeling the touch of warm and passionate male lips on hers. Maxim's kiss began as a gentle touch on the lips, but soon it became more intense and his tongue lingered, demanding and hungry, in Raya's partially open mouth.

So, this is what Manya felt so many years ago at the train station. Although Maxim's kisses began to stir deep-seated emotions, Raya's thoughts still remained relatively detached and noncommittal.

Maxim's lips were now fondly kissing her neck and her shoulders; his hands were urgently unbuttoning her blouse and then Raya felt the warm touch of his hand on her breast.

He's going way too far, Raya thought indignantly, but she said nothing and did nothing to dissuade him. Rather, she had another thought: *this is my one and only opportunity, maybe my only opportunity, to experience those feelings and to know what it is like to be desired. Why not let this foolish, love-struck boy show me what it's all about?*

Maxim's hands freed both of Raya's breasts and began cupping and caressing them. Then she felt him kissing her aroused nipples. *Okay, that's enough, a* suddenly alarmed Raya decided.

But another voice in her head, filled with latent curiosity, protested strongly. *Raya, you know that it's your destiny to live and die as a spinster, but surely you don't have to die a virgin.*

And so, Raya allowed Maxim to proceed unimpeded.

Afterwards, she lay very still, trying to comprehend the variety of feelings she had just experienced, and listening to the sweet words of affection that Maxim was whispering in her ear.

The next morning, Raya awoke filled with a resolve to put aside yesterday's events and to concentrate on the task at hand, her studies. She was expected to be in Kazan for the next month and she knew very well that it would be an extremely intense period, academically speaking.

The *extern* education program in the Soviet Union included two one-month-long overview sessions for each academic year that had to be conducted on the university campus and the students were obligated to attend in person. At the beginning of each session, the students were required to pass the exams for the previous half-year of studies. Only successful students were then allowed to proceed to the next session.

The most critical session was the very first, and it was scheduled to start almost immediately after the results of the entrance exams were announced. This session would determine who was suitable to be deemed a worthy student and who was not. The students were going to be studying three new subjects and there were going to be three exams at the end of the session. The average expulsion rate at the conclusion of that first session was usually between fifteen and twenty percent. Raya was determined not to become a part of that statistic.

She went to the university early that morning and was one of the first to register and to buy her books. With a certain bemusement, Raya realized that she was actually more thrilled when the administrator called out, "*Student Kushnir, please receive your schedule,*" than she had been from her first love-making experience with Maxim.

When Raya emerged with her arms loaded with books, Maxim was waiting for her on the steps of the main campus building.

"Raya," he said, "today is only Friday. Your studies start on Monday. You have a full weekend ahead of you. Let's go to the river again."

"Maxim, you can't expect me to show up on Monday without knowing something about what the new subjects are about. I'm planning to read the first several chapters of each of the textbooks before then," Raya explained by way of mild protest.

But somehow they found themselves on the shores of Volga again. They made love, and afterwards Raya started reading her books while Maxim was contentedly carving a figurine out of a block of wood.

Such was their routine for the next month – Raya would spend the day at the university and then they would retreat to their favourite secluded place by the river and make love. Afterwards, Raya would read her books and Maxim would carve another figurine for her.

One day, Raya was startled to learn that another girl was vacating the rooming house. She had declared that the studies were too difficult, the teachers were too demanding and pushy, and that the stress was too much for her.

"To be accepted as a student and then to give it all up so quickly, so easily..." Raya was discussing that girl's decision with Maxim. "How could she do it? Would she ever be willing to voluntarily go through the hell of those entrance exams again, or has she just decided that she'll never be getting a higher education? Who knows, but I just can't understand that girl."

For Raya, that month of intensive study was akin to a dream come true. Finally she could abandon once and for all the tedium of the high-school books and concentrate on learning exciting and challenging new material. Most of the topics she was already familiar with from attending the evening lectures in Kiev University, but others were totally new for her. Raya enjoyed every minute she spent at the university and when she was immersed in her books. Meanwhile, Maxim was a charming diversion on the side during this wonderful time.

Before she knew it, the month was almost over. Raya's roommate failed one of the exams, packed her bags, wished the remaining girls good luck and left Aunt Dasha's house for good.

Raya excelled in all her exams. Three more days of lectures, in which the teachers would give an overview for the next half-year of studies and explain their assignments, and then it would be back to Kiev.

In the morning, Raya awoke with a wholly unexpected thought. *I'm going to miss Maxim. I'll miss our times together and the feeling of being loved and desired.*

She glanced at her bed-side table which was littered with carved wooden figurines, and then she smiled to herself, thinking, *at least I'll have my treasures. These statues will help me to remember Maxim forever.*

That day, when Raya was leaving the university with her schoolmates, Maxim was waiting for her nearby with flowers. He had a profoundly serious and stern expression on his face.

"Maxim, what's happened?" Raya inquired with some anxiety. "Why are you looking so sombre?"

"Raya, marry me," he said without prelude.

"What?" an astonished Raya reacted. "But..."

"Raya, please, just wait and hear me out. Let me say what I need to say.

"I understand the differences between us. You'll become a fully-qualified biochemist in five years; and later on, I've no doubt, you'll become a Doctor of Science. I'm a furniture maker and will always remain so. You are a sophisticated, educated and intelligent woman. I'm just a simple man. I do appreciate all of that.

"But I love you, Raya. I can't imagine a day of my life without you. I can't bear the thought of parting with you. I love you, Raya, with all my heart. Please, marry me. I promise to be the best husband any woman could wish for. I'll look after you and protect you, and I'll help with all the chores at home so you can study as much as you want. Just marry me, my darling," Maxim pleaded.

Raya regarded him incredulously, uncertain how to react or what to say. It was one thing to have an affair with Maxim, but to marry him? The thought had never even occurred to her. They were so different in so many ways - their backgrounds, their interests, and their nationalities! Yet that inner, rebellious voice was already whispering to her, *Raya, don't be foolish. This is your chance to have your own family, and not to be just an 'auntie' and live only observing the happiness of others. It's your opportunity to become a wife and a mother. This boy loves you; let him take care of you.*

And to her utter amazement, Raya heard the stammering sound of her own voice, "Okay, Maxim, I'll marry you."

Maxim embraced her, lifting her off her feet, and whirled her about as she laughed heartily at his happiness and unbounded enthusiasm.

"Maxim, where are we going to live?" Raya's well-organized mind was already thinking about the immediate future. "My life is in Kiev; I must go back. My family is there, and of course there's my work. I'm finally a university student, so they'll promote me quickly. I'm sure of it. I'm doing the work of a biochemist anyway. I can't just give up seven years of hard-earned seniority. And even more importantly, I can't live without my brothers and Manya. Manya's more than just my sister-in-law, she's my blood sister and I can't imagine ever living far away from her. I've told you our story, so I'm sure you understand."

"Then we'll live in Kiev, Raya," a resolute Maxim replied. "I'm not attached to the house here. It's more of a hostel anyway, where I'm just one of the tenants. And my mother might then feel free to marry Uncle Konstantin."

"Maxim, we only have a small, two-room apartment in Kiev. My mother and younger brother live there as well. We share the kitchen and the bathroom with two other families. It's not exactly a palace," Raya cautioned. She didn't want Maxim to be deluded with too high expectations.

"With you, darling, any place will be a palace," Maxim assured her, all the while tenderly kissing the fingers of both her hands.

"Our factory is starting to build a new apartment building for the employees. I can apply, but it will only be ready in three years," Raya mused.

"We'll do the best we can in the meantime, Raya. Don't worry about an apartment. We'll be very happy, you'll see," Maxim assured her. He couldn't fathom how Raya could even think about such a mundane consideration as an apartment at this moment. All that he cared about was Raya and he was ready to follow her to the ends of the earth.

They made their way back to Maxim's house and made their announcement to his mother. A thrilled Aunt Dasha kissed Raya and enthused, "I couldn't imagine a better wife for my son. You're going to make a real man out of him. I bless you with all my heart."

"Thank you very much, Aunt Dasha."

"You're very welcome, niece Raya," Aunt Dasha responded teasingly with a broad smile.

"Umm," Raya stammered, somewhat taken back. "I'm not actually your niece."

"And I'm not actually your aunt! You must call me Mama. I want you two to be married tomorrow here in Kazan. I raised one son all by myself. I deserve to witness his wedding."

Maxim and Raya went to the telephone station in the post office again in order to call to Kiev. They had to wait more than an hour for a connection, and meanwhile Raya was becoming increasingly nervous. She knew that the conversation with her family wouldn't be an easy one, so she asked Maxim to wait for her outside the booth.

Finally she was connected to her mother's apartment number and she heard Vera's voice, "Rayechka, why are you calling? It's so expensive. Did something happen?"

"Yes, Mama. I'm getting married tomorrow. His name is Maxim Sokolov and he's the most wonderful man in the world," Raya announced, speaking in a tone as confident as she could muster.

"Oy... Dima and Manya are here."

"Dima, it's good that you're here today," Raya heard her mother saying. "Please, talk to Raya. I had better sit down. My heart..."

"Raya, what's going on? Mama's about to faint," Dima asked worriedly.

"I'm getting married, Dima. I met a wonderful man here; he's the son of my landlady. We've been dating for the past month. Dima, I'm so happy!" Raya exclaimed.

"What's his name, Raya, and what's his occupation? Is he a student at the university like you?" Dima's voice was cautious as he posed those questions.

"No, Dima, he's not a student. He's a furniture maker and a very talented one at that. His name is Maxim Sokolov." Raya decided that she had better hold the bit of information about Maxim's age for later.

"Russian?" Dima half-inquired, half-stated.

"Yes. So what does that matter?" Raya responded defensively.

"Raya, are you sure you know what you're doing? Aren't you rushing it a bit? You've only known him for a month," Dima cautioned.

"Dima, not everyone has the privilege of dating for ten years like you! He's a good man and he loves me and that's the only thing that really counts," Raya shot back.

"And why wouldn't he? You're smart, interesting, exciting. Of course he loves you. But do you love him, Raya? And what have the two of you got in common? What will you both talk about?" Dima asked with genuine concern in his voice.

"Oh, Dima, stop it! Did you ever see a line-up of men waiting to marry me? As if I have hundreds of boyfriends to choose from!" Raya exclaimed. Dima's sceptical reaction had started to really irritate and frustrate her.

"It doesn't mean that you have to marry the first..." Dima continued with the same line of thought, but Raya cut him short.

"Dima, I don't want to hear it. Why can't you just be happy for me?"

Raya heard the phone changing hands and then the soft, melodic voice of Manya came on the line.

"Sister, don't listen to that grouch. I'm very happy for you. Mazel Tov! I wish you all the happiness and can't wait to meet this Maxim of yours."

Raya and Maxim were married the next day in a simple civil ceremony. There was no white dress for Raya and no black-tie suit for Maxim, but his mother prepared a scrumptious dinner and her student tenants, friends and relatives all gathered together to congratulate the newlyweds.

Two days later they boarded the train for Kiev. At home, Vera was making her own preparations to receive her newly-married daughter and son-in-law. She packed up all her clothes from her room where she had lived with Semyon and moved them to the living room which she would share with Misha from now on. Maxim and Raya would live in her room, which would give them some degree of privacy.

A festive dinner was prepared to celebrate Raya and Maxim's arrival. As Raya had expected, in addition to Dima and his family, Aleksander was also invited for the festivities.

Aleksander arrived, not alone, but accompanied by a pleasant-looking woman. "Alla Andreevna," he introduced her. "She's teaching Russian to junior high students at our school."

It seemed to Raya that Aleksander looked better than he had in years. He was clean-shaven, wearing a freshly-pressed suit, and what was most important, bearing a cheerful grin on his face! The sisters had concluded long ago that their dear friend was a very handsome man when he was smiling.

Manya and Raya looked at each other and nodded their heads in agreement. The woman looked just the way that the wife of Aleksander should look - pretty, pleasant, open-faced, kind and with wise eyes.

Dima did his best to engage his new brother-in-law in conversation. He tried to talk about politics but Maxim was under the distinct impression that politics was best left in the hands of the government. Dima also talked about some recent popular books but Maxim had never been keen on reading. Then Dima tried other subjects, including science, theatre, art, and so on and so on, but he didn't find a single common thread of mutual interest between himself and Maxim.

Maxim in turn was trying to talk about the things that interested him - fishing, hunting, and soccer, but Dima considered these sorts of activities to be an idle waste of time. Soon Dima excused himself and went to talk with Aleksander instead.

That first conversation determined the state of the relationship between Dima and Maxim for years afterwards: civil and polite, but devoid of any closeness, kinship, or genuine warmth.

Maxim was quite relieved when Manya made an approach to talk with him. He found her easy to speak with, not like that aloof and snobbish brother of Raya.

Alla Andreevna became friends with Manya and Raya before the evening was over. They talked openly about her relationship with Aleksander (diplomacy never was Raya's strong suit) and the sisters were gratified to understand how deep and sincere Alla's feelings were for him. They didn't have to ask anything of Aleksander. They knew their friend well enough to appreciate that he was hopelessly in love.

"When's the wedding?" the girls wanted to know. They didn't leave poor Aleksander alone until he formally proposed to Alla right then and there to the delight of everyone.

The Price Of Success

A TRIUMPHANT RAYA returned to her workplace the very next day. The first thing on her agenda was a visit to the Human Resources Department. She informed the head of the department of the change in her marital status and provided him with the required paperwork from the university. She applied for a change of name and then asked to be added to the list of employees waiting for the new staff apartment building expected to be completed in about three years.

"I want to apply for a two-room apartment," Raya proudly announced.

"But a couple without children only qualifies for one room," she was informed.

"I understand," a confident Raya replied as she meaningfully patted her stomach. "Before the building is ready, we'll qualify."

The ladies of the laboratory enthusiastically congratulated Raya on all of her achievements. Someone rushed off to the bakery and returned with a cake. This was the day that Raya had been dreaming about for seven long years. At last she was no longer the *eternal lab-technician* and as an added bonus, no longer *an old maid in the making* either.

At the end of the day, the entire female contingent of the laboratory was gathered near the windows, curious to catch a glimpse of the new husband that would be meeting Raya. After Raya and Maxim left the premises, the ladies stayed behind for a long while, busy discussing and exchanging opinions amongst themselves about the newlyweds and the new stage in Raya's life.

The next morning, the women sat Raya down in a chair in the middle of the laboratory room and surrounded her with grim expressions on their faces.

"Who was that handsome young man that was waiting for you yesterday?" the oldest biochemist, Nina Arkadyevna, inquired pointedly.

"My husband, of course," Raya answered with pride.

"And how long are you planning to stay married to him?" the matron continued.

"I beg your pardon?" an indignant Raya exclaimed.

"For about as long as it takes for that handsome fellow to look around and compare Raya with some of the other girls of Kiev," one of the ladies chipped in.

"That's enough! Stop insulting me." Raya made a move to get up from the chair.

"Sit down and just listen, Raya," Nina Arkadyevna brusquely instructed. "You're one of us and it's our responsibility as your co-workers to look out for your best interests."

"Thanks, but I don't need your help. Maxim loves me. He thinks that I look stately, even regal, and those are his own words."

"Exactly! You've lost weight – you always do during exams – so you do look stately right now. Take a look at Marina here," the older lady said, pointing to the other lab technician, a petite blonde. "Marina," she continued, "can gain ten kilograms and still look pretty. Plump but pretty. But with your large, big-boned frame, one kilogram can make all the difference between stately and massive. You always want to be on the side of stately."

"So, what do you suggest?" a bewildered Raya asked, quite taken aback by the ladies' unexpected concern about her weight.

"Watch what you eat," a chorus of ladies responded in unison.

"I take it," Nina Arkadyevna continued relentlessly, "you were working so hard to get into the university because you want a promotion, right? You want a more senior job in our laboratory, correct?"

"Yes, of course," Raya responded in a low voice.

"Then start to dress seriously! All those flowery dresses, casual skirts and loose blouses must go. Straight to the garbage!

"Tamara," she gestured to a well-dressed lady, "you're in charge of Raya's new wardrobe and her fashion education."

Nina then addressed another woman. "Larissa, tomorrow you're taking Raya to your hairdresser. That silly ponytail must go. And see what can be done with her nails at the same time."

Nina then turned back to Raya and proclaimed, "Now you're a woman and wife to a handsome young husband. Learn to look after yourself. I don't ever want to see you in this laboratory without fresh lipstick, mascara and face powder. Is that understood, Raya?"

The woman was speaking with the confident tone and authority of the *mother-hen* of the laboratory, and whose directives were not to be ignored. She had been handing out advices (both solicited and volunteered) to the young ladies of the laboratory for ages. Some of the women couldn't tolerate Nina, while others loved her dearly and considered her to be their best friend and advisor.

Raya felt resentful and more than a little angry. How could it be that these ladies who paid her so little attention before, apart from mocking her behind her back, now thought that they had the right to instruct her how to live, how to dress, and how to wear her hair? But her quick, analytical mind acknowledged that there was some validity in their comments and advices. She had two choices: to snap back, reject them, and make enemies of her co-workers; or, to accept the offered assistance for what it was worth and perhaps derive some benefit from this unsolicited, free education.

"Understood," Raya acceded meekly.

Within a week, Raya's makeover was complete. With her intelligence she only had to be told once and she got the message. Never again did she come to work dressed casually or looking unkempt.

Maxim was thrilled with Raya's transformation. In his eyes she was a queen in any clothes and with any hairdo, but the fact that she tried so hard to please him with her appearance made him feel loved and important. He needed that reinforcement of his confidence too, because in the presence of Raya's more sophisticated relatives he felt quite inadequate.

After Semyon's death, Vera had dedicated virtually all of her spare time to the theatre and never missed any important ballet, opera or drama performances. She tried to introduce Maxim to these higher forms of art. She bought tickets for herself, Raya, and Maxim for performances of *Tosca* and *Swan Lake*.

During the opera, Maxim turned to Raya and whispered, "I don't understand a word they're saying."

"It's in Italian, dear," Raya explained.

"Then what are we doing here? I don't know a word of Italian," Maxim responded with obvious frustration.

Vera glared in his direction, so after that he kept quiet and did his best not to fall asleep. But he did fall asleep during the ballet performance.

"All those white shapes moving so slowly to that tedious music – how could anybody stay awake? I'm not into fairy tales," Maxim asserted, and so Vera soon abandoned her efforts intended to foster Maxim's cultural education.

One day Raya overheard her mother saying to the neighbours, "My daughter has married way below her station. He's simply a peasant! Definitely not the proper match for my Raya."

What station is mama talking about? Raya wondered. A *lab-technician living with her mother and brother in a small apartment – quite the princess!*

Despite the rather frigid reception from Raya's relatives, the newlyweds were happy. Maxim secured a job in the Kiev Experimental Furniture Factory and enjoyed his work there immensely. Raya was carrying on with her work at the lab and with her part-time university studies.

In November, Raya learned that she was expecting. "Manya," she was confiding to her sister, "I'm so happy, and Maxim is even happier! I know that it's going to be difficult coping with university and a baby, especially in our small apartment. There's not even enough room for the four of us as it is, so can you imagine how it's going to be with a new baby here too!"

"I can," Manya encouraged Raya. "I remember when you and Dima and Mama Vera and Semyon were all living there together. And I remember the arrival of baby Misha too."

"Well, he's not a baby any longer. He's twelve now and needs some privacy of his own. Anyway, we'll manage somehow," Raya sighed.

It was a difficult pregnancy and through the entire winter Raya suffered from severe morning sickness. Despite the difficulties with her pregnancy, she passed the winter exams with flying colours.

Raya gave birth to a baby boy just one week after her twenty-fifth birthday. It was at a time when she was in Kazan for the university exams and summer session. Maxim had accompanied her on this trip from Kiev. She had started to feel the contractions the day of the biology exam.

Wait, baby, she willed, and she went to write the exam. As soon as Raya had handed in the completed examination paper to the biology professor, she asked Maxim to take her to the hospital.

Raya always remembered that day as a noisy and chaotic affair. She was assigned to a room with seven other women who were in labor and they were all moaning or screaming to varying degrees. One of them was cursing her husband, while another was crying and swearing never to have sex again. Raya thought that all of them were being quite silly and was proud that she was suffering in silence. In fact, in her case the pain was not that burdensome and Raya couldn't see what the fuss was all about.

However, after being in the labor room for several hours, Raya joined the chorus of the other suffering women. The pain became excruciating and by then the only thought in Raya's head was how any woman could knowingly subject herself to such pain. If she managed to survive this day, she decided that she would not be having any more children. Never again!

In the early evening, Raya was taken to a delivery room. Three doctors were working there, tending to her and two other women who were also on the verge of giving birth. Raya's delivery of a baby boy progressed quite quickly and he was born before night fell over the city. The baby was washed, weighed, wrapped in a blanket, and placed in her arms. Raya proudly looked at her son and said, "Thank you, my love. Thank you for letting me write my biology exam before you came along."

"You were lucky," another new mother and fellow student said while looking at her own new baby girl. "I missed the algebra exam today."

"What a bunch of silly women you are!" the doctor exclaimed in exasperation. "Can't you focus on your babies right now instead of thinking about university exams?"

In 1961, it was conventional that women were confined to the hospital for seven days after childbirth, but just three days after their son was born, Maxim brought Raya some clothes and she made an escape from the hospital for several hours. She arrived at the university just in time for her next exam. She wrote the test as quickly as she could and was back in the hospital before the next feeding time for her baby.

They named the boy Boris, after Raya's father, and immediately started to call him Borya, the familiar form of that name in Russia and the Ukraine. Maxim's mother was the happiest grandmother in the world and between Raya, Maxim and his mother, they managed to take care of the baby, even while Raya attended the summer university session.

One week after Boris's birth, Raya received a telegram from Kiev – Aleksander and Alla had a baby boy whom they had named Misha after Aleksander's father.

When Raya thought about Aleksander's dismal living quarters, she shuddered. How could they all possibly live in that small room of his? Where would they put a crib? How could Alla possibly manage to cook in that unheated, so-called summer kitchen? Compared to Aleksander's dwelling place, Raya and Maxim had luxury quarters, not to mention a heated toilet room so they didn't have to run to an outhouse in the middle of winter. Raya was well-aware that Aleksander wanted to extend the house again, but the new city council had rejected his application. According to the new by-laws, Aleksander couldn't make any further additions or structural changes to the house.

It was only after the young family returned to Kiev that Raya fully appreciated all the difficulties that were awaiting her. The flannel diapers had to be boiled and then ironed on each side; the water for the baby's bath had to be boiled in advance; the baby had to be walked outside in order to get enough fresh air; and furthermore, the second year university course material still had to be studied.

One day Raya took little Borya to the laboratory for a visit and the ladies in her workplace presented her with a nice gift for the baby. Of course they also volunteered lots of advices: how to nurse the baby, how to eat properly, what to drink, what to do in case the baby sniffles, and last but not least, how to prevent another pregnancy.

That last subject was of utmost concern to Raya because there was simply no place for another baby in their small quarters. For the first time in her life, Raya realized that there was no straightforward solution to this birth control issue and none of the recommended methods afforded any absolute guarantee against another unwanted pregnancy. From Raya's viewpoint, the ladies' recommendations in that regard seemed more like warnings that actual practical advice.

"Don't even think about condoms. Russian-made condoms feel like sand-paper and break all the time. I have two sons to prove it," one woman said.

"You can try a diaphragm but you must get up immediately after making love and wash yourself thoroughly," another woman advised.

At that point, Raya imagined herself preparing the hot water in advance, storing it in her room, and rushing to the shared bathroom in the middle of the night. She could just imagine her teen-aged brother's sarcastic remarks, not to mention how Maxim might react to this decidedly unromantic procedure.

"*On the side* is the only proven method," was another piece of helpful advice offered by yet-another of the women.

"What do you mean, *on the side*?" Raya inquired innocently.

In response to that, the ladies began to giggle. "You'll figure it out."

"Why are you all making such a big deal out of this?" pretty Lidochka asked. "You get pregnant; you have an abortion. It's as simple as that. I've had eight abortions already."

"No way! I would never do that. It's like murder!" Raya hotly protested.

"Don't be silly. If it comes to that, you'll have no choice. If you have to choose between aborting an unwanted pregnancy and not being able to properly take care of another baby, what would you chose, eh?" Lidochka retorted.

Raya broke into a cold sweat. "Is it really true? You've all had abortions?" That question kicked off a multitude of responses.

"I've had five."

"I'm lucky. Only two...so far."

"My husband has a friend who's a gynaecologist. Every time I get pregnant he comes and scrubs me out on the kitchen table. No big deal."

"The real problem is not whether or not to have an abortion. The problem is having a good doctor who'll do it for you in time. Raya, whenever you need the procedure, just speak to me and I'll give you the name of my doctor. He's reliable, discreet and not too expensive," Lidochka offered.

"Expensive? You have to pay for it?"

"Of course you do. And if you want to have it done without a lot of pain, you have to give extra cash to his nurse assistant to get an injection."

Virtually every woman in the laboratory had something to say on the subject and Raya's head was spinning.

"Girls, stop frightening poor Raya," Nina Arkadyevna finally interjected. "Don't worry, dear. While you're nursing you won't get pregnant anyway, so you don't have to worry, at least not for now."

Raya's 'educational' lab visit was finally over and she went immediately to talk with Manya. "Is it true what all those women said?" she asked.

"Well, it's not quite as bad as they suggest. You just have to be careful. I've been lucky so far," Manya replied in a moderately encouraging tone of voice.

After that, love-making ceased being fun anymore for Raya. She was constantly worried about becoming pregnant. What's more, she was uncomfortably conscious that each of their movements or anything that they said, even in hushed tones in their confined quarters, could readily be heard through the paper-thin walls by her mother and young Misha in the next room. It was not as if they were living in the privacy of their own apartment.

All that Raya could recall from the first year of Borya's life was her constant state of exhaustion. The baby had to be fed in the middle of the night, and sometimes more than once. She had had only one burning desire - to get a good night's rest once in a while.

During the winter exams Raya had difficulty concentrating and she even surprised herself with the high grades she received. Throughout the month in Kazan, she had a hard time just staying awake during her lectures. Her mother-in-law did her utmost to help, but Raya was still perpetually tired. She was very much relieved when the university session was finally over and they could return to Kiev.

On the first Sunday after their return, Raya and Maxim dressed little Borya warmly and went to Manya's place for a visit. Aleksander and Alla were there with their new son too. The two boys were placed together in one playpen and the parents were able to relax for a bit.

"I have some great news to announce," Aleksander said proudly, all the while looking affectionately at Alla. "We're expecting again!"

"Where can you possibly put a second crib?" Raya wondered.

"Oh, we'll find a place," Alla said as she smiled in return with her typical outward aura of calm and happiness.

"You're brave," Raya acknowledged. "I don't think that we'll consider having a second baby for quite a few more years! Maybe after we get a new apartment and I finish university. I'm very tired all the time as it is. I barely survived the winter session in Kazan, even though I managed to get good exam results. I never realized that raising a child would be so time-consuming and utterly exhausting."

"Have you been to the doctor lately?" Dima asked caringly.

"Half-a-year ago. I don't have any need to see a doctor right now, Dima. I'm just tired, that's all," Raya replied dismissively.

"Raya, go to a doctor," Dima insisted. "I think that you're pregnant again."

"Don't be silly," Raya scolded him with heightened agitation. "Don't invent things! Just because a woman is tired, it doesn't mean that she's pregnant. I've got more than enough reasons to be tired these days. And what do you know about these things, anyway? You're a paediatrician, not a gynaecologist. And besides, I'm nursing! Don't

166

you know that a woman doesn't become pregnant while she's still nursing?"

Manya and Dima exchanged furtive glances. "Raya, there's no need to get angry at Dima. He loves you and cares about you very much. Why don't you go to the doctor tomorrow? I'll go with you. Maybe you just need some vitamins," Manya suggested soothingly, and Raya relented grudgingly.

The visit to the doctor resulted in bad news for Raya... as a matter of fact, the worst news she could possibly have received. Dima was right after all; she was expecting again. And since she was already more than eighteen weeks pregnant, an abortion was clearly out of the question.

Just a year ago, when Raya had received the news of her first pregnancy, she had been elated. This time she was devastated.

"This is the end, Manya! This is it." Raya was crying in consternation on the shoulder of her sister. "I can't possibly carry on studying with two young ones. Not only that, if I don't go back to work soon they'll take my name off the waiting list and I won't get an apartment when the staff building is finished. And the worst of all, there isn't even any space for another crib in our cramped room. What am I to do now?"

"Calm down, dear heart. We'll think of something. You shouldn't give up on your university studies. Be strong," Manya was saying caringly.

It was Vera who came up with the solution. "I'm almost of retirement age, so I'll retire. Sure, I wanted to work several more years but your future, Rayechka, is much more important. Go back to the factory and continue working as long as you can. After the baby's born, you'll go back to work again after a couple of months and I'll be with the children. That way you'll be able to keep up with your university assignments too. You mustn't sacrifice that now."

"Raya, I'll help as much as I can too," Maxim was saying, hugging and kissing his wife. "We'll manage."

For the next several months, Maxim was busy making a custom crib for the new baby and a small bed for Borya. Then he completely rearranged the furniture in their small room and somehow everything fit in.

Elena Maximovna, or simply, Lena, was born in early June and Raya then traveled to Kazan for her summer session, accompanied by Maxim and their two children.

After they returned to Kiev at the end of July, Raya confessed to Manya, "I don't know what I'll do this time when Maxim wants to resume our intimacy. I can sense he's starting to get impatient and I'm terrified. I'm scared of getting pregnant again, and I detest the idea of mama and Misha hearing the sounds of our love-making. Besides, I'm afraid that we'd wake up Borya, and with his loud cries he'd wake up Lena too. It's a vicious circle. I certainly don't want to lose Maxim, so what am I to do, Manya?"

The always faithful and empathetic Manya offered a good solution. "Come to our apartment every Sunday. Dima and I will take the kids and we'll go out so you two can have privacy in our apartment for a couple of hours."

"Manechka, this would be great! That would save my marriage! And I could even take a hot shower instead of wasting time in the public baths. But what do you think Dima will say to that idea?" Raya fussed.

"You leave Dima to me. I'll manage him," Manya responded with a reassuring smile; and so, it was all arranged.

For the next year, the Sokolov family was going to the Kushnir apartment every Sunday morning, and then later in the afternoon a contented Maxim and Raya would help Manya to prepare dinner for everybody.

It was an expedient temporary solution, but Raya knew that it couldn't last forever. And if she had previously been obsessed with the notion of becoming a university student, now she was equally obsessed with obtaining a decent apartment and with gaining the long-awaited promotion to a biochemist position at her factory. Enough of being a mere lab-technician! Raya felt that she had earned the title of a biochemist and was more than ready for it.

Two landmark events related to Raya's work took place in the same week. Nina Arkadyevna unexpectedly announced her retirement, thereby freeing up a biochemist position; and, the coveted staff apartment building was finally completed and ready to start accepting the lucky ones among the long list of applicants.

The HR Department, together with factory management, the factory union, and the local Communist Party cell engaged in a long meeting, allocating apartment units to selected employees. The next day, the lucky employees were called to the HR Department one by one.

Raya could hear the exclamations of some of her fellow employees. "I got a corner unit! Corner units are the biggest! Well, it's on the first floor, but who cares – beggars can't be choosers, right?"

"I got an apartment on the fifth floor. I wonder who my neighbours are going to be. Do you know who else got placed on the fifth floor?"

All day Raya was impatiently waiting for her turn to be summoned, but alas, it never came. Finally, around four o'clock, she knocked on the office door of the Head of the HR Department.

"Oh, Rayechka, my dear child, what can I do for you?" the manager asked, greeting her with a disarmingly innocent smile.

"Yuri Ivanovich, I was wondering which apartment I got? I haven't been called yet."

Yuri Ivanovich made a show of being surprised by the question. "Raya, you didn't actually get an apartment. Didn't anybody tell you that you didn't qualify?"

"How can that be? I've been working in the factory for almost ten years and I was one of the first to apply. What do you mean I didn't qualify?"

"Raisa Borisovna," Yuri Ivanovich intoned slowly, all the while trying to making a show of sounding formal, "you applied for a two-room apartment, correct? But you have two children of different gender. On that basis, you would only qualify for a three-room apartment."

"Okay, I'll take a three-room apartment then!"

"But you never applied for a three-room apartment."

"I don't care which apartment. Please just give me a two-room unit then. It'll still be a thousand times better for my children that what we have now."

"But it would be unlawful to give you two rooms and you can't expect us to break the laws of our country, can you?" Yuri Ivanovich responded sternly.

"My daughter is already one year old. How is it that nobody ever mentioned such a law to me?" an indignant Raya asked in a tone of voice conveying her rising frustration.

"Well, Raisa Borisovna, it's not my responsibility to instruct every employee of our large factory about their rights and benefits," the manager responded pompously.

Raya wanted to ask him what his responsibility *actually* was, but she couldn't bring herself to pursue the argument any further. She sat dejected in a chair and stared back at him with a look of helplessness.

"Rayechka, there's talk of starting another building. It'll be ready in a mere five of six years. You're still young, so five or six years are nothing at your age." Yuri Ivanovich was trying to mollify Raya and suggested, "You can apply for one of those apartments and I'm quite certain you would qualify the next time."

It was all too much for Raya to bear - six more years in one tiny room with two growing children. Another six long years of standing in line for the use of a stove burner in the kitchen. Six more years of living in such confined quarters together with her mother and brother.

Raya began sobbing in earnest, almost beyond control.

Yuri Ivanovich considered himself to be a genuinely sensitive and good-hearted person. He abhorred it when people broke down in his office, and he absolutely couldn't cope with women wailing in his company. In this case, nothing could be done and he knew it.

He rose from his chair, intent on making it clear that their meeting was over. At that very moment, Yuri Ivanovich happened to take notice for the first time of Raya's soft white neck and her bountiful, heaving breasts. The sight of this alluring *damsel-in-distress* had a wholly unexpected and surprisingly pleasant effect on the aging manager.

He gently placed one of his hands on the back of Raya's neck, slowly caressed it, and then confided in a hoarse low voice, "There are several apartments left in reserve 'till the end of the week. There'll be a further meeting of the committee on Friday morning to finalize those remaining allocations. Why don't you come by my office Thursday evening around seven o'clock and we can discuss your particular situation again? Perhaps I can do something for you after all, Rayechka."

Did she perceive his intentions correctly? Raya lifted her head and looked up at the leering older man. She felt that she was about to become ill. She couldn't speak. Hastily, she got up and ran from his office directly to the ladies' room. She barely made it.

On her way back to the laboratory, Raya noticed that the door to her boss' office was ajar. Resolutely, Raya asked for permission to enter.

"Gregory Mikhailovich," she said, addressing her boss courteously, "Nina Arkadyevna is retiring. I was wondering if I'm going to be promoted to take over her position."

"Rayechka, it's an engineering position and you have two more years until you graduate. Please be patient. You should finish university first and then we'll see about a promotion," her boss dispassionately advised.

"But Gregory Mikhailovich, you promised! I know the work! I've been doing it for years already! There's nobody else as qualified as I am. I'm quite certain you know that. I've worked for you for almost ten years. Doesn't my seniority mean something?" Raya was trembling with a combination of distress and rage.

"Of course it does! But this position has already been taken. I'm sorry, Raya. I'm sure there will be other opportunities," her boss stated unceremoniously.

For the second time within the hour, Raya started to cry. And for the second time her despair elicited a similar response. Her boss approached her, patted her gently but deliberately on the shoulder and suggested with barely disguised subtlety that she should be nice to him.

Incredulous after the day's events, Raya went to see Manya that evening. Her despair had been supplanted by seething anger and determination. She was not about to give up now.

"Manya, what's the matter with those two men? Why such an interest in my body all of sudden? They've known me for almost ten years, so why now?" Raya fumed.

"Because now you're desperate and they know it's an opportunity to take advantage of you," Manya replied matter-of-factly. "Raya, you have to leave that factory. You've overstayed your welcome there. With your education and experience you'll have no problem finding a new job, and a better one at that."

"And give up the staff apartment that's rightfully mine? And let them get the better of me? ' Raya retorted hotly.

"Raya, listen to me. Don't do anything that you'll be ashamed of later. Don't do something that would keep you from looking honestly at Maxim straight in the eye," Manya was pleading with her sister.

"But if I don't do something, the next thing you know I'll have no husband to look in the eye at all," Raya countered. "I've got an idea though," she mused before suddenly dropping the subject. Manya refrained from asking for any details.

Raya thought through her idea all night, and the next morning she was ready and reconciled to going forward with her plan. She knew that time was running out. On Friday the remaining apartments would be allocated and unless she managed to secure one of them, that would be the end of her ten-year career in the factory and the end of her dream of a normal life.

Raya dressed in her best dark, navy-blue business suit and an embroidered white blouse, buttoned to the very top. She put on the stylish, high-heeled shoes that she had never worn to work before now, and finally, applied a soft touch of make-up. Her hair was piled high into a bun, fully exposing her long, graceful neck.

She went to see the secretary of the Factory Director, the famous (or infamous, depending on one's point of view) Vasily Andreevich Kovalenko.

"I need an appointment with Comrade Kovalenko today please," she appealed to the secretary.

"Comrade Kovalenko is an extremely busy man. I don't think he can see you until next week at the earliest," the secretary responded indifferently.

"Irina, dear, I only need five minutes; no more! I've worked here for ten years and I've never asked for an appointment until now, but this is an urgent matter." Raya then casually placed a box of expensive chocolates on Irina's desk.

"Okay, wait here. I'll see what I can do," the secretary said as she discretely hid the chocolates in the lower drawer of her desk.

While Irina was in the director's office to arrange the appointment, Raya was revisiting in her mind everything that she knew about their formidable Director. He was a no-nonsense type and everyone in the factory feared becoming the object of his wrath.

Feared, yes, but at the same time respected. He was actually a good manager, a good chemist, and he had navigated factory politics quite successfully over the past ten years. Vasily Andreevich was quite young to be holding such a privileged position, being in his early forties. But people were saying that his father-in-law was some important figure, a local Party boss or some sort of government official. Nobody knew for certain, but the right connections were far more important than age or job experience in the Soviet Union. Therefore it was commonly assumed that his father-in-law must be quite an influential person in order to have placed Kovalenko in his current post.

Vasily Andreevich was a tall, athletically built, and exceptionally good-looking man, with dark brown eyes and a strong, chiselled chin. The thing that distinguished him remarkably from the rest of the men among the management of the factory was the fact that he was always well-groomed and impeccably dressed. He was always clean-shaven, with his hair cut short and styled, and he wore expensive, freshly-pressed suits with crisp white shirts and tasteful ties. All in all he was not hard to look at.

His one weakness was women. He was married to a beautiful, elegant lady (Raya had seen her from a distance during some official factory celebrations). Yet, despite having a gorgeous wife, Vasily Andreevich had reportedly not missed one single skirt in the factory. His affairs were never longer than three months, often shorter, and in the end, the dismissed mistress received a handsome present and was supplanted by another favourite. The women in the factory who had fallen under his spell furtively compared stories about his sexual prowess and the gifts they each had received, but always very discreetly. There had never been a scandal, a fight, or a clash related to the office affairs.

Everything that transpired was conducted with mutual understanding and by mutual consent.

In fact, Raya thought, *he has missed one skirt. Mine! Let's see if we can correct that oversight.*

Meanwhile, Irina was doing her utmost to persuade the Director to see Raya. "Vasily Andreevich, please, only five minutes."

"Why does she want to see me, do you know?" the Director inquired.

"Of course I know. Everybody knows. She was expecting a promotion and she was supposed to get an apartment in the new building. She got neither," Irina stated matter-of-factly.

"And why are her problems any of my concern? Let the Head of HR take care of this," Irina's boss said dismissively.

"I understand your point, Vasily Andreevich, but please take into consideration that she's been with our factory for ten years and everybody agrees that she's an excellent worker." Irina was not about to give up easily.

"If she's such an excellent worker, why wasn't she promoted?"

"Vasily Andreevich, you promised the position to the niece of Comrade Ilchenko, from the Ministry. Surely you remember that," Irina reminded him.

"Ah, yes! And the apartment?" Vasily Andreevich probed further.

"The niece got that too," Irina confirmed.

"I see...but why don't I have any recollection of this woman? Did you say she's been working here for ten years?" Vasily asked.

"Not your taste," Irina answered boldly. After all, as the director's personal secretary and as one of his former favourites, she could permit herself to speak boldly once in a while. "So, I'll call her in. Okay?"

"If you must..." and with that Vasily Andreevich cast his eyes down to the stack of documents littering his desktop.

Irina eased her way out of his office and with a quick nod motioned Raya towards his door. Just before entering the office, Raya made two quick adjustments, unobserved by Irina. She undid the two top buttons of her blouse and tucked in the waist-band of her skirt, thus making it shorter so that it now rode well-above the knees.

The Director slightly lifted his head and observed Raya as she approached his desk. He immediately noticed the long and shapely legs coming into close-up focus. *It would really be a shame to say 'no' to those legs*, he thought.

"Vasily Andreevich, thank you so much for seeing me on such short notice. My problem is that it's difficult for me to focus on my regular work because I can't think about anything else except this new enzyme that I've discovered," Raya said bravely.

"What?" a bewildered Vasily Andreevich asked as he carefully scrutinized Raya's appearance – too tall, large-boned, sharp features and the nose was way too big. *Irina is right*, he reflected, *not my taste.*

"May I take a seat?" Raya asked politely, and before he could respond she promptly sat down in the chair across from the director's desk. Her skirt rose a bit higher, revealing an amble portion of her shapely thighs.

"I know that I should have discussed it first with my own superior, but you're recognized as the best enzyme specialist in our factory. All my life I've wanted to be a scientist and this is my first serious undertaking."

After pausing sufficiently to be sure she had his undivided attention, Raya pushed on. "Here, Vasily Andreevich, as you can see I've outlined the formula and the expected properties and the anticipated benefits. Of course there'll need to be many more experiments conducted in order to validate my theory, and that's why I'm here. I can't take on anything this significant and potentially important without your explicit authorization," Raya intoned. "Wouldn't you agree?"

She leaned forward across the desk to show him the formula, offering Vasily Andreevich an inviting glimpse of her shapely breasts. He suddenly felt as though it was getting stuffy in his office and he loosened his tie. Within the five minutes that Raya had requested, Vasily discovered three things: the woman had legs worthy of his further attention, she had spectacular breasts that begged to be fondled, and as an added bonus, she was incredibly clever.

"It's a serious matter, to be sure, Raisa…?"

"Borisovna."

"Raisa Borisovna, I have to read your documentation carefully and consider all the pros and cons. Why don't you leave your papers here with me and come back, let's say around six o'clock this afternoon? That is, of course, if you can stay behind after regular working hours," Vasily suggested, looking at Raya with a countenance that spelled volumes.

"I can definitely stay. I'll be seeing you at six," Raya affirmed while smiling charmingly at the Director.

As she made her way out of the office, Raya discretely nodded in the direction of the old, well-worn couch that was positioned along one wall. *I'll be seeing you too,* she thought with some amusement.

Not a word had been spoken about the apartment or about her promotion.

Ascent To Prominence

RAYA'S THIRTIETH BIRTHDAY party was an impressive and prestigious event. All the important people from the factory were there, including the Director, Vasily Andreevich, with his ravishing wife. Everyone in the management group of the factory had been vying to receive an invitation to this party. After all, Raisa Borisovna was a woman to be reckoned with.

Just three years ago she had been promoted to the position of biochemist (after her ten years of gruelling tenure as a lab-technician).

And then, only one year after her first promotion, Raisa Borisovna became a senior biochemist. Nine months ago, when the laboratory had been divided into separate Quality Assurance and Research and Development departments, she was appointed as the Head of the R&D Department. This didn't surprise anybody, except perhaps her former boss who had to be content to lead the sub-divided QA Department.

And who else was better qualified for the R&D position than Raisa Borisovna? After all, she graduated from Kazan University in four years with outstanding grades and immediately after that was admitted to the graduate program of Kiev University. In a year or two she was expected to earn her PhD degree.

Furthermore, this woman was now being invited to all of the factory management meetings and her frequent input was never dismissed or taken lightly. She was one of the few people who were influencing both the present and future direction of the factory and (as everybody knew) was the trusted right-hand of the Director himself.

The party was held in the Sokolovs' luxurious three-room corner apartment in Rusanovka, which was one of the most prestigious new suburbs of Kiev. Three years prior, at the same time when she was first promoted to a biochemist position, Raya had been awarded a modest, two-room apartment from the last few reserved units in the factory's residential building. But several months ago, the factory was allotted five premium apartments restricted for management only in a brand new building and Raya was one of the lucky recipients of this windfall.

Maxim was busy showing off the apartment to all of Raya's colleagues. The unusual, elegant and expensive-looking furnishings became the talk of the party.

"It looks a bit like the Romanian set that my father has," the director's wife was saying. "But no…German? Definitely not. Polish… Italian maybe? How could that be? Where would you get such fine Italian furniture in Kiev?" she inquired.

"Actually," a highly pleased Maxim explained, "it's from the Kiev Experimental Furniture Factory."

"No way! Domestic furniture looking like that? You must be joking!" another surprised woman exclaimed.

"I bought the unfinished pieces from the factory and finished them myself," Maxim was explaining with the pride of a master craftsman.

"Maxim, dear, are you taking any custom orders?" several of the ladies asked in unison.

Vasily's wife took Maxim aside to discuss her own particular furniture suite requirements with him.

Raya was pleased beyond words with the entire proceedings. The party turned out great. Everybody was there: her family, Aleksander with his family, and all her management level co-workers. There was more than enough scrumptious food and drink for everyone. The children behaved perfectly and all the guests were admiring them for their good manners.

Aleksander was in one corner of the living room talking with Dima. Both men were subdued and feeling a bit sad. Manya had certainly never revealed Raya's secret relationship with the Director to anyone, but these two intelligent men didn't need to have it spelled out for them. They had eyes and were quick to observe and reach their own conclusions.

Aleksander didn't care to judge Raya harshly, yet he was disturbed that such an exceptional woman had to demean herself by stooping to such contemptible means to secure from life all the things that she otherwise so justly deserved.

After the party, an elated Maxim was kissing his wife and telling her, "I always knew that you were going to achieve everything you set out to accomplish! You're the smartest and most admirable woman in the entire world. All those years of studying and working have really paid off. Two more years and you will have your PhD too! Then we'll have so much more time to enjoy our lives. We can go skiing every weekend in the winter. We'll go to Kazan every summer, not to study, but just to relax! Raya, I love you so much! You're the best wife a man could possibly dream of. I'm so proud of you!"

Later, when they were in bed and Maxim was already sleeping peacefully, Raya pondered, *I must finish the affair with Vasily. It was never supposed to last this long. All his previous affairs didn't last any more than two or three months but we've been together now for over three years. I must find a way to stop it, but how?*

Raya had to admit to herself that from many points of view it wouldn't be easy. Vasily was not simply her lover; he was her friend, her confidant, and all in all a very dear person to her. And as for the sex… At the beginning of their affair, Raya felt like a virgin when they were together. He introduced her to pleasures that she didn't know existed. He could evoke such incredibly strong feelings and responses from her body. Even so, she inwardly knew the time had come when their affair had to end.

Raya reflected on her easy admission to the grad school of the same university that had unceremoniously turned her down seven times previously. "Well, Rayechka," her academic advisor, Dr. Sinitsin, had confided outright, "with your connections…we received a phone call from above…" Dr. Sinitsin pointed heavenward.

Raya still needed those connections to be sure of successfully defending her PhD dissertation, but she had to put a stop to her affair with Vasily regardless.

Poor Maxim, Raya thought. *I'm so guilty before him and it's not just because of Vasily. Maxim thinks that after I get this PhD, I'll be satisfied and ready to take it easier. But it's only the beginning for me. I'll never be content to be a mere Candidate of Science. I want to be a recognized Doctor of Science. And that means a second dissertation. Maxim is married to a scientist. When will he ever understand that it will never be an eight-hour working day for me?*

And the kids are growing up so fast! They need me too. I feel that I'm betraying not just Maxim but the children as well with this affair. It has to come to an end. But how can I still face him in the factory and continue to work closely with him after it's over? I must be really careful to find the right way to resolve this problem.

Vasily and Raya were seeing each other in an official capacity almost every day: meetings, new product discussions, laboratory inspections, and so on. He was always formal with her and referred to her only as *Raisa Borisovna* in the presence of others at the factory. But then, two or three times a week, Vasily would call her and in a very different voice say, *"Raisochka Borisovna, I've missed you."*

This was her *mating call*. She would rush to the apartment Vasily had discretely rented not far from the factory. They would make love and then they'd talk of many things. Sometimes the most important decisions affecting the factory's future were discussed and decided upon in that bed. They debated the issues, and even fought sometimes. But in the factory they always presented a unified front. Raya could give Vasily a hard time when they were alone but she always supported him fully in any public forum.

But it must stop. It must stop… but how?

When Raya closed her eyes she could think of nothing else but Vasily's strong hands and warm lips.

In the end, Vasily actually made it easy for both of them. Raya had recently noticed how he had been looking fondly at a new accountant, a young and attractive brunette. So one day, Raya boldly marched into his office and said, "Vasily, you're not married to me. If you're interested in that brunette, feel free to go after her. Don't restrain yourself on my account."

"Raya, you're my dearest friend and you are the closest person to me in the whole world. I can't lose our friendship. I will always need you," Vasily responded hesitantly.

"Why would you lose my friendship? I'm not going anywhere," Raya said.

"Friends?" Vasily wanted to be sure that there would be no lingering hard feelings or regrets.

"Friends," Raya assured him.

Raya felt an incredible sense of relief and smiled back to him. But later on that day when she was alone, she cried bitterly.

Vasily Andreevich started to date the brunette, although that relationship didn't last for long. After her it was a blonde, a red-head, another blonde, another brunette, and so it went. Following the unusually long and intense relationship with Raya, Vasily had reverted to his old, familiar ways.

His relationship with Raya changed, yet in a way their bond became even stronger. They remained genuine friends and trusted colleagues and very dear people to one-another.

In 1967, Raya successfully presented and defended her PhD dissertation. Without any break to relish her success, she immediately started to work on her next dissertation. She might have had a slow start, but she was on a roll now and compensating for all those lost years.

Raya had over thirty employees reporting directly to her, and her research laboratory was heavily involved in a number of serious and challenging projects. Her frequent articles were published in a number of prestigious Soviet and foreign scientific journals. She was frequently invited to attend international conferences (although permitted to attend only those that were taking place within the Soviet Union). Raya was enjoying a satisfying and happy life and felt very secure in her own world.

Maxim loved her as much as ever and she had beautiful, strong, healthy and intelligent children. Raya cherished her dear friends, Aleksander and Alla, and she was close as always with her own family – her mother, her brothers, and her beloved sister Manya.

Raya just wished that Maxim wouldn't be so insistent about all those sports and recreational activities that he was so fond of. She didn't mind skiing once a month or so in the winter or even going fishing occasionally in the summer, but every weekend? It was a bit too much.

Eventually, the spouses reached a compromise. On Saturdays, depending on the season, Maxim would take the children to ski, to fish, or to hike in the forest, while Raya would remain at home. She would quickly prepare a simple dinner and then spend the better part of the day working on her second dissertation, taking advantage of the solitary peace and quiet.

In the evenings they sometimes entertained. When Maxim invited his co-workers, the party was usually quite lively – his guests ate a lot, drank a lot, and enjoyed singing songs. On those particular evenings, Maxim was happy but Raya was quite miserable. She would make an effort to be civil and friendly, but she found Maxim's friends to be shallow, primitive and utterly boring.

On other occasions, Raya would invite her colleagues from the factory and from the university. Dima, Manya, Aleksander and Alla usually attended those evenings as well. Their intellectual conversations often became heated debates, in a respectful fashion of course. The range of discussion topics typically included politics, science, medicine, and most importantly – the arts. This crowd considered it a heresy to miss the performance of a guest singer in the opera or a famous piano or cello soloist. They read mostly the same books and magazines and disagreed amongst themselves about most everything. Raya loved those evenings but not surprisingly, Maxim despised them. He found that crowd to be pompous snobs, unapproachable, and boring beyond words.

It saddened and worried Raya that after so many years, Maxim wasn't any closer to Dima and Manya. The brothers-in-law still barely tolerated one-other. Manya tried to bridge the gap, but Maxim found her soothingly sweet words to be condescending and patronizing.

Sunday was always the most important day of the week for Raya. This was the day when her family spent time with Aleksander's and Dima's families. In the winter they were gathering at Manya's and Dima's apartment, while in the summer they would meet outdoors in Aleksander's backyard. Maxim reluctantly tagged along with Raya for those unbearably long outings.

In addition to the usual three families who continued to convene regularly, in this particular year the other frequent attendees for those Sunday get-togethers included members of the *Aleksander Society*.

The Aleksander Society

THE ALEKSANDER SOCIETY was comprised of Aleksander and a closely-knit group of seven of his students. Sometimes other teenagers would tag along, but the seven inseparable friends were always present together. Their so-called *society* had formed unexpectedly and was comprised of an eclectic crowd of characters.

It all began when a new luxury apartment complex was built near Aleksander's boarding school. It was much more luxurious than the typical Soviet 'cookie-cutter' structures that were being erected at that time in Kiev. This building belonged to the Soviet Army and the apartments were given out exclusively to the families of officers stationed in the countries of the Eastern Block: East Germany, Romania, Hungary, Poland and Czechoslovakia. No officer with a lesser rank than major merited consideration for an apartment in that prestigious building.

The laws of the Soviet Union permitted the children of the officers to live with their families and study in junior schools abroad. However, at the age of fifteen, these young people were required to return to the Soviet Union and attend high school in their homeland. The government's rationale was that this policy would ensure that the officers' children would mature as upstanding and loyal Soviet citizens.

In many cases, the officers' wives preferred life on the military bases in Eastern Europe with all the available perks, as compared with their relatively bleak lives at home. And so, the officers' teenaged children were enrolled in boarding school in Kiev so they would be under constant supervision.

When Aleksander learned that for the upcoming school year he would be the home-room teacher in charge of a grade nine class consisting of both the usual under-privileged boarding school kids and the pandered children of military families, he became quite worried.

One Sunday during the summer, while he was sitting in the backyard with his family, together with the sisters and their families, Aleksander voiced his concern.

"I just can't imagine how those two groups of students will ever get along with each other. My class will consist of sixty percent of 'have-nots' and forty percent of spoiled military brats that have everything they've ever desired.

"I personally know all of those 'have-nots' that will be in my class. After all, they've been at this school since they were seven years old. It's simply not going to work out.

"Let me give you an example," Aleksander was explaining. "The student leader of the class has always been our famous, or should I say infamous Konstantin, or as he's called by everyone, *Kostya*."

"So why do you say he's infamous?" Manya asked.

"If some mischief has taken place at the school, look for Kostya; he's usually not far away from the action. He's the biggest prankster in the school: disappearing textbooks, blackboards covered with wax, prickly objects on teachers' chairs, broken windows, and so on. Almost invariably it's Kostya who's behind it in some way, shape or form. However, he's also the school's star soccer player, a talented goalkeeper.

"The boy is smart and witty but with a strong rebellious streak about him too. His parents are hopeless alcoholics and can't look after the boy, not even on weekends when he's supposed to go home. For years, Kostya has preferred to stay at the boarding school quarters during weekends, rather than to go home and have to face his drunken parents.

"Throughout his school life the other children have always looked up to him to organize their games and activities, whether to lead them through the forest on a field trip, or to initiate some form of mischief. Kostya is a natural leader and now it's inevitable he's going to be challenged by some rich kid, if only because of the influential status of the child's father. I can just see it coming! It won't be easy for Kostya to relinquish his undisputed leadership role.

"And then there's his girlfriend, Olya. One way or another, a change in Kostya's status in the school is going to affect her too."

"Why is Olya in the boarding school?" Raya inquired.

"The guardian of Olya and her younger sister is their aunt. She has three kids of her own and can't afford the burden of two additional children."

"So what happened to the parents of those two girls?" Dima asked.

Aleksander's face clouded. "The father murdered their mother with an axe during a drunken rage. It's such a shame that drinking problems are so common in our country. I'd say one in three of the kids in our school are here because their parents are abusing alcohol on a regular basis.

"Anyway, at the time when that tragedy happened, seven-year-old Olya grabbed her three-year-old sister and ran to the neighbour's house. She had witnessed her father's horrendous crime first-hand and still has nightmares about it. Her worst fear in life is her father. One day he'll be released from prison and Olya's terrified over the prospect of having to face him again someday. She's actually a wonderful girl and takes good care of her younger sister. But what's Olya going to talk about with some girl from a military family who has never experienced anything but unwavering support and love from her parents? They'll have absolutely nothing in common."

"I agree with you completely," Alla chimed in. "What about Olya's closest friend, Polina? She's the best-looking girl in the school and she's only fifteen. She has huge blue, almost violet eyes, the face of Rafael's *Madonna,* and a gorgeous figure. With the military kids around, Polina is going to be trouble in the making."

"Why trouble necessarily? Just because she's so attractive? Manya's pretty and she never gets into trouble," Raya commented.

"Polina's mother is a prostitute and her father is unknown," Alla explained flatly. "Every time she's home on the weekends she sees things that she shouldn't be seeing. Once the military kids get wind of it, they'll likely start making assumptions about Polina too and she'll have a hard time dealing with that. It's so unfair. The girl's ambitious and smart, and I really believe she wants to do something worthwhile with her life. The last thing she needs right now is some unwanted suitor or some inappropriate temptations."

"So these three kids are all going to be in your grade nine class?" Dima asked.

"Yes, the class leaders. I anticipate problems between them and the newcomers, especially so with Kostya." Aleksander's face grew stern.

"You make it sound like you don't really like Kostya very much," Manya commented.

"Actually, I think he's a remarkable boy. I could really get to like him if it wasn't for the way he persists in treating Lev, another boy in our school."

"Who's Lev?" Maxim asked.

"Lev's the class nerd. He's the smartest kid in the class, but he's the smallest and never takes care of himself. He always looks untidy. His father's paralyzed and his mother is looking after the father so she's not working. In addition to Lev, there are three other boys in the family, although Lev is the only one who attends the boarding school.

"Lev can't stand this place! Why would he? For years he's been snickered at, punched, bitten, and generally bullied, and Kostya's one of the worst offenders. What I don't know is whether Kostya has an ingrained evil streak in him or is just trying to show off and reinforce his influence in front of the other boys." Aleksander shook his head and then added, "Lev's going to find it even tougher now with some of the new kids bound to abuse him."

"What do you know about those teenage newcomers from the military families?" Alla asked in a concerned voice.

"Well, I've read their files and it's quite a crowd! There's Tamara. She's the daughter of one of the top honchos in East Germany; and then there's Oleg, the son of a top general stationed in Romania. The fathers of the other children are not far behind in rank: generals, colonels, majors... G-d help me and the rest of the class!"

Aleksander's misgivings were proven to be valid beyond a shadow of a doubt as soon as the new school year began. The reality was even more brutal than he had anticipated. The military kids came to the school and immediately established themselves as a dominant force.

The smartly-dressed boys brought with them foreign-made tape recorders and flaunted their access to western music that was prohibited, locally inaccessible, and of course highly desirable.

The girls arranged an assortment of expensive perfumes and skin care and make-up products on their bedside tables, the likes of which had never been seen or heard of by the rest of the girls. Under their prescribed brown uniform dresses, the officers' daughters wore high quality silk and nylon underwear – foreign-made to be sure. They were envied by the poor local girls in their cheap cotton garb. Even the uniforms of the military kids were fashioned from expensive pure wool.

Tamara, an imperious looking girl with a tall slim body, gorgeous face and practiced poise, established herself as the recognized leader of the 'haves' within the first several days. She had a side-kick, Nastya, a big, heavy-set girl whose father was actually an adjutant of Tamara's father. Nastya behaved more like Tamara's bodyguard than as a friend.

Tamara promptly organized the clique of military children, first by the ranks of their fathers and secondly based on their own merits. She designated the 'have-nots' as serfs, not to be friends with, but to be used in a servitude capacity: to do personal laundry, to carry heavy things, and to write their essays. They were paid off with a pack of gum, or a cheap scarf, or a bright pen - things of that nature. These trinkets were of no value to the military kids but were absolutely unobtainable in any other way for most of the poor youth at the school.

The military children soon discovered that the majority of the teachers could effectively be bought off too (just at a bit of a higher price). Whenever Oleg didn't feel inclined to do his homework or came to class unprepared for a test, a bottle of perfume or a pack of imported cigarettes was usually enough to resolve the issue. Aleksander was the notable exception among all the other teachers.

Every Saturday evening, Oleg threw a party in his apartment, and for the week afterwards, the 'have-nots' would hear about nothing else but the exotic drinks that were served at the party and the foreign music that was played there. The 'have-nots' were never invited to any of those parties.

The girls of the class flirted shamelessly with the handsome Oleg, and the behavior of some of the female teachers wasn't much better.

For the first time in his student life, Kostya experienced what it was like not to be regarded as 'king of the hill' at the school and he didn't like the feeling of being pushed aside one little bit.

He resented the fact that whenever he misbehaved and did something wrong, the teachers would reproach him with a warning that there was a cell in the prison waiting just for him; or would remind him that he'd never amount to anything worthwhile and was likely destined to become an alcoholic like his parents. If some similar misdeed was done by Oleg, the teachers would giggle and say, "Oleg, dear, you're such a joker! You just have a bit too much energy."

For the first month of the school term, Aleksander left matters alone to observe how the mixed class of children would cope with their new situation. Then, slowly but surely, he purposefully began to steer the two groups within the class in a direction of greater understanding and tolerance.

One day, he was walking in the corridor when he passed by an enraged Kostya whom Olya and Polina were trying to calm down. "I'll kill her! I'll kill all of them!" Kostya was repeating aggressively.

Aleksander stopped and calmly said, "Instead of planning a murder, Kostya, why don't you take a few lessons from Lev?"

"What are you talking about? What lessons?" the bewildered Kostya stammered.

"Lessons in survival – how to cope with being constantly abused. Lev's had a lot of years of practice to master that skill."

"Don't compare me with that dweeb!" Kostya shot back.

"And why not, Kostya? You're in the same boat now, aren't you?" Aleksander pointed out.

Kostya fell silent and Aleksander continued. "Let's think about why you and your friends are here in this school and why the military kids are here."

Kostya and the two girls were taken aback; their personal backgrounds were well-known but not a subject for open discussion, especially with the teachers.

"You're here because your parents really can't afford to look after you, isn't that right? I sincerely hope that you have no doubt that your parents, and in your case, Olya, your aunt, really do love you and would prefer to have you living at home if that was possible.

"But why are those military kids here at all? It's because their mothers prefer their carefree and frivolous lives, instead of taking responsibility for looking after their own children. It's as simple as that," Aleksander asserted.

"So now we have to feel pity for Queen Tamara and her court?" Kostya asked bitterly.

"I don't ask you to feel anything like pity, Kostya. I just suggest that you try to look at the military kids as normal teens with their own problems and hurts. You don't have to submit to them, but you don't have to fight with them either. Just think about it, okay?" Aleksander suggested, and then he continued on his way, leaving Kostya, Olya and Polina pondering his words.

Another time, Aleksander came upon a sobbing Lev in the school hallway and stopped to ask him what was the matter. He was shocked by the degree of anger and bitterness that the boy expressed. Strangely enough, Lev's anger was not so much directed against the bullies of the class, but rather towards his own parents. There were four brothers in his family. Why was it that he, Lev, had been singled out and sent off to this cruel place away from home?

Aleksander logically pointed out that the older brothers could soon start working and help the family, while Lev's younger brother was not yet old enough to be sent off to boarding school. None of this was of much consolation to Lev. His frustration and anger against both home and school had been accumulating for years, so one empathetic talk with Aleksander wasn't going to easily wipe away all of those ingrained feelings. Aleksander understood very well that this boy was badly in need of warmth and love of family, and that the process of building a level of trust with him would be long and arduous.

To Aleksander's genuine surprise, however, Lev was the first among the students to cross the line between the two groups in the class. As it happened, this was because Lev had fallen head over heels in love with Nonna, one of the military girls. Nonna had a mane of curly blonde hair, big blue eyes, and the face of a china-doll. As far as Tamara was concerned, however, Nonna had about as much brains as a *mute* china-doll.

It was to this empty-headed but pretty girl that Lev started to write and dedicate poems. He was keeping them hidden away, but one time he impulsively slipped one of the poems into Nonna's notebook.

That day, before gym class, the girls in the change room had the laugh of their lives. A half-dressed Nonna climbed up onto a bench and started to read Lev's poem aloud. Each and every word was mocked derisively. Suddenly, Nastya approached Nonna, snatched the slip of paper from the girl's hands, and passed it over to Tamara.

Tamara read the poem aloud slowly, in the way the rhyming was actually meant to be read, and then she remarked, "This is good. It's very good." Tamara then turned towards Nonna and reproachfully added, "And you're stupid."

From that day onward, Lev became Tamara's friend and protégé. Nobody dared to taunt or abuse Lev anymore.

The next transition step amongst the class members was taken by Oleg. A mediocre soccer player himself, he admired Kostya's superior talent and decided that Kostya was the only boy in class good enough to be his friend. Furthermore, Oleg had taken notice (and who wouldn't?) of the dazzling Polina, and he recognized the fact that the girl was under Kostya's protection. Before long, the famous trio comprised of Kostya, Olya, and Polina received an invitation to one of Oleg's parties.

The merging of the two diverse elements of the class continued to evolve slowly. To speed things up a bit, Aleksander proposed that Tamara be elected as the class president. The other teachers thought that this idea was ludicrous.

"The girl thinks that she's the Queen of Sheba as it is, and a formal designation as class president would just make her all the more arrogant," objected Marina Petrovna, the head of the mathematics department.

"Tamara is a born leader," Aleksander countered. "She'll take the lead in any situation, whether elected or not. So, let her take on responsibility for the entire class, not just her own 'court'."

Aleksander prevailed in the debate with the other teachers and introduced the idea to the young people of his class. Tamara was duly elected in a unanimous class vote.

One Sunday, seven students showed up unannounced at Aleksander's place to discuss some particular situation at the school. They arrived in two separate groups. First, there was Lev with his two new friends, Tamara and Nastya; then Kostya who was accompanied by Polina, Olya, and Oleg. With Aleksander acting as mediator, the students spent hours discussing, debating and arguing their different points of view, and eventually they left together. Thus the *Aleksander Society* was born.

The seven students were introduced to Raya and Manya and their families and the presence of those young people soon became a constant at the Sunday afternoon get-togethers.

Manya, Raya, and Dima were quite fascinated by the student group – such different backgrounds and social standings, and yet so many common interests. Under Aleksander's careful guidance, they were changing, growing up, maturing and becoming genuine friends. For these children Aleksander became much more than a teacher; he was their mentor and a source of sound advice and mature friendship.

Maxim, however, was bored by the presence of all those teenage kids. He was working hard during the week and didn't want to spend his precious Sunday time listening to the debates of those brats. He voiced his opinion rather strongly to Raya. "I don't know what you can possibly see in them. Those military children are self-indulgent snobs and the other four kids are simply pathetic in their attempts to be their equal. I don't think it's good for Borya and Lena to spend their Sundays in Aleksander's backyard doing nothing. I prefer my children to be doing something more active."

Raya decided it was best not to argue the point, and so when the weather was good on Sundays, Maxim started taking his children to picnics with his own friends, while Raya continued to go to Aleksander's or Manya's place, but on her own. To Raya's dismay, Borya and Lena preferred to accompany their father rather than play with Sasha and Misha, Aleksander's children.

The first year of the class integration had passed by very quickly. In June, the officers' children left to join their families abroad for the summer, and then in September they returned, happy to see one-another and their beloved teacher again.

Meanwhile, Aleksander was becoming increasingly concerned about his family situation. He had foolishly surrendered his house to Lisa and now he was paying the consequences. It was bordering on impossible for his growing family to live in one small room. It was tolerable in the summer months because they would put up a tent in the backyard and the boys would spend a lot of time there. The rest of the year, however, a tent was hardly a feasible solution for their oppressively crowded conditions.

Misha developed chronic bronchitis and was constantly coughing. Living in such conditions, cooking year-round in the cold summer kitchen, and running to the outhouse in the middle of winter didn't do much for Alla's health either.

Something drastic had to be done about their living quarters. Aleksander had a serious talk with the principal of the school and then with the district's Board of Education officials. Finally he was promised an apartment in a building that was under construction and was expected to be ready around the time of the beginning of the school year in September of 1970, one year hence.

"One more year, Alla, and before the next winter we'll start to live properly like normal people," Aleksander assured his wife. The apartment issue notwithstanding, Aleksander was basically a happy man. He loved his job. He loved his family. He was proud of his *Society* and his entire class which continued to come together more and more harmoniously in their second year together.

The one individual close to him and who caused Aleksander a great deal of anguish was his eldest daughter, Tanya. Aleksander, who enjoyed the profound respect of students and teachers alike, and whose opinion and counsel were sought-after by so many, was regarded by Tanya as an old-fashioned fool and an abject loser. She had no problem telling him so, or rather, shouting her opinion straight to his face. She was living with her mother just behind a wall in the main part of the house, but it might as well have been on a different planet.

Aleksander tried desperately to reach some kind of reconciliation with her. He invited Tanya to join him and his friends on Sundays, but she invariably had more important things to do. He offered her help with her studies too, but she declined his assistance. What's more, Tanya despised Alla and didn't much care about her younger brothers either.

Father and daughter remained estranged. Lisa had won that battle.

A Year Of Dramatic Events

1970 BEGAN AS a year of hope, joy and great anticipation. It was not destined to materialize in that way.

On the eve of the New Year's celebration, the *Aleksander Society* contingent came to Manya's apartment to extend their best wishes to their friends and their teacher, before going on to Oleg's New Year's bash.

"I've decided what I want to do with my life," Tamara proudly declared. "I'll become a biochemist like Aunt Raya. I want to be a research scientist."

"I want to become an aviation engineer. I want to build airplanes and maybe even rockets," Kostya proclaimed with conviction.

"And I'll go to some technical school and get a profession within a year or two. Somebody has to support the family," Olya commented, all the while looking earnestly in Kostya's direction.

"I want to be an actress and live in Moscow. I mean, I love Kiev and all, but I want to get away from... you know... I know that it's very hard to get into the Theatre College in Moscow, but I'll try anyway. Do you think I have a chance?" Polina asked hesitantly.

"You have every chance in the world, Polina. I've seen you perform in the school plays," Alla assured her. "You're really very talented. If you wish, I'll help you get ready for the entrance exams."

"Oh, will you?" Polina rejoiced. "Alla Andreevna, you're the best!"

"What about you, Oleg?" Dima inquired. "Any plans?"

"Oh, yes, lots of plans and all of them are my father's. He's already spoken with his friend who works at the Kiev Military Academy. After

I'm done with high school, I'll be going there and become an officer, just like my father."

"But do you really want to be a military officer, Oleg?" Manya asked.

"Why not? It's a good life, especially when there's no war going on. Papa will help me to get a good assignment. Life is good!" a carefree Oleg responded.

In August, Raya defended her second dissertation with great success and became a Doctor of Science. It was an amazing accomplishment. At the age of thirty-four, she was one of the youngest scientists ever to achieve this feat in her specialty field of biochemistry.

Her laboratory staff increased to almost fifty people and she became involved in some ground-breaking research there.

The one thing that bothered Raya was that Manya and Dima had grown somewhat distant, as though they were holding something back from her. For the first time since the age of five, Raya felt strangely alienated from Manya. She couldn't bear to live with this feeling and so she confronted her blood sister.

To Raya's horror, Manya, who had always been very straightforward, was somewhat evasive and seemed sad. But finally, Manya acknowledged, "You're right, sister. There is something I want to tell you, but let's talk about it on Aleksander's birthday. I would prefer to tell this news to everyone at the same time."

Raya was incredulous - Manya was harbouring some sort of secret from her. However, Raya had no choice but to wait. Luckily, Aleksander's birthday was coming up soon on September seventh, so the wait wouldn't be that long in any event.

On the first day of September, Aleksander's class commenced its graduating year. The children were happy to see one-another again after the summer recess. The girls were showing off their new outfits, while Lev was going out of his way to point out that he was no longer the shortest boy in class.

Oleg returned to school dressed in American jeans and a stunning cashmere pullover. Around his neck he wore a gold chain with a huge, half-moon pendant.

"Is it ivory, dear?" Marina Petrovna asked as she gingerly lifted the pendant with her fingers. But almost immediately she recognized what she was holding and exclaimed, "Ugh!" and indignantly walked away.

"Oleg, what is that thing?" Kostya inquired.

"Ivory indeed! It's my toe-nail. I didn't cut it for half a year; then I clipped it off, boiled it for two hours and drilled a hole through it so I could put it on the chain. The other boys laughed heartily.

"Kostya, look what I've got!" Oleg ceremoniously removed a new soccer ball from his bag. This wasn't just any soccer ball; rather, a genuine professional ball that his father had procured for him from a major league soccer team.

"Let's try it out!" Oleg ran off with the ball and an enthusiastic Kostya scurried after him. Oleg started to kick the ball around inside the school building. The boys raced through the corridors and came upon the Great Hall. Usually the hall was closed, but on September first it was wide open, ready and waiting for the celebration marking the start of the new school year.

"Hey, let's play here! Defend your gates!" Oleg exclaimed as he gave a ball a mighty kick and ran into the hall to chase after the ball.

"Oleg, stop! Not in the Great Hall!" Kostya shouted as he scrambled after his friend. But it was too late. The ball, having been launched into the air by Oleg's powerful but inept leg, arched across the entire auditorium and smashed directly into the huge portrait of the General Secretary of the Communist Party, Leonid Ilyich Brezhnev, on the opposite wall. The heavy wooden frame and glass-encased portrait came crashing down from its place on the wall, falling over the large red hammer and sickle flag of the Soviet Union that was mounted below it. The remnants of the flag, which had been shredded by the flying pieces of glass, then tumbled down onto the floor.

The noise when the ball crashed into the framed portrait was tremendous, and a moment later Marina Petrovna came running into the hall to find out what all the commotion was about. She gasped in horror when she caught sight of the mutilated portrait and the shredded remnants of the flag. She clasped her hands together over her heart in shock, and then glanced intently at the two boys. One was the favourite of the school and the son of the school's biggest benefactor;

while the other was the well-known, rebellious hooligan of the school. Without giving the matter of responsibility for the incident a second thought, the teacher firmly took hold of Kostya's arm and marched him into the principal's office.

When the principal was informed of the horrific incident, he became terrified. After all, he was personally responsible for his school's students, for their political education, for their loyalty to the Soviet State, and for their devotion to the leaders of the Party and the government. It was his own career, reputation and even his freedom that would be on the line. In view of everything that was at stake, he saw only one way out of this incredibly awkward situation and that was to lay the entire blame for the incident on the rogue of the school. Given his reputation as an incorrigible 'bad apple', Kostya was the obvious culprit.

The principal looked at Kostya sternly and with fury in his voice said, "I hope you realize, boy, that what you have done is a criminal offence. The desecration of the Soviet flag and the portrait of the Leader of the Soviet People is a blatant political act against our society. Konstantin, as far as I'm concerned you should spend the rest of your days rotting in prison for such a horrendous misdeed."

Kostya maintained a stoic silence. In accordance with the traditional ethics of the school, it was Oleg's duty and moral obligation to come forward and explain what had really happened. Kostya had no doubt that his friend would clear his name. But Oleg failed to make an appearance. And so, Kostya was escorted to the detention room and locked inside.

Soon afterwards, Aleksander Mikhailovich came to see him. "Kostya, I need to know what actually happened. If you want me to help you, please talk to me truthfully."

Kostya remained silent. It was one thing to commit some harmless prank or to make fun of an inept teacher or a nerdy student, but it was quite another to betray one's best friend. Besides, although Kostya was intelligent enough to recognize the gravity of the situation, he also understood that in reality the proverbial ball was not in his hands, but rather in Oleg's.

The teacher and the student sat facing one-another in uneasy silence for a long while until finally Aleksander tried again. "I want you to tell me all the details of the incident. All I was told by the boys is that Oleg ran with the ball and that you ran after him into the Great Hall. Who kicked the ball and hit the portrait? Was it you, Kostya, or was it Oleg? Don't you understand that I must know who was responsible?"

"What difference does it make? Nobody would believe me anyway," Kostya replied bitterly. And then in desperation he turned to his teacher and pleaded, "Aleksander Mikhailovich, please help me. I don't want to go to prison."

Aleksander summoned Tamara and Nastya. They discussed the incident and then together the girls went looking for Oleg. But Oleg was nowhere to be found at the school. Finally, the girls ran to their building and found Oleg sitting and drinking in his apartment.

"Oleg, you must go and tell the principal right away what happened before it's too late. Please, Oleg, go and do it before the authorities and the militia are informed," Tamara pleaded. "Your father can get you out of this mess, but nobody's going to help Kostya!"

"I can't! I can't!" Oleg protested. "You don't know my father! He'll kill me!"

No matter what the girls said or how they pleaded, they couldn't persuade Oleg to come forward and confess. They eventually returned to the school feeling downcast and betrayed by their erstwhile friend.

The mess in the Great Hall was cleaned up and the school received a new portrait of Brezhnev and a new flag. The militia came and took Kostya away, but the mood in the school remained gloomy and the teachers had difficulty getting the students to focus on their work. Olya was crying virtually non-stop. The students stopped speaking to Oleg and kept their distance from him. The teachers ignored him in class too, but Oleg remained unmoved.

Aleksander discussed the predicament at home with his wife and his friends. He remained determined to find a way to save Kostya but couldn't think of anything he could possibly do without Oleg's co-operation.

In the early afternoon of September seventh, a staff meeting was called. The principal of the school stood and made a short but powerful speech.

"It is the responsibility of each of us to put this shameful, anti-Soviet incident behind us. The school and its reputation should not be made to suffer because of one 'rotten apple'. We have been instructed to prepare a school profile of Konstantin for the criminal investigation. I've written a document outlining his rebellious behaviour throughout all his years at this school. I've listed all the official reprimands that the school's authorities have given Konstantin up until now. We've tried everything, but some people are just incorrigible. Let the correctional services authorities deal with him now. We need my signature on this document and the signatures of all the Department Heads, as well as that of his Homeroom Teacher. Please come forward to sign, each of you."

"Just a second!" Aleksander intervened. "Marina Petrovna, when you came into the Great Hall, what precisely did you see? Who was in the room and where exactly were they?

"I can't recall the precise position of the two boys in the room. What difference does it make?" Maria Petrovna replied defensively.

"But isn't it true that Oleg was standing in the middle of the hall and thus in the obvious position to have been able to kick that ball; and isn't it also true that Kostya was standing close to the entrance and therefore not in a position to have been responsible for making that kick?" Aleksander persisted with this line of logic.

"Aleksander Mikhailovich," the principal cautioned, "kindly drop that line of thought immediately. The situation is bad enough as it is and I'll not allow you to drag the leadership of our Army and their families into this incident. There was enough time for the boys to alter their positions in the room and for Kostya to try to move away from the scene of his horrific crime. There's no possibility that such a fine, upstanding boy as Oleg would ever allow himself to do something this despicable. As I said before, the faster we put this incident behind us, the better it's going to be for the school and for all of us."

One after another, the Heads of the Departments came forward and signed the document. Only one more signature was required to make it official. But Aleksander remained seated in his chair without making a move.

The principal tried a different tact. "Aleksander Mikhailovich, it's your birthday today, right? Happy Birthday! Oh yes, and we have a fine present for you too - a present that you've been waiting for all these years! Your very own two-room apartment. So please just come forward and sign the document now and then we can get on with the celebration we've planned for you."

"And if I don't sign?" Aleksander stubbornly retorted.

The principal's face clouded. "Kostya's profile history will go forward with or without your signature. It will make no difference. It will not save that criminal student. But surely you understand that the school cannot reward any member of the staff who is opposed to supporting the best interests of our school and who condones any form of anti-Soviet behaviour."

Without responding or looking at the principal or anyone else, Aleksander got up, turned his back and strode out through the door. Tamara, Nastya, Olya, Polina and Lev, who had been eavesdropping just outside the staff meeting room, had scarcely enough time to jump aside as Aleksander briskly marched past them.

He left the school, got onto his motorcycle, and drove off at a high speed. It was less than a ten minute drive from the school to his house, but Aleksander wanted to clear his head and to get control of the surge of rage that he was feeling. He wasn't sure at whom he was most angry - whether at the irresponsible and cowardly Oleg; or at the principal of the school along with Marina Petrovna; or at the rest of the teachers who acquiesced to the principal's demands and made no attempt to come to the defence of the innocent boy. Perhaps he was most angry at himself for his inability and absence of power to do anything about the injustice of it all.

I've failed, Aleksander thought. *I've failed Kostya and I've failed Olya who can't imagine her life without him. I've failed my entire class. They were looking up to me. But the worst thing is that I've failed Alla, Misha, and Sasha. Now we'll all be stuck in our pitiful living quarters forever. I've failed my family...*

His distress and anger veiled Aleksander's sense of vision and awareness of his surroundings like a heavy mist. He was driving the motorcycle almost subconsciously without being aware of anything around him and never noticed the intersection, or the large truck turning around the corner, directly into his path.

Meanwhile, the sisters took a half-a-day off work and rushed to help Alla with the preparations for the birthday party. They knew that despite the fact that Aleksander never invited anybody, there would be a large gathering of at least fifty or sixty people present: Aleksander's former students, his friends, some of the teachers from his school, and their neighbours. Today was Aleksander's fiftieth birthday, so they expected the crowd to be even larger than usual.

The three women were in the midst of chopping salads and cooking when five dejected members of the *Society* arrived. "Where's Aleksander?" Lev inquired.

"I don't expect him for at least another thirty minutes," Alla replied, somewhat confused by the question. "He had a class this afternoon."

"But he left the school right after the staff meeting and never came back!" Olya exclaimed.

Tamara, trying to remain outwardly calm, told everyone about the meeting proceedings, about the principal's request and his offer of the apartment, and about Aleksander's reaction.

Alla slowly lowered herself into a chair, clutched her apron in her hands and said in a desperate voice, "How could they? How could they do that to Kostya? How could they use our promised apartment as a wedge to force Sasha to betray an innocent student? Don't they know him well enough by now to understand that he would never compromise his principles and submit to such despicable tactics?"

The guests started to gather. By six o'clock the backyard was crowded with guests and by this time everybody had heard about the events at the school. The mood of the gathering was tense and gloomy. *"Where is Aleksander? Should we go and look for him?"* people were asking one-other.

A short while later, a militia vehicle pulled up to the front on the house. A militiaman rang the front bell and spoke for a moment with

Lisa. Then he went around to the backyard and stopped abruptly when he observed the large gathering of people. It was always hard enough to deliver bad news to the direct family alone, but to have to convey his horrific news before such a large group was going to be all the more difficult.

"I'm looking for the wife of...," he began hesitantly, but before the officer had an opportunity to finish his sentence, three of the women suddenly cried out in unison.

The militiaman faltered and quietly announced, "There has been a most unfortunate accident. Somebody has to go with me to identify the body."

Never before had he seen such a reaction of total grief. The entire backyard was engulfed with crying and exclamations of shock and consternation.

Dima gently placed his hand on Alla's shoulder and said, "Allochka, I'll go with you." He looked at his wife and sister and added, "Take care of the boys."

The birthday party had suddenly become a wake.

Three days later, the open coffin containing Aleksander's body was reverently set upon a table in his own backyard. His many grieving friends and neighbours came to bid him a final farewell. Almost all of his fellow teachers and students from the school seemed to be present too. Four individuals were distinguished by their absence: the school principal, Marina Petrovna, Oleg, and Kostya.

Alla was totally overcome with grief. She was holding the hands of her sons and looking down at the face of her beloved husband. *Several more minutes and the lid of the coffin will have to be closed and I'll never see his face again*, she thought.

Manya and Raya were standing near the coffin too, crying and holding onto each other for support. Aleksander had been so much more than just a friend to them; he was family and they grieved for him as only sisters can grieve for their big brother.

Aleksander's oldest daughter, Tanya, stood nearby, clasping the hand of her new husband. "Your father must have been a remarkable man to have had so many friends," he was saying. "It's just too bad I never had the opportunity to get to know him better."

Lisa remained inside the house near a window where she could observe the backyard scene. *I always knew that loser would come to a bad end. Now I just have to find a way to get rid of his bastards and that stupid wife of his and then the entire house will be mine,* she thought callously, without the slightest remorse for Aleksander's untimely death.

All at once the crowd parted to give way to a small contingent of new arrivals. The downcast principal of the school and Marina Petrovna were approaching Alla. Marching behind them was a tall, imposing-looking, uniformed general who was holding the hands of Kostya and Oleg.

The procession stopped before the bewildered Alla and Oleg's father urged the principal, "Go ahead."

"Alla Andreevna," the principal began in a trembling voice, "we are all truly sorry for your loss. Aleksander Mikhailovich was our best teacher, respected and loved by everyone. I never meant... I never thought..." He paused for a moment, searching for the right words, and then added, "Please, take this. It's yours. It's a document entitling you to an apartment." And with that he placed the document in Alla's hands.

"I don't want it. My husband died on account of this apartment," Alla said. She attempted to hand the document back but Dima intervened.

"Alla, you have to think about your boys. They need a decent place to live. Take it," he insisted.

"Alla Andreevna, I'm sorry; I'm so sorry," Marina Petrovna blurted out and then hastily ran from the backyard. The principal turned and followed slowly after her and nobody stepped forward to stop them.

Kostya then came forward to the grieving widow. "Alla Andreevna, Aleksander Mikhailovich died because of me..."

"Kostenka, please don't think that way. He loved you so much. Are you free now?" Alla asked through her tears.

Kostya nodded his head silently and quickly went to join Olya and his other friends who were standing nearby. Olya hugged him and continued to cling to him as though she would never let him go. Kostya in turn held her tightly and they both started to cry.

The general shoved Oleg forward somewhat roughly and said, "Alla Andreevna, I'm deeply sorry for your loss. I consider myself responsible. I was planning from the beginning to send Oleg to live with my sister in Zhitomir, but then I had thought that he was mature enough to live on his own at the boarding school. I was wrong. Two days ago I received a phone call from General Smirnov, the father of Oleg's classmate, Tamara. He told me all about the most unfortunate incident. I immediately contacted my son and confronted him.

"What can I say? I'm ashamed of the irresponsible act my son committed and his cowardly behavior. That's not how I raised him or what is expected from a future Soviet officer. Oleg should be punished properly and I intend to make sure that he will be. But he's my only son and I don't want him to rot in prison. I have vouched for him before the authorities and now I'm taking him away. He'll live with his aunt and believe me, his life will be quite different from his carefree existence here in Kiev.

"To see to it that the innocent boy Kostya was freed, and to make certain that you got your so well-deserved apartment – that was the least I could do."

Oleg timidly looked up at Alla and spoke up briefly, barely above a whisper, "I'm very sorry." He glanced toward his old friends, but their return stares were clearly unsympathetic and unforgiving. At that point, the general took a firm hold of Oleg's hand and marched him out of the yard.

"Thanks, Tamara," Kostya said and looked at his friend gratefully.

"Don't mention it, Kostya. I should've been smarter and called papa sooner." Tamara responded.

Finally! Lisa thought, all the while observing the proceedings in the backyard. *Finally the house is mine! The entire house and the backyard! I deserve every bit of it.*

So, the back room is free at last, Tanya was thinking at the same time. *That's good. When I have children, mama will need her privacy, so I can move her into that room. Not right away, of course. But this house was built by my great-grandfather and now it's really mine!*

The Beginning Of Emigration

AFTER THE BURIAL of Aleksander at the cemetery, everyone made their way to Manya and Dima's place. The wake lasted a long time and it was only by late evening that the grieving sisters and their husbands were finally left to themselves.

"You were going to talk to me about something, Manya. What is it?" Raya asked.

"Not today, sister. You've had a hard enough time as it is today," Manya said, avoiding Raya's eyes.

"Manya, you're making me really nervous. What can be so bad that you can't tell me? After Aleksander's death, nothing can upset me. Unless you're seriously ill or something like that. Or is it Dima? Is somebody ill?" Raya persisted in a worried tone of voice.

"Nobody is sick." Manya said, as she looked at Dima, imploring him to say something.

"Raya and Maxim, we're going to be leaving for Israel," Dima announced slowly and solemnly. "That's our news."

"What do you mean, *leaving*?" Raya wasn't prepared to grasp the full implication of Dima's surprise pronouncement. "Are you going for a vacation? How did you obtain the visa? For how long are you going to be away?"

"It's forever. We're emigrating, Raya," her brother answered firmly.

Raya looked blankly at Manya, then at Dima. She started to feel an uncontrollable panic. This couldn't be happening to her; it was just too much.

"You can't do this! Dima, you can't just leave. You know that Manya and I can't live apart from each other. You know that you two are my closest friends. You know that I can't and I won't leave. How can you possibly do this to me?"

"Raya, please calm down. I'm not doing it to you. I'm doing this for my family - for my wife and for my children," Dima was trying to explain compassionately. He felt as distressed by the situation as Raya but his mind was already made up.

"Dima, I'm sorry but I just don't understand," Maxim said. "You and Manya have good jobs and you have a nice apartment too. So why would you want to leave your city and your country?"

"It's not *my* country!" Dima retorted passionately. "It's yours! You're asking why I'm leaving. It's because I want my children to be proud of being Jews. I want them to be judged based on their own merit when applying to universities and for jobs, and not according to a notation in their passport where the offending word, 'Jew', is written. People tell me that being a Jew means to observe Judaism. Maybe so - I don't know. I was never exposed to Judaism before, but now I'm going to have that opportunity and so is my family.

"Maxim, you need to understand that I want my children to learn about their religious heritage, and I want them to appreciate that being a Jew means something much more than a notation in a passport.

"And you, Raya... I had hoped that you would understand me better than anybody else after everything that you've been through."

"Oh, please stop it! Don't use me as an excuse to justify your horrid scheme! I would never even consider leaving my sister behind!" Raya was hysterical, while Manya remained subdued and crying quietly as the heated and emotional exchange between Raya and Dima carried on.

"Aleksander would never forgive you for such treacherous behaviour," Raya protested again in desperation.

"Aleksander knew all about it," Dima countered. "We told him about our plans in August. He approved by the way, but he wanted to be present when we told you."

"You informed Aleksander before you even told me? So much for us being sisters, Manya. I'll never forgive you two for this!"

"Maxim, let's go!" Raya commanded as she stomped out the door.

All the way home, Raya sobbed while trying to rationalize what she had heard. "They won't do it! Something will happen to make them change their minds. They just can't leave!"

But two months later, Raya with her husband, children, mother and younger brother were all at the train station saying their final farewells to Dima, Manya, Anna and Mila. The girls were excited; for them this trip to a foreign country was some kind of an exciting adventure. Dima was checking all the bags, while Manya was kissing Raya and saying, "This isn't goodbye forever, dear sister, it's just goodbye for now. I don't know where or when, but we will see each other again. I know that much."

"It's just words, Manya. We both know that I will never leave and I won't ever be permitted to go for a visit. It's a final farewell, let's admit it." Raya remained inconsolable. "I feel abandoned and lonely already."

"You're not alone, Raya. You have Maxim and Borya and Lena. You have a great family who love you very much and they need you," Manya was consoling her sister. She felt sad and miserable leaving Raya and her family behind. At the same time, Manya felt an incredible anxiety about whatever might be awaiting her in Israel. What did she know about the land of the Jews, the country that was now destined to become her new homeland?

It was only when the train had left the station that Raya suddenly realized something and exclaimed, "Maxim, she said that I have you and the kids!"

"Of course you do. You'll always have us. What's upsetting you so much now?" Maxim asked. Privately he was relieved that Dima and Manya had left and that he no longer had to compete with them for Raya's attention.

"But Manya didn't say that I have mama and Misha too! I suspect that means they're also planning to emigrate!" Raya blurted out.

"Raya, what are you talking about? I think that's nonsense. Emigration should be the last thing on Misha's mind right now. He's still in college and he has one more year to go before he graduates. And did you see that girl that he brought with him to the station? I think he's much more concerned about her than about moving to Israel at this stage of his life!"

It seemed that Maxim was right after all. Misha remained focussed on his studies, while still finding time to date his new girlfriend, Lily. Vera and Misha were still living in the same downtown apartment too, although Misha was so rarely at home that his mother often felt very forlorn.

Despite having her husband and children close to her, without Aleksander or Dima and Manya to reach out to, Raya felt a great deal of emptiness, and to compensate for that she needed her mother more than ever.

Every Friday after work, Raya would meet Vera near the metro station and together they would go to Raya's apartment. On Saturdays, Raya did her housecleaning and her mother helped with the cooking. Vera became much closer to Borya and Lena and spent countless hours with them. On Saturday evenings, the family often went to the downtown to see a performance at the Opera House or at the Russian Drama Theatre. Vera had incredible connections in the world of the arts and invariably could secure tickets to even the most sought-after performance. Maxim rarely joined the family for these cultural outings. There was nothing new about that.

During those days, Raya was also finding more time for her family, especially for the children. She had always tried to be a good mother but when they were small she didn't have the time or the patience. It was usually Maxim who would tuck them into bed and read them bedtime stories.

Raya had now come to the realization that her children had become interesting individuals, each in their own way. Boris looked a lot like his mother but had the easy-going manner of his father. He loved sports and wouldn't miss a single game of soccer in the summer or hockey in the winter. His grades in school were quite mediocre, but that was not because he couldn't do better. Boris had a good head on his shoulders; it was just that school didn't interest him in the slightest. Books and homework were such a bore! Boris' attitude at this stage of his young life was not to spend one extra minute longer than was absolutely necessary on studying.

Lena was quite different. She was a beautiful child with huge blue eyes and ash-blonde hair; tall and slim like a Russian birch tree.

Outwardly she looked more like Maxim but she had Raya's inquisitive, analytical mind.

The children were proud of their mother-scientist, although they were much closer to their father. It was Maxim whom they were running to whenever they had a scraped knee or some seemingly insurmountable problem with their friends.

When Raya began to spend more time with them and even offered to help them with their homework, they reacted to her unexpected overtures with a degree of surprise and even a touch of resentment. But Raya was persistent in her quest to establish a greater closeness with her children and indeed, with her husband too. She joined her family in all their activities, took the kids to the famous Kiev Circus, and even attended the Kiev Dynamo games with Boris, trying her best to comprehend the rules of soccer.

Lena refused to waste her time on such folly as sports, but she did love attending the theatre with her mother and grandma.

Maxim didn't mind Raya's new-found interest in the children at all; in fact he embraced it. His dream had finally been realized. Raya had finished her studies and her dissertations, and so now belonged solely to him and the children. But Maxim couldn't even begin to imagine how much Raya sorely missed her brother and her blood sister, her dear Manya.

Raya practically lived for the letters from Israel. When a letter would arrive, it was read and re-read many times over, and then compared with the letters received by Vera. Usually, Manya wrote one letter for Raya and a separate one to Vera. But Raya and her mother had decided that only by comparing the contents of each of their letters they could deduce just what was really going on in the lives of their loved ones in Israel.

At first, the letters from Manya were sad and remorseful.

"Dear sister, I miss you! I've missed you more than I can describe. Life is so different here... everything is so confusing. If only you, my bright sister, could be here to advise me and help me! It seems to me that I've traveled not just thousands of miles, but also across time and into some other era that I can't even comprehend.

"*People are different here, entirely different. Relationships between people are distinctly poles apart from what we've been used to; manners, customs, and the culture are so foreign to me. But the worst thing for us is the absence of common language. It's horrible not understanding what people around you are saying. We will be studying Hebrew for the next several months in a special school called an 'Ulpan'. I hope that will help!*"

And then some weeks later, in another letter, Manya wrote, "*I'm getting a bit more used to this country... Do I have a choice? You know, Raya, compared to life in Israel, our lives in Kiev were dull and boring. What were our problems: to stand in line to buy groceries? To obtain a decent piece of meat for dinner or fruits in the winter? Well, I can go to a store here and buy anything I want now. But we're still trying to come to grips with a myriad of other problems. Miss you.*"

It was only after several months had passed that the mood of Manya's letters reflected a change for the better.

"*Rayechka, you know how it is with close relatives: you may love them or despise them, or sometimes you may be angry with them — but they're still your relatives, a part of your life. And that is exactly my feeling about Israel. I may be angry at its convoluted banking system, crazy politics and complicated education system, but it's my country now. I feel it more and more with each passing day. My family and I really do belong here. Wish you could be here too!*"

Soon after that, Manya wrote enthusiastically, "*Raya, immigration is over for us and now normal life has begun! Dima got a good job in the children's ward at the Haifa hospital and I got a job as a nurse in the intensive care unit at the same hospital. Would you believe it, I can actually speak Hebrew now! Well, at least some Hebrew. I understand more than I can say and I have a horrible accent, but the people here seem to understand me. Miss you lots!*"

The next letter conveyed another new development. "*Raya, we've changed our given names. 'When in Rome...' as they say. Dima is now David, Anna is Hannah, and Mila is Malka. And I'm Miriam! In a way I feel that we didn't actually change our names but simply reclaimed them. As you know, the girls were named after our grandmothers and their real names were Hannah and Malka. Dima was named after his grandfather who was also David. And me? Do you remember when my papa was screaming at me that I was not a*

Russian Maria but a Jewish Miriam? I decided that for once he was right. Therefore, you could say that it's my father who gave me this name of Miriam.

"Raya, it's not such an easy transition. The girls are still calling each other 'Anna' and 'Mila' and I still sometimes call David 'Dima'. So, please help us! Please refer to us by our new names from now on."

"The hell I will!" an indignant Raya was telling Maxim. "She can call herself whatever she wants but for me she'll always be Manya."

For a while, Raya was taking the children and going to see Alla in her new apartment quite often. But the pain was just too great for both women to cope with. The absence of Aleksander, Dima, and Manya was felt acutely, and so Raya's visits became less and less frequent.

Raya concluded that she needed to occupy her mind and her spare time with something more constructive. Her mind had been constantly working on a very demanding regime for all these years: studies, dissertations, and the demands of the managerial position in her laboratory. So it was understandable that any period of unfamiliar idleness of the mind caused Raya to feel edgy. To be sure, she still had interesting work and her laboratory was involved in fascinating research, but for her that alone was not enough. She just couldn't adjust to slowing down, even if only to relax.

Raya approached Vasily with a fresh idea. "Vasily, I want to write a book. The textbook still being used for the first-year university biochemistry program is based on a combination of largely outdated facts and theories. Science has progressed a great deal in recent years and is now far ahead of anything you can find in that old textbook. Students are getting an archaic view of the subject. I want to write a textbook that will reflect the current state of scientific knowledge and understanding."

"Excellent idea!" Vasily enthused. "I can help you publish the book. I have some good connections. But I think you need a co-author, somebody with a well-established name in academia."

And then with a sly grin, Vasily added, "Poor Maxim! His dream of scrumptious dinners every day and a spotless house will have to remain on hold for a little while longer."

0

Raya went to present the proposal to Professor Sinitsin. "Your proposition, Raya, is truly an honour, but I'm thinking more about retirement now than about starting a new project," he said.

"Professor, I'll do all the writing. I just want you to edit it and allow me to consult with you when I need advice. And of course your name will be on the book as my co-author," Raya asserted, seeking to cajole him into acceptance.

After some reflection, the professor eventually agreed to Raya's proposal and work on the new book began.

At home, Raya didn't reveal the nature of her new project right away, instinctively feeling that it would only upset Maxim. In the evenings, after the kids had gone to bed, Raya didn't read or watch TV. Instead, she sat at her desk working on the outline of her book. Even during Sunday picnics with Maxim's friends, Raya would find a quiet place under a tree and continue her writing, all the while claiming that she was working on urgent factory assignments.

Maxim's friends didn't think much of Raya at all. They regarded her as snobbish and distant. Raya knew that, of course, but she couldn't have cared less. There was nothing of common interest that she could talk about with them in any event.

Eventually it came to the point where Raya had to let her family know about her new project. The children were extremely excited – their mother was a writer! Somewhat surprisingly, Maxim assured Raya that he was very proud of her and that he was resigned to the fact that with a scientist as a spouse, he shouldn't be expecting gourmet meals every day.

The year 1972 started off with a bang. Raya's baby brother Misha finally got married. Lily's parents arranged a lavish Jewish wedding and afterwards Misha moved into Lily's apartment.

By early spring, Raya had completed her book and the publisher promised that it would be in print on a timely basis before the new academic year began in September.

Then news arrived of Manya's pregnancy. She was expecting another baby in August.

One weekday Raya came home and found her mother waiting there for her. Her heart skipped a beat. Raya intuitively knew what her mother was going to say, even before Vera had an opportunity to utter a word.

Vera kissed her daughter warmly and said, "Rayechka, darling, we need to talk."

"Is Misha emigrating?" Raya half-guessed, half-asked.

"All of Lily's family is leaving. Lily is expecting and they want their child to be a *sabra*. That means a child who's born in Israel."

"I know what it means, Mama. What about you? What have you decided?" Raya asked in a hushed voice.

"I'm going with them, Raya. Please understand me. I love you and the kids very much, but I'm lonely in my flat and I would never be able to live in the same apartment with…" Vera paused and blushed.

"With Maxim, you mean. Still a stranger even after all these years," Raya acknowledged with a noticeable touch of sadness. She tried to stay calm in the face of this latest news since she didn't want to upset her mother, but it was hard, so hard!

"Oh, Raya, please don't misunderstand me. He's a wonderful man, a good husband and a loving father to your children. You were quite right to marry him. But you don't need me now. I'm not getting any younger and I don't want to be alone. And with Manya and Lily both pregnant, I'll be needed and feel useful in Israel. I'll babysit the children and help Misha and Lily; they've asked me to live with them. Raya, don't be angry with me!" Vera was looking earnestly to her daughter, hoping for some sign of understanding and acceptance.

"I'm not angry, Mama, just sad," Raya said gently. Then she got up and embraced her mother.

In July, the new book, *Biochemistry 101,* was published, well-timed as had been promised for the upcoming university season. The book cover prominently displayed the two co-authors' names: Drs. Sokolova and Sinitsin.

That September, Raya and her family found themselves standing on the station platform again and waving goodbye to the train leaving for Chop, a town on the border between the Soviet Union and Czechoslovakia. That was the first leg of the journey to Israel for Vera, Misha, and Lily.

"That's it," Raya was saying to Maxim on their way back home. "That was the last time I'll ever have to see that accursed train. I have nobody left who can emigrate. We're done with witnessing emigration and that departing train!"

But Raya was wrong.

Vasily's Confession

IN LATE NOVEMBER of that same year, Raya received a totally unexpected call at her office. "Raisooochka Borisovna, how are you?"

It was that intimate tone of voice and that oh-so-familiar way of addressing her; it was her 'mating call'!

What's going on? an alarming thought flashed through Raya's mind. *I hope Vasily isn't intending to revive our relationship. That's the last thing I need right now.* Aloud she scrupulously acknowledged his call. "Yes, Vasily Andreevich, what can I do for you?"

"You can meet me in half-an-hour at the Beryoska restaurant. I'm taking you out for lunch today. We need to talk," Vasily replied insistently.

A short while after receiving his call, Raya was sitting across from Vasily in a quiet corner of the small restaurant. *He's as charismatic as always. And as good-looking as always too,* Raya decided. *It's strange... I still see him almost every day in the factory, but when we're alone I feel the desire to touch him, to hold him, to...*

Vasily was beaming. In fact, Raya couldn't remember when she last saw him looking quite so happy, for whatever reason.

"Vasily, did you win the lottery or something? You're shining like a brand new kopeck!"

"Even better! Raya, I'm in love!" Vasily announced proudly.

"You're always in love!" Raya shot back as she started to chuckle. "But usually it doesn't last long. So who's the current favourite?"

"No, Raya, it's altogether different this time. For the very first time I've met a woman that I truly love and want to spend the rest of my life with."

"Vasily, are you kidding me? What about your wife, your daughter? Are you actually planning to divorce your wife?"

"Raya, you've known me for many years. But I never told you much about myself or about my family. I don't think you know how it came about that I married *Princess*?"

"No Vasily, you never did say anything about that. And by the way, why do you always refer to your wife as the princess? I've never once heard you refer to her by her real name."

"Listen to me for ten minutes and I'm sure you'll understand," Vasily said dryly.

"I'm just a village bumpkin; a mere peasant. I was born in a small rural village, three hundred kilometers from Kiev. Raya, have you ever been to a remote Ukrainian village? Not one close to the city where people can grow fruits and vegetables in their private gardens and then take them to sell in the city market. I'm talking about a *really* remote village, with no other city or town anywhere nearby. If you haven't ever visited one then you don't have any idea what real poverty is all about.

"I hated it there and always had just one dream ever since I was a small child - to get out of that village and to move to a big city. Fortunately, I had the brains and the desire to study hard and I was admitted to the Kiev Polytechnic Institute, in the faculty of Chemistry. Why chemistry? Because the competition was less than in the mechanical or electrical faculties. Raya, I didn't much care what I studied at that time, just so long as it gave me a one-way ticket out of my village."

"Do you have parents still living, and siblings?" Raya inquired.

"My parents passed away years ago. My sister still lives in the same village with her family. I haven't seen her for ages. I send her money a couple times a year and that constitutes the extent of our relationship.

"Anyway, here I was in Kiev, in one of the best engineering colleges, dressed like a peasant, behaving like a peasant, and talking like a peasant. The girls paid no attention to me but I didn't care about that. I was there to study, not to date or to party.

"As you are well-aware, at the end of the five years of studies when the students receive their diploma, they are given a designated work assignment where they are required to work for the next three years. I was terrified that I would be given an assignment at some factory in some obscure place. That would have been the end of all my dreams. I knew that the choicest placements were awarded to those with connections, but I hoped that if my grades were among the best in the faculty, as they were actually, then at least I would be awarded a decent work assignment. So I concentrated on studying very hard," Vasily explained.

"There was a beautiful girl in our faculty. Not only far better-looking than the rest of the girls, but better dressed, and decidedly more poised. She stood apart from all the other students in the faculty like a princess among her courtiers. And so we all started to call her *Princess*. All of the students and even the teachers addressed her and referred to her as *Princess* throughout my five years there. It just so happened that her father was the Second Secretary of the Kiev Party Committee."

"Wow!" Raya exclaimed. "A real VIP!"

"Oh yes! He has been promoted since then, and I can assure you that you know his name and have seen his portrait. But my story is not about my distinguished father-in-law but rather about his daughter. She had money and she had connections. She could get tickets to any performance, admittance to any restaurant, obtain any imported booze… well, you get the drift. As you might expect, all the male students at the college were at her feet, seeking her attention. She dated a lot, changing her boyfriends frequently. But for me she was unreachable. I think I was probably the only guy who wasn't after her. It was like noticing an expensive diamond in the shop window, but not actually lusting after it because it's way too far out of reach.

"Anyway, in the middle of the fifth year I was informed of my mandatory three years' work assignment at a fertilizer plant near Lugansk. I wasn't at all happy about that but I had no choice in the matter. The very next weekend I went there to see with my own eyes where I would be living.

"The nocuous yellow cloud from the plant's exhaust tower was constantly hanging above the town. The workers in the plant looked sickly and pale, and many of them were constantly coughing. For me, Raya, this was little better than a death sentence. I couldn't understand why I had been given the worst possible assignment in spite of my excellent grades.

"After my return from Lugansk, Princess approached me quite unexpectedly and inquired how my trip was. She was so understanding, so sympathetic, and so kind. She then asked why I'd never invited her out for a date. I was too shocked to reply, so she asked *me* out. We started to see each other quite often after that. Everything we did was at her initiative – where we would go, what we would do. She took me to the restricted store, the one where only government and party officials were permitted to shop. The store was like a treasure cave to me. I had never seen such luxuries in all my life.

"Raya, I was quite literally in a daze those days. On the one hand, the most desirable girl at college was dating me; on the other hand, I felt I was doomed to live in the worst possible place for the upcoming three years.

"Princess initiated her own personal campaign of remaking me. She told me what to buy, how to dress, and how to properly use all the cutlery in the fine restaurants. I was a quick study and a couple months later I was deemed presentable enough for Princess to introduce me to her parents.

"That first evening with her father was more like a formal interview interrogation than a friendly dinner. After the meal he ushered me into his office and said that he was pleased that his daughter had finally fallen in love with a decent man with serious intentions. He acknowledged that he knew that his daughter was spoiled rotten and it was entirely the fault of himself and his wife. He said Princess needed a strong and decisive man to control her and to lead her and that he believed that I was just that man. And then, to my delight, he confided that he didn't want to part with his daughter and therefore I would be receiving a different work assignment right here in Kiev. Raya, at that moment I felt as though I was living in some kind of a fairy tale world," Vasily confessed.

"We got married right after we received our graduation diplomas. For our honeymoon, my father-in-law presented us with a vacation package in Evpatoria at one of the most posh resorts in Crimea.

"Please don't ask me if I was truly in love with Princess. Was Cinderella in love with her Prince Charming? It's assumed that because he was a prince and of charming character that she must have loved him, wouldn't you say? Well, it was the same story with me. That short time that we were dating before we got married had been magical: restaurants, theatres, exclusive parties... I was proud as a peacock that from all the men she knew, she had chosen me. And of course I was physically attracted to her too, so I suppose I thought that I was truly in love. But I was stupid and naïve!

"The first week of our honeymoon was absolutely perfect. We behaved like any other newlyweds: made love, sunbathed, and went for moonlit strolls. But one day during our second week when I woke up after an afternoon nap, Princess wasn't in the room. I didn't see her until late that evening. I was afraid that she might have drowned or fallen victim to foul play. I was out of my mind with worry and had spent all afternoon frantically looking everywhere for her. Eventually she returned to our suite a little tipsy. When I asked what had happened, she looked at me askance and said, *"I met an interesting man and we spent a pleasant afternoon together."*

"I clenched my fists and I was just about to give her a piece of my mind but she laughed and callously said, *"I did hope that you were smarter than that, my peasant boy. Did you really think for one second that I was actually in love with you?*

"Silly boy! Let me be straightforward with you and explain the basis of our marriage. My papa was after me. He didn't like me constantly playing the field. He insisted that I get married and settle down. I wasn't anywhere near ready for that, but I decided that the easiest way for me to gain my freedom was to get married and escape from being under his prying eyes. My father rejected several candidates that I thought would suit me and whom I'd already introduced to him. He wanted me to marry a serious, solid man, or so he said, and you were the ideal candidate! All I had to do was make sure that you were desperate

enough to go along with my little scheme and you certainly made that easy for me."

I was in a state of shock. "Was it you who arranged that terrible Lugansk assignment?" I asked.

"But of course, who else? A nice gift to the right person and off to Lugansk you were going!" she giggled.

"We're through! I'm going back to Kiev and applying for a divorce immediately. You and your father can go to hell with your shameful and deceitful games!" I shouted.

"Calm down, you peasant," Princess commanded with disdain. *"You have two choices. Your first choice is to divorce me and go to Lugansk. In that case, I can assure you that you'll never work in Kiev. Not ever. You'll live and die in that horrid fertilizer plant.*

"Second choice, we stay married and allow each other our freedom to do as we please. Papa told me yesterday that he had secured an important position for you at the Kiev Vitamin Factory. You behave and your career's guaranteed. You'll live in a nice apartment that papa has just arranged for us. You'll shop in those elite stores closed to the public and you'll have access to all the other places where only the privileged people of Kiev are admitted. Not bad for a peasant boy, eh?

"And all you have to do is let me live my life as I desire and accompany me to official events when necessary. If you want another woman you can go right ahead and find one, as long as there's no scandal around your affairs. If I want to sleep with you, I'll let you know; if I want to sleep with someone else, then I will," Princess stated categorically.

Vasily fell silent for a moment, then looked directly at Raya and concluded his startling confession. "Raya, I agreed to her terms. I sold my soul to the devil. Princess made only one miscalculation of a sort, not that it mattered to her, at least not at that time. We village peasants are very possessive people and we don't like to share. Since that fateful day in Crimea I've never touched my wife."

"Vasily, you have a daughter!" Raya exclaimed, while still trying to come to grips with the enormity of Vasily's shocking tale.

"She has a daughter. When we were both thirty her father informed us in his typically overbearing way that it was about time for us to have

a child. So we did. Or, should I say, *she* did. Raya," Vasily added, "I can't bring myself to do it with her."

"What?" an incredulous Raya exclaimed. "You of all people? You can't be serious! You can't do it?"

"Not with her. She hurt me and deceived me too much. My body quite simply feels frozen when she's around. By now I'm sure she hates me as much as I hate her. She's not getting any younger and I suppose it's not as easy as before for her to find a suitable lover. Actually, I don't hate her anymore. I'm simply devoid of any emotion other than utter disdain," Vasily explained.

"What about the girl? Does she know that you're not her actual father?" Raya inquired.

"I think she's guessed the truth. She lives with her grandparents. Princess never cared much or had time for her and I certainly didn't want the responsibility for somebody else's child. Her grandparents love her and give her all the care and attention that a child could ever need. In fact, I think they want to redeem themselves as parents by raising their granddaughter better than they managed to accomplish with their own daughter," Vasily said.

Vasily pressed on with anxiety in his voice. "Raya, I know that I'm a cynic and a sexist pig, but all I want is a woman that I can call my own and a child that is of my own flesh and blood!"

"My G-d, Vasily! I can't imagine how much you must have despised all of us for cheating on our husbands and jumping into bed with you!"

"Well, I confess I didn't have a great deal of respect for any of my mistresses, except of course for you, dear Raya."

"But I was the worst of them and you know it, Vasily! I became involved with you, at least in the beginning, for my own selfish purposes - to obtain an apartment and an important position in the lab."

"And whose fault was it that you had to resort to those means? If I hadn't promised that position so carelessly to someone connected to the Ministry, and if I had taken some interest in that staff apartment building and the living conditions of my employees, you wouldn't have felt compelled to press on with your scheme. Nobody can understand you as well as I can because I know what it means to be desperate. But I'm grateful that it happened anyway, because I gained a long-lasting friend. I don't have too many friends in this world and you're my closest friend, Raya. Well, at least that was the case until very recently," Vasily said with a tell-tale, broad smile.

"Who is this remarkable woman that stole your heart?" Raya gently prodded.

"She's a biochemist and she recently received her Candidate of Science designation. I met her in Leningrad last summer during a conference. She's divorced; has been for years. No children either. Her name is Rimma Berman and she's the loveliest lady in the world. Rimma is smart, witty, beautiful, kind, gentle..."

"Oh, stop it!" Raya laughed, "I get the picture. Rimma Berman – sounds Jewish."

"Yes, she certainly is a Jew and I almost lost her because of that. We were together during the conference and then I took a month off work, as you may recall, and I stayed with her in Leningrad. It was a magical time. For the first time in my life I felt totally content. But at the end of that wonderful month, Rimma informed me that she couldn't see me anymore. Raya, I almost lost my mind! I couldn't understand what was going on. One day we were proclaiming our love to each other, and the next day – it's over. Just like that!

"When I pleaded with Rimma for an explanation, she informed me that her parents and her brothers had decided to emigrate to the United States. She said she had made up her mind to leave the country with the rest of her family.

"The next several weeks were a time of much soul searching for me. In the end I decided that I couldn't live without Rimma and therefore I had no choice other than to leave this evil empire too. That's how they refer to our country abroad – *evil empire*. Did you know that? Well, they're right, Raya. Let's be frank. Our government, the Party officials and all the other bureaucrats are blatantly corrupt and downright evil," Vasily asserted.

"Vasily, please quiet down! You don't want anybody to hear you," Raya whispered as she looked around nervously for any nearby eavesdroppers.

"You're right. But it's not about myself that I'm worried, it's about you, my dear Raisa Borisovna," Vasily said in a hushed voice.

"Me? What does your decision to emigrate have to do with me? Of course I'm sad, very sad about the prospect of losing you. I'll miss you very much, Vasily. But I'm happy for you and wish you and your Rimma all the best that life has to offer. Have you applied for the divorce yet?"

"No, not yet. I wanted Rimma to be out of the Soviet Union before I made my move. And I haven't told you the most important news of all. Rimma's expecting! I'm going to be a father!

"Raya, I can tell you that when I ask Princess for a divorce and then apply for emigration, I'm afraid it's going to be ugly. Really ugly! Honestly, I'm hoping the authorities will let me go without too much noise or interference, but in the worst case I have a couple of aces up my sleeve," Vasily confided.

"You mean you're planning to blackmail Princess and her father?" Raya ventured.

"Raya, I don't relish the idea and I hope that it won't come to that, but one way or the other I intend to get out of this country and to be with Rimma, no matter what it takes," Vasily asserted.

"Anyway, yesterday I received a message from her. She's in Italy now, so I can go ahead and start the process. I want to do it as soon as possible because I don't want her to worry or to be left on her own in her condition. But I'll wait for a week or two until you find a new job away from our factory. With your outstanding qualifications it shouldn't take you more than a couple of weeks."

Raya was stunned. "But Vasily, I'm not looking for a new job. I'm very happy here at the factory," Raya assured him.

"Raya, please hear what I'm saying. They won't be able to stop me but they're sure to take their vengeance out on my close friends and associates. You're particularly vulnerable. Please resign today or tomorrow and find yourself a new job. Everybody knows that you're my close friend and my loyal associate. I'd even prefer it if you left Kiev altogether. Why don't you go to Kazan? They'd be thrilled to have you at the university there," Vasily suggested.

"Vasily, my laboratory is in the midst of several ground-breaking research projects, as you're perfectly well-aware. I intend to see this work through to a successful completion. It means a lot to me and I'm not going to just quit and walk away now. After all, what can they possibly do to me? I don't deny that there might be several unpleasant months but I'm a strong woman and I'll manage.

"Vasily, please don't delay on my account. I can just imagine how poor Rimma must be feeling, pregnant with your child and sitting alone in Italy, worrying whether you're going through with it and joining her or not. So don't delay or worry yourself about me," Raya admonished him.

"Raya, please reconsider," Vasily pleaded. "If the authorities blacklist you, which they could easily do, you won't be able to get work anywhere."

"Stop being so dramatic!" Raya retorted. "I came to work at this factory for the first time when I was seventeen years old. The factory's so much more than a job to me; it's a part of me. I'm not going to quit and that's the end of it,"

"In that case, so be it and good luck to you, my dearest Raya."

"Good luck to you too, Vasily. And please try to let me know when you'll be leaving. I hope to see you one more time before you go." Raya smiled and looked compassionately into the eyes of her dear friend and former lover.

"I certainly will, Raya. You know, I have this odd theory. Every person automatically inherits a bowl of tar at the time of their birth. Until the person finishes consuming the contents of the bowl, he or she can't truly enjoy a decent life. I feel that I'm finally about done with my bowl!" Vasily laughed heartily. "I'll be in touch."

✑Maxim's Decision

R AYA DIDN'T COME into contact again with Vasily in the factory. For two weeks everything was quiet, and then...

There was one meeting committee after another! Posters were placed prominently on the walls of the factory. One such poster said: *Vasily Andreevich Kovalenko has been terminated from the position of Director of the factory for mismanagement of national resources and funds.* Another poster pronounced: *For behaviour which is a disgrace to the proud title of Communist, Vasily Andreevich Kovalenko has been expelled from the Communist Party of the Soviet Union.*

Rumours were flying in abundance. Pretty Lidochka, who always seemed to know everything that was going on inside the factory, came running into the laboratory one day with a sensational announcement. "Our Vasily was arrested for embezzlement!"

Raya's heart skipped a beat. "When did that happen?" she asked.

"Oh, three or four days ago, I think," Lidochka replied. "I overheard a conversation between the Head of HR and the Chief Engineer."

"I don't know what you heard, Lydia, but I saw Vasily Andreevich earlier this morning here in the factory," another biochemist countered.

Raya felt that she could breathe again. She wanted to see Vasily, or at least hear his voice. She wanted to know what was really going on but he hadn't called her since their lunch meeting. *He's trying to protect me,* Raya thought, but her anxiety wasn't at all diminished by this rationalization.

Another day passed and then, quite unexpectedly, there was a sudden outward calm in the factory. The posters disappeared, the committees were disbanded, and the Assistant Director assumed de-facto leadership. From that moment forward, there was never another reference to Vasily's name. It was as if he had never existed. *He must have played one of his aces,* Raya mused.

There were no other changes to factory management for a month, until an excited Lidochka rushed into the laboratory one day with another announcement, "We have a new Director!"

"Who is he and what's he like? Did you see him yet?" several people asked simultaneously.

"Let me tell you one thing," Lidochka contemptuously responded, "our husbands have nothing to worry about!"

When Raya finally met her new boss, she had to agree wholeheartedly with Lydia. The new Director was physically altogether different from Vasily: a slight, austere man, much shorter than Raya, with a receding hair line, thick glasses, and a long, narrow nose. *I hope,* Raya thought, *that his management skills are rather better than his looks.*

One day he made an appearance at the laboratory, but stopped near the entrance and without acknowledging anyone in particular, he remained standing there for five minutes or so, observing everyone going about their work. Then he turned away and walked off without a word.

"Rat! We have a rat for a director!" Lidochka exclaimed.

Raya instructed everyone to ignore the incident and to continue normally with their work. But she was thinking, *Lydia's absolutely right! What an unpleasant man they've bestowed upon us!*

Life in the factory started to change and more than anyone else, Raya felt the impact of those changes. She was no longer invited to management meetings and when the daily planning meeting, mandatory for everyone that was either a supervisor or in some higher position, was rescheduled, Raya wasn't informed of the new time and place. The laboratory's budget was severely slashed and some important projects had to be closed down. The message was clear – Raya had been ostracized. And so, with each passing day, she reflected more and more on Vasily's advice and contemplated starting to look for a new job. The vexing issues were that she wasn't by nature a quitter and she loved her laboratory.

I shouldn't rush into any decisions. Things will change. The Director will see that we're doing good work here and he'll mellow out with the passage of a bit of time, Raya thought, trying as best she could in the circumstances to reassure herself.

At the end of January, the Director finally made another appearance in the laboratory. This time he was accompanied by a stranger. The Director asked all the workers of the laboratory to gather and then announced, "Comrades, allow me to introduce your new Head of Department. Please welcome him and make him feel comfortable."

Then turning to the newly-appointed manager, the Director said, "Igor Ivanovich, this is your domain now. Good luck, and if you need anything just ask me. Our factory management places a lot of importance on the success of this laboratory."

The Director turned and headed towards the door. Then, as if it was an afterthought, he twisted his head around and said, "Raisa Borisovna, would you please follow me to my office."

The astonished workers silently stood aside to let Raya pass. As she followed after the Director, Raya hastily marshalled her thoughts about everything she was intending to say to this despicable man – about her nineteen years of service with the factory, about her superior qualifications, about the successes of her laboratory and the many awards which the lab had received during the years of her management.

When they reached the office that was so familiar to Raya, the Director sat down in his chair and quite out of the blue asked, "Raisa Borisovna, where's your mother living right now?"

"In Israel," a bewildered Raya stammered.

"Ah! In Israel… and I think you have an older brother, isn't that right? And where is he now?"

"In Israel."

"Fascinating. And do you have other brothers or sisters?"

"Yes, as I'm sure you're well-aware, Comrade Director, I have a younger brother."

"And where is he?"

"In Israel."

"What a coincidence! It seems that your entire family is in Israel. And what are your intentions? When are you planning to join them?"

"I have no plans to emigrate."

"Not yet, right? Very well… and do you know where your good friend citizen Kovalenko is?"

"I have no idea where the former director, Vasily Andreevich, is right now. He was my boss and he was as much my friend as anybody else's, but I haven't seen or heard from him for at least a couple of months."

"Well, you are right about one thing. I have heard that Kovalenko had many friends… lady friends… but, Raisa Borisovna, let's not diminish your own role. My understanding is that you were his closest friend and most loyal associate. Isn't that so?"

"Will you please explain where you're heading with this line of questioning? What are you trying to say?" Raya shot back defensively.

"I just want to point out to you, Raisa Borisovna, that you currently represent a security risk. I would even say an enormous security risk for the laboratory and for the factory. I hope you understand that under the present circumstances, I cannot allow you to continue to work in such a strategically important place as the research and development laboratory. However, our Soviet Government has spent a lot of money to educate you: four years in university, three years in grad school, and all of that at the expense of the State. We can't afford to simply terminate you. So I've reviewed the organization chart of the factory and identified a suitable position for you as supervisor of the packaging department. It's very important that when our product reaches the pharmacies and the stores it is undamaged and looks presentable, don't you agree?"

"I'm a scientist, not an operational manager."

"That may be, but this is the only position that's available and it's for the evening shift: four PM to midnight."

"Well, that might be the good part, since at least I won't have to face my family! I'd be too ashamed to look them in the eye!"

"So is it agreed, Raisa Borisovna?"

"Absolutely not! I decline your ridiculous offer!"

"Well, that's the only position that I have available for you. But of course we're living in a democratic country and there's no slave labour here. You're always free to resign at your own initiative," the Director prompted.

"Where's a paper and pen?" Raya demanded.

"Here you are." The Director motioned to a pen and a blank sheet of paper that were already conveniently laid out on his desk. *He knew very well that I would resign,* an outraged Raya thought.

She hastily scribbled out and signed a terse resignation letter. The Director signed his acknowledgement just as quickly. It was done, and Raya was unemployed.

At home, Raya's family didn't take her resignation as a tragic event at all. The children were confident that their smart mother would have no difficulty in finding another worthwhile job.

Maxim offered words of encouragement. "Good! It's about time you got out of that factory! You've been with them for too long anyway. And trust me, they'll be sorry. Before long they'll come crawling back to you, begging you to take your position back!"

With fresh enthusiasm, Raya started looking for a new job. She applied to all the scientific R&D Institutes that were working in her field. Unfortunately, from every place she received the same response: *Dr. Sokolova, we would love to have you, but not now. There are no openings at the present time.*

She paid a visit to the University of Kiev. At first she approached her old friend and advisor, Dr. Sinitsin. "Rayechka, my dear girl," the Professor said enthusiastically, "I'm so glad to see you here again. How can I be of help?"

Raya explained her situation but the Professor shook his head. "Raya, I never had a lot of clout here. You should know that. Now I have even less influence than before since I'm about to retire. You'd better go to see the Dean."

The Dean looked Raya straight in the eye and categorically stated, "You've been blacklisted. We've received a phone call from…" and he gestured heavenwards. "I'm sorry but there's nothing I can do for you."

Raya resolved not to become depressed about her unsuccessful job search and decided to devote her time to editing a second edition of her book. Since the first edition was published she had a lot of new ideas and she also wanted to incorporate some corrections and updates.

There was plenty of work to be done. Something would come up on the job front sooner or later, she concluded.

At the beginning of March, Raya received a phone call in the middle of the day while Maxim was at work and the children were in school. "Raya, I'm leaving today – my train leaves in two hours. I just wanted to say goodbye and wish you well," she heard the oh-so-familiar voice.

"Vasily, just tell me where you are now and I'm on my way! The phone is not the proper way for us to bid farewell to one-other."

"Raya, I'd love to see you, but is that wise? I'm already at the train station."

"As I have recently discovered, I'm not such a wise woman. See you soon."

When Raya arrived at the station, the platform was crowded with Jewish families. Some people were already boarding the train, while others were still gathered on the platform and saying goodbye to their loved ones. Everyone had misty eyes.

Amid this sea of Jewish families, a lone Ukrainian man looked very much out of place. He was standing near one of the passenger cars, looking about absently. When Vasily noticed Raya, he broke into a broad smile. Raya rushed along the platform to him and gave him a hug and a kiss. Then she presented him with a bouquet of yellow mimosas.

"Well, this is the first time I've ever received flowers," Vasily laughed.

They spoke mostly about Vasily's plans. "One of Rimma's brothers is already in California. The rest of the family is heading there as well. Just imagine - Los Angeles, USA, instead of Ukraine! Quite the move, no?" Vasily enthused. Then he added, "Raya, may I give you one more piece of advice? The last bit of advice, I promise."

"I'm listening."

"Leave this country. The sooner the better," Vasily said with a tone of voice exhibiting passion and conviction.

"Vasily, you know I can't do that. Maxim…"

"Then leave your Maxim here," Vasily interrupted. "You aren't suitable for each other anyway."

"Please don't say that. He's a wonderful father and husband. He loves me and adores the children. Maxim deserves my loyalty and devotion. I'm never going to leave him," Raya protested.

"In that case, good luck again and farewell," Vasily replied with resignation.

"Farewell, Vasily. I worry about how you'll cross the border. They can still play one last trick on you. Please send me a postcard or something from Rome," Raya implored him. He nodded slightly in return.

Vasily climbed the steps onto the train and went to a window where he stood waving to Raya.

It was a sad throng of people that were gradually drifting away from the train station to return to their homes. It seemed everybody was thinking about their loved ones and had but one other common thought: *Will I ever see them again?*

Everyone, that is, except for Raya. She knew full-well that she would never see Vasily again.

One day, Maxim came up with an unexpected suggestion. "Raya, there's nothing that holds you in Kiev now. Why don't we go to Kazan? I'm sure they'd be happy to have you there at the university. We could go during spring break, the kids would spend time with my mother, and you could try your luck at the Kazan University. What do you say?"

Raya, who wouldn't have even considered leaving Kiev just a year ago, promptly agreed without the slightest hesitation.

Several days before their departure, Raya received a postcard from Rome. "*Walking on the streets of the Eternal City. It's even more beautiful than I ever imagined. The weather is nice here and everyone is doing fine. Love, Rimma.*"

"Who's this Rimma?" Maxim asked when he saw the postcard.

"Oh, a girl I knew from grad school," Raya quickly replied.

"And not a very bright girl," Maxim intoned angrily. "The last thing you need right now are cards and letters coming from Rome."

"She won't be writing again," Raya tersely replied.

At the end of March the family arrived in Kazan and Raya made her way to the university that same day.

The Dean was exceedingly pleased to see her. "Dr. Sokolova! The pride of our university! I want to congratulate you on your book. Excellent piece of work and sorely needed, I might add. What can I do for you?"

"We're considering relocating to Kazan. Maxim has a house here and his mother isn't getting any younger," Raya explained.

"Great idea! And don't you even think about looking for a job anywhere else. You belong right here. In September you'll start teaching, but for now you can work with us on some interesting research projects. Rayechka, why don't you go home and relax and come back tomorrow? We'll discuss your first assignment."

The next day, a confident Raya appeared at the Dean's office at the appointed hour. However, this time the reception was decidedly cooler. The Dean looked sternly at Raya and said in a formal tone of voice, "Raisa Borisovna, I'm afraid the university can't offer you a position at the present time." Then he continued with marked consternation in his voice. "Raisa Borisovna, how could you do that to me? Don't you realize that I could lose my job? Yesterday you didn't even say a word about your tenuous situation."

"I didn't know that in our country it's a crime to look for a job or that I should be ashamed of doing so. After all, I didn't steal from anybody and I didn't murder anybody; I'm not a spy and I don't have an infectious disease," Raya responded fiercely. Without waiting for a response from the Dean, she turned and strode quickly out of his office.

Maxim was waiting for her in the main lobby of the university building. Just like that occasion so many years before, he had with him a full knapsack and he was smiling broadly, but when he caught sight of his wife's expression, his smile promptly faded.

"Maxim, let's go to the Volga and get drunk!"

They reached their favourite place near the river where they had made love for the first time. Notwithstanding her audacious suggestion, Raya didn't really feel much like drinking. She rested her head on Maxim's shoulder and cried bitterly.

"Raya, my love." Maxim was bravely trying to comfort her. "Why don't you simply relax for a while? Stay home; let me provide for the family. Just be a wife and a mother for a bit. Things will change, you'll see."

A week later they returned to Kiev and Raya tried to get accustomed to her new domesticated lifestyle. It wasn't easy for her. She had trouble adjusting to the role of a homemaker. Even the letters from Israel didn't help to improve her mood. There were two new boys in Israel with strange names, Aryeh and Jonathan. Those boys were her nephews, but she would never see them.

At the beginning of June, a new second edition of her book was published. All of Raya's changes, corrections and additions had been incorporated in the latest edition. The cover and title pages had undergone a change as well. Now there was only one author's name listed: Dr. Sinitsin.

That bitter pill was the last straw. Feeling utterly defeated, Raya lapsed into a deep depression. The children and Maxim saw her dressed in the same bathrobe all day long. She stopped going to the hairstylist and her hair took on the appearance of a wild mane. She didn't read or watch television. She would prepare simple meals, make the beds, and then sit idly near the window, thinking about her sister and brothers, and about her mother.

Somewhere, far away from Kiev in a foreign land there were people near and dear to Raya's heart. She needed them so much! If only she could see her Manechka and Dima! Calm Manya and wise Dima – they'd have the answers to her problems. They would tell her what she should do to overcome her disastrous situation.

Maxim couldn't bear to see his energetic wife become so lethargic and so despondent. He racked his brain trying to think of any way to cheer her up. Finally he decided to take her out to dinner at Kiev's best restaurant to celebrate her upcoming birthday. He insisted that Raya buy a new dress and go to the beauty salon to be pampered for the occasion. On June twenty-second, Maxim and Raya went out for their celebratory dinner.

But even the gourmet food and pleasant music failed to alter Raya's downbeat mood. She didn't feel like drinking or eating much of anything and she refused to get up to dance. There was not much the spouses could talk about, even though Raya forced a smile on occasion and attempted to keep the conversation going. She felt utterly despairing and guilty before Maxim who was trying so hard to please her and lift her spirits!

By the time they were served dessert and coffee, they were both relieved that the long dinner was almost over. It was then that a foreign gentleman quite unexpectedly approached their table.

"Dr. Sockolove, how are you?" the man addressed Raya in broken Russian. "Do you remember me? I'm Dr. Kevin Jones."

In spite of her depressed state of mind, Raya immediately recalled meeting this man previously. "Oh yes, of course, Dr. Jones, I do remember you. You came to the factory last summer with the Canadian delegation."

"Yes, that's right. And I was very impressed by all the work that you were doing in your laboratory. The firm where I'm working now is engaged in similar research but you're miles ahead of us. My company sent me back to Kiev to see if we couldn't arrange something mutually beneficial. But my trip has been a total failure, at least up until this point when I happened to notice you here in the restaurant!"

"Did you go to the factory?" Raya inquired.

"I certainly did. But instead of that charming fellow with good English, I was greeted, in a manner of speaking, by a very unpleasant man. He had no interest whatsoever in doing any business with Canada and furthermore, do you know what he said? He said that the laboratory had been downsized and now consisted of only five people. And he said that the mission of the factory was not to squander national funds on dubious research, but rather to deliver proven products of good quality to the Soviet people."

"Five people! My entire laboratory consists of only five persons now?" Raya exclaimed in dismay.

Dr. Jones redirected the conversation. "Dr. Sockolove, you're a fine scientist. Your articles have been published in many prestigious magazines and your textbook is a wonderful and most-needed publication. You must consider translating it into English. You have a widely known and highly respected name. Have you ever considered emigrating to Canada? You'd have no trouble securing an excellent position there. In our country, your impeccable qualifications would be truly appreciated."

Dr. Jones glanced briefly at Maxim and then back to Raya, hastily adding, "In Toronto we already have a large Ukrainian community and there's a growing Russian community too. Here's my card. If you ever decide to come to Canada, please be sure to give me a call. I'm certain that my company would be most interested in employing you."

That being said, Dr. Jones wished Raya and Maxim both a pleasant evening and returned to his own table where his business colleagues were patiently waiting for him.

On the way home, husband and wife were quiet. They were strolling at a leisurely pace through the beautiful streets of downtown Kiev, engrossed in their own thoughts. Suddenly, Maxim said, "Canada might be all right for us. I'd never want to live in Israel or in America, but Canada is quite different."

Raya looked at him incredulously and said, "Maxim, what are you talking about? Emigration is a very big decision. Let's not rush into it. Let's sleep on it and talk it over tomorrow, okay?"

Not another word was said on that subject as they made their way home, but when they were eventually settled in bed, Raya spoke up in a voice filled with a mixture of hope, anticipation and anxiety. "Maxim, did you really mean it? Would you like us to emigrate to Canada?"

There was so much hope in his wife's voice that Maxim responded without hesitation, "Yes, Raya, I did and I would." With a heavy heart, a suddenly frightened Maxim came to the realization that he had committed himself beyond recall.

The next morning, Maxim awoke to an enticing aroma. He ventured into the kitchen and found his wife preparing a delicious breakfast and wearing a pretty dress, fresh make-up...all in all, looking her best.

Raya presented him with a fresh cup of coffee and asked, "So, what do you think about Canada, now that you've had a chance to sleep on it? I really don't want to push you, but..."

Raya sounded so enthused that Maxim, who had been contemplating saying, *I was too drunk last night*, incredulously found himself saying instead, "Start packing, wife!"

The Sisters Reunite

THERE WAS NO stopping Raya now. She had once again been transformed into her most energetic and most efficient self. She was on the phone with Israel in a matter of minutes on that same decisive morning. "Send me an invitation! Now!" she instructed Manya in no uncertain terms.

There was quite a lengthy process involved in assembling and preparing all of the required documents, but by the time the invitation arrived, Raya was ready. Before the end of July, the Sokolovs' application for permission to emigrate to Israel was in the hands of the authorities.

By this time in 1973, the emigration procedure was well-established. Jewish families that wished to leave the Soviet Union presented an invitation from Israel, asking the authorities to allow their family to re-unite. After several months of deliberation, the authorities were issuing Israeli visas. Recipients of these visas were then required to leave the country within a month. After crossing the border, quite a number of families headed west: to the United States or to Canada, whichever was their true intended destination. Those families who didn't wish to settle in Israel were met in Vienna by representatives of the Jewish Immigration Aid Society (JIAS), which arranged their transfer to Italy. It was there that they waited for the country of their choice to grant them landed immigrant status. While in Vienna, and later in Italy, and even while in-transit to their final destination, JIAS fully-supported these families.

Everything proceeded smoothly for Raya. She received the invitation from Israel quickly, thanks to Manya, and her papers were accepted by the Soviet authorities without question right away. Now that she had a goal and a set purpose, Raya was brimming with energy and filled with anticipation.

It seemed that all of Maxim's energy had been transposed to Raya and it left him feeling deflated and depressed. His happy, content, and secure life was falling to pieces right before his eyes.

Every day he came home to find that one more piece of custom furniture, which he himself had crafted with such passion, had been sold. One day the hutch was missing, the next day the china cabinet was gone…and so it went.

Meantime, the house was getting filled up with cameras, linens, dolls and even boxes of condoms!

"Raya, what are you going to do with all this stuff?" a bewildered Maxim asked.

"Sell it in Italy, what else? I have a list of the kinds of items that people who left before us recommend that we bring," Raya explained. "This merchandize is in high demand and can be sold quickly for a good price."

"Since when has my highly intelligent scientist wife become a common peddler?" Maxim inquired in dismay.

"Since the Soviet government made a silly rule that people are only allowed to take ninety U.S. dollars per person with them when they leave, that's when. We were working hard all our lives. Do you want to leave everything behind, Maxim, and start your new life like a pauper? I'm sure you don't want to arrive in Canada with only three hundred and sixty dollars between us in your pocket, do you? When we sell all this stuff we're going to have some savings to start us off when we get to Canada." Raya added impatiently.

"Whatever. But I have no intention of standing in the middle of Rome with a collection of silly children toys and all that other junk, trying to sell it on the street!" Maxim objected.

"Maxim, stop worrying! I'll be doing all of the selling. I'll do what everybody else is doing," Raya assured him. She wasn't going to take his skeptical mood seriously. Of course she noticed that Maxim wasn't at all happy in those days, but Raya was certain that as soon as they left the Soviet Union, he would get over his gloominess.

"Don't worry, everything will be alright," Raya kept repeating again and again.

But Maxim did worry – a lot. His last hope was that they would be refused their visas. Then he could say to Raya that he tried, that he had been willing, and that it was not his fault that things didn't work out. To his chagrin, they received their visas in record time.

Maxim still couldn't understand how Raya could so easily abandon their home. Not so long ago, she was dreaming about their apartment and had fought for it long and hard. They'd spent years acquiring their household items and decorating the place. Didn't she feel any remorse about leaving it all behind? What about his friends and what about all of the children's friends? But Raya remained undeterred in the face of all his objections and second-guessing.

In mid-October, Maxim found himself standing on the platform of the train station with his family, bidding farewell to all their friends and acquaintances.

Alla and the members of the *Aleksander Society* (apart from Oleg and Lev) came to see them off and that gave Raya a final opportunity to hear all the latest news. She learned that Polina was living with Alla and her two boys in their new apartment; and that Polina was studying in the Theatre College and was well on her way to becoming an actress. Raya also heard that Kostya and Olya were engaged; that he was studying in Aviation College and that she was working. Raya was pleased to learn that Tamara and Nastya were now students of Kiev University in none other than the biochemical faculty. Lev, she was told, was studying in Kostroma to become an engineer. Raya didn't need to ask why Lev had gone all the way to a small city in the middle of Russia to study. She knew very well the answer to that.

The farewells were tearful, but finally the time had come for them to leave.

For one last time, Maxim looked at the cityscape that he had learned to love, and at the faces of the people that he had known for so many years, feeling an impulsive urge to say, *Raya, you go. Let me stay. It's my country and I don't want to leave it.* But Maxim glanced at the excited faces of his wife and children and understood that there was no turning back. It was with an emotional state of profound resignation that he despondently boarded the train with them.

The family would always remember their eventful trip out of the Soviet Union as a series of anecdotes, one after another.

On the train, Lena befriended a little girl named Emma. While they were standing in the lineup for customs clearance at Chop, Emma started to scream at the top of her voice, "I don't want to go to Sochi; I want to go to Vienna with Lena!"

Emma's mother quietly explained to Raya that she hadn't wanted her daughter to alert everyone in their apartment building of their impeding emigration, so they had told little Emma that they were going to Sochi for vacation. Now, the entire large gathering in the train station was listening to Emma's squeals of protest and laughing amongst themselves. Chop was definitely not en-route to a resort in Sochi on the Black Sea.

Clever Lena, realizing that she had unwittingly made a mistake by revealing her family's destination, promptly reacted by explaining to Emma that Sochi was actually a suburb of Vienna and that they would travel on the same train and later on they would live in the same city. Pacified with this explanation, little Emma quieted down. But for years afterwards, Raya and her children were jokingly referring to Sochi as if it were a part of 'greater Vienna'.

Not long after that incident, Raya was startled to hear a familiar voice. "Raisa Borisovna, you're here! What a pleasant surprise to find you going on this train," said the former manager of the factory's cafeteria who clearly was emigrating with his family too. He opened his arms to give Raya a bear hug and then introduced himself to Maxim as *Grisha*. In a somewhat conspiratorial tone of voice, Grisha asked, "Are you going to Israel or to some other country in the West?"

"We hope for Canada," Raya answered carefully.

"Great, then we'll see each other in Rome!" Grisha glanced at their belongings and asked, "Where's your electric heater?"

"Heater? Why do we need a heater?" a bemused Maxim asked.

"The winters in Italian apartments can be quite unpleasant. No heating. I'm taking two heaters with me - one for my wife and myself and one for the kids' bedroom. Actually, you could do me a small favour and I would be much obliged. You see, the authorities are only allowing one heater per family. So, if you don't mind taking my extra one through the Customs…"

"Grisha, it's not a big deal," Maxim responded graciously. "Just put one of your heaters on top of our stuff. No problem."

Maxim and family made it through customs clearance in record time and without incident. Apparently the authorities didn't think that a worker from a furniture factory with a scientist as a spouse would be carrying anything of particular value.

Just before they boarded the train, an exasperated Grisha finally emerged from the customs hall with his family. "They gave us the third degree search," he lamented. "Anyway, we're here now so may I have my heater?"

The heater changed hands again and the incident was forgotten. The next stop was Bratislava, and from there the train took them on to Vienna.

Upon arrival in Vienna, the immigrant families were separated into two groups. Those who were officially en-route to Israel were whisked away to some mysterious castle where they would await their turn to board an El Al flight to Tel Aviv.

The families who wanted to try their luck in seeking entry to the United States or Canada were taken by bus to a cheap hotel that was actually a closed-down, former bordello, belonging to one Madam Bettina. The proprietress had apparently decided that she could make better money by renting her sparsely furnished rooms to Jewish immigrants and getting paid reliably by the Jewish Immigration Aid Society.

The next day, these newly-arrived families made their way to the Vienna branch of the Israeli Immigration Center SOCHNUT, as they had been instructed to do. There, the SOCHNUT representatives did their utmost to convince them to change their minds and go to Israel instead. Some families were driven to the castle immediately after their meeting with the SOCHNUT officials, because now they were destined to immigrate to Israel after all. The more stubborn families that couldn't be swayed were given a stamped slip of paper that stated that they had been cleared by the Israeli Immigration Center. With this precious document in hand, they could proceed to another office where they would register with JIAS and receive their first support allowance.

When Raya and her family arrived, the entrance door to the interview room of the Immigration Center was closed. They waited patiently for over twenty minutes until eventually little Emma and her parents emerged from the office. Emma's mother was on the verge of tears.

"I was almost convinced. I was so tempted! If my sister wasn't living in Winnipeg we'd be flying to Israel right now! But she's waiting for us. Raya and Maxim, good luck and stick to your story if you're absolutely sure of where you want to go. That woman in there really knows how to put the pressure on!"

The Sokolovs weren't given the opportunity to exercise their determination, one way or the other. The immigration officer silently studied the Jewish-looking Raya, and then almost longingly looked at young Boris, before glancing quickly at Maxim and the blonde, blue-eyed Lena. With that, she promptly made some notation and stamped a document which she then handed over to Maxim and said, "Okay, you're free to go."

Raya was relieved but Maxim reacted with irritation. "She didn't even try to convince us to change our minds! It was as if she was saying, *who needs you in Israel anyway?*"

"Oh, Maxim, never mind about that! We got what we wanted. Let's go and get the allowance money and then we can start seeing the sights of Vienna."

For the next three days, the enthralled Sokolov family walked the streets of the beautiful city. They shopped for fruits in the open market and visited the local supermarket. Everything about Vienna excited them. The storefront windows of the shops were filled with displays of attractive merchandize; the architecture on every street was a sight to behold (*"Mama, look, their Opera house is even more beautiful than ours in Kiev"*); and an enormous number of well-groomed dogs were being walked by their well-attired owners in the spacious parks.

On the fourth day the Vienna sightseeing came to the end and they boarded the train for Rome. By now they felt as though they were on a giant processing belt, moving along from one work station to another, and then to another. It seemed as if the Soviet Visa Department, the Israeli Immigration Center and the international arm of the JIAS organization were all integral parts of the same network, simply handing off migrant Jewish immigrant families from one organization to the next.

Upon arrival in Rome the immigrant families were immediately surrounded on the train platform by several burly men carrying semi-automatic weapons (*"Our guards,"* somebody whispered). They were escorted to a small hotel and instructed where and when they were expected to go to the Rome branch of JIAS for their first interview with their counsellor; they were also told to start looking for apartment accommodations in the meantime.

"We have to go to Ostia de Lido," Emma's mother had told Raya and Maxim. "It's a sea-side resort, not far from Rome. All the immigrants are living there. There's a central post office in the town which I've been told is some kind of meeting place. We'll go there and then we'll see what happens."

"What I can't understand," Maxim mused, "is how we're going to talk to the local Italians about an apartment? We don't know a word of Italian!"

The next day, after fumbling their way within the vast Termini Railway Station and then taking a thirty minute ride on a commuter-train, the Sokolov family arrived in Ostia de Lido. There were quite a few other Soviet immigrants on the train and they had no problem locating the famous post office. Upon arrival there, they immediately realized that there was no need for Italian. The square in front of the post office was swarming with immigrants. It looked more like a Kiev flea market than an Italian post office courtyard.

In the crush of the crowd, the Sokolovs became separated from their new friends, and in no time at all a young man with crafty eyes accosted them and asked, "Are you looking for an apartment? You've lucked out! I have an incredible apartment for you! Built to fit your family perfectly! Great area of the city... great view...two bedrooms. It's everything that you need. Good price too, and I mean, a really good price. I already have two other takers for this place but I really like you and I want you to have it. Only fifty dollars commission for me. Do we have a deal?"

"I don't think so." The calm and confident, oh-so-familiar voice had come from just behind where they were standing. "Not before we examine the place and verify that there are no outstanding utility and telephone bills. We wouldn't want my sister to be stuck with somebody else's debt, now would we?"

"Dimka!" Raya exclaimed, forgetting altogether about the apartment and turning to embrace her brother.

"Grandma!" she heard the kids screaming and then Raya saw her mother standing aside. After she hugged and kissed Vera and Dima, Raya turned around again and there she was: the woman that she had missed the most - her Manya!

While Dima and Maxim continued the search for a suitable apartment, Vera was checking out the children (*How much did they grow? Are they both healthy? Did they lose, G-d forbid, any weight?*) The sisters, meanwhile, became deeply engrossed in their own conversation. There were so many things to tell one-other; so many things to discuss! Three years had passed since Manya and Dima had emigrated so there was a great deal for the sisters to catch up on.

Eventually the entire family went to investigate a prospective apartment, but definitely not in the company of that original broker who had promptly disappeared as soon as Dima had come upon the scene. Raya and Maxim liked the place that was destined to become their home for the next several months and arrangements were made to secure the apartment. Dima accompanied Maxim on the train back to Rome to pick up the family's belongings. Vera took the kids for a walk on the beach, leaving the sisters alone to continue their own conversation.

"We took a three-week vacation so we could come here," Manya informed Raya. "Misha and Lily are looking after our kids. The girls are old enough now to help with Aryeh. And please," Manya practically begged, "don't forget to address us as David and Miriam. It took quite a long time for us to get used to our Hebrew names, so let's not create any extra confusion now. That would be a great help to us."

Raya was left with no choice but to promise to comply with Manya's wishes.

"Hannah is sixteen now and oh-so-beautiful," Miriam (aka Manya) was saying proudly. "She's dating an Israeli boy, Ilan. But I think she takes it way too seriously. She's much too young for a serious relationship."

"Look who's talking," Raya chuckled. "You were in a serious relationship since you were ten years old!"

"Well, that was different," Miriam primly replied, and then she joined her sister in laughter.

The next day, the Sokolovs made the trip to Rome and registered with the local branch of the JIAS. They were quizzed about their interest in Canada.

"Why Canada?" their counsellor was asking in Russian. "There's so much more work opportunity in the United States and it's easier to get an immigration visa too. Canada uses a merit-grading system and is looking for very specific skills, so you may not even qualify. The business card that you got from that Canadian scientist isn't exactly a firm employment offer."

Raya and Maxim remained adamant. They were determined to apply for Canadian Landed Immigrant status and eventually their counsellor relented and agreed to support their wishes. She suggested registering Raya as head of the family because of her superior education and work experience. Maxim grumbled to himself, "*What else is new?*"

The counsellor was an astute woman. She scrutinized this unlikely couple and concluded that they'd probably have a difficult time with immigration no matter where they went. However, she discreetly kept that thought to herself.

Then, without warning, the counsellor switched to speaking in English and Raya easily made the transition. Maxim, who was now listening to his wife speaking in an unfamiliar language and not understanding a word of it, was becoming increasingly frustrated by the minute.

The counsellor eventually addressed Maxim in Russian. "I'm sorry, Mr. Sokolov, I was testing your wife's English. We have a tremendous amount of paperwork to process and we could use some help, so I've offered her some temporary work with us here at the JIAS. Your immigration proceedings can take six months or longer in any event, so why not make some extra money while you're waiting? Your wife has graciously agreed."

Without even consulting with me, like always, Maxim thought irritably.

David and Miriam had been waiting outside the JIAS office for them and after the interview process was over and done with, they all decided to go and explore a bit of Rome together. The sights were so awesome and the weather so perfect that after a while Maxim's bad mood dissipated.

The next decision they had to make was concerning the children. The kids needed to start learning English as soon as possible. There were two options: there was the ORT school in Rome (but the kids would have to spend over two hours each day traveling back and forth on the train); or alternatively, there was a small synagogue right in Ostia where an immigrant teacher of English was offering free lessons. It was actually a full-day program since, in addition to the English classes, a Rabbi was teaching the Jewish immigrant children who knew nothing about their heritage, the history of their people and the religion of their ancestors.

"I don't want my kids to be brainwashed by some Rabbi," Maxim declared. "They'll learn English when they get to Canada."

"And what are they going to do here for half-a-year?" Raya countered. "Roam the streets of the town? It's not good for the children to be idle. Let's have them try this place for a day or two. If they don't like it, then we'll think about some other possibility."

Reluctantly, Maxim acquiesced, as usual.

Lena loved the small school. Within a day she had made some new friends. She liked the old English teacher with her easy-going manner and she loved the Rabbi and his interesting stories about the long and complicated history of the Jews. She was immediately fascinated by a world that before-now she had no knowledge of whatsoever.

Borya, on the other hand, tried his utmost to avoid attending the school. He found all that talk about religion to be boring and couldn't concentrate on his English language studies either, knowing that outside there was glorious weather, a spectacular beach that was beckoning, and an Italian town to explore! However, he soon found out that there was nobody else to play soccer with, or to accompany him to roam the streets of Ostia in the middle of the day, because all the other immigrant boys were in school too. Grudgingly, Borya started to attend the classes regularly, but as soon as the school day was over he and his new buddies would run off to the closest park to play soccer.

Raya and Maxim only saw Borya first thing in the morning before school and in the evenings when he eventually returned home. It was a hopeless cause to get him to do any homework!

A week later, Raya, Miriam, Maxim and David (it took some effort for Raya and Maxim to get used to the Hebrew names of their relatives) were seriously caught up in exploring Rome. They went to the Vatican; they spent hours sitting on the Piazza Navona observing the bustling daily life around them; and before long they discovered a Russian library. It was operated by an elderly Russian immigrant who had been living in Italy since 1922. They also traveled to nearby Tivoli and spent a whole day exploring the spectacular, manicured gardens.

They learned that some immigrants had started a small travel business. Three-day tours to Tuscany or to Napoli/Capri were being offered. David purchased everyone's tickets for the Tuscany tour. The cost was a modest twelve dollars per person, yet Raya and Maxim were affronted by such an outrageously high price.

The first stop on the tour was Florence and they were all enamoured with the city and its culture. They saw Michelangelo's famous *David*. They went to Ponte Veccio and strolled across the famous bridge and gazed at the amazing window displays of expensive jewellery.

They toured the Uffizi Museum and spent hours closely observing the famous paintings. Their tour guide had apparently done his homework, because his knowledge of the city and its history was impressive.

In the museum, he took his group to see the most remarkable paintings and rendered an informative narrative about the artists, the history, and the significance of each masterwork. Whenever someone inquired further about any particular painting, the tour guide always had a knowledgeable answer. All the while Maxim, not surprisingly, was bored stiff, but he was obliged to tag along nonetheless.

In one of the exhibit halls of the museum they encountered another group of Russian émigrés. They were evidently not as fortunate with their guide. This hapless group was being rushed through the exhibits with barely enough time to catch a glimpse at the works of art on display. When an elderly lady tried to slow down the pace and asked her guide about a particular marble statue, he gave it a quick glance and responded, "It's a famous Italian general." Then, as he was quickly passing another nearby bronze statue of a horse, he added, "And that was his horse. Anyway, do you want to go shopping or not? Move it, move it!" and that group quickly disappeared from the museum.

For days after this episode the sisters and their husbands were having great fun recounting the story of the *Italian general and his horse*.

That evening after the tour was finished, the two couples came back to the famous Ponte Veccio Bridge. It looked completely different after dark. The expensive jewellery shops were closed; and instead, the street vendors had taken over the area. There was a carnival-like atmosphere with little street bands, crowds of locals and tourists milling about, and inexpensive, tacky trinkets on offer.

The foursome stopped to watch a blind young guitar player. He was singing some Italian folk song and had such a captivating voice that quite a large throng of passers-by had gathered around him. When he finished the song, many people generously dropped coins onto his offering plate. Then the young man removed his dark glasses, opened his large, sparkling blue eyes, winked to the gathering around him, and smiled. There was so much charm in the manner by which he had carried out this ruse that the crowd actually started to laugh and applaud.

While their parents were experiencing the charms of Italy, the children were making discoveries of another kind.

"Grandma," Lena asked, "what are our Hebrew names?"

Vera looked at the children with bemusement. "I don't believe you or your brother have Jewish names. Your parents just gave you nice Russian names, ones that they liked."

"But Grandma," Lena persisted, "wasn't Borya named after our grandfather? What was his Jewish name? Wasn't it Baruch?"

"Well, actually," Vera explained, "his name was Benyamin. His father's name was Leib. Benyamin Leibovich was not a politically suitable name for a Soviet officer, so when he joined the army he changed his name to Boris Lvovich. Much more dignified."

"Benyamin," Borya repeated, "that's weird."

"What about me?" Lena wanted to know. "Didn't you have some female ancestors with a name that started with the letter 'L'?"

"Of course we did. My grandmother was Leah Tzeitel," Vera laughed as she replied, amused at Lena's persistence.

"I love it! Leah Tzeitel!" Lena shouted in triumph.

"Hey, how come you have two names and I only have one?" Borya protested.

Lena generously suggested, "Well, you can be either Baruch Benyamin or Benyamin Baruch. What do you think?"

"Okay, so why don't you go and ask the Rabbi which one is better?" Borya prompted.

"Why can't we go together?"

"Can't. The boys are waiting for me. There's a game starting in about ten minutes."

"You and your stupid soccer!" Lena exclaimed, and with that both children ran off in different directions.

Vera shook her head and wondered with some trepidation how Maxim might react when he heard about the new Hebrew names of his children.

The three weeks of vacation for David and Miriam passed by all too quickly. On their last evening in Italy, the entire family went for a leisurely stroll on the popular Ostia boardwalk. The evening was lovely and the boardwalk was crowded with tourists and immigrants. David bought a gelato treat for everyone and the family sat relaxing on a bench, enjoying their ice cream.

All at once they heard a nearby, animated voice of a woman. "Sisters! Look there, Yuri, it's the blood sisters that I was telling you about. I can't believe you girls are still together!"

Raya and Miriam looked askance at the elegantly-attired and confident-sounding lady who was addressing them as she approached. Accompanying her was a finely-dressed gentleman. A step or two behind them was another couple, evidently fresh immigrants from all appearances.

The lady gushed, "Don't you two ladies recognize me? We spent two years in that wretched cellar together!"

"Yulia!" Miriam and Raya exclaimed in unison.

"Yes, it's me!" Yulia responded enthusiastically.

"You're looking quite spiffy," Raya observed. "You must have emigrated some while ago. Where do you live now?"

"We're living in West Germany. It's the best country in the world and with the highest standard of living. My husband's family was living in Riga before the war so he qualified for German citizenship," Yulia boasted. "So I'm a German citizen now. We just came to Italy to help our friends here to get through the border. "

"How can you do that without papers?" Raya asked.

"Oh, there are ways," Yulia replied rather evasively.

Miriam had a different question on her mind. "Yulia, how does it feel to be called a German and to live in Germany after your horrendous war experience? Do the German people consider you to be a German or a Jew? After all, you don't exactly look too German!"

"Manya, please! Don't be such an old-fashioned prude! The German people are very kind and treat us nicely. I wish people would forget about the war. As far as my war experience... you mean all that dreadful homework?"

Yulia clarified her comment for the rest of her entourage. "We stayed with this grouchy old teacher and he forced us to study seven days a week! Sometimes I considered running out into the streets to be killed, just to avoid the homework!"

Yulia's companions dutifully laughed.

A visibly upset Miriam was about to respond but David laid a restraining arm on her shoulder.

"And where are you planning to go?" Yulia asked, changing the subject.

"Raya and her family have applied for immigration to Canada but I live in Israel now with my family," Miriam answered proudly.

Yulia looked at Miriam with open disdain and said, "Canada should be fine, but Israel is definitely a mistake. Try to escape from there as soon as you can. Anyway, we must be going."

Yulia nodded her head in parting and without waiting for a response walked away, leaving Miriam and Raya fuming.

David sympathetically said, "Girls, quite honestly I feel sorry for both of you. I wouldn't have been able to tolerate staying in the same room with that unpleasant woman for two long years, even if she was only a child at that time."

The family promptly agreed that Yulia wasn't a topic that merited any further discussion. After all, the evening was so beautiful with the balmy temperature and a gentle breeze off the water, and they wanted to be in a good frame of mind on their last evening together.

A short while later, they happened to notice Raya and Maxim's old acquaintances - the former factory cafeteria manager and his wife. The couple was just leaving a nearby restaurant. Grisha looked like a new man. He and his wife were dressed from head to toe in brand new, expensive-looking Italian clothes. He cheerfully greeted the family when they called out to him.

"Wow!" Maxim exclaimed, "you must be getting a different allowance than us."

"The allowance is the same," Grisha chuckled. "However, I just sold a couple of stones and now I can afford to live and look like a normal person, not like some poor immigrant."

"Stones?" Maxim asked.

"He means diamonds," David said wryly.

"How did you smuggle diamonds through the border?" Maxim inquired.

"I didn't. You did, actually. They were hidden inside the heater you carried for me," Grisha explained casually and started to laugh heartily.

The instantaneous realization that he had been unwittingly involved in a smuggling operation, and that his family had been jeopardized and could easily have been arrested and sent to Siberia instead of Italy, hit Maxim like a brick. He rose up from the bench, clenched his fists and moved menacingly towards Grisha.

"Hey man, take it easy," Grisha admonished him smugly. "What are you planning to do? Beat me up, eh? Then kiss your Canada goodbye! And don't make such a big deal out of it! It worked, right? No harm done." With that, Grisha and his wife proceeded to make their way towards the boardwalk, while David, Miriam, and Raya were doing their utmost in trying to restrain and calm down the highly agitated Maxim.

"What's the matter with those people? Does the immigration process bring out the worse in them or is this some form of your 'Jewish solidarity'?" an aggrieved Maxim asked with marked sarcasm. "We've just witnessed two fine examples of Jewish gratitude and Jewish camaraderie!"

"Maxim," David said calmly, "the Jewish people are a nation. Just as it is in every other nation, there are good people and there are bad people. I live among Jews in Israel and I can tell you that the vast majority of them are very fine people. Please don't judge us collectively based on the despicable behaviour of those two rotten apples."

The next day, the Israeli guests departed. On the Monday following, Raya boarded the commuter train to Rome to start her temporary job with the JIAS organization. After the children went off to the synagogue-school, a bored Maxim went to the beach.

For the next several days while the rest of the family was absent, he sat idly on the beach, contemplating the sea. But then one day he came upon some driftwood and became engrossed in carving small figurines, just as he had done years ago.

An Italian couple who were walking on the beach stopped near Maxim who was absorbed in his craft. The gentleman withdrew a ten mille lira banknote from his pocket and offered it to Maxim in exchange for one of his carvings.

Maxim looked up, shook his head, and addressed the gentleman curtly in Russian. "My work is not for sale."

The couple stood aside in discussion for several minutes and then the man stepped forward again and added another ten mille lira, and then five more.

Astonished by his unexpected good fortune, Maxim accepted the money and handed over a figurine. Twenty-five mille lira! He could hardly believe it.

The next Sunday, Raya took all of Maxim's newly-carved figurines with her to the flea market and returned home with a substantial sum of money. "Everything is sold!" she proudly announced.

Maxim started to carve his figurines in earnest now. He was a bread-winner again! He was in business!

It seemed that some kind of mystical force was helping the Sokolov family in their quest, because in record time they were called to the Canadian consulate for an interview, and then for their medical check-ups. Before the end of March they were scheduled to fly to Canada. Their Roman holiday was over.

A New Life; New Challenges

U PON ARRIVING AT the Toronto Pearson International Airport, the family was met by a representative of the Toronto JIAS branch, a pleasant, middle-aged woman with a kind, open face. She was an immigrant from the Soviet Union too and introduced herself as Inna.

Inna drove them to a motel and cheerfully said, "It's getting late and you must be tired. I'll order you a pizza so you don't have to worry about supper. Relax tonight and tomorrow I'll pick up you in the morning. We have a busy day ahead of us."

After their meal, the children turned on the television, while Raya and Maxim went for their first walk in their new country. However, they couldn't comprehend whether they were situated within the city or somewhere beyond. Nobody was walking on the streets. On one side of the roadway there was an empty field; on the other side, some small, non-descript houses. The street looked bleak and unattractive. They came to an intersection and Maxim read slowly, "*Batoorst.*"

"Maxim, the letters *t* and *h* together sound more like *s* than *t,*" and Raya enunciated the street name as "*Bathurst*".

"Weird word and even weirder language," Maxim commented. "I liked it much more in Europe. I wish we could have stayed there," he grumbled.

"We're here now, so let's make the best of it and see how it goes," Raya replied encouragingly, and then she proffered a kiss to her husband. She understood how difficult it was for Maxim to leave Kiev and felt an enormous sense of gratitude and fondness towards him. She was a lucky woman to have been blessed with such a devoted husband as Maxim.

The next morning, Inna arrived early to pick up the new Canadians. "First we have to rent you an apartment," Inna announced. "You can't be staying in a motel for long!"

They drove less than five minutes and the appearance of the street changed dramatically. Now they were on a busy suburban thoroughfare, bracketed by tall apartment buildings on both sides of the street.

"We just passed Steeles Avenue, so now we're in North York, part of the Greater Toronto metropolitan area. Bathurst always was the main Jewish street of Toronto. The Jews began living on Bathurst in the downtown area, close to Lake Ontario, and then slowly through the years many have moved north. There are an amazing number, more than fifty synagogues on this street," Inna was explaining to them with pride in her voice.

"So who's pushing the Jews out of downtown Toronto?" Maxim asked.

Raya sucked in her breath and kicked Maxim in the leg. The children looked askance at their father and Inna tersely laughed. "Nobody is doing that. It's just that as the city grows, the demographics change."

Inna fell silent, evidently having lost her desire to continue with the local geography lesson. Before long they were parked near a large, high-rise apartment building with black balconies.

"There are traditionally a lot of immigrants, many of them from the Soviet Union, living in this area," Inna explained. The majority of us are starting here. It's easier. Families are helping each other to settle. Some immigrants are even starting small businesses. You'll find a Russian deli nearby, a Russian barber shop, and even Russian doctors. After you learn your way around the city, then you can decide where you eventually want to live. For now, I suggest you rent an apartment here. There's a two-bedroom unit available in this building. I talked to the superintendent yesterday," Inna informed them.

The apartment was rented within fifteen minutes, thanks to Inna's no-nonsense efficiency, and Raya marvelled at the speed with which the rental was arranged. "I spent years waiting for an apartment in

Kiev and here we get an apartment better than our old one with no effort or delay at all."

Inna smiled but made no comment.

Next, Inna drove them to a large warehouse and invited the family to enter with her. "The well-established Jews of Toronto have donated their used furniture to our organization. Please go ahead and select whatever you want. Well, within reason of course. There are many Jewish immigrants arriving in Toronto who need our assistance. Okay, let's start with beds…"

While Inna led them towards the selection of beds, Maxim looked aghast. "Hand-me-down furniture? Do you really expect me to sleep on somebody else's mattress?" Maxim implored his wife.

Inna overheard him and felt an increasing dislike towards that handsome-looking man. While managing to control her temper, she rebuked Maxim rather sternly. "Mr. Sokolov, people whom you don't even know have contributed all of this furniture in good faith. They didn't have to do it; they could have sold it or just thrown it away! They wanted to make sure that you and your family didn't have to sleep on the floor and that you had chairs and a table to sit at to eat your meals. The least you can do is to stop complaining about their charity!"

Raya glared at Maxim and he responded by saying, "You go ahead and select whatever you want. I'll be waiting outside."

Raya apologized profusely to Inna. "I'm so sorry. I don't know what's gotten into him today. Maxim is a very accommodating man. It's just that he's a furniture maker by trade and really particular when it comes to furniture."

"That's okay," Inna replied, and then asked, "let me guess - you're the one that wanted to emigrate and he didn't. Am I right?"

"Yes, that's correct," Raya acknowledged.

"I'm sorry to say this, but that usually spells trouble. I've seen quite a few families like yours and often things didn't turn out well. You'll need to help him adjust," Inna cautioned Raya.

"Oh yes, I will. I know how to handle my husband," Raya replied confidently.

Raya and the kids quickly selected an assortment of furniture pieces and Inna then drove the family back to the motel.

"Okay," Inna began after they had all sat down in the lobby of the motel, "let's talk about your job prospects. Raya, you're on your own. We have no contacts within the scientific world of biochemistry.

"Maxim, I understand that you're a master furniture maker and highly qualified in that field. But you don't have Canadian experience and you don't have any English either, so for now you may have to accept some employment below your skill level. JIAS will support your family for two months, but then you're on your own."

"Thank you very much," Raya said with heartfelt gratitude. "Nobody invited us to come to this country, nobody owes us anything, and this organization has already done so much for us! They supported us in Italy, and then they brought us here too. It's very generous of JIAS and we are so grateful."

"I'm glad to hear that," Inna replied. "We're trying to do whatever we can within our limited budget. Anyway, I called around yesterday and found a small furniture shop that needs another worker. They're only paying their employees the minimum wage, but I haggled with them and got you an extra fifty cents per hour. If you want it, it's yours, Maxim."

"I was making wooden figurines in Italy and selling them for good money," Maxim probed.

"Maxim," Inna responded cautiously, "you definitely can try to offer your carvings to gift shops or even get a booth in the flea-market. However, it may take time for you to establish a clientele. I would suggest you take the job and consider your carvings as a possible additional source of income."

"Inna, thank you for finding a job for Maxim. Of course he wants it!" Raya enthused.

Maxim's response was much more subdued. "Yes, thank you, I'll take it."

"Maxim," Inna cautioned, "please remember that your first job is like your first apartment and the used furniture. It's something that's needed in the beginning, but not necessarily for long. Just take advantage of the opportunity you've been given for now. And here's a list of English language evening courses being offered in this area. I've underlined the most popular of them for you.

"Now, let's talk about the children. I have some good news for you," Inna declared. "Really good news! There are public schools in Toronto and there are also private schools, some of which have a religious affiliation. Private schools are quite expensive but they definitely deliver a higher standard of education. The Jewish community has made arrangements to provide free education at the Associated Hebrew School for one year for the children of new immigrants. In your case, it's going to be for more than a year. They offer this consideration for you until the end of this current school year and for the entire next year too! You're very fortunate."

"What's wrong with the public schools?" Maxim inquired sceptically. "Why can't my kids go to a public school like most everybody else's children?"

"They can if you wish," a deflated and somewhat frustrated Inna replied. "It's your choice."

"Oh no!" Raya intervened. "The Jewish private school would obviously be the best and the education of our children is of utmost importance to us. We're sincerely grateful for the offer."

"You can discuss it after I leave and let me know tomorrow," Inna suggested.

"Papa, can I go to the Associated Hebrew School, please?" Lena asked.

"Do you remember Ira and Tanya that I befriended in Italy? They're both coming to Toronto and they'll be going to that school too. We talked about it back in Italy. Papa, please!" Lena pleaded.

"What about you, Borya?" Maxim asked.

"I don't know," Boris hedged. "It might be fun to learn Hebrew. Then when I go to Israel to visit Uncle Dima and Aunt Manya I could talk to everybody. But it might he hard, right? Inna, is this school much harder than the public schools?"

"There are some additional classes, yes. I'll be honest with you, Borya, there will be more homework, that's for sure."

"Borya, why don't you try it? It's only for three months until the end of this school year. Then next year you can decide where you want to go. You might like it, you never know," Raya suggested.

"I suppose," Borya replied hesitantly.

"Maxim," Raya said sweetly, "let's have the children go to the Hebrew school for the rest of this year and then we can better decide during the summer what we want to do for next year."

"Whatever. Apparently you all have already decided. I have a headache. If you don't mind, I'm going out for a walk," Maxim mumbled and he marched out the door of the motel.

Maxim returned an hour or so later in a mollified and apologetic mood.

"Raya, I don't know what was wrong with me today. I'm sorry for being so difficult. Maybe it's all because I didn't like that Inna woman very much. As a matter of fact, I don't like Canada so far either. It's so different from Kiev, or even from Rome! And about that job - I'm not a young boy who should be starting at an entry-level. I realize that I have to take it for now but it doesn't mean I have to be happy about it."

That evening, Maxim and Raya discussed the children's schooling again. Maxim was still in favour of a public school where his children could meet other Canadian children, become integrated in the community more easily, and most importantly from his viewpoint, not be brainwashed by the Rabbis as was the case in Italy. Nevertheless, Raya prevailed and eventually convinced him to yield and to give the Hebrew school a try.

Raya and the children had different perspectives, each for their own innate reasons. Given her upbringing and intelligence, Raya couldn't resist the prospect of a superior school for her children. A good academic education was essential to her way of thinking. Lena was infatuated with Judaism and refused to even consider public school. Borya was mildly interested in learning Hebrew, although he was otherwise essentially indifferent.

The following Monday, Maxim started work at his new job, while Lena and Borya began attending the Associated Hebrew School. Meanwhile, Raya went to buy some dishes and other household essentials for their new apartment.

The family was slowly settling into their new neighbourhood in their new country, but everyone was on edge for one reason or another.

Lena couldn't fathom her father's apparent resistance to her interest in Judaism. After all, he had married a Jewish woman! Maxim was angry at Lena's disobedience and Raya's implicit encouragement of her behaviour.

But the worst aggravation for Maxim was his mindless, monotonous work at the factory. He was used to performing the most difficult and challenging tasks of the furniture craft, but in this job he was now limited to mechanically assembling cheap kitchenettes. In his shop there were four other co-workers, all of whom were immigrants from different countries. None of them had any useful knowledge of English and therefore were unable to communicate normally. Maxim loathed this job.

Raya was doing her best to organize the new apartment on their limited budget. She wanted to make the place as cheerful as possible. She was doing everything in her power to accommodate each member of her family. Only after she was satisfied that the apartment was looking presentable, Raya placed a call to Dr. Jones.

To her disappointment, nobody answered his extension, and after several more unsuccessful attempts she called the company's main switchboard number.

"Dr. Jones is not with this company any longer," a pleasant female voice advised.

Raya had not anticipated this eventuality and when she recovered from this surprising setback, she asked, "Do you happen to know where he's working now? Could you please provide me with a forwarding number?"

"Sorry, I don't have that information," the lady replied politely.

Quite frantic by now, Raya tried another approach. "But I'm sure Dr. Jones must have had some friends and associates that are still with your firm. Can you please connect me with somebody who may be able to help me?"

"I think not. Dr. Jones didn't leave the company on the best of terms," the woman responded coldly. "Is there anything else I can do for you?"

Terrified that the woman would hang up the phone, Raya hurriedly explained her situation and asked whom she should be speaking with about employment possibilities.

The woman's response was quite indifferent. "I'm not aware that we're looking for any new research specialists at this time, but if you wish you can bring in your resume and leave it with me. I'll pass it on to our HR department."

Raya was devastated by this wholly unexpected development. She had been counting on Dr. Jones' assurance during their chance encounter in the Kiev restaurant that her name was well-known and that his company would most likely be more than happy to employ her. Now she wasn't sure where or how to begin looking for a job in her field of biochemistry.

Raya called Inna and related the story to her. "What's a resume?" Raya asked quite innocently.

Inna sighed, thinking that this was an unfortunate, but not entirely surprising turn of events. "Raya," she said, "there's nothing more important for you than to have a good resume. It's a document that describes your work experience and educational qualifications. It should be put together in a proper format too. It should contain terminology familiar to Canadian employers. I'll get you a couple of names. These are people who are immigrants like us, and they're scientists like you. They should be able to help you out."

When Raya informed Maxim about the untoward development, he shrugged his shoulders and reacted angrily. "He got what he wanted; he tricked us out of our country. Well, Raya, you wanted to emigrate; congratulations, we emigrated. Welcome to Canada and a world of unlimited opportunity," he concluded sarcastically.

"Maxim, stop acting like that. We need to do something. April's almost over. JIAS will pay the rent for May and after that what will we do? If I don't get a job then how can we possibly pay for the apartment? Your wages won't even cover our basic expenses," Raya said with mounting consternation.

"Well then, Raya, you had better find a job. I'm working eight hours a day as it is, so what else do you expect me to do?" an annoyed Maxim shot back.

It seemed to Raya that her husband was covertly relishing this unexpected difficulty so he could rationalize and re-assert his original objections to abandoning their comfortable way of life in Kiev.

Raya managed to maintain her composure. "For a start, Maxim, I expect you to start learning English and start looking for another part-time job or a better-paying full-time job," she challenged him.

"Raya, I'm working in the place where your good friend Inna placed me. I'm doing my bit." Maxim wanted no part of a further conversation on the subject and stomped off to watch television.

Raya, who was always confident about their relationship, felt that she was losing her grip. Maxim's emotional state of mind these days was up and down like a rollercoaster. One day he was his old, easy-going, caring self. He would help with the household chores and accompany Raya for long walks in the neighbourhood. Other days, he would be aloof, objectionable, cold and depressed.

Another thing troubling Raya was the fact that Maxim was spending much less time with the children than previously when they were living in Kiev. He never asked them about their new school and seldom proposed any activities for the family to do together. It was so unlike him!

One Sunday, Raya suggested that Maxim and Boris should go to the park and play some soccer together.

Maxim agreed, and so father and son took a ball and set off for the park. Less than fifteen minutes later Maxim returned home, slumped down onto the sofa and turned on the television without saying a word.

"What happened, Maxim? Where's Borya? Why aren't you with him?" Raya quizzed.

"He's with his buddies. A few minutes after we started to play by ourselves, five other boys showed up at the park. Such an obnoxious and loud group! They didn't even ask for permission and just joined our game, screaming all the time. Borya said that they were from his class, immigrants from Israel. Somehow he managed to communicate with them. They couldn't care less that I didn't understand their language…I guess it was Hebrew. Anyway, Boris doesn't need me there."

"Maxim, they're just boys, and boys will be boys – you know that."

"And I'm not one of those boys," Maxim shot back curtly and directed his attention towards the television again.

Lena was at home and just looked bemused at her father and didn't comment or intervene in the conversation between her parents. Maxim's relationship with Lena had started to subtly change too, just as it had with Raya.

Raya of course knew that Maxim was unhappy in Canada and she resorted to blaming herself for their immigration. She desperately needed to find a decent job as soon as possible. That would allow Maxim to escape from the small factory that he hated so much and find something more suitable and to his liking.

There was still no doubt in Raya's mind that as soon as her husband had a decent job and she was gainfully employed, Maxim would adjust and be as happy in Toronto as he had been in Kiev.

The gruelling and often frustrating search for a job in the scientific community began in earnest. It was progressing much slower than Raya had hoped or anticipated. It took her almost two weeks to create a resume that she was satisfied with. Then she went to York University and applied for equivalency certification documents for all her diplomas. After that, she went to the library and compiled a list of the Canadian companies that were working in her field. Raya even located some magazines containing a number of her scientific articles and made copies as support documents for her resume. However, by this time the month of May was almost over and she still had no job.

Inna called and offered her a temporary, part-time job in a bakery, five to nine AM, minimum wage. The bakery was within walking distance from their apartment building and it would still leave Raya most of the day to continue searching for a proper job. She accepted the position and graciously thanked Inna for her assistance.

Not long after that, Raya unexpectedly received a second job opportunity, if one could call it that, while standing near the elevator of their apartment. Inna was right; there were quite a few immigrant families living in their building and Raya had already met the majority of them. One of the neighbours saw her when she entered the building and asked, "Raya, are you busy tomorrow? Can you help me?"

"Sure," Raya replied politely. "What can I do for you?"

"Can you clean the house of one of my clients tomorrow?" the woman asked.

"Are you cleaning houses for a living?" a startled Raya inquired.

"Please don't look at me like that," the neighbour sighed. "What else can I do? I was a meteorologist back in Moscow, but without a Canadian diploma I can't even apply for a job in that field. We decided that my husband had to get a good job first and then I'd be able to go to the university for a couple of years to study. Meanwhile, he's delivering pizzas and I'm cleaning houses. Anyway, Raya, I'd arranged to clean a large house tomorrow but one of my old clients really needs me to come to her residence instead. Can you do it? It's fifty dollars cash."

"I can use fifty dollars," Raya agreed without hesitation.

"Great!" The neighbour looked relieved and proceeded to explain to Raya about the house and its mistress. "I'll be frank with you, Raya," she added at the conclusion of their conversation, "I don't like the woman at all. She's too finicky for me. If you two get along nicely then you can take over the future cleaning of that house if you wish. I have seven other houses to clean weekly as it is. It's more than enough to keep me busy."

The next day, Raya worked hard and performed her task well. She was as organized and diligent in cleaning house as she was in staging and conducting scientific experiments. At the end of the day the satisfied hostess offered Raya a regular weekly job.

That's how it all started. Within a couple of weeks Raya had four more cleaning assignments. The immediate money problem had been resolved. Maxim's disgruntled reaction was quite predictable. "I suppose, Raya, you find it more fun to clean toilets in Canada than to be a supervisor in the Kiev factory."

Raya didn't have a good answer for that so she just bit her tongue and kept her counsel so as not to aggravate Maxim further.

Borya and Lena had challenges of their own to cope with. They were trying to learn English and study all the other academic subjects in this unfamiliar new language. They were learning Hebrew at the same time, and combining the study of academic subjects with the study of Judaism. Raya's children were not dull and under the circumstances they were coping rather well.

But a greater problem for Lena and Borya derived from being poor, immigrant children in a private school amongst mostly privileged children, and having come from a different society with quite different values and principles.

They were dressed much more plainly than all the other children. Borya didn't care about that, but Lena felt this difference acutely, as most any girl would. The teachers babied them and tended to talk down to them patronizingly, and that caused Lena to fume inwardly. After all, her lack of knowledge of English didn't mean that she was dull or diminish her knowledge of math and science. In fact, she decided that academically speaking, she was far ahead of many of the other children in her class.

For Borya the most difficult part was the tattle-tale behaviour of other kids who were resorting to almost any means to gain the favour of their teachers.

"They're all rat-finks!" he declared at home. "Back home in Kiev we managed to solve all are problems ourselves. If somebody would rat to a teacher, we would beat him up and stop talking to him. But here it seems they're expecting you to go running to the teacher about every little thing! I would never do that!"

Lena encouraged Borya to get started on his Bar-Mitzvah lessons. He was almost thirteen years old and all the boys in his class, apart from the newer immigrants, were more or less ready for their own Bar-Mitzvahs. They had been preparing for years but the immigrant boys had to start from scratch.

A small Bar-Mitzvah study group was formed and Borya attended one lesson. After the lesson, he categorically stated that he didn't need that *stupid* Bar-Mitzvah. "The other boys are studying just because they hope to have a big party and receive lots of presents," he said.

Besides, who could they possibly invite to his Bar-Mitzvah party, other than some of the other immigrant families, and how could his parents find the money to make a party anyway? That was his attitude.

Borya figured he had more than enough other problems without those additional lessons.

Borya's objections to the Bar-Mitzvah lessons started an immediate heated argument with his sister; that is until Maxim put a quick stop to it. "Lena, if you enjoy being brainwashed, then fine, but leave your brother alone!"

Lena just shrugged her shoulders and answered sulkily, "As you wish, Papa!" She turned away and retreated to her room.

By the end of the school year it had become readily apparent that Borya had no intention of going back to the Associated Hebrew School for the next full school year under any circumstances. He had befriended several other neighbourhood immigrant boys and spent nearly all of his spare time with them. As a result, his school marks were mediocre at best.

On the other hand, Lena's grades were excellent. She loved the school and even managed to make some new friends. She ceased eating pork, insisted on not mixing the milk and meat products in the same meal and frowned disapprovingly when anyone else in the family was eating those non-kosher 'forbidden foods'.

As usual, Raya was caught in the middle, trying to satisfy Lena's new dietary restrictions while still accommodating Maxim's traditional preferences. He liked his pork dinners at least three times a week. He enjoyed pork sausages, salami, and ham, and saw no reason whatsoever to be deprived of his favourite foods.

As much as anything, Maxim became irritated that Lena was often invited out to dinner on Friday evenings and didn't return home until Saturday after sunset.

"It's wrong for young people of your age not to sleep at home," Maxim insisted.

"Papa, what do you expect? I want to have a proper Shabbat dinner but we're not having Shabbat dinners or observing the Sabbath at home," Lena protested.

"Then let's have one. You know what to do – you organize it," Raya suggested.

Lena became excited about the prospect of having a proper Shabbat dinner at home with the family. She discussed the menu with her mother all week, and on Friday evening her parents arrived home to a festive atmosphere. On the neatly-set table, there were two large challahs covered with a white serviette, along with a bottle of red wine and a bottle of grape juice. On the kitchen counter five candles had been readied for lighting to mark the beginning of Shabbat.

"Mama," Lena explained, "you'll light four candles - one for each member of our family – and then I'll light the last one. The men don't light candles. Then we'll say a prayer in honour of the lighting of the candles. You can repeat after me. Then you bless us. Usually, it's the father's responsibility to bless the children, but because Papa isn't a Jew, you'll do it for him. Then Borya will bless the wine mixed with the juice and we'll all drink a bit of this wine. After that I'll show you how we wash our hands and we'll say the prayer for hand washing. Then Borya will bless the bread and we'll be ready to begin our meal."

Lena handed the matches to her mother and for the first time in her life Raya lit Shabbat candles. After Lena lit her solitary candle, she started reciting the prayer, which Raya dutifully repeated after her daughter. *"Barukh atah Adonai..."*

Maxim couldn't handle it. He turned and withdrew to his bedroom, soundly closing the door behind him.

"You keep going, Lenochka," a distressed Raya said, interrupting the prayer. "I'll see what's going on with your father."

"Maxim, what's wrong?" Raya asked.

"What's wrong?" Maxim hissed.

He mimicked Lena's voice: "You light the candles and bless the children, Mama. Borya will do this, I'll do that.

"Where does that leave me, Raya? What is my role in this family anyway? Are you happy now? Better education indeed! Look what it's done to our kids! Because that school is too difficult, Borya isn't studying at all and his pitiful marks show it; Lena is completely brainwashed. Is that what you wanted? Is that why we emigrated?"

"Maxim, would you please stop overreacting. The immigration process is difficult for everybody, including the children. They're trying to find their identity and trying desperately to fit in. Granted, Lena is fascinated with religion and that's a bit frustrating, I agree. However, if religion helps her through this transition period, so be it. It's not such a big deal; it's probably only a stage she's going through. Borya will go to a public school next year. I agree with that too and I will work with him over the summer. I'm sure he'll be able to do better next year. But for now, come back to the table so we can have a nice dinner together. Lena worked so hard to prepare everything for us."

"I'm not hungry," Maxim grumbled, turning on the small TV in the bedroom that Inna had recently given them as a present.

Raya returned to the kitchen and silently shook her head; Maxim wasn't joining them for dinner. Lena was crestfallen by the turn of events and politely asked if she could go and spend Shabbat with her friends instead. Her mother simply nodded her head in reluctant agreement.

Borya quickly ate his own dinner and disappeared with a soccer ball under his arm, leaving his mother sitting alone at the festive table. Raya tried to eat some of the food so carefully prepared by her daughter. Tears were slowly rolling down her cheeks and falling onto the dinner plate. *What am I to do now? How can I put this family back together again?*

Early on Sunday morning when Raya awoke, Maxim was already dressed in his best clothes and getting ready to leave the apartment.

"Where are you going so early?" she asked.

"To church," Maxim replied evenly.

"Maxim, you never went to church before! Why now?" a startled Raya exclaimed.

"Well, I have to start someday, so why not today? You guys are all going to synagogue, so why can't I go to church? Do you have any objections?" Maxim asked. There was a thinly veiled challenge in his tone of voice.

"Of course not, Maxim. If you want to go, by all means go. By the way, I've never gone to synagogue myself," Raya replied.

"You will," Maxim curtly retorted as he stepped out of the apartment.

Raya made a call to Israel. It was quite expensive, even with the Sunday discount rates, but she desperately needed to talk with Miriam and David.

"It was a dumb idea for us to come to Canada in the first place," Raya started, without any preamble. "Maxim is constantly in a foul mood; he hates his job and he hates everything about Canada. He hasn't made any friends, even though there are so many nice families from the Soviet Union in our building. We were invited several times to visit other families but he refused to go. I don't know what I should do. He's blaming me for everything and he's right in a way because it was me who pushed our immigration onto him."

"How is your job search going?" Miriam asked cautiously.

"Oh, I'm a professional house-cleaner now and I have quite a few clients. As far as biochemistry – nada, zip, not even a hint of any opportunity. I sent my resume to a number of places where it seemed to make sense - nothing. I would give anything just to get any job in some laboratory and to work with other scientists, if only to get back to some semblance of my former way of life."

"Raya, you can't go back to your old life so you have to be persistent. Something will turn up eventually. And be patient with Maxim; it's not easy for him either. Study English with him and help him to find a better job. And don't let the kids rattle him," Miriam advised.

"Speaking of the kids…" Raya briefly described the events of the past Friday evening and then added, "Imagine! Maxim went to church this morning – that's a first!"

"Well, that may spell trouble of a different sort," Miriam mused. "Not church by itself – it's his right to practice any religion he wants. But if Maxim would find new friends there and get really involved in church activities, it would drive the two of you even further apart and who knows how that might affect the children. It's unhealthy for a husband and wife to have entirely different circles of friends and to live essentially different lives."

"Well, that's basically what we had back in Kiev. He had his friends and I had mine. But still, in those days we were usually happy when we were together.

"But you're right, Miriam. I have to find the right approach and spend more time with him. I'm sure that given time we'll be okay. But the biggest problem right now isn't even our relationship - it's his relationship with Lena. He insists that she's totally brainwashed. She drives him crazy and frankly, me too sometimes. I can't forgive myself for sending the kids to that Jewish school, all in the name of a better education."

"Well, at least they're with you and they're safe. Hannah is going to the army soon. I'm already losing my mind worrying about her."

"Let's hope there's peace in Israel while she's in the service," Raya said earnestly.

"There's never lasting peace in Israel, Raya. It's a fact of life here."

"Oh, poor Miriam!" Raya sympathized. Suddenly, her own concerns seemed insignificant by comparison. *Hannah is going to active army duty and she could get seriously injured or even killed*, Raya was thinking.

The sisters talked for a bit longer, cried together, and offered each other consolation and some advices and they both felt somewhat better after their conversation.

Maxim arrived home from church in a positive frame of mind and was particularly congenial with Raya for all of the following week.

The next Sunday morning, bright and early, Maxim went off to church again. When he eventually returned home he informed Raya that there were English courses being conducted at the church three times a week and that he intended to participate in them. The church was quite far from their apartment and he indicated he was thinking that it would be useful to buy a used car.

Raya was pleased – Maxim was coming back to life! The next week, Raya and Maxim took all the money that they had earned and saved while in Italy and bought a car. It was six years old and a bit dented and scratched here and there, but it was a car!

Apparently there were quite a number of activities at the church every Sunday in addition to the service, because Maxim was routinely coming home quite late in the afternoon. Raya volunteered to accompany him one Sunday but Maxim politely rejected her offer. She tried to talk to him about his classes and tried to help him with English, and also suggested some recreational family activities, but her overtures were all to no avail. Maxim remained polite but if anything even more distant.

He's still punishing me for leaving Kiev. I should be patient and it will pass, Raya decided.

Under the circumstances, Raya took on one more cleaning job to earn extra money for the family.

One day she tried to discuss with Maxim what to do with the children during the summer holidays. "The cost of a summer camp, even a day-camp, is out of our reach. We can't afford a hundred and fifty dollars a week!" Raya sighed.

"What do you want me to do about it?" Such was the predictable response from the 'new' Maxim.

Raya called Inna, seeking her advice. Several days later, Inna located a position of junior counsellor in a sports camp, which was ideal for Borya. That same day, someone slid a brochure under Raya's door and it presented the perfect solution for Lena. The Bais Yaakov School for Girls was advertising a day-camp for girls aged eleven to fourteen years. The subsidized cost was a mere seven dollars per week for a two-week period. Raya was jubilant; if this camp worked out it would be a great solution, at least for part of the summer.

Lena attended the camp and liked it very much. It was operated by the senior students of the school and Lena felt comfortable and happy with that crowd.

One day that summer, there was a phone call, and when Maxim picked up the phone, a young girl's voice asked, "May I speak to Leah Tzeitel, please?"

"Is no Leah Tzeitel here," Maxim responded in his broken English and was about to hang up when Lena said, "Papa, it's for me."

Maxim looked askance at Borya who was engrossed in a book at the time. "And how do they call *you* at school, Boris?"

"Ben," his son replied.

"Why Ben?" Maxim wanted to know.

"Because Ben is cool. They can't pronounce Borya properly anyway; they say *Borjya*. Sounds awful. And when they say *Boris*, they make the wrong accent. Sounds strange. In the Hebrew school they called me Benyamin because it's my Hebrew name, but the boys just call me Ben. I like the sound of Ben, so I hope you don't mind, Papa."

"Why should I mind? Leah Tzeitel, Benyamin - nice to make your acquaintance." Maxim proffered his children a mock salute and slammed the bedroom door behind him.

The Crumbling Of Raya's Family

THERE WEREN'T ANY employment ads for scientists during the summer and Raya still hadn't had any success with her job search. She made a number of phone calls and sent her resume to several places that she hadn't submitted-to already. But the only kinds of responses she was getting were: *We are only looking for people with Canadian experience;* or, you *are over-qualified for our position.*

Determined not to abandon her field of expertise, Raya continued to read all the periodical journals in her scientific specialty and even began to translate her book into English.

Maxim spent little time at home that summer. He dedicated his time primarily to learning English and establishing himself with the community at the church. He informed Raya that he was making good friends within that community, although he never undertook to introduce any of them to her. Raya had a difficult time assessing his mood. Was he still depressed or simply being remote with her?

He needs a better job where he can make proper use of his skills, Raya rationalized. *As soon as he has a good job, things will be different.*

Raya continued to peruse the newspapers on a daily basis, looking for job ads suitable for both herself and for Maxim. In September, when the children were already back in school, Raya came across a promotional ad for a Home and Furniture show. She carefully cut the ad from the newspaper and showed it to Maxim.

"Let's go this Sunday to the show," Raya suggested. "You'll meet people who are working in your trade. You can talk to them and maybe make some connections."

"Raya, you know that I'm busy on Sundays. And in any case, I have no intention of going, just to be reminded of how real furniture masters are working and then returning to my sweat-shop the very next day. I hate my job enough as it is. Thank you very much but this just proves that you don't understand me at all," Maxim replied sullenly.

In spite of his rebuke, Raya re-arranged her schedule and went to the show on her own.

She observed the tradesmen, examined the furniture on display, and finally singled out a booth being manned by an older gentleman. His display poster read: *Robert Smythe, Antique Furniture Restoration.* Raya was attracted by his relaxed manner and his kind face.

She bravely approached the booth and asked, "Mr. Smythe, do you need an assistant?"

The man looked startled. Sometimes he had inquiries from job seekers, but this lady hardly seemed the type.

"Are you skilled at furniture restoration?" he asked.

"Not me," was the quick answer, "but my husband certainly is. He's a real professional, a master with the highest qualifications and many years of experience."

Mr. Smythe was mildly amused. "So, where is the master himself? Why does he send his wife to look for a job for him?"

"He didn't send me, sir. We immigrated recently and all that he could find was work in a small kitchenette assembly shop. I'll be honest with you, Mr. Smythe. My husband is a true specialist, a skilled and diligent worker and a very good man. But right now he's a bit depressed. Immigration hasn't been easy for him. His English is far from perfect at this stage, so he doesn't have the confidence to start looking for another job on his own."

"I understand, madam, but how is it then that your English is so good?" the furniture maker asked.

"I'm a scientist in the field of biochemistry, and in the Soviet Union knowledge of English is a prerequisite for completing grad school and earning a PhD, as I have done. I was studying English for many years. In addition, I have had to read English language scientific journals and sometimes meet with other English-speaking scientists."

"Anyway, it's not about me. Maxim, my husband, attends ESL classes several times a week. I'm sure his language skills will improve as soon as he has an opportunity to practice every day. Mr. Smythe, would you please give him a chance? If you could just meet him..."

More out of curiosity than anything else, Mr. Smythe handed his business card to Raya and said, "Bring this master of yours to my shop tomorrow after six PM and then we'll see."

That evening when Maxim arrived home from his Sunday activities, an excited Raya told him about her meeting and his upcoming interview with the furniture maker.

"I'm not going anywhere," was his unexpectedly curt reply. "Thanks for embarrassing me before that man. What would he think about a man who enlists his wife to arrange an interview for him?"

Utterly deflated, Raya began to cry, and seeing her mother so distraught, Lena became angry.

She started to scream at her father. "Somebody has to do it, Papa! You're never home anymore; you don't care about us any longer!"

Maxim retreated towards his bedroom and started to shut the door behind him. These days, this was his usual response to any unpleasant situation that he wasn't prepared to deal with.

He stopped when he heard the calm voice of his son. "Papa, why are you so mean to mama about us being in Canada? You agreed to come too. But now you're always angry and hurting her. You're hurting us too. I know you don't like it here but you're still our father!"

Maxim looked at his distressed family and grumbled, "Okay, I'll go to the stupid interview. Nothing will come of it anyway, but at least then all of you will leave me alone."

The next day, Maxim and Raya travelled to the address listed on the business card. Raya had been given general directions and in due course they located the house. She stepped forward onto the porch and bravely rang the bell.

Mr. Smythe opened the door, smiled at Raya, and offered her a brief hug. Then he extended his hand to Maxim. "Bob Smythe. Please, call me Bob."

"Maxim."

Instead of inviting his guests into the house, Bob led them directly to his spacious backyard where there was a separate building that looked like an oversized barn. He pulled the heavy door ajar and Raya and Maxim were presented with the sight of a large workshop that was jammed with a large assortment of antique furniture. Some of the pieces looked finished and polished, as if ready to be delivered to clients. But numerous other pieces were in really rough shape. Bob led them to a large, dark dining table with a huge white, heat-infused stain on the surface. "Raya, ask your husband what he'd do with this."

Maxim methodically examined the table and spread his hand over the surface. Then he asked Raya, "How do you say *gretsky orech* in English?"

"Walnut," Raya replied and Bob nodded in acknowledgement.

Maxim had noticed a shelf on the wall with a row of numerous jars and bottles. He started opening one after another. He smelled the contents and sometimes gingerly touched the liquids with one finger in order to judge their consistency. Eventually he replaced some of the jars and bottles back on the shelf; others he set aside. Finally, he selected three particular jars and a bottle and set them down on the walnut table. Bob remained silent but was consistently nodding his head affirmatively during this selection process.

Maxim carefully arranged the containers he had selected into a particular sequence and said in Russian, "This can't be done in a single day. I have to treat the heat-stained area with this paste and then wait for several hours. After that, I'd apply this liquid and wait for a whole day. Only after that I would use these other two, with a few hours between them. I don't know the English names of any of these things."

Raya dutifully translated.

Bob looked approvingly at Maxim and then motioned them to a chair with three legs (the fourth was lying on the floor nearby) and with ripped upholstery.

"Raya, please tell that master of yours to repair this chair by replacing the missing leg, using this new upholstery for the seat, and then to treat that table top with the paste which he selected. Meanwhile, you and I will have some tea."

Bob showed Maxim his tools so he could begin the restoration tasks and then he led Raya out of the barn and into his house.

Raya had a pleasant and relaxing time, chatting and drinking tea with this gentile Englishman and his wife. An hour later, they returned to the shop.

Bob carefully inspected Maxim's progress and said, "If Maxim's interested, I just might have a position for him. I suppose he'd need to give some notice to his current employer and then he could start working here next Monday. I'm afraid the most I could pay him to start would be ten dollars an hour. But if he works as professionally and efficiently as he has in his trial today, I'm certain he could expect that his wages would increase before too long.

"He needs to improve his English, of course. Quite frankly, if he's studying as hard as you say he is, I'm surprised his English isn't a bit better by now. I will need to see how quickly he picks it up. When he demonstrates that he can converse with my clients and help me to acquire new customer orders, then we can talk about more serious money."

The spouses drove home in a celebratory mood – the best news from Raya's point of view was that Maxim seemed genuinely enthused. He acknowledged that he really liked Bob and couldn't stop talking about the variety of quality pieces he had seen in the shop. Maxim was explaining what he could do to restore each of them to their natural, original beauty.

Raya was thinking to herself, *I was right after all. He just needed a good job. Everything's going to be fine now.*

When they arrived back home, a triumphant Raya retrieved a bottle of sparkling wine from the fridge. "Maxim, I bought this wine today, just to show my confidence in you. Let's open it and drink to our family, for our success in Canada and most importantly, for you!"

Maxim's face clouded and he replied in a restrained voice, "Raya, let's not open it just yet. Let me start working there first and then we'll see."

For the next two weeks, Maxim looked gloomier than ever, if that was possible. He had started his new job with Mr. Smythe, yet clearly it hadn't improved his ongoing mood in the slightest.

Feeling despondent, Raya called to Israel again. Miriam and David picked up the two phone extensions at the same time and listened patiently to Raya's latest tale of woe. "I don't know what else I can do now. He has good, interesting work suited to his skills and he should be happy, but for some mysterious reason he's just as depressed and melancholy as ever," Raya lamented.

David cautiously responded, searching for the right words. "Raya, please don't take offence or get upset at what I have to say, but perhaps he resents the fact that it was you who found that job for him."

"What difference does it make who found the job? I'm his wife, so what's the big deal?" Raya failed to detect the subtle implication and possible significance of David's words.

"Raya," David pressed on, "it may be that Maxim doesn't want to feel obligated to you in any way, or owe you anything."

"David, what are you trying to say? Where's this leading?" Raya asked tensely.

"Rayechka, if you don't mind me asking a personal question, when was the last time that you two made love?" David was prodding as gently and compassionately as he could.

"That is none of your business! There's nothing wrong with my relationship with Maxim; he just got overly depressed because of all the difficulties with our immigration. I called you as my brother, as my friend, and here you are making wild insinuations!" Raya had become almost hysterical and promptly slammed down the phone, thus severing the connection.

Miriam never had a chance to say anything at all.

When she eventually calmed down, Raya thought to herself, *I can't even remember the last time we made love.* She stared at her reflection in the mirror - hair gathered in a loose bun, no make-up, short-trimmed nails without polish... nothing glamorous to say the least. What's more, she was still wearing the same tired clothes that she had brought with her from Kiev.

At that moment, Raya recalled the warning of her old colleague, Nina Arkadyevna, and concluded that the time had come to do something drastic about her appearance.

"Lena," Raya asked her daughter, "do you know where I can get my hair done properly? You had a haircut recently and I really liked it. I remember I only had to give you five dollars for it. Where did you find such a good hairdresser at such a bargain price?"

"Mom, go to Rita. Everybody goes to her. She's very nice and you'll like her. She lives right here in our building, two floors above us."

Lena was right. Raya liked the easy-going and fast-working Rita. She cut and set Raya's hair into a fashionable new style, manicured her nails, and even quickly (as an added bonus) applied some discreet make-up.

Maxim apparently didn't notice any of these changes...or if he did he didn't say anything at all to Raya.

That night, Raya gently laid her hand on Maxim's shoulder and then slowly brought it down his back, tracing along his spine. Maxim mumbled something to the effect of, *"I'm tired, Raya. I worked very hard today. I want to sleep,"* and then he pushed her hand away and settled on the far side of their bed.

Raya had never before felt so rejected and so humiliated. She was a married woman with a husband and two children, but she felt incredibly alone at that moment.

Raya's children were pursuing lives of their own. Borya had started at a neighbourhood public school in September and was pre-occupied with making new friends. Lena had somewhat unexpectedly changed her school too. She was so enthralled with the summer camp that she begged her parents to be allowed to transfer to the Bais Yaakov School.

Raya was reluctant to agree. That school was quite far from their apartment – almost half-an-hour ride on a bus. Furthermore, it was a girls-only school and that didn't sit well with Raya either. But Lena persisted and finally persuaded her mother to go for an interview with the school authorities. Raya was actually quite impressed with the school and when she was assured that the payment of fees for the upcoming year would be waived, she acceded to Lena's wishes.

Maxim had outright refused to accompany Raya for the interview and had declared that whatever Raya decided would be good enough for him, and thus the matter was settled.

Lena was keeping busy with school activities and with her Bat-Mitzvah lessons. In addition, the Bais Yaakov School handed out a tremendous amount of homework and Lena preferred to study with her friends until late evening.

Maxim and the children, each in their own way, were moving forward with their Canadian lives. But Raya was still stuck in a rut - cleaning houses and working odd hours in the bakery. *At least my clients like me,* she reflected.

"Raya, dear," a client told her on one occasion, "I know how busy you are but I have a friend who needs someone to clean his house. It would only be for several months. His wife went to Europe with their children and my friend Peter is all alone. He's a doctor, works crazy hours, and worries that the house will become an absolute mess. His wife will kill him when she comes back if he doesn't do something to maintain it properly. So, Raya, would you mind if I gave him your phone number?"

"I don't mind at all," Raya replied agreeably. "The kids need new winter clothes, so the extra money wouldn't hurt."

A day later, a gentleman called and introduced himself. "Hello, my name is Dr. Peter Kolinsky. I understand you are looking for a job. Is that still the case?

"Yes, I am," Raya acknowledged.

"Would you mind coming in to discuss a potential opportunity with me?"

"What is there to discuss?" Raya asked in a surprised voice. "Just tell me when you want me to start and what your address is."

Now it was Dr. Kolinsky's turn to be surprised. "But we didn't even discuss anything yet about your responsibilities or your salary."

"My wages," Raya said, "depend on the number of toilets and mirrors. Do you have a lot of mirrors, Peter?"

"Yes, I think so," he stuttered.

Raya persisted with her interrogation about the good doctor's cleaning requirements. "How many toilets do you have?"

"I never actually counted." His voice now sounded amused and Raya thought, *Men!*

"Okay, Peter," she continued patiently, "should I bring my own cleaning rags and chemicals or do you provide the supplies?"

"We usually give our biochemists everything they need for their work. I'm sorry, ma'am. Evidently I dialled the wrong number," at which point the man severed the connection.

Raya was left standing aghast in her living room, clutching the phone and not quite knowing whether she should laugh or cry.

Finally, at the beginning of December, Raya had a more-promising employment interview. She met with a well-groomed, tall woman who was looking only slightly younger than herself.

The woman appeared to be very businesslike. She wore her brown hair short and neatly styled, and was dressed in a dark pantsuit with a white, silk blouse. Raya immediately felt comfortable with her. The woman introduced herself courteously as *Pamela*, smiled indulgently, and asked Raya to tell her in detail about her work experience.

While Raya was speaking about her laboratory in Kiev and the type of advanced research work that she and her staff had performed there, Pamela was leafing through Raya's resume. She interrupted and said, "Very, very impressive, but we have a full contingent of scientists on our project."

"Then why did you invite me for an interview?" a suddenly crestfallen Raya inquired meekly.

"Raisa, I see from your resume that you have ten years' experience as a lab technician," Pamela commented.

"For the last five of those ten years I was actually working as a biochemist," Raya politely clarified.

"Then you should update your resume to reflect that fact. Anyway, Raisa, I hope you understand that the levels of scientific advancement in Canada and in the Ukraine are quite different from both an academic and technical standpoint. You graduated from where? Kazan University? Never heard of it," Pamela commented bluntly.

"It's a large and famous university in our country and well-respected throughout Europe too," Raya explained.

"Apparently it's not famous enough. In any event, you are starting in a new country. I hope you realize that you would need to begin at an entry level. If you're interested, I can offer you a position as a lab technician. After you prove yourself, I'd expect that something better could be arranged. My project is extremely important and complicated and I'd be taking a big risk by hiring an individual with no Canadian experience. I hope you appreciate that. But I do like you and I'd be willing to give it a try, that is if you're interested."

"I agree," Raya responded without hesitation. "Thank you very much for placing your confidence in me. I'll be happy to take the lab tech position and I'm confident that I won't disappoint you."

"Very good! Can you start tomorrow?"

Raya was making her way home after the successful job interview with mixed feelings. The position was not exactly what she had been hoping for, and the starting pay was even less than she was making now. Transit was also something of an issue; she would have to take a bus, a subway train, and then another bus just to get to work, and then again to get back home.

But at least the job was in a scientific laboratory! She would work on a serious project among other professionals. She would prove to this Pamela woman that she was highly capable and indeed a knowledgeable specialist. Raya concluded she wouldn't mind working several months as a lab technician, especially if it opened up other doors for her in Canada.

At home she announced to the children, "I got a job! Well, I'm starting as a lab technician but it's only the beginning. My boss promised me that she would promote me before too long, after I've demonstrated my capabilities and knowledge level."

The kids were jumping up and down with excitement.

Raya went to the kitchen, took that bottle of sparkling wine out of the fridge again and proceeded to the bedroom. "Maxim, I got a job! Time to celebrate!"

Raya hadn't seen Maxim react quite so enthusiastically in a long time. His varying facial expressions exhibited a whirlwind of emotions, but more than anything he looked relieved.

"That's great, Raya. When are you starting?" he asked.

"Tomorrow! They offered me a position as a lab technician because I don't have Canadian experience yet, but that's only temporary until I prove myself," Raya enthused. She hoped that he wouldn't start with the same old tune again by asking, I*s it better to be a lab technician in Canada than a supervisor in Kiev?*

He didn't. In fact, Maxim sounded practically ecstatic when he responded, "I'm sure of it, Raya. I know you and I have always believed in you. You are a strong, smart, and independent woman. In two years or less you'll be leading projects. So now you won't be needing me anymore. I'm sure you're going to be just fine."

"Maxim, what are you saying? Slow down. Why are you talking about my independence, and whatever do you mean about me not needing you any longer? Of course I need you! We've had a rough beginning here in Canada but we're past that now. We'll be happy here, just as we were back in Kiev, you'll see," Raya said, trying desperately to reassure her husband.

"But Raya, you've never really been happy with me, even when we lived in Kiev. You're an intelligent and educated woman, but I'm just a simple, blue-collar worker and always will be. You'll find somebody much more suitable for you than me.

"Raya, I'm leaving you. It'll be far better for everybody," Maxim quickly stammered through his well-rehearsed speech.

"Maxim, why are you doing this? For whom will it be better? For the children? I don't think so. Maxim. We have a family; we've been together for over fourteen years," Raya started to plead desperately with her husband.

"Raya," Maxim responded frantically, "please let me go. Please don't hold me any longer. I've met another woman whom I love very much and I can't live without her. She's only a saleslady in a deli store but what's important is that she understands me and appreciates me for what I am, as you never could."

"Maxim, you were always telling me those very same words - that you needed me, loved me, and couldn't be without me," a desperate Raya appealed to him.

"Raya!" Maxim was practically screaming by now, "Natasha's pregnant. She's expecting my child!"

"Your Natasha means nothing to me! What about *our* children, Maxim?" Raya asked, feeling tears welling in her eyes. The reality of the situation was gradually coming to the fore in her mind at last.

"We'll be fine, Mom." Raya looked behind her. Both of the children stood framing the doorway of the bedroom. They looked sad but resolute.

Maxim bent down to reach under the bed and retrieved his fully-packed suitcase.

"I have to go now. I'll phone you guys and I'll see you soon," Maxim hastily said to his son and daughter, and then he quickly strode out of the apartment, without so much as a partying 'goodbye' to his suddenly estranged wife.

Raya slumped down onto a chair, cradling the unopened bottle of sparkling wine and staring at her children with a look of apprehension and shock.

Borya came forward and hugged his mother, while Lena knelt before her. Lena laid her head onto Raya's lap and cried out, "It's entirely my fault, Mama. I'm the one that drove Papa away."

"Don't say that, baby," Raya consoled her daughter. "It's life. He met someone else that he fell in love with. It happens, Leah." Without realizing it, Raya had sub-consciously addressed her daughter by her Hebrew name for the very first time.

"We'll be fine, kids. You'll see that we're going to be just fine." But Raya's hands were trembling and all the while the tears were streaming down her cheeks.

That sleepless night, Raya remembered her old friend Vasily, and their last lunch together. She silently addressed him in absentia. *"Maybe you were right, Vasily, that everybody has been given a bowl of tar they are destined to eat before they can have a decent life. But why is my bowl so deep?"*

The next day Raya started her new job in the laboratory. To her considerable disappointment, the work was mundane and tedious. Because the work routine didn't occupy her active mind to any great degree, Raya found herself rehashing the same lingering questions. Why did Maxim leave her? How was it that she didn't detect or pay any attention to all the signs of his infidelity?

Indeed, there had been plenty of tell-tale signs. Dima had immediately surmised the problem based on one short, long-distance conversation with her. How could an intelligent woman like herself have been so naïve and so blind? Why didn't she insist on going to church with Maxim? Why didn't she notice that his English had hardly improved at all in spite of his alleged ESL lessons?

There was no end to Raya's myriad of questions and feelings of self-doubt. And now, as a result of her stupidity, the children would suffer the most. The children!

Over the next several days it became apparent how markedly different Borya and Lena's reactions were to their father's sudden departure.

Lena was maintaining a brave front, pretending that she was not really affected by the split-up of the family, yet the typical spark in her eyes was gone.

Borya was angry and that was predictable. However, notwithstanding his initial display of solidarity with Raya, surprisingly he actually seemed less angry with his father than with his mother.

A week after Maxim's departure, Raya arrived home to a shouting match between the children, some of which she overheard outside the door before she entered the apartment.

"Nobody cancelled schoolwork, Borya! It's hard enough for mom as it is. If you fail she's going to totally collapse. Do you think I don't know that you haven't been in school for the past three days? The school office called here to inquire about your health. Wait until mom finds out about this!" Lena yelled at her older brother.

"Stop telling me what to do! Mind your own business and stop bossing me around! If *she* hadn't bossed dad around all the time he would be still living with us!" Boris was shouting back.

"What's going on here, children?" Raya asked in a stern voice as she walked in. "Boris, is this true that you've been skipping school?"

Boris glared at his mother but didn't offer a reply.

"Borya, Lena, let's sit down and talk. Borya, I feel terribly about what has happened and I'm prepared to accept some of the responsibility, but let's not play the blame game. We need to be strong and help each other because we're still a family and always will be. Lena loves you very much and cares about you and so do I. You must go back to class. Find out tomorrow what you've missed and I'll help you to catch up," Raya said, taking care to sound calm and reasonable.

"Why?" was the unrepentant response from Borya.

"Why what?"

"Why should I go to school every day? They're studying the same things now that I already studied in grade five in Kiev. This school is totally boring," Borya insisted stubbornly.

"Borya, one day they will move along to new topics, things that you don't know; you don't want to miss it, do you? Education is the most important thing for you right now."

"It isn't for me." Borya paused and then carried on with his rationalization. "Don't worry; I'll finish the school somehow. But that's it. I'm not planning to go to any college, so my marks don't really matter very much anyway."

Raya felt the anger welling up inside but she was still controlling her temper. "So what are you planning to do after you're done with school?"

"I'll be a furniture maker like dad," Borya declared.

"Ha! That's a laugh!" Lena interjected. "You can't even hammer a nail straight into the wall! You're such a klutz."

"And you're a bossy, stupid brat! Let's have a Shabbat dinner... let's eat this, but don't eat that! Dad hates you and so do I!"

"Borya, stop talking like that! How could you say such a thing to your sister? Her father loves her very much and..."

"Yeah? Then why isn't he here to tell her how much he loves her, eh?"

By now Borya was completely out of control. "Do you want to know why he left? Because of the two of you! Did you ever ask dad where he wanted to live in Toronto? This is a big city, but you decided where we should live and which school we should go to. You never cared or paid any attention to his opinion! Why did you force him to take that stupid job? Why didn't you give him time to find a job that he liked? Your friend Inna conveniently forgot to mention that we could go on a welfare program so there was no need for him to go to work in his very first week in Canada. How come I've heard about the welfare program and she hadn't? She just wanted to humiliate dad! Even with his second job, you found it for him! How do you think he felt about that?"

"Borya, please listen to me. Only recently you said..."

"I know what I said! I wanted everyone to be happy and I wanted us to be together! But you pushed him way too far. You were always pushing him, Mama, even in Kiev! You never cared for his interests or his friends who were actually nice people, but they were always scared to be anywhere close to you. You treated them like low-life morons. It's as simple as that."

Borya wasn't done yet...

"Did you think I don't know that Grandma Vera didn't like dad? Or that Uncle Dima couldn't stand him?" As for Aleksander, he was just patronizing him! Dad never could please you or any of your snobby friends! And dad was the one who was looking after us when you were studying or working ridiculous hours! He was always taking care of us and he was always available for us when we needed him and now he's not!"

Boris was ranting at the top of his lungs. His accusations came randomly, and sometimes he didn't sound coherent, yet the barrage of words and feelings hit home and left Raya feeling utterly deflated and shattered.

She sat down on a sofa, her face tense and drawn. Her hands were clasped tightly together and she looked at her son with a profound sense of shock. She had never realized how much he resented her and the manner in which she had treated his father, or that his emotions ran so deep.

Finally Boris stopped venting, walked off to his room and slammed the door. Lena had stood quietly aside during her brother's tirade. Now she came close and sat down on the sofa beside her mother. She laid her head on Raya's shoulder and for a long while mother and daughter sat together, comforting one-other without saying a word.

The next day, Maxim finally called.

"I want to see the children," he began. "Can I take them next Sunday?"

"Yes," Raya answered simply. "You don't have to come here. They're big kids now. Give me an address and they'll be there."

""I'll meet them Sunday at ten in the morning near the Bloor metro station."

"I'll let them know."

"Raya, I want to get a divorce as quickly as possible. You know, Natasha..."

"I understand. There will be no delays from my side." Raya interjected.

"That's fine. Now, about the financial arrangements. I definitely want to support the children but I'm not making a lot right now and Natasha will soon have to stop working."

"Maxim, whatever you can provide will be fine. I know that you love our children and will do your best. Is there anything else?"

"No, that's all."

The conversation was abruptly over and Raya went to speak with the children. They were eating their supper in sullen silence, not even looking at each other.

"Your father wants to see you next Sunday," Raya announced.

"Good!" Borya beamed.

"I'm not going," Lena stated categorically.

"Lena, he's your father. You have to go to see him."

"I'm not going and that's final. And it's Leah, Mom. You're calling Uncle David and Aunt Miriam according to their proper Hebrew names and I want you to do the same from now on with me, please."

"I'm trying, but it's not always easy to remember."

"Well then, please try to remember for my sake. Everybody else here calls me Leah. I understand that it's confusing, but please try."

"Okay, Leah, but you're changing the subject. We were talking about your father."

"This is the apartment that we rented as a family and it's my home. If he wants to see me then he can come here."

Raya was too upset by the whole ordeal to fight this battle with Lena/Leah. *Maxim wants to see his daughter, so let him find the correct approach and mollify her*, Raya thought. And so, on Sunday morning Boris set out from the apartment on his own to spend the day with his father.

By seven o'clock in the evening, Raya had begun to worry. It was pitch-dark and quite slippery outside with a cold winter wind howling. Her imagination was running wild, conjuring up all kinds of worst-case scenarios.

The phone eventually rang at about eight o'clock.

Raya anxiously answered and when she heard Maxim's voice she immediately asked, "Where is Borya? I was expecting him to be home long before now."

"Raya, Borya has decided to stay here."

"Maxim, it was your responsibility to make sure that the boy would be home in good time. How can he go directly to school tomorrow morning? He didn't take a change of clothes with him. Can't you drive him home now?"

"Raya, you misunderstood. Borya has decided to live with me... with me and Natasha. He's very unhappy in your place. I think it's the best for everyone if we split the children. You'll have Lena and I'll have Borya."

"It's totally out of question!" Raya exclaimed indignantly. "The children love each other, they must be together and they must live with their mother. You're starting a new family – fine, but don't destroy what's left of mine. Borya will continue to live with me and that's all there is to it."

"Why don't you talk to him then?" Maxim asked, and he passed the phone over to Boris.

"Borya, sweetheart, I know that you've been unhappy since papa left. But we're a family and we need to be together."

"Mom," Borya interrupted her, "I want to stay with dad. At home I would just be fighting with Lena and you. I like it here. Dad is so cheerful, just like he was in Kiev. Please, Mom, let me stay."

"But Natasha..."

"She's actually very nice and she likes me. It was her idea that I should move in with them. And they have a school real close. I'll come next Sunday. I'll be coming to see you very often. Okay, Mom?"

And Raya heard herself saying, "Okay, baby... as you wish. But if something doesn't work out you can move back here anytime. It's your home and always will be, so please remember that."

"I know, Mom. Good night, Mom... One second, dad wants to say something."

Maxim took the phone again. "Raya, I was thinking… Now that Borya will be living with me and Lena with you, I hope you don't expect any support money from me, do you?"

"No, Maxim. I don't expect anything from you. Just make sure that Borya attends school and does his homework."

"I know how to handle my son," was the cold retort, and with that the conversation was terminated.

Raya felt utterly defeated and trapped. She had neither the will-power nor the energy left to start a battle over Borya's custody. She was ready to fight with Maxim, but how could she possibly fight her own son?

Leah was standing nearby and had been listening to the entire conversation. Raya had never seen her daughter so beside herself with anger. Leah clenched both of her hands into tight fists, stomped her feet, and kept repeating, time and again, "How could he? How could he?"

If Raya had thought that she couldn't have been any more unhappy after Maxim left her, now she knew otherwise. Without the presence of Boris their apartment was hauntingly quiet and empty.

The Depths Of Raya's Despair

ON THE SUNDAY morning following Borya's move to live with Maxim and Natasha, Leah excused herself and left the apartment early. An hour later, Borya arrived for a visit with his mother. He didn't even inquire where Leah was and avoided making any comment about his sister.

Raya had prepared his favourite dishes and planned the entire day for them. She had investigated what movies were playing at the nearby theatre and made a booking at the bowling alley. She wanted this day to be as pleasant and memorable as possible for her son. Raya hoped that perhaps some of these shared new experiences would help overcome the unhappy memories that Borya associated with life in her apartment.

But sad to say it didn't turn out as Raya intended.

"Mom, I'm not hungry right now," Borya said as soon as he arrived and noticed the table setting. "I had a humongous breakfast of homemade fries, salad and chicken cutlets. Can I go to see the boys? I'll be back soon, okay?"

"As you wish, Borya," Raya answered meekly. Her pancakes apparently paled in comparison with Natasha's hearty meal.

Borya finally returned around four o'clock in the afternoon. They had a hasty meal together, avoided talking about anything sensitive, and then he left. The visit left Raya feeling even more lonely and despondent than before.

On Wednesday of the following week there was a call from Borya who asked, "Mom, you're not celebrating Christmas, are you?"

"Borya, you know better than to ask a question like that."

"Yeah, sure. But dad organized some parties and some outings during the holidays and we're planning to go skiing right after New Year's. So that means I'll be seeing you again right after the holidays, if that's okay with you."

"Borya, you have two whole weeks of holidays from school! Aren't you going to show up here at all to see me?"

"Well, Mom, Natasha's friends have a cottage not far from Toronto and they've invited us there for a few days. I'll try to come and see you after we get back. Please don't be angry with me. And say hello to Leah. I don't hate her, actually. I just said that when I was angry. Anyway, I'll see you soon. If I don't talk to you before then, have a happy New Year's, Mom."

Boris eventually did make an appearance to see his mother again on the second Sunday of January. That visit was essentially a replication of the previous one. After her son had left, Raya sat alone in her apartment and cried bitterly.

With the winter skiing season in full swing, Raya saw her son quite sporadically. Boris seemed to be happy, assuring her that school was going fine, that his relationship with his father and Natasha was good, and that he had made friends with some of the boys in his new neighbourhood.

If everything in Boris' life was going *fine,* then why was Raya's heart aching? She was feeling increasingly apprehensive as though some unexpected disaster was about to happen. But was it truly female intuition, or merely a manifestation of a mother's shattered nerves? Raya was unable to come to grips with her feeling of foreboding, and it continued to linger and haunt her.

Leah was still ignoring her brother and refusing to see her father. The adjustment was not easy for her, either at home or at her new school. Bais Yaakov was a school where Orthodox Jews were sending their daughters. All of her new classmates were living in kosher homes, observing Shabbat scrupulously, going to synagogue every Saturday morning, and were surrounded by religious-minded parents, relatives and friends. In every respect they were living *Yiddisher kite* – a Jewish life.

Leah found herself co-existing in two very different worlds. In school she was learning Jewish traditions, while at home she was living with her mother who didn't care to light the Shabbat candles or to go to synagogue, and who saw no merit in adopting kosher food rules.

Raya considered herself to be an atheist and saw no reason to change her viewpoint. In fact, she had decided that religion was one of the contributing factors in turning Maxim against her. After all, he had started attending church on the Sunday immediately after that ill-fated attempt at a Shabbat family dinner. And it was there at the church that he had met Natasha, or so Raya assumed.

In spite of the religious factor, Raya and Leah actually became closer as mother and daughter during that difficult winter. Leah started to come home earlier after school and was doing her homework at home instead of with her classmates. Raya enjoyed helping her with her studies, especially when it came to mathematics and science.

They liked to go for long walks in the neighbourhood park and to spend Sundays together (excluding those occasional Sundays when Boris was visiting). They chatted openly about everything except religion.

The stubborn and persistent Leah even managed to manipulate quite a few dietary concessions from her mother. Raya stopped buying pork and pork products. Kosher products were quite expensive, but knowing how important it was for Leah, Raya was always on the lookout for kosher items and trying to buy them whenever they were on sale.

Eventually Raya acceded and bought Leah her own set of dishes (just a couple of plates, some utensils, two pots and two pans); a grateful Leah koshered them properly and after that began to cook some kosher meals for herself.

Occasionally Leah stayed at home on Saturdays, but more often than not she was spending Shabbat with her school friends and their families.

One of Raya's greatest ongoing concerns was money, or rather lack of it. She soon realized that on her modest salary she couldn't afford to pay the rent for the apartment and still properly support Leah and herself. She considered moving to a smaller, less expensive flat but couldn't bring herself to do that. What if Borya changed his mind and decide to return home? Raya wanted Borya to know that he would have his own room and to feel that he was always welcome in the unlikely event that he really did come back to live with her and Leah.

Raya called several of her former clients and resumed cleaning houses on Saturdays to earn a bit of extra money. And so, on Saturday mornings when the festively-attired Jews were walking to synagogue, Raya was passing them on the street in her coveralls, heading off to start her working day at the home of one client or another.

One day in March, Leah arrived home looking radiant and announced that on the upcoming Saturday she would be having her Bat-Mitzvah. There were several girls that had finished their Bat-Mitzvah instructional classes with Leah and there was going to be some special ceremony in the synagogue, after which there would be a special lunch sponsored by the parents of the other girls.

"Mom," Leah pleaded, "please, please come and join us for the celebration!"

For countless years afterwards, Raya felt ashamed that she'd missed Leah's Bat-Mitzvah, but on that day she was fearful of losing a regular client and unwilling to forfeit the fifty dollars that she needed so badly. And so, with regrets, she had said *"no"* to her daughter.

Raya poured her heart out to Miriam in her letters and in some ways that seemed to help her to cope. The letters coming back from Israel and the brief, long-distance Sunday phone conversations helped keep Raya afloat.

"The difference between my situation as it was in Kiev and here in Toronto is that now I can't allow myself to be depressed," Raya wrote. *"Leah needs me; she has nobody else in this country except me. Well, that's not exactly true; she does have a lot of friends, but a mother is a mother, right? She suffers a lot - I can see it and I can feel it. She misses Borya and Maxim but she refuses to compromise her attitude towards her father and her brother as a matter of principle. She reminds me of you, Miriam! You were just as stubborn at her age.*

"But Maxim and Borya are not her enemies! Honestly, I can't understand Maxim. He never calls here. I know that he's preoccupied with his new family and that he's angry with Leah for not visiting him, but can't he at least make an effort to talk to her? Why should I have to fight his battle? Assuming he

still wants to see his daughter, then he has to find the right approach and take the initiative, don't you think?

"*I know that I have to be strong for Leah's sake, but it's so difficult, Miriam, so very difficult!*"

"*Raya, you were never a quitter, you'll make it,*" Miriam was constantly encouraging her in her own letters and whenever they spoke on the phone.

The work at the lab continued to be tedious and disappointing. Soon after her separation from Maxim, Raya went to the HR Department and changed her last name. Now, instead of Dr. Raisa Sokolova, she was to be known simply as Raisa Kushnir. Nobody bothered to ask her what happened to her hard-earned title of *Doctor,* and in any event Raya wasn't even sure if anyone but Pamela was even aware of her professional designation.

Pamela, who had seemed so sweet and had smiled so nicely during the job interview, was, as it turned out, a petty and narrow-minded bureaucrat. She was a good organizer and from outward appearances it seemed that the team was performing well; but from what Raya could see the project was not going well at all. Even as the project deadline was rapidly approaching, the same experiments were being performed again and again, sometimes with only slight variations, and always with the same inconclusive results.

As far as Raya was concerned, Pamela didn't possess any of the three critical qualities which Raya deemed essential for a bona fide scientist: an analytical mind, a broad vision, and an innate ability to be humble and self-critical at times.

Raya cautiously broached her concerns to a young biochemist, Shelly, a co-worker who also reported to Pamela.

"Pamela did quite a good job when she was working closely with our Director, Dr. Griffin. Apparently he felt confident that she could lead this project on her own, so he went to our branch in the States and won't be back for a couple of more months. Pamela still has weekly conference calls with him but I have no idea what she's reporting," Shelly was saying. "What I can't understand," she added ruefully, "is why Pamela was doing so well when Dr. Griffin was here but is struggling so much now on her own."

Raya intuitively knew the answer. There are some people who are excellent followers and capable of performing exceedingly well when someone else is leading them and providing ongoing direction; but those same individuals are out of their depth when it comes strategizing and leading others. Raya had already concluded that Pamela was just such a person, but she kept her counsel and didn't share her observations or feelings with Shelly or anyone else in the office. After all, she was only a lab technician and Pamela was reminding her of her place almost daily. Several times Raya had tried to initiate a discussion about some scientific aspect related to the project with Pamela to no avail. Pamela merely instructed her to focus solely on her own direct responsibilities.

"Shelly," Raya asked, "am I permitted to read through the project documents?"

"Definitely, Raya. After all, you're part of the team. However, there are a lot of technical terms in those documents, so I'm not sure if you would understand all the biochemical terminology," Shelly advised her innocently.

"I'll give it my best try," Raya said, and she reflected, *Pamela never told anybody about my background. Maybe she just doesn't believe me. The time has come for me to prove to that woman that I can do more than clean test tubes around this place.*

And so, in the evenings while Leah was doing her homework, Raya was carefully reviewing all the project documentation. She analyzed the theory and the assumptions on which the project was based; then she scrutinized all the documented experiments and the respective results to date. Raya also went to the library to obtain some highly technical reference texts on the subject matter, after which she reviewed all the documents again for a second time, all the while looking for possible shortcomings or outright scientific errors.

A week later, Raya suddenly realized that one of the key assumptions inherent in the foundation for the project was fatally flawed. It wouldn't have mattered what parameters Pamela might have changed or how she might stage the next experiment. Raya was now confident in her belief that it wasn't going to work. For the time being, however, she kept her findings to herself while she considered a possible solution.

It took Raya two more weeks of studying and researching the subject matter to establish a viable alternative approach. During this intensive time, she encouraged Leah to spend Shabbat with her friends. Leah, who loved those outings, was overjoyed.

Raya stayed late after work one Friday and discreetly staged some experiments on her own. On Saturday morning she cancelled her cleaning appointment scheduled for that day and spent the entire day working on her own in the lab. She had become totally preoccupied with validating a breakthrough solution and was thinking about little else. Every evening after Leah went to bed, Raya would spend long hours into the night researching technical books, making calculations, trying and then rejecting certain assumptions. Finally, late one evening some days later, she struck upon the solution she was looking for.

Raya was ecstatic! She neatly documented all her findings, organizing the material logically as she was used to doing back at her lab in Kiev, and then scheduled an appointment to meet with Pamela. Raya was immensely proud of her work. It would literally save the project and it would prove to Pamela once and for all that she, Raya, was in fact a highly capable scientist. This was going to be the career breakthrough that she had been looking for.

In Pamela's office, Raya began by summarizing her findings; she handed over a thick file with all of her documentation, and then proceeded to start outlining the details.

Pamela interrupted her almost immediately. "Thank you so much for your efforts, Raya. It's great to see a lab tech taking the initiative and trying to work on advanced biochemistry. I appreciate all of your efforts. Of course I'm not sure you quite grasp what we're working on here, but I will certainly take a careful look at this next time I have a free moment." Pamela paused – she could detect that Raya was crestfallen.

"Raya," she continued, "I want you to understand something very clearly. We are at a critical stage of a very difficult project. There are a number of experienced scientists working on our project, and quite frankly we aren't in any position to entertain another opinion or to make any drastic, ill-conceived detours from our well-thought-out plan. However, as I said, I will definitely take a look. Was there something else you wanted to speak to me about?"

"No, ma'am," Raya replied disconsolately. She was too disappointed and upset to even become angry. She was almost out of Pamela's office when she was stopped short.

"Raya," Pamela said crisply, "I'm sorry to have to point this out, but you were not hired to advise me what to do, rather to do exactly what I tell you to do. Is that understood?"

"Yes, ma'am."

Pamela picked up the file so carefully prepared by Raya and shoved it randomly into the middle of a large stack of papers on her desk. She hoped that she had made it abundantly clear to Raya that her advices were not welcome and that those alleged findings and recommendations of hers were not going to see the light of day.

"By the way, when did you do all of this documentation? During working hours?" Pamela asked, with transparently feigned innocence. Raya could now see through the false pretense behind her innocuous smile. Why were these Canadians always in the habit of smiling when they didn't mean it in the slightest?

"No, ma'am. I was doing it entirely on my own time," Raya replied.

"Okay, then go and get back to your own job now," Pamela instructed her condescendingly.

"Yes, ma'am."

As soon as Raya left the office, Pamela retrieved the file. She was furious. *Who does she think she is*, Pamela fumed, *to sneak behind my back and do her own research? It was a big mistake to hire her in the first place.*

Pamela decided that she must have been dealing with a fraud and a pretender from the moment Raya accepted the position. After all, there was no possibility that a legitimate scientist, particularly a specialist with a PhD degree in biochemistry, would ever consent to work as a simple lab-technician in the first place.

But the budget of the project had been tight and that woman had agreed to work for an exceedingly low salary. So Pamela had risked hiring Raya against her better judgement. When she made that lowball salary offer she had expected at least some attempt at negotiation, yet

Raya had agreed immediately without hesitation. Dr. Sokolova indeed! As a matter of fact, Pamela was vaguely familiar with that name. Dr. Griffin had mentioned it to her at one time and had recommended one of Dr. Sokolova's articles for her reading.

If the esteemed Dr. Sokolova had indeed come to Canada, the major biochemistry companies would have been fighting for the privilege to hire her. What's more, not long after she was hired, that woman had gone to the HR department and inexplicably changed her last name. How convenient! No, this was not the *real* Dr. Sokolova!

Pamela thought for a moment that she should've fired Raya right then and there. But now, the three-month employment probation period was past, so terminating her would require a little finesse. Still, it shouldn't be that difficult to arrange, Pamela concluded.

All the same, she was still tempted to open the file and glance through it. What if there was something of actual merit in Raya's report? The project was proving to be much more challenging than Pamela had anticipated and the completion deadline was looming.

Pamela was already frustrated and well on the way to feeling desperate about the status of her landmark project. Why was it that all of her experiments failed to produce a substantive breakthrough or even any vestige of the expected results? She was rigidly following the protocol established by Dr. Griffin and had executed all procedures correctly, strictly by the book, yet she couldn't get past first base, as it were. How could this be?

Pamela tentatively opened the file cover, but then she promptly stopped and admonished herself. She was a *cum laude* graduate of the best Canadian Universities; she had earned her Bachelor's degree at Waterloo University and her Master's degree at the University of Toronto. How could she possibly consider wasting any of her valuable time to undertake even a cursory examination of the document of that immigrant with a dubious education and more than dubious credentials? It would just distract her and lead her off in a wrong direction.

Pamela tore off the first page and then shredded it into tiny pieces. She continued to tear apart page after page of Raya's document and strangely enough, was feeling greater and greater relief and satisfaction with each successive mutilated page. It was only after the last page was in shreds and discarded in the waste basket that Pamela got a grip on her emotions and calmed down again. Now that that was over and done with she could refocus and concentrate on the task at hand.

But the burning question ultimately remained. Why couldn't she get any satisfactory results? Was her prized project doomed to imminent failure?

When Raya returned to her own workplace her hands were shaking uncontrollably. At that moment she understood what a terrible mistake she had made in the first place by accepting Pamela's insulting job offer. She had recently learned that prospective employers usually didn't read beyond the most recent position on the applicant's resume. So if she didn't want to be a lab-technician forever, it seemed she couldn't have this mundane work experience listed on her resume. But that would mean that she had no references to cite and still no Canadian experience to speak of. Besides, regardless of how much Raya detested Pamela and her job and how much she wanted to quit, she was obliged to accept the reality that she wasn't in any position to simply walk away; she still had to provide for herself and for Leah.

The next Sunday during her weekly call to Israel, Raya related the disastrous incident with Pamela to Miriam and David.

Miriam immediately responded, "Raya, please move to Israel and be done with it. You'll work in a senior position befitting your expertise here. There's no doubt about it."

"Are you kidding? Without Borya? I can't," Raya replied with considerable frustration and anguish in her voice. "Besides, there's a provision in our separation agreement that I won't take the kids out of Ontario until they're eighteen. I can only take them for vacation and even then, for no more than thirty days at a time. I haven't actually signed the agreement yet, but anyway, I'm hardly in a position to do anything that drastic right now."

"Raya," David contemplated aloud, "I hope Borya will come to his senses soon. In any case, be careful what you sign. You should wait until Maxim is happily married and has the child. Then he may be more amenable to the prospect of your moving to Israel with both of the children."

"I'm not so sure. And besides, Leah has a lot of friends here in Canada now. She's finally settled. I'd hate to put her through another disruptive immigration," a reluctant Raya responded. "In any case, I won't be moving anywhere without Borya."

The separation agreement papers, ready for execution, had arrived from Maxim's lawyer in mid-February. Raya's first inclination was to sign and return them as soon as possible, but then she read the provisions more carefully and decided to consult with someone whom she could trust.

She called Inna and was relieved to hear her cheerful voice and astute words of advice. "Finally you're getting smarter, Raya. Don't sign anything until you talk to a good lawyer. There's a recent immigrant I know who just passed his Canadian bar exam. He's a very nice, intelligent man and right now he needs the experience more than the money. Actually, I think he's from Kiev too. Let me give him a call. He wouldn't charge you for the first consultation. After that we'll figure something out."

"I'm glad that you've decided to meet with me," Alex Katz said at the onset of his first meeting with Raya. "Stop thinking like a Soviet woman and start thinking as a Canadian citizen who has legal rights.

"The divorce provisions where we came from typically stipulated some monetary compensation for the children but left the custody issues mostly up to the parents to work out for themselves. Some fathers chose to actively participate in their children's lives, while others rarely saw their children after their divorce was finalized. Believe me, I know.

"Here in Canada your separation and divorce documents are binding agreements that aren't so easy to change once they have been certified by the courts. The justice system works entirely differently here.

"I see that your husband asked for custody of your son and is granting you custody of your daughter; plus there would be mutual visitation rights.

"Have you considered the possibility that your son, who is a minor and isn't even fourteen years old yet, might change his mind and decide he wants to return to live with you after all? That can't happen – as it stands now, it would be a violation of this legal agreement; only if you sign it, of course. You would have to start a fresh custody battle and you can be sure that this would cost you much more than my fee, whether you were successful or not.

"Here's another problem. You said that your daughter doesn't want to see her father. If you sign the agreement as currently written, she'd have to visit him every two weeks until she's of legal age as an adult, assuming he wants to see her. If she chooses to continue ignoring her father and avoids meeting him, it might very well be you who could be deemed in violation of the agreement for supposedly interfering with his visitation rights. You're not in any position to sign these papers, Raya, until you resolve these issues regarding your children.

"Furthermore, there is no provision whatsoever for support of Leah or for you - no alimony, no medical or dental benefits, no insurance – no nothing. This is totally unacceptable."

"I want nothing from him," Raya countered.

"What about your daughter? You're not being noble; quite frankly, you're being irresponsible if you think that way. Please leave these papers with me and I'll see what I can do to improve the terms, not just for your own sake, but especially for the sake of your children."

"But Maxim's girlfriend is pregnant and he wants to marry her before the baby is born," Raya objected.

"And why is that any of your concern, Raya? Think about your own children and their future. Surely that is your highest priority, is it not? "

The draft agreement was left with the lawyer and Maxim was informed there would be a delay while the terms were negotiated. He protested vigorously, tried to put pressure on Raya, and then tried to cajole her, but he always received the same response. *"It's out of my hands, Maxim. We have to wait until my lawyer contacts your lawyer and they come to some reasonable resolution that we both can live with."*

By the end of March, Boris' mood was not as upbeat as before. He didn't seem inclined to meet up with his old friends any more, and so Raya finally had the opportunity to spend some worthwhile time with her son when he came for a visit. They went to the movies and to the bowling alley, just as Raya had planned three months ago. Leah obstinately still chose not to participate in any of those activities with her mother and her brother.

The very next Sunday, Boris arrived with his school-books in hand and asked for Raya's help with a couple of minor questions. As it turned out, they ended up studying together for the entire day. Despite Boris' assurances that he was doing well in school, Raya was anything but convinced. On Monday, she called to his school and made an appointment to see the principal.

When Raya arrived at the school on Wednesday of that week, there were several teachers along with the principal waiting for her in his office. The news about Boris was much worse than Raya had suspected.

"Your son has missed more than half of his classes. He didn't turn in any of his essays and he skipped all his term tests. It seems he was not feeling well for almost the entire winter. We have notes from home to that affect. Was he always a sickly child?"

Startled by this revelation, Raya said, "Boris is a very healthy boy. I'm not aware of any illnesses that he might have had over this past winter. In fact, every time I saw him he was looking quite healthy.

"You see, he lives with his father now. We're separated. I should've had better control, but Boris and his father assured me that he was doing well here at the school. However, last weekend my son asked me for help with his homework. His questions were all over the place, so that's why I decided I should check on his progress. Have you informed his father of Boris' poor attendance and his unsatisfactory grades?"

"We called his father and spoke with him a week ago. He came to the school with a young lady whom he introduced as his wife."

"Technically, that's not so, at least not yet. But who was signing all those absence notes?"

"Mrs. Sokolov," the principal replied, all the while looking at Raya with an expression indicating both scepticism and concern.

"Can Boris still pass this year? Please be honest with me," Raya pleaded. "I need to know how far behind he is."

The teachers looked hesitantly at one-another and then directed their attention to Raya. The meeting that ensued for some while longer was distressing and painful for all concerned.

Raya decided it was best to wait until Boris' next visit to confront him about his school situation. This was not a telephone conversation, she concluded. Meanwhile, she saw no point in raising the matter of Boris' schooling and his dreadful grades with Maxim. He would most likely stonewall her and nothing helpful would be accomplished.

The serious talk with Boris took place sooner than Raya had anticipated. Thursday evening, just a day after her meeting with the school authorities, she came home and encountered a shouting match in progress between brother and sister. In a somewhat perverse way it actually made Raya quite happy. At least Leah was communicating with Boris instead of ignoring him altogether. But what on earth was he doing in her apartment on a Thursday evening?

Boris was clearly agitated. "How did I know that the stupid plate was kosher and meant only for milk? I was hungry and there was a piece of chicken in the fridge so I took it! Stop making such a big deal out of it."

"Mom!" Leah exclaimed when Raya entered, "look what this traitor did!"

"Okay, guys, chill out," Raya said with a smile. "Borya, I'm very happy to see you but what are you doing here in the middle of the week?"

Leah demonstratively pointed at the large back-pack and the school-bag standing in the corner but offered no comment.

"You decided to move back! Oh, sweetheart! I'm so happy!"

"But tell her to stop calling me a traitor," Boris grumbled.

"Traitor," Leah said, trying to sound menacing.

"You see? I just came home and she started a fight right away!"

"Traitor," Leah repeated, but Raya noticed that her eyes were shining and she was actually brimming with happiness over the unexpected return of her brother.

"Okay, you two! Come and kiss each other. That's enough squabbling; let's celebrate instead."

Boris and Leah stared intently at one-another and then Boris ran towards his sister and embraced her tightly, lifting her feet off the floor and swirling her around several times.

"Traitor, traitor," Leah kept saying, but by now she was giggling and kissing her brother exuberantly.

While Borya was unpacking his bag, mother and daughter were preparing a meal. Finally, the reunited family sat down together for the first time in a long while.

"Borya, have you washed your hands?" Raya asked, more or less automatically.

"It's Ben!" Brother and sister both responded simultaneously.

"Mom, really! You call her Leah, so why do insist on calling me Borya? All my friends call me Ben now."

"Okay, okay, I'll try to stick to Ben," Raya promised. "It seems that only your father and I still retain our original names.

"Not really," Ben smiled. "Natasha calls dad *Max* and sometimes *Maxick*.

"No!" Raya exclaimed. "He had always hated to be called Max!"

"Maxick!" Leah chuckled and then asked, "okay, Ben, what made you change your mind all of a sudden and move back home with us? You seemed to be quite happy living with dad and Natasha."

"She's stupid!" Ben declared. "Well, in the beginning everything was swell. Dad made a grand speech right after I moved in. *"You have to be responsible and you have to do well in school, blah, blah, blah."*

"Ben," Raya interjected, "let's at least be respectful!"

"Yeah? Well, I wish *he* would be respectful! Anyway, dad warned me that he had to work long hours because he was responsible for two families now and that he still had to help support my mother and my sister."

I wonder, Raya thought bitterly, *did he say that before or after he told me that he wouldn't be helping us?* She didn't share this question with Ben or Leah.

"Natasha was a great cook and always making huge, delicious meals," Ben continued. "She tried to be nice and sweet with me in the beginning, but that didn't last for long. It sort of got to me how she was always fawning over dad. As soon as he came home from work, there was always a dinner on the table and she was treating him like a king. Honestly, 'his majesty' was looking like the cat that swallowed the canary. So I started to make some comments."

Raya refrained from saying anything in response to that revelation. She looked aside and then rose from her chair and carried some of the dirty dishes into the kitchen.

"Okay, we got your point," Leah hissed. "I wouldn't have lasted there a single day! But you – you sold your mother for a bowl of soup!"

"Oh, come on!" Borya retorted defensively. "That's not true."

Raya returned to the dining room with their dessert and took her seat again.

"Well anyway," Ben continued on a different note, "the school was stupid. It's even worse than the one I was going to here. And the boys were so stupid! They were all one year younger than me because we started school at age of seven and they started when they were six. I was bored out of my mind there. Then I had a fight with three of the boys from my class. It was so stupid! Anyway, I ended up with a black eye but they were in far worse shape than me!"

"Borya! I mean Ben!" Raya exclaimed. "How many times have I told you not to get into a fight? Why did you get into a squabble with those boys?"

"They tried to tease me," Ben replied without elaborating.

"Anyway, I didn't feel like showing up at school with a black eye so Natasha gave me a note. Besides, it was almost Christmas-time, so the school term was nearly over."

Ben pressed on with his story. "After the holidays I went back to school for a little while but I couldn't stand it. I already knew all the stuff they were learning in math and science, but I couldn't understand half of the things the teachers were talking about in history and social science classes. All I knew was that they were talking about some native Indians. And I had nobody I wanted to hang around with either, so I told Natasha that I had a cold and she gave me another note. Her signature was so primitive that I didn't have to ask her for notes any more after that."

"Ben, are you telling me that you were writing all those notes yourself and forging her signature?" Raya was aghast.

"Uh-huh," Ben mumbled sheepishly. "But it's not like she didn't know! I wasn't ever doing any homework; I was spending most of the time in the evening watching TV instead. Natasha loves TV too, especially those shows where the audience is laughing and clapping in the background and all those stupid game shows. So we even started to fight over using the TV."

"But what were you doing in the daytime, Ben?" Raya wanted to know.

"On the days when Natasha was working, I would leave the apartment, walk for a bit and then come back home. I went to the library a few times but they didn't have any books in Russian and it was hard for me to read in English. Sometimes I went downtown and hung around the Eaton Centre mall with a couple of other guys," Ben added casually.

"Then we started to fight more and more...Natasha and me. Not even fight, just constantly bicker about this and that. And another thing – Natasha and dad were always smooching and that was getting on my nerves too. You know, like I wasn't even there with them! They were all over each other, kissing and hugging and all that stupid stuff."

"Ugh!" Leah exclaimed. "How disgusting is that?"

Ben ignored Leah's remark and carried on. "What really annoyed me the most was how she was always putting *you* down, Mom. Like, she would say, "*Oh, you poor boys, go ahead and eat these cabbage rolls... I bet you never had such good cabbage rolls before.*"

"Whenever we went skiing with dad, Natasha would sit in the lodge and wait for us with a warm lunch and a thermos of hot coffee. That's fine, but then she would say, "*I want you to be warm and comfortable. I have a dry change of clothes for you. I just love taking care of both of you.*" And dad would reply, "*Nobody ever treated me like you, my dearest.*" It would be okay maybe for one weekend, but they repeated the same stupid routine every time we went skiing!

"So, one day I told her to stop it. I told her that we've had perfectly good cabbage rolls before and that we were used to taking a thermos of tea or coffee with us on all our outings. And I said that dad wasn't exactly starving and he wasn't mistreated or anything like that at home either before the two of them met. Natasha went into a sulk and didn't talk to me for days after that.

"Another irritating thing was that she was yakking on the phone for hours at a time, although she would usually hang up whenever I showed up. One day I came into the room and heard her saying, *"You wouldn't believe what she used to do!"* Then she saw me standing there and shut up. So I asked her what it was that *she* used to do. Natasha didn't answer that one. Anyway, we were always having these petty quarrels when dad wasn't at home, so he didn't know... unless of course she told him," Ben added before changing the subject.

"Two weeks ago, the principal asked dad to come to the school, and after their meeting dad was furious with me. He shouted that I had betrayed his trust and that he had had a better opinion of my maturity, blah, blah, blah. Then he started to yell at Natasha, saying that she was supposed to supervise me while he was working long hours trying to provide for their family. She started to cry; then he started to apologize and it was a big mess! The next day after dad went to work, Natasha claimed that I did it all on purpose to submarine her. She stopped talking to me after that and what's more, didn't let me to come close to the TV any more either. It was all so stupid!

"Then this morning dad asked me if I was doing any better in school. I told him that I had missed too much and needed lots of help. What else could I say?

"Natasha informed me that they had no spare money for a tutor, so I told her that if she spent less money on shopping they could afford to hire one for me. Then she said, in that annoying sarcastic way of hers, that it made absolutely no sense to hire a tutor since my mother was supposed to be a highly-educated scientist.

"Oh boy, it became really ugly after that comment! She claimed that my mother couldn't possibly have the brains of a scientist if I was so stupid that I needed a tutor. And she also said that if you were a real scientist, Mom, you would be working in that position, not just as a lab-technician, unless of course you were deliberately staying in that low-level job just for the purpose of getting a higher support payment from dad.

"After all those stupid comments I told her she was the one that was stupid and that you would be working as the head of a laboratory in a year or two, but she would be cutting salami in her stupid deli store forever. Then I told her that she wasn't even capable of reading the book that you wrote.

"Everybody was screaming - dad, Natasha, and me. Finally dad shouted that I had to apologize before Natasha; that she was going to be my step-mother and the mother of his child, so I was obliged to respect her. So I said that *you* are the mother of two of his children; that *you* were his wife for more than fourteen years; and that *he's* the one that needs to apologize for allowing his floozy to talk about you disrespectfully and put you down. Anyway, bottom line, I had no choice other than to leave after all that," Ben concluded. "It was all too much and I'd had more than enough of all that stupid stuff."

Raya didn't offer any comment whatsoever concerning Ben's long and winding story and instead just asked him to get re-settled at home. She retreated to her room to lie down on the bed and digest everything that she had heard. In spite of it all, she couldn't juxtapose the Maxim in Ben's story with the husband with whom she had lived for fourteen years, or with the young man who many years ago had professed his undying love to her on the shores of the Volga.

Okay, he didn't love her anymore; Raya had come to terms with that. But the children! How could he trust a stranger, a woman who never had any children of her own, to supervise Ben? Did he really believe that an adolescent boy of thirteen years of age was actually mature enough to be independent and responsible? Especially when it came to Ben who had habitually tried to dodge his homework! And what about Leah? Why wasn't he making the slightest attempt to re-establish some relationship with her?

The phone rang as if on cue. Raya knew who it was before she even picked up the receiver.

"Is Ben at home with you?" Maxim asked. His manner was gruff and direct.

"Yes, Maxim, he's here."

"His behaviour this morning was despicable. You can tell him for me that he's not welcome back in my house until he apologizes to Natasha."

"Maxim, do you really believe that I would do that? He's back in his proper home now and this is where he's going to stay. Frankly, I'm much more concerned about his situation at school than about his relationship with your girlfriend. And if you still want to be part of

Ben and Leah's lives, you'll have to work it out yourself from now on. I have no intention of intervening one way or the other."

"Oh yes you will!" Maxim replied angrily. "I will not pay a single cent of support for a girl who refuses to see me or for a boy who is dishonest and disrespectful and behaves outrageously!"

"It's your choice, Maxim," Raya responded in a tone of voice tinged with frustration and anger. Then she hung up the phone so as to terminate the hurtful exchange with him.

I wonder if all divorces are this ugly, Raya mused, and then her thoughts reverted to her more pressing problems with Ben.

She remembered herself as the ten-year-old girl who considered school, the teachers, and the other children to be dull and stupid. But that girl had a wise Aleksander to counsel her. Ben had nobody else to turn to but her alone, his mother. Raya understood his issues very well. He was too bright and impatient for a regular school curriculum. If he knew the subject matter, he was bored; and if he didn't, then he wasn't interested in the slightest.

In Kiev everything had been quite different. Ben was a part of the ingrained system and he knew very well the minimum that was required from him in order not to fail in school. He at least put in this minimal amount of effort and otherwise focussed on what was most important to him — his soccer and his friends.

Here in Canada everything was totally foreign to him. He didn't fit in well in the public school system or in a private Jewish school. Raya was determined to find some other solution, realizing that otherwise her son would probably become a drop-out statistic and more than likely get into some serious trouble. But the first step was to transfer him back to the local school and hope to help him enough to salvage this academic year. There were still two-and-a-half months before the end of the school year. Would it be enough time for Ben to make a miraculous recovery?

The very next day after Ben's return, Raya requested a day off from her work and with Ben in toe they went to re-register him in the neighbourhood school. She discussed the problem with the principal and his teachers at length and together they formulated a plan. Ben was informed in no uncertain terms that he would have to work very hard, and quite likely through the summer too, if he hoped to be advanced to the next grade.

"Mom, I promise I will work hard," Ben told her after the meeting with the school authorities. "I don't want to be in a class with kids two years younger than me. I'll do my best but you have to help me too, okay?"

Raya promised that she would.

Perhaps for the first time in her life, her own work ceased being of greatest importance to her. Raya was still going to the lab every day and performing her job adequately, but afterwards she was hurrying home to work with Ben in the evenings. She ceased concerning herself with the ongoing problems of the project and didn't even worry about Pamela's increasingly obvious disdain for her.

At the lab, her co-worker Shelly would sometimes ask her a question related to biochemistry and Raya would provide an intelligent and comprehensive answer. Despite her low-level job ranking, Raya's superior skills and technical knowledge could hardly go unnoticed for very long by the other members of the team.

One time, an agitated Pamela summoned her to the office and demanded that Raya stop answering Shelly's questions.

Raya stared at Pamela in disbelief and calmly responded, "Pamela, I don't volunteer. But if any of the staff asks me something related to work, then I'll answer to the best of my knowledge and ability as a good team player. I may be just a lab-technician around here but I'm not an idiot. Is there anything else?"

Raya returned to her desk after that daring outburst and once again contemplated that she really ought to start looking for a new job. But not right now, she concluded, because she had to help Ben as much as possible. *As soon as the school year is over, I will definitely start looking,* Raya vowed to herself. Pamela and her petty objections were forgotten and as Raya was washing the laboratory dishes, she focussed on just one concern: *How can I make sure that Ben manages to pass this school year?*

One day in May, Raya ran into Rita near the elevator and the hairdresser asked why Raya wasn't coming to see her any longer.

"I've meant to," Raya apologized, "but I never seem to have time. Besides," she added, "I have nobody to impress with my hairstyle anymore."

"Nonsense! A good hairdo will cheer you up. You have to do it for yourself, not for anybody else. I'll be waiting for you tomorrow at seven PM. I'll make you look absolutely gorgeous," Rita promised.

"That'll be the day," Raya chuckled, but she agreed to show up for the appointment nonetheless.

When Raya entered Rita's apartment at the appointed time, there were already three other women sitting in the room.

One woman with nicely-styled dark hair was finished and waiting for her blonde friend, who was sitting in Rita's chair and having her own hair styled. A third woman, with her hair dyed and wrapped in a towel, was patiently sitting on a sofa and leafing through a magazine.

The brunette looked at Raya and curiously asked, "So, that handsome husband of yours finally left you, did he?"

"I beg your pardon? I'm not sure that we've met before. How would you know anything about my husband and my personal affairs?" Raya asked, feeling affronted.

"Honey, just chill. We're a tight little bunch here and everybody knows everything about everyone else in this building," the woman replied, laughing heartily.

"Well, I don't," Raya shot back crisply, taking up a magazine to indicate that the brief conversation was over.

"It's too bad for you. If you weren't so high and mighty with your attitude, then people would have told you last September that your husband was already fooling around and cheating on you."

"Last July, actually," her blonde friend chimed in from Rita's chair. "Do you remember when we saw him at Kensington Market with that willowy blonde? He was so lovey-dovey with her. Did he leave you for that chic?" the blonde asked Raya unabashedly.

Incredulous, Raya forgot about her indignation and replied in a controlled voice, "I've never seen his girlfriend, so I wouldn't even know what she looks like."

"Then let me tell you," the brunette volunteered, all the while staring critically at Raya. "Much younger than you; no more than thirty. Not as tall as you but with a great figure and *much* slimmer. Long, platinum-blonde, straight hair. Cute button nose too. In a word, she was definitely attractive and incredibly sexy."

"I get the idea. Compared to her, I'm an old, unattractive, overweight hag with a beak for a nose," Raya responded sullenly.

"Raya, cut it out," Rita interjected. "You have a very interesting, even exotic appearance, so don't put yourself down."

"It's not the looks," the blonde declared. "It's the immigration. It changes everything: values, priorities, relationships. Do you think your case is unique? You wouldn't believe how many divorces there have been in our community... including mine.

"We met this nice couple in Italy and spent all our time together. We even came to Canada on the same flight. Two months later, my husband moved in with my 'Italian' girlfriend and left me to look after our nine-year-old daughter by myself."

"How about you, Rita?" the brunette inquired. "I've never seen your hubby around here."

"That's because I left my loser husband back in Leningrad and emigrated with my two boys and my brother's family," Rita explained.

"Why do you call him a loser?" the blonde asked, looking at Rita with obvious curiosity.

"Vodka," was the cryptic reply. That, actually, explained a lot.

"Men have to be kept on a short leash – a very short and tight leash. How come your husband was gallivanting downtown every Sunday and you didn't do something about it?" the brunette asked Raya.

"I always trusted him. Marriage has to be built on mutual trust and respect, don't you think so?" Raya advocated.

"Absolutely not! I monitor my husband's every move. Even today I gave him a list of errands to do and then told him to wait for me. Right now he's sitting outside of the building, patiently waiting," the brunette replied self-confidently.

"Hey," Rita joked, "do you know what they call a woman who always knows where her husband is?.. A widow!"

Raya joined the other ladies in laughter that served to release much of the tension in the room.

"At least each of you has somebody to blame for your troubles, ladies. I have only myself to blame," the woman with the dyed hair joined the conversation. "I was a dentist in Riga. Here, I'm a nobody. I emigrated with my husband and two kids. He started to look for some job while I went to clean houses."

"Familiar story," Raya sighed.

"One of those houses belonged to a very handsome man. He worked quite close to his house, so he'd come home during the lunch-time while I was cleaning. We started to talk. Before long he was telling me how much he admired me and how much he liked me."

"How long did it take before you spread your legs?" the brunette crudely inquired.

"Not too long." The woman paused and sighed. "But my biggest mistake was to take the guy seriously. I started to compare. On the one hand, I had a husband who wasn't capable of finding a job and was always whining, "*Canada's a country with a cold climate and colder people... Canadians are stupid and primitive... Nobody appreciates or understands me here...*", and on, and on, and on. From another side I had a dashing, confident, romantic lover. So, one day I said to my husband that I didn't love him anymore and that I was in love with someone else. Then I told my lover that I'd left my husband for him and was ready to start a new life together with him."

"What bravery!" the blonde exclaimed.

"Such stupidity!" the brunette expounded.

"Let me guess," Rita laughed wryly. "After that revelation you lost your lover and that place of employment, right?"

"I lost much more than that!" the woman said despairingly. "My husband took my children and moved in with his mother. My mother-in-law doesn't let my children take the phone when I call, and she's told them such things about me that now they refuse to even see me. I lost my husband and my children, all at the same time. And for what?" Her lips started to tremble.

"So what are you doing now?" Raya asked in a hushed voice.

The woman regained her composure and explained, "I enrolled in college. I'm studying in the daytime to become a dental hygienist and I work as a waitress in the evenings. I live in a small room in the basement of a house and I'm still calling my husband daily, asking him for forgiveness."

The room fell silent and everyone except the brunette looked at the woman with empathy. The brunette said nothing but callously stared at that poor woman with unsympathetic, ill-disguised amusement.

Evidently the woman with the dyed hair suddenly became embarrassed that in a moment of weakness she had bared her soul before strangers and she buried her face behind a newspaper.

Those revelations, which she heard quite by chance from the other women during that visit to Rita, in some way helped Raya come to grips with her own troubles. If that poor, naive woman with the dyed hair had found the strength to start college and keep going, then surely she had no excuse to remain depressed, Raya decided. She had her children and that was the most important thing.

Raya still thought a lot about Maxim and about his betrayal and double life during the past summer. However, she was no longer harbouring any anger towards him. It was time to move on.

The duly revised separation agreement and then the divorce papers were signed by the middle of May. The weekend after, Leah and Ben went downtown together for a visit with their father.

After the children had left for the day, Raya felt restless and forlorn. She tried to study some scientific papers and then to work on the translation of her book, but she couldn't seem to concentrate. So she quickly dressed and left the apartment. For the first time since arriving in Toronto, Raya went for a walk on her own - not running for work or rushing off to do some errand; just for a solitary, unhurried stroll.

She made her way south along Bathurst Street and soon reached the grounds of a large cemetery on the west side of the street. No, Raya decided, that's not what she needed in her present mood and she promptly crossed to the other side. It wasn't much of an improvement, she concluded. That side of the street was lined with drab, low-rise residential buildings, and modest, unappealing storefronts.

With a sense of nostalgia, Raya thought of cheerful and beautiful Kiev, where she knew each street, each park and every public square. She could still feel that sense of an intimate relationship with her home city. She thought fondly of the ostentatious Khreschatik and the many roads leading to that vibrant main street of the city.

It certainly wouldn't win any awards in the *Architectural Digest*, but the street had its own undeniable charm and vitality. It was almost a given during her strolls on Khreschatik that Raya would meet up with some friends. It had even been much the same whenever she went for a walk during her short sojourn in Rome. On the other hand, it was virtually a given that she wouldn't meet any acquaintances on the street here.

This Toronto... the city was still such an enigma to Raya. Sure, she had been in the downtown on a few occasions, and had even gone to the O'Keefe Center once with Leah to see some performance. Yet she didn't sense the pulse of the city, didn't feel its soul, and didn't understand its people. *This has to change*, Raya mused. *This is my city now and the least I can do is to explore it properly and try to understand its character. It's time for me to start living in the present again.*

After a leisurely, two-hour stroll, Raya returned home. She quickly prepared a simple meal for herself and began to idly browse the current issue of a scientific magazine that she had picked up at the office. But her mind was not focussed in the slightest on the latest discoveries in biochemistry; her thoughts remained fixated on her children. She sincerely hoped that they would have a good day and that Leah would somehow reconcile with her father. Even so, Raya had difficulty suppressing what she knew was an unwarranted jealousy towards Maxim and of his day with the children all to himself.

As it happened, Raya had nothing to be jealous about. The get-together between Maxim and the children didn't go as smoothly as everyone was hoping. Maxim showed up with Natasha at his side and her very presence started the visit off on a distinctly sour note.

They had agreed to meet in a Druxy's deli in the downtown. Leah and Ben arrived first and Leah was visibly anxious and excited. She had missed her father more than she was prepared to acknowledge, although at the same time she still felt resentful. She wanted to finally tell him how much he had hurt her; to let all that pain and anger out; and maybe then, she hoped, she would be able to face him and talk with him once again as daughter to father.

But when Leah spotted Natasha accompanying her father, her desire for a frank talk and reconciliation immediately dissipated. She didn't even get up from her seat to greet Maxim. Instead she said,

"Hello, Papa," in a chilly tone of voice, as she stared at Natasha with obvious loathing.

Maxim, taken aback by Leah's demonstratively cool greeting, managed to say, "Hello children. I'm very happy to see both of you. Leah, please meet Natasha, my soon-to-be-wife."

Natasha smiled in a friendly fashion and said, "Hello Ben; Leah. And Ben, I'm sorry for our last squabble. I didn't really mean the things I said. We've missed you."

"Yeah, I'm sorry too. I didn't mean all that stuff. But I like it at home and I'm doing much better in school now. Mom and I are working together every evening. I may have to study all summer too, but I think I'm going to pass. I hope so anyway."

Nobody said anything further for an awkward period of time after Ben's apology. Eventually the silence became oppressive and needed to be broken.

"I'm really glad to meet you, Leah. I've heard so much about you from your father. I do hope we can be good friends," Natasha finally said.

"Why?"

"Why what?" a frazzled Natasha asked.

"Why would I become friends with the woman who destroyed my family?" Leah's voice was calm and dispassionate.

"Leah, stop that!" Maxim interjected. "You're not old enough to understand and make judgements. Your mother and I had our problems long before I met Natasha."

"I know that. I'm not blind. But I'm also old enough to know that there are problems in every marriage, Papa. Usually it takes two, both a husband and wife, to resolve those problems together. But it's much harder when a third person interferes. And whether you want to admit it or not, for years you were happy most of the time when you were with mom!

Leah bravely continued with what she had to say. "Immigration is painfully difficult for everyone. At least half the residents of our apartment building are immigrants like us and everybody struggles at first. If it was not for *her*, you would still be at home where you should be with your own family!"

"That's not fair, Leah," Natasha said, seeking earnestly to reason with the emotionally charged girl. "When I met your father he was deeply unhappy and…"

"And you took it upon yourself to make him happy, is that it? Why would you ever think that my father's happiness was any of your responsibility? Didn't he tell you that he was a married man with a family?"

"We love each other!" Natasha exclaimed, as if that line of reasoning was going to mollify an angry and bitter teenage daughter.

"Oh well then, I suppose that makes all the difference," Leah said sarcastically. "And because of that big love you've decided to come here today and provide moral support to daddy, is that it? Haven't you considered that I've not seen my father for almost half-a-year? Didn't you even consider that I should become friends again with my own father first, before even thinking to offer me your friendship?"

"Leah, that's quite enough!" Maxim admonished his enraged daughter. "Have some compassion! Look at Natasha's condition! You're talking to the soon-to-be mother of my future child!"

"And you're talking to your *living* daughter! Apparently that future child of yours is more important to you than your existing children! That's it; I'm going home.

"Ben, are you coming with me or staying?" Leah asked impatiently as she got up from her seat and turned towards the exit.

"Leah, wait. Please sit down," Natasha said in deflated voice. "I will leave now so you children can be alone with your father. I hope the next time we meet you will be more accepting.

"I'll see you later on at home, Maxim."

"Will you be okay?" Maxim asked in a concerned tone of voice.

"Yes, of course. Don't worry." Natasha moved closer to Maxim with the apparent intent of giving him a parting kiss but then she glanced in Leah's direction and hastily walked out of the restaurant.

"After Natasha was gone, we had our own time with dad," Ben was saying, after relating to his mother the essentials of the brief morning encounter with Natasha.

The children had arrived home somewhat sooner than expected and Raya was extremely relieved to see them.

"So, how did it go on your own with your father?" she asked.

"Well, at first Leah was screaming at dad, then he was screaming at her, and then we left because everyone in the deli was staring at us. We went to the park where Leah and dad yelled at each other some more. But eventually they were both done with their shouting, and after that they hugged and cried on each other's shoulder. After everybody had calmed down we had a good lunch in Swiss Chalet, and then went to the movies," Ben concluded.

"Are you hungry now?" Raya inquired.

"Yeah, Mom, the lunch was ages ago," Ben replied.

"Mom, can I go to see Orit after dinner?" Leah asked.

"Who is Orit?" Raya wondered. "Is she a new girl in your school? I don't think I've heard you mention that name before."

"No, Mom, she's been in our class since the beginning of the school year. But she likes being alone, doesn't have any other friends, and usually looks downcast," Leah explained. "We tried to involve her in some activities but she declined and the teachers told us to just leave her alone. Anyway, she's on my bus and always keeping her nose in a book. A couple of weeks ago, I sat next to her and we started to talk. She's actually a very sweet girl when you get to know her, but outwardly very withdrawn and sad."

"Why's that?" Ben wanted to know.

"Not sure. She doesn't like to talk much about herself. All she said was that she lives alone with her father and that her aunt lives here in our building."

"Who's her aunt?" the ever-curious Ben inquired.

"I have no idea, Ben."

"So, Mom, can I go for a visit?"

"Yes of course, Leah. You did right to talk to her. It sounds like that girl is badly in need of some compassion from a friend."

"Maybe her mother found her one-and-only true love and disappeared," Ben speculated with a touch of sarcasm.

"It's not our business, Ben," Raya admonished, "but the social studies homework due tomorrow *is* our business."

The Birthday Party

THIS YEAR'S BIRTHDAYS for Raya and the children were fast approaching. Ben was going to be turning fourteen and Leah would be thirteen, while Raya herself would be thirty-nine on June 22nd. She decided to put all of her problems aside and plan a nice celebration that they could enjoy together as a family. June 22nd in 1975 conveniently fell on a Sunday, so Raya told the children that she would take them to see Niagara Falls and they'd spend the entire day sightseeing there.

"I'll clear the day with your father in advance," she informed them. "The school year will finally be over and Ben's getting passing grades on most of his subjects now. And with your excellent marks, Leah, we'll have lots of reasons for our celebration, including your upcoming birthdays, as well as my own."

Ben and Leah looked at each other, not quite knowing what to say until Leah spoke up and asked, "Mom, can we do it on some other Sunday please? We're both busy on the twenty-second."

"What's so important that you can't spend the day with your mother on her own birthday?" a disappointed Raya asked.

"Dad's wedding," Ben replied sheepishly.

"Your father's getting married on the twenty-second? Did he choose the day of my birthday specifically to humiliate me or does he simply not care that he's going to hurt me again?" a dismayed Raya cried out.

"Mom, please don't take it personally," Ben said, hoping to reason with his mother. "Natasha is due soon and she wants to get married

318

before her baby is born. I really don't see what difference it makes, but she has 'a bee in her bonnet' about that."

Ben momentarily felt proud of himself. Did his mother or his sister notice that he had actually invoked a Canadian colloquial expression? But they both looked gloomy and downcast, so he pressed on. "Their priest happened to be available on that day. We can always go to Niagara on a different weekend, if that would be okay with you, Mom."

She should have been thinking about this before sleeping with a married man! Raya was tempted to say. But then she looked at the concerned faces of her children and hastily said, "I'm sorry, kids. I didn't know about your father's plans until now and it's not fair to put you in the middle. You go to your father's wedding and we'll go to Niagara another time."

"Thanks, Mom, you're the best!" Leah smiled and the matter was settled.

Several hours later, Rita called. "Raya, what are you doing on the twenty-second?"

"Being miserable, I expect," was Raya's disconsolate response.

"My goodness, aren't *we* cheerful today. Why such a dire prediction?" Rita inquired.

"My dear ex-husband is getting married on that day and the children will be going to his wedding. That day just happens to be my thirty-ninth birthday," Raya explained.

"Your *ex* is really being Mr. Sensitive, that's for sure," Rita commented. "However, coincidentally I'm celebrating my birthday on the same weekend. I was born on June 20th, 1935. It's going to be my fortieth birthday. I'm making a small party on Sunday evening and I'd like to invite you to join us," Rita said.

"Thank you very much, Rita. That's very kind of you but I don't think so. It's your party and you shouldn't have to share the occasion with anybody else. Besides, I wouldn't feel comfortable because I don't know any of your friends," Raya politely declined.

"You know *me*, Raya, and what's more, it's wrong to be alone on your birthday. Here's the deal: if you aren't in my apartment by seven,

I'll come down with several of my guests and we'll drag you out!" Rita mockingly threatened with a chuckle.

"Okay, okay. I'll come then," Raya promised. She was somewhat bemused by Rita's insistence but grateful all the same. Anything would be better than to be sitting at home alone during her own birthday and on the very day of Maxim's wedding.

On the appointed Sunday morning, the children got dressed early in their festive clothes, kissed their mother and wished her a happy birthday, and then they left the apartment. Raya kept herself occupied during the daytime with household chores of cooking and cleaning. Just before seven o'clock that evening, she quickly changed her dress, brushed her hair, retrieved the modest gift she had purchased for Rita, and headed for the door.

At the very last moment, she glanced at her image in the mirror and was not at all pleased with what she observed - a severe brown dress whose shape and colour made her look dull and matronly, way beyond her thirty-nine years. Her face was looking much too pale too. The only good thing about her appearance was that Raya had had little appetite ever since her separation from Maxim and had lost twenty or twenty-five pounds. *At least I am looking stately again*, she reflected.

Raya resolutely returned to her closet and scrutinized her limited wardrobe. Eventually she selected an attractive black dress with finely-woven white trim. It was the dress that Maxim had bought for her birthday two years ago...her last birthday in Kiev. That was the day when they had met Dr. Jones and the subject of emigrating to Canada had been raised by Maxim for the very first time.

Raya changed into the black dress and played with her hair for the next five minutes. She applied light make-up under her eyes and a touch of lipstick. Then she took another look in the mirror. *Much better*, she thought.

The party was already in full swing by the time Raya arrived. Rita's living room, kitchen, and even the hallway were crowded with guests.

To Raya's mild surprise, she noticed the three ladies whom she had met at Rita's during her hairdressing session a couple months prior. The brunette was tightly grasping onto the hand of a gentleman, apparently her husband, who was struggling to get to the bar to get a drink. *Still on a short leash,* Raya mused.

The blonde was standing nearby with a Canadian gentleman who was looking around at the exuberant Russian-speaking crowd with wide eyes. The blonde introduced her companion to Raya. "I'd like you to meet my new boyfriend. We've been dating for a month already. Please speak with him in English; everyone else is speaking only in Russian and he feels quite lost amongst our crowd."

Raya acquiesced and engaged in some small talk with the man who seemed like quite a decent chap.

The third acquaintance from Rita's salon, the woman with the dyed-hair, had come to the party with a middle-aged man who had a receding hairline and a visible pouch of a belly. This man didn't exactly have a movie star appearance, but the lady was holding his hand fondly and glowing with apparent happiness. She introduced her escort to Raya. "My husband," and then confidentially whispered, "he forgave me!"

The husband seemed to be as happy and relieved as his wife with their reconciliation and Raya responded with genuine warmth, "I'm so happy for both of you."

There were numerous toasts proffered by Rita's guests: to Rita's health and happiness; praise for Rita's kindness; compliments about Rita's hair-dressing skills…The numerous toasts continued one after another for quite a while.

Then Rita rose and proposed a toast of her own. "There's one more birthday-girl here with us this evening. I invite you all to drink to my good friend and neighbour, Raya."

Raya was embarrassed and grateful at the same time; it was heart-warming that at least somebody cared.

By the time the lengthy round of toasts was over and done with, Raya felt that the party was getting rather raucous. The noise was beginning to get to her. Dinner was being served buffet-style in the living room and the majority of the guests were crowded around the table, chatting rather loudly and partaking of the abundant amount of food. Raya noticed, however, that the balcony was presently unoccupied and decided that this was an ideal opportunity to get a bit of fresh air and a little respite from the din of conversation within the apartment. She stepped out onto the balcony and looked down absently at the busy street below.

For some inexplicable reason Raya started to think about her work, and about Pamela and their latest unpleasant encounter on the previous Friday. *"Raya, if you were more organized and neat, I expect that our project would be more successful,"* Pamela had been saying in an accusatory tone.

Now it's my fault that the project is a failure, a bemused Raya had thought at that time, although she had politely responded, *"Yes, ma'am, I'll try harder, ma'am."*

Raya thought about her own research and the documentation she had worked so hard to prepare. Of course she had taken the precaution of making a duplicate copy before presenting the originals to her boss. Not that she was expecting such an adverse reaction from Pamela, but because it was second nature to an experienced and well-organized scientist to retain a second copy of all source documents. *What should I do with them now? Will they ever see the light of the day? Why am I still keeping all that paperwork?*

Raya was deeply engrossed in her thoughts when she heard a jovial *"Happy Birthday!"* greeting. She turned and standing there before her was a gentleman who was holding two glasses of red wine.

He offered Raya one of the glasses and introduced himself. "Joseph."

"Raya," she smiled gratefully as she accepted the glass of wine.

She casually assessed his outward appearance without being too conspicuous about it and liked what she saw. He wasn't overly tall; rather, he seemed to be about the same height as her. *I wouldn't be able to wear high heels on a date with him*, Raya thought, and then inwardly smiled. *Where did that silly idea come from?*

The gentleman was dressed in freshly-pressed dark slacks and a light, button-down shirt, open at the neck. He was neatly groomed and clean-shaven. He projected the distinct impression of being a professional who was accustomed to dressing impeccably for work.

Joseph appeared to be in his early forties and his facial features bore all the hallmarks that identified him as a Jew: dark, curly hair; long, pointed nose; and large, dark-brown, soulful and sad-looking eyes.

"I hope you don't mind my interrupting your solitude," Joseph ventured.

"Oh no, not at all, Joseph. I was just thinking about my job. It didn't turn out to be what I was expecting," Raya was saying.

"It must be a bit difficult for you to celebrate your own birthday at someone else's party," Joseph commented carefully. "Do you have any family here in Canada?"

"My two teenage children – a son and a daughter," Raya responded.

"And being typical teenagers, I take it they didn't feel inclined to spend the evening with their mother," Joseph guessed.

"Well actually, it's not that. They're really great kids. It's just... they had to attend their father's wedding today," Raya explained, trying all the while to sound as casual as possible.

"I'm sorry, Raya." Joseph said simply, and then he promptly changed the subject. "You said you were thinking about your work out here on the balcony. What's your line of work, if I may ask?"

"Here or there? In Kiev I was a Doctor of Science, specializing in biochemical research; here I'm working as a lab-technician. From what I can tell," Raya nodded toward the room, "the majority of people here this evening have had to step down a notch or two after their immigration."

"That's quite true, but not many women as young as you have earned a doctorate degree. That's quite an accomplishment," Joseph said with admiration.

"It doesn't mean anything here, Joseph. My boss thinks that the Soviet Union is a backwater country and Kazan University, from where I graduated, provides only a dubious quality of education," Raya responded dryly.

"Raya, you shouldn't judge everyone on the basis of one ignoramus. I know how difficult it is to get to a level of employment as we were used to in the Soviet Union, but all we can do is continue trying and one day each of us will succeed," Joseph said in a manner that led Raya to believe that he was trying to convince not just her but himself too.

"Well, Joseph, I suppose you're right about that and it's something worth keeping in mind. So what's your occupation?"

"I'm a doctor, a gastroenterologist by specialization. Or rather, I *was* a doctor. I've already passed my medical exams here in Canada, but I haven't been able to get an internship appointment so far. I have another interview tomorrow, so please wish me luck."

"Good luck, Joseph! Which hospital are you trying to get into?"

"My interview is all the way to Oshawa, which would be quite a long daily commute, but I don't mind provided they'll accept me," Joseph said wistfully.

"Maybe you'll move there, at least temporarily. Would your wife object to your moving?" Raya asked, keeping up the conversation.

"My daughter's attending a Hebrew school here and I'm not going to disrupt her education. Sadly, my wife passed away almost two years ago," Joseph explained.

He was looking directly at Raya as he spoke and she could detect enormous suffering and loneliness in his eyes.

There was a brief pause in the conversation and then Raya sympathetically said, "I'm so sorry, Joseph."

"Thank you, Raya. It was very difficult in the beginning but we're doing fine now, my daughter and me." Joseph was silent for a moment and then offered a suggestion. "Raya, I'm not really in the mood for such a loud party. Would you like to go for a walk?"

"I'd love to," Raya responded without any hesitation.

They left the apartment unnoticed by the rest of the party crowd, other than Rita who glanced in their direction, and upon seeing them walking out together, smiled to herself and nodded her head in satisfaction and approval.

The evening was warm and the slight breeze made the weather perfect for a casual stroll. Joseph and Raya headed towards the nearby park.

"What was the subject of your dissertation?" Joseph wanted to know.

"Enzymes," Raya replied.

"Ah, so you're the creator of those products that cause people to have expensive urine," Joseph attempted to joke.

Inadvertently he had hit upon Raya's hot button. "At least we're doing less harm than all you doctors with your antibiotics and steroids," she replied a bit curtly.

"Just a second, dear lady. Tuberculosis was not defeated with enzymes," Joseph pointed out in defence of modern medicine.

"I'm not talking about tuberculosis, Joseph. Don't take it personally but I'm talking about all those doctors who perpetually prescribe antibiotics when raspberry jam and a mustard plaster would suffice. Why don't they just give every new mother a large pail of Amoxicillin and be done with it?" was Raya's passionate retort.

Joseph had no comeback for that, or if he did, he didn't say so.

For the next several minutes Raya continued to lecture Joseph on the benefits of natural enzymes and vitamins and the frequent harm to the human body caused by strong medications.

Joseph meekly attempted to respond in defense of his professional training but then he started to laugh. "Raya, my congratulations! We've just had our first disagreement!"

Raya cut short her commentary and joined Joseph in laughter. "I'm so sorry," she said, "my brother's a doctor too and we always have these debates. I miss my brother and our friendly little fights."

"I do understand, Raya. So where's your brother living now?" Joseph asked.

"He lives in Israel. He's married to my sister and I miss them both terribly."

"You mean, your sister-in-law," Joseph corrected.

"No, Manya, or I should say Miriam, is much more to me than just a sister-in-law by marriage. She's my true blood sister."

Joseph looked at Raya with a bemused, puzzled expression.

Raya hadn't felt so much at ease in a very long while, perhaps not since her last meeting with David and Miriam in Rome. It seemed as though she'd known this kind man for years; there wasn't the typical wall of caution in their interaction as one might expect on a first date... not that their chance meeting was really a date.

So Raya told Joseph all about meeting Miriam (Manya at that time) in Kiev in 1941; about their escape from Babi Yar and their life together with Uncle Misha and later on with Aleksander; and about their eventual reunion with their parents. Joseph was an excellent listener and quite fascinated by Raya's compelling saga. She also told him about David and Miriam's young love and eventual marriage, about her own seven attempts to become a university student, and how her first encounter with Maxim had come about in Kazan.

They eventually concluded their leisurely stroll in the park and made their way back to the apartment building. Instead of rejoining the party, however, they sat down on a bench near the entrance and continued their dialogue.

Now it was Joseph's turn to tell Raya how he, with his sister and his mother, had escaped from Leningrad before the German blockade. He related how they had lived in Samarkand and how, when they were eventually able to return to Leningrad, they learned that their uncles and aunts and cousins had all perished from hunger during the blockade.

"In spite of this tragedy, I did have a happy childhood after the war," Joseph related. "My father returned from the war alive and unharmed, thank G-d. He was a doctor and my mother was a teacher of music. We had a cheerful family life and maybe that's why Rita's always has such an optimistic and joyful outlook on life."

"So Rita's your sister? I didn't realize that. You don't look at all alike," Raya remarked

"You're quite right about that. We certainly don't look alike but Rita truly is my one and only sister. We're really close. She's been a great source of support to me during these past three years," Joseph added.

"I like Rita very much," Raya said. "She's a wonderful woman and a great hairstylist too, as every one of her clients will attest."

"Except for the fact that she was a civil engineer back home, she's not doing too badly here," Joseph commented.

"What's your daughter's name?" Raya then asked.

"Svetlana."

"How is she managing?"

"It was bad for her at first after her mother passed away, really bad. She shut out all of her friends from her life. She even insisted on changing her school so she could be among strangers. I was against it but she was adamant. I believe she felt very much pained by the fact that all her friends still had their mothers. That was certainly difficult for her to cope with.

This year she started at a new school but even there she was not doing very well at the beginning. It's only recently that Svetlana has started to communicate more with other children her own age and she's even managed to make one good friend."

Raya noticed her children approaching the apartment building and Leah addressed them both. "Hello, Mom. Hello, Dr. Feldman."

"Hi, kids. How do you know Dr. Feldman, Leah?" a surprised Raya asked.

"Mom," Leah replied, "he's Orit's father! She's my new friend that I told you about."

"Dr. Feldman, this is my brother Ben," Leah said while looking back and forth between her mother and the father of her friend with open curiosity.

"Hello, Dr. Feldman," Ben said politely, although he looked tired and somewhat dejected.

"I didn't make the connection," Raya said. "I'm confused, Joseph. Leah said her friend's name is Orit. But you said that your daughter's name is Svetlana."

"Orit means *light* in Hebrew, the same as Svetlana," Joseph clarified.

"Now that's a familiar story! Joseph, please meet Lena and Borya, aka Leah and Ben.

"Well, we'd better be going. The children look tired. It was very nice meeting you, Joseph."

"Likewise, and thank you for the conversation, Raya."

"And Leah, I'm very glad to know that Orit has such a nice friend as you. Good night."

After saying goodbye to Joseph, Raya and the children entered their building. When they were in the elevator Raya took the opportunity to ask the children, "So how was the wedding?"

"It was okay, I guess," Leah replied laconically.

"Dad got married," Ben said matter-of-factly. "Natasha was looking huge and silly in her white dress. And by the way, Mom, we didn't have a good time thanks to *Miss Ice Princess* here. She was constantly glaring at everybody with looks of disapproval."

"I was not!" Leah objected.

"Oh yeah? I thought that the priest was going to choke during the ceremony!" Ben exclaimed.

"Mom, I think Dr. Feldman likes you," Leah said, deliberately changing the subject.

"Oh, never mind about that, Leah. We happened to meet at Rita's birthday party and we went out to have a bit of fresh air, that's all," Raya explained, lightly brushing off Leah's remark.

That night, Raya found herself lying awake and thinking about Maxim and his wedding night with his oh-so-pregnant new wife. She tried to visualize his face, but when she closed her eyes all that she could see instead was the vision of Joseph's kind face.

Good Fortune Smiles On Raya

T HE NEXT DAY in the laboratory, Pamela was in a murderous mood. Raya had never seen her quite like that before. She was hissing at the employees and asking for reports that nobody had heard of before now. She demanded the documentation concerning the most recent series of experiments, and when Shelly tried to explain that it had not been prepared yet, Pamela started to scream at the young woman. The words *ignorant, stupid, sloppy and clumsy*, amongst others, were uttered in a loud voice and heard by the entire team.

A devastated Shelly began to cry uncontrollably.

That was too much for Raya and she accosted Pamela in a firm voice, "Don't try to push your project failures onto somebody else's shoulders!"

It was so unusual and out-of-character for Raya to speak up assertively, that the entire team immediately fell silent, and then everyone cautiously edged their way closer to the center of the confrontation to observe the impeding cat-fight.

"How dare you! What do you know about science, never mind this project?" Pamela exclaimed in a voice seething with anger. "I've had more than enough of your meddling in my project. I will be reporting your insubordination to HR, along with the fact that you are deliberately and maliciously sabotaging this project by giving unsolicited and ill-informed advices to other members of the team.

"If you performed your direct responsibilities diligently and we had clean equipment to work with and a well-organized working space, there's no doubt we would be in a much better position! You leave me no choice, Raya. I will discuss your performance and unacceptable behaviour with HR and then they can deal with you. As far as I'm concerned, your days on this project, and for that matter in this company, are over."

At this point, Raya threw caution to the wind - she had nothing to lose any longer. "You do that!! But before you have me fired, I'm going to explain something to you about your project and about the science."

"I don't want to listen to you and I don't need to listen to you. You had better return to your own tasks immediately, since for the moment at least, you're still on our payroll!" Pamela instructed.

"Oh yes, you will listen to me." This was not the meek lab-technician speaking any longer; rather, it was Dr. Raisa Sokolova, the renowned scientist and head of a well-regarded research laboratory in Kiev.

Raya went directly to the blackboard and wrote out in concise terms the key failing in Pamela's theory. Then, in a confident and authoritative manner, she proceeded to outline how the fundamental problem could be resolved and thus how the project could be reoriented towards success. By the time Raya was done, the entire board was crammed with notes and formulae. All the while Pamela stood rigidly with her arms folded, her face a deathly ashen white.

Raya then turned to face Pamela and said sternly, "My professor always taught me that the most important quality of a good scientist is constant self-examination and self-criticism. You're way too self-assured and arrogant to be a legitimate scientist. When I was the Head of Research at my laboratory in Kiev, I didn't allow incompetents like you anywhere near serious research experiments."

"Shelly, erase this rubbish from the board immediately!

"Raya, you will follow me. We're going to HR right this minute to deal with your intolerable, unprofessional behaviour once and for all." Pamela had completely lost control of her emotions and was screaming hysterically.

"Shelly, please don't touch that board." Everyone present heard the calm male voice which seemed to have come out of nowhere. It suddenly became deathly quiet in the laboratory and everyone looked towards the man who was now standing just inside the lab entrance.

"Dr. Griffin! Hello, and welcome back, sir. I'm so sorry for this incident. I hired this woman last December and I've had nothing but grief from her. That'll teach me never to hire Russians again," Pamela said in a feigned apology to her boss.

Without so much as acknowledging what she said or even looking in Pamela's direction, Dr. Jeremy Griffin spoke again, clearly and dispassionately. "Shelly, I want you to carefully copy down everything that is written on this board. Don't miss a thing."

"That won't be necessary," Raya said in a disconsolate voice. "I have it all documented."

Dr. Griffin turned and addressed Raya.

"I haven't caught your name?"

"Raya Kushnir."

"I've never heard anything about a biochemist by the name of Raya Kushnir and ours is a fairly narrow field. I pride myself on knowing about all of the leading biochemists. Have you ever published anything, Raya?"

"Yes, sir, I have." Raya's voice was very controlled by now. The passion was spent and she already regretted her outburst. "I was published extensively under the name of Dr. Raisa Sokolova."

"I've read every one of Dr. Sokolova's publications – all of them quite impressive, I might add. So why is it that you changed your name?"

"There's another Mrs. Sokolova now." And then, to her own surprise, Raya blurted out bitterly, "as of yesterday."

Somebody whistled under their breath.

"Pamela," Dr. Griffin asked, "didn't you know that this woman was the internationally known Dr. Raisa Sokolova from the Ukraine?"

"Jeremy, I haven't become familiar with everyone in our scientific community to the same extend as you," Pamela responded defensively. "I'm sorry I didn't recognize her name and verify her credentials, but sometimes things written in a resume are false. I was just trying to exercise normal due diligence, start her from an entry position and monitor her progress to see how things would work out. Unfortunately, Raya is not a team player and doesn't fit well with the rest of our group. That's what this is all about."

Dr. Griffin looked intently at the two warring women and then at the rest of the team before he said, "Pamela, Raisa, would both of you ladies please follow me to my office." Then he turned on his heel and strode out of the laboratory.

Pamela cast Raya a murderous glare and ran after her boss. Raya trailed slowly behind. Dr. Griffin opened his office door, beckoned Pamela to enter, and as Raya approached, he politely asked her to wait.

Raya took a seat on the chair outside Dr. Griffin's office, feeling deflated and very angry with herself. What had possessed her to open her big mouth? Did Shelly or anyone else ever try to defend *her* when Pamela was on the attack? Who really cared about her laborious research and ground-breaking findings that could salvage the project? Certainly not Pamela.

As she awaited the expected verdict from Dr. Griffin, it seemed to Raya at that moment that the only thing she had accomplished in the end was to get herself fired. *How will I put food on the table and pay the next month's rent?* Raya contemplated in a state of mounting desperation.

After what seemed like an eternity, the door to the office came ajar and Pamela emerged in tears. Without so much as glancing at Raya, she headed off in the direction of her own office.

Raya rose from her chair but Dr. Griffin smiled kindly and asked her to wait a bit longer. The wait was unbearable. Time seemed suspended. At long last, the Director opened the door of his office again and invited Raya to come in and close the door behind her.

"Raisa, I'm truly sorry that we had to be introduced under these unpleasant circumstances. I really could have used your talents on this project! It was my mistake to leave the office for so long and to trust Pamela entirely on her own. But let's talk about you. From what I understand, you were a manager in a large laboratory. How many people reported to you?"

"I managed over fifty, highly-qualified employees," Raya replied.

"In that case, you of all people should understand that the morale of the team, especially after today's unfortunate incident, is my utmost priority. Under the circumstances I simply can't permit you to remain on my team, as much as I would like to," the Director explained apologetically.

Raya was genuinely confused. She knew it would come to this and hadn't expected anything better. But why had he asked her to wait almost an hour? Just to apologize? *I'll never understand these Canadians,* Raya pondered, but she said, "I do apologize for today's incident, sir. My nerves were frayed after yesterday but I know that's not an excuse. With your permission, sir, I'll just go and pack up my things."

Raya started to get up from her chair but Dr. Griffin motioned her to take her seat again. "That's not necessary, Raisa. I've already spoken to Shelly and asked her to pack your belongings and bring them here for you. The reason I asked you to wait is twofold. First of all, if you would, please tell me more about the investigative research you've conducted with regard to this project."

"I wouldn't call it *research* as such, because I couldn't conduct enough meaningful experiments. But here's what I've determined," Raya calmly stated, and for the second time on the same day she outlined in detail her theory as to why a basic premise of the project was fatally flawed and her proposed solution.

There was a knock on the door and Shelly sheepishly entered. She placed the box with Raya's belongings on the floor and then looked regretfully in her direction before retreating from the office without speaking a word.

"Are the documents in that box?" Dr. Griffin asked. "May I see them?"

Raya retrieved the thick binder containing the backup copy of all her documents, handed it over to Dr. Griffin and sat down again.

Dr. Griffin scanned the documentation for some time and then said, "Raisa, you can't even imagine how much I need you now! But what's done is done. You did a lot of extremely fine work here, and as I understand it, you even did it all on your own time. As far as I'm concerned you've acted diligently and professionally as an independent consultant. I would like to award you five thousand dollars for this outstanding piece of work. Would that be satisfactory?"

An astonished Raya was speechless but nodded her head in acceptance of the wholly unexpected offer. The binder disappeared into Dr. Griffin's desk. Then he called down to the accounting office and had a brief conversation with a staff member of that department.

"They'll mail the check to you within a week. Now then, about the other reason you're here. I want to introduce you to the son of a good friend of mine, Dr. Peter Kolinsky. Peter is working in a company much smaller than ours, but he's quite a brilliant scientist and they're doing some innovative research in his laboratory. I've already spoken with him and he's waiting for you to come for an interview. He suggested meeting you at this restaurant."

Dr. Griffin handed Raya a slip of paper on which he had written the restaurant's name and address. He pressed on. "It's almost lunch-time and Peter is anxious to talk with you over lunch today. Here's a chit for a taxi. Please take it, since you have no time to wait for the bus. Good luck, Raisa. I'm sure you and Peter will get along just fine."

"Thank you so much for everything, Dr. Griffin. I really appreciate your help and your kindness. I'll do my best," a grateful Raya responded.

"You are most welcome, Raisa, and hopefully, when this incident is long-forgotten with the passage of time, I'll have an opportunity to hire you back again someday," Dr. Griffin said wistfully.

Raya's few personal belongings that Shelly had packed in one carton consisted of pictures of the children, a small plant, and her lunch-box. Dr. Griffin picked up the carton and they walked towards the building exit together. The taxi was already waiting outside. Raya turned to Dr. Griffin, smiled, and said, "It's too bad you didn't come back sooner, sir. I would have enjoyed working with you very much."

"So would I, Raisa, so would I. Good luck again," Dr. Griffin said as he opened the rear door of the taxi for her.

Raya felt numb. She had just been released, to put it delicately, from her first real job in Canada. Now she was already on her way for an interview with another company that she knew nothing about, although it was apparently held in high esteem by Dr. Griffin. Well, one way or the other she was unexpectedly five thousand dollars richer and that certainly lightened the burden of her financial worries, at least for the next little while.

Something was nagging at Raya in the back of her mind about the name of the man she was about to meet. It sounded all too familiar, although try as she might she couldn't place it. *I've heard this name before. Dr. Peter Kolinsky... Dr. Peter Kolinsky... Where have I heard it? I must have read some of his publications,* Raya finally decided.

Twenty minutes later she was entering a small, pleasant restaurant. She left her box of possessions at the coat-check booth and proceeded to the main dining lounge. Raya detected Dr. Kolinsky's presence right away. He was quite young, not more than thirty-five years old, she guessed. He was wearing a casual shirt and tweed jacket without a tie, khaki slacks, and he sported a full beard and a large mane of brown, curly hair. All in all he exhibited the classic look of a scientist or perhaps a university academic. He rose from his table and smiled. "Dr. Raisa Sokolova, I presume? Or should I call you Dr. Raisa Kushnir now?"

"It's Dr. Kushnir, but please call me Raisa." This was the second recent occasion when Raya had cause to re-iterate her new professional identity.

They took their seats and Raya immediately noticed the English language transcriptions of some of her old Russian scientific papers that had been laid out on the table.

"Raisa, please do call me Peter," Dr. Kolinsky said.

"Okay, thank you, Peter. It seems you have read some of my articles," Raya commented, pointing at the journals and the translation documents.

"Yes indeed, and I have several questions about them that I wanted to ask you about in person too, so this is an ideal opportunity if you don't mind," Peter replied with measured enthusiasm.

For the next half-hour they discussed not only Raya's articles but also her book and her laboratory work. It didn't feel like an interview... more like an engrossing academic discussion between equals. If Peter had harboured any doubt that he was talking to the actual author of those publications, any such doubts would have been quickly dispelled.

Then Peter began speaking about the projects he was responsible for and the research that his team was undertaking. He went on to describe in greater detail the main challenges of a specific project that had recently been initiated but didn't have an assigned project manager as yet.

Then it was Raya's turn to pose the questions. Meanwhile, the food was served but remained untouched as their highly focussed dialogue continued.

Finally, Peter came to the point. "Raisa, I would like to engage you as manager to lead this project. I have a tight budget and a non-negotiable deadline. Before you answer, I should forewarn you that there will be many long hours and an immense amount of pressure. That being said, will you accept this position with my company?"

"Oh yes, I certainly will, Peter, and I sincerely appreciate the opportunity. Thank you very much. Rest assured that I won't disappoint you. I'll do everything humanly possible to make certain this project is a success," a radiant Raya enthused.

"That's wonderful! Now, about your salary..." Peter slyly grinned and said, "I still haven't counted the toilets and I have no idea how many mirrors we have either!"

Raya blushed and then covered her face with her hands. She had never felt quite so embarrassed in all her life. Now she remembered very clearly how and when she had previously heard the name of Dr. Peter Kolinsky.

"Please don't remind me!" she blushed. "I'm so ashamed."

"There's nothing to be ashamed of, Raisa. The fault was all mine," Peter said soothingly. "After I hung up the phone that day, I realized what was going on but I felt too uncomfortable to call back. I certainly didn't want to cause you any embarrassment. But if a woman with your qualifications and experience was prepared to clean houses to support her family, I know that such a person is capable of making my project a resounding success."

Peter wrote a proposed salary number on the back of one of his business cards and showed it to Raya. She beamed with happiness and gratitude.

"I accept your generous offer, but please, Peter, let's not tell anybody else about that original phone conversation of ours."

"Okay, agreed! It'll be our little secret. If you're not busy now, I would like you to accompany me back to the office so I can introduce you to our team. Then I'll take you to our HR department so you can fill out all the usual employment paperwork," Peter suggested. "In that case you'll be able to start working tomorrow."

Soon after leaving the restaurant, Peter and Raya had made the short walk to his company headquarters and they went directly to his laboratory.

"Attention everyone, please. I have an important announcement to make," Peter said in a moderately raised voice so as to garner the attention of the staff. "I would like to introduce you to our new Project Manager, Dr. Raisa Kushnir."

Raya was introduced to so many people from the project and from other projects which also fell under Peter's jurisdiction, that she soon lost track of who was whom. But she smiled congenially as she exchanged greetings with each new staff member whom she met. Peter showed Raya to her new, tastefully-appointed office and then escorted her to the HR department where she spent the remainder of the afternoon filling out employment forms.

At five o'clock Raya rushed home. She was so excited that she could hardly wait to relate her good news to the children.

"Ben, Leah, I got a new job today, and a very nice one too! I'm a Project Manager in a biochemical lab. I was even addressed as Dr. Kushnir today! I'm going to be receiving a starting salary that's more than twice the money I was making before," Raya enthused.

"Hurrah! That means I can get a new pair of running shoes," Ben exclaimed.

"It means that you're a selfish brat," Leah snapped in jest as she rushed to embrace her mother. After all the kisses and hugs were done with, Leah ventured, "Mom, I do need some decent new summer clothes."

"Okay, kids! I almost forgot to mention the other great news. I've received a five thousand dollar bonus from my previous employer for that research work I was doing on my own time. As soon as the check arrives, I'm taking you both shopping," Raya promised jovially.

After dinner, the children left with Raya's blessing to see their friends. She was still feeling supercharged and wanted to talk with somebody to share her good fortune. It was too soon to call Israel; it would be the middle of the night there. So Raya called Rita but she was too busy with her clients to engage in a chat, and nobody picked up the phone at Inna's residence. Raya even thought about calling Maxim, but that would be decidedly inappropriate, she concluded.

Just then the phone rang and Raya quickly retrieved it.

"Hi, Raya, this is Joseph calling. We met yesterday. I hope you remember me."

"Of course I do, Joseph! And I have such wonderful news to tell you!" Raya gushed.

"I have some good news to report myself. Can you come by the Riva Bagels cafe on the south-west corner of Bathurst and Steeles?" Joseph asked.

"I can be there in half-an-hour," Raya agreed.

"Wonderful! See you there," Joseph affirmed.

Should I change? Raya thought about that and then reconsidered. *It's not a date, after all. He just wants a friendly ear, and so do I.*

Confessions

BEFORE LONG RAYA and Joseph were sitting in the café and drinking tea together.

Raya had already guessed Joseph's news - he received the internship he was seeking. Raya's news by comparison was a total surprise and Joseph's reaction was very gratifying.

"You didn't! You wouldn't! How could you?" he exclaimed at various points during her story. He laughed boisterously when Raya related the part about her first phone conversation with Peter and his sly remark when they met earlier this day.

Joseph picked up his cup of tea with a flourish and proffered a toast: "To the continued success and good fortune of Dr. Raisa Kushnir."

Raya raised her own cup and responded in turn: "To the long-lasting success of Dr. Joseph Feldman."

When the initial flurry of excitement had subsided, Joseph looked intently at Raya and said, "I can't even fathom how any man could leave such a woman as you, Raya. So smart, witty, exciting, and beautiful. And a devoted mother too."

"That's very kind of you to say those things, Joseph, but you don't know me well enough to render such a generous verdict," Raya responded modestly.

"Well, I saw you yesterday with your children and that was enough for me. I've no doubt you were also a devoted and loyal wife."

Something snapped in Raya's mind. Joseph's warm words had had a startling effect. She had felt on edge during the entire day and this unexpected praise caused her to say, "Joseph, I was never really such a good wife to Maxim. I married him impulsively because I was twenty-four at the time and I had never dated before. He swept me off my feet and he was the first man to propose to me. I always cared more about my education, my career, my children, and my friends than about him. To be totally frank I even cheated on my husband."

No sooner had Raya uttered those words than she regretted it, but it was already too late.

Joseph's face clouded and he guardedly said, "I don't think I need to know everything about your private life, Raisa."

"No, you don't, Joseph. But I have to tell somebody. Maybe I need to make a confession. Maybe today is my day for stupid outbursts, but I'll not be able to become as your friend unless I share with you the entire story," a resolute Raya replied.

Joseph kept silent to allow Raya to continue as she wished.

It took her less than fifteen minutes to relate to him about her struggles to receive an apartment and a promotion, about her seduction of Vasily, and about becoming his friend and lover in a relationship that had blossomed and lasted for more than three years.

Raya concluded her story. "Maxim never knew about Vasily and he left me for other reasons, but even-so, I always instinctively felt that I deserved that. He was always a caring father for our children and a good husband. I took him very much for granted and I never properly appreciated him when I had him.

"The man who saved my life many years ago once told me that the end never justifies the means. His son Aleksander proved it with his life. My sister Miriam understood those wise words and always led her life accordingly. It took me many more years to learn this lesson. I finally understood it, but only after it was too late."

Raya then got up quickly from her seat and implored her companion, "Joseph, please don't walk me back home. I just need to be alone right now. Goodbye." And with that she hastily made her way out of the café, leaving a bemused Joseph sitting alone at their table.

Raya walked for several minutes towards her apartment building and then abruptly stopped. *What's wrong with me today? I've met a decent man who wasn't looking for a relationship, just for a friend and some companionship, and I had to burden him with my stupid confession! As if he doesn't have enough problems of his own! When will I smarten up and learn to control my emotions and my tongue?* Raya admonished herself.

She had really liked Joseph and now it seemed that she had destroyed the possible opportunity for a genuine friendship. Raya began crying as she resumed her solitary walk back to the apartment, all the while thinking that she would never see this kind man again.

Raya endured a sleepless night, but bright and early the next morning, a resolute Dr. Raisa Kushnir walked into her new office for the very first time. Her new life with its new responsibilities and challenges had begun.

Raya devoted the entire morning to conversing with individual members of her team. She avoided calling them into her office; rather, she sat at the desk of each employee and had a brief, informal conversation about the state of the project from their viewpoint and how they understood each of their own roles. By lunchtime Raya felt confident that she could now match the names with the faces and she concluded that it was an impressive group. She joined two ladies from her team for lunch and mostly just listened politely to their light gossip.

After lunch, Raya undertook a detailed review of the project documentation. By the end of the day she felt that she had still not accomplished as much as she would have liked, so she took several binders of project papers home with her. She resumed her reading on the bus and was planning to continue with her familiarization of the documents all through the evening if necessary.

But right after supper, Joseph called, quite unexpectedly given the conclusion of yesterday's encounter in the cafe. "Raya, can we meet at the same café? Please come because I need to talk to you."

When Raya reached the café, Joseph was already there and waiting for her. Two cups of tea had just been served. She took a seat opposite of Joseph, not quite knowing what to expect.

"Raya," he began, "yesterday I listened to your story and I could tell how upset and confused you felt about it. If you'd told me this tale back in the Soviet Union, I would have just shrugged my shoulders and passed it off by saying you did what you had to do. The cards were stacked against you but you had enough brains and guts to outmanoeuvre the bastards. As far as your husband was concerned, I would have said that he should be happy to have had you as a wife for as long as he did. And that would have been the end of it."

Joseph paused and then carried on with what he was anxious to say. "Raya, I've changed a lot since I came to Canada. I'm looking at life quite differently now. Believe me, I can understand and appreciate your anxiety and I'm certainly not the one to judge you. But this evening I'm asking you to listen to my story and I hope you would not judge me too harshly."

Joseph looked earnestly at Raya for some sort of acknowledgement. She wasn't terribly anxious to listen to the story of Joseph's past transgressions, but he had patiently listened to her the previous day so what choice did she have? Raya remained silent and simply nodded her head, almost imperceptibly.

"I met Nelya when we were both at the Medical College. I was studying medicine and she was studying dentistry. I noticed her for the first time at a large party. She was surrounded by lots of guys, which was hardly surprising. Nelya was such a sweet, pretty, petite girl. I was one of those guys going out of their way to be noticed and it so-happened that it all worked out for me. In my case, what helped me was the endorsement of her parents. As far as they were concerned, I was a nice boy from a nice Jewish family, ideally suited for their daughter.

After I introduced Nelya to my own family, my parents fell in love with her too, and my sister became best friends with her in no time at all.

"We married after we finished our third year of college and our parents got together and bought us a condo. Raya, we had it very easy compared to most of our friends. I wasn't in a hurry to start a family. I wanted to establish myself as a doctor first and I presumed that Nelya wanted to concentrate on her dental career too.

"After college graduation, I started to work at the hospital. In those early years I was working long and crazy hours and spent quite a few nights there. As a young specialist I was scheduled for a lot of overnight shifts.

"Late one evening when things were unusually quiet and I was relaxing on a couch browsing a magazine, one of the nurses came into the doctors' sitting room. She was some years older than me but still very attractive. I'd heard that she was divorced but I didn't know much more than that about her. In any event, she sat down quite casually right beside me on the couch and promptly unbuttoned her blouse. Raya, I loved my wife and I wasn't looking for an affair, but then again, I didn't say *no*."

"You started to date her on the sly after that," Raya guessed.

"Actually, no I didn't. Let me explain. Not all of the nurses were like her and not all the doctors were like me. But there were several of us, young and stupid, who didn't mind having a little fun on the side and there was a female pool, shall we say, of available nurses.

We didn't date the nurses and had little concern about their lives or about their feelings, but whenever the opportunity presented itself, we would sleep with them. It was as simple as that. Most of those nurses were single and we consciously rationalized that we were actually doing them a favour. Those women had their needs and we were satisfying them. They certainly didn't complain. And if you'd heard us comparing notes in the doctors' room, I imagine you would have been mortified."

"For us," he continued, "those women were simply convenient sex objects, nothing more. If somebody had asked me at that time if I was cheating on my wife, I would have just said *no*. I had convinced myself that what I was doing wasn't actually cheating at all. I didn't date any of those girls and I didn't take any actual time or money away from my family. It was simply innocent and available entertainment, or so I thought.

"In the morning when I came home from a night shift, I would go straight into the shower to wash away the smell of the hospital, and the sex if that had happened, as it often did. When I emerged from the shower, Nelya was always waiting for me, ready with a hot cup of tea and a warm smile. There was never any suspicion on her part and never any questions. She loved me and she trusted me wholeheartedly.

"By the time she reached her thirtieth birthday, both of our families were starting to become concerned. We'd been married for a number of years and still had no children. So we decided that one child wouldn't be too disruptive to our careers or our lifestyle. Within a year after that we had our dear daughter, Svetlana.

"After the birth of our daughter," Joseph continued, "I realized that Nelya was a born mother and that she had wanted to be one for a long time. It wasn't that she was a bad dentist. It was just that her career no longer seemed as important to her as having her own family. I'm quite sure she would've been happy to have had more children, but I decided that one was enough and took the necessary precautions. She didn't voice any objections.

"Nelya was the most agreeable and complacent wife, that is until 1970. That was the year she became obsessed with the idea of emigration. She was talking about it incessantly. Her parents and my father were no longer alive by that time. But Nelya finally convinced my mother and Rita to emigrate from Russia, and that left me with little choice in the matter.

"Raya, we had a good life in Leningrad. We had enough connections to gain easy admittance to college, to have a good job, and to procure good food and nice clothes. We never actually suffered from anti-Semitism like many other Jews. Sure it was there, just below the surface you could say, and we felt it up to a point, but we had our secure jobs, a nice apartment, and great friends. We were living in an exciting and beautiful city. Why give it all up? I was exceedingly reluctant to part with my comfortable life but eventually I grudgingly agreed.

"One time I asked her, *"Why would we want to emigrate? Why the insistence and such urgency?"*

"Nelya answered simply, *"I want my daughter to grow up to be a better Jew than we are."*

"Raya, I was astounded. You know how it was there. We knew that we were Jews. It was even written in our passports. The majority of our friends were Jews and we were trying to marry other Jews, but that was about it. We never discussed or even thought about religion, observance of any traditions, or about G-d. I hadn't even heard the word *kosher* until after I left the Soviet Union. I didn't know a word of Yiddish and my parents didn't even celebrate any of the major holidays; neither did Nelya's. That's why I thought her new-found passion to emigrate was so strange. But she won the debate of course, and so in due course we emigrated.

"At first we were planning to go to Israel. During those times most of us didn't know that it might be possible to go to the United States or to Canada instead. On the train to Vienna we met another family and started to talk with them. They told us that they were intent on trying to get accepted into Canada. When I asked them why, they explained that they had two young boys who would be required to go into the Israeli Army as soon as they were old enough. The parents were very concerned about their boys' future safety. Rita looked at me and said, *"I have two boys as well,"* and in that instant we changed our intended destination."

Joseph paused for a minute or two and sipped his tea. Raya didn't say a word. In her mind, however, she was digesting his story and at the same time trying to envisage how a much younger, carefree, and rather selfish Joseph might have looked and behaved. The more mature and reserved man now seated directly across from her appeared to be altogether different. It seemed apparent to Raya that there was more to it than just the passage of time that had contributed to such a dramatic change. And so, she waited patiently until Joseph was ready to resume his story.

"We had a great time during our temporary stay in Italy. I suppose everybody did. I would've preferred to stay there even longer, but Nelya was behaving like a woman possessed. She wanted to get to Canada as soon as possible. She called almost every day to JIAS, asking when we might be permitted to go. To this day I'm still amazed that she passed the medical examination, but she did. I didn't suspect anything untoward at that time.

"But soon after we settled in Toronto, Nelya asked me to examine her breasts. I, who had caressed them so often, had never put my hand a bit further toward the underarm, so I hadn't noticed the pronounced lump until that evening. The very next day we went to the doctor and a new, frightening stage in our life had begun – first the tests, and then waiting for the results. That was followed by more tests and more waiting; then surgery, chemo, and another succession of more tests. Ultimately we were informed by the doctor that her cancer had metastasized and that she only had several more months to live.

"Raya, I was devastated and went absolutely berserk. I blamed myself for her illness, and for letting it become so far-advanced without being detected. As it turned out, Nelya had noticed the lump at first while we were still in Italy, but her desire to see her family get settled outside of the Soviet Union was so strong that she chose to ignore it. But how could I have been so blind?

"Anyway, I made a complete nuisance of myself in the hospital. I insisted on reading all of her test results and I argued with the doctors about her treatment, critiquing their every step. At first her doctors were sympathetic with me as a fellow-doctor, but eventually they became totally frustrated with my behaviour and interference.

"Finally I was summoned to the office of the head of the department and he issued two threats in no uncertain terms. First of all, he said that if I continued to harass his staff he would make sure that I never practice medicine in Canada. Frankly, I didn't care about practicing anything at that time.

"But his second threat cooled me down. He asserted that he would take steps to make sure that my visiting hours were severely restricted. I couldn't allow that to happen. I wanted to spend every possible minute with Nelya.

"My mother and Rita were helping to take care of Svetlana. We all lived in the same apartment at that time and Rita opened her hair-styling business there too. My mother worked as a babysitter for other children as well. I didn't look for any work during that time; I just couldn't. I must say JIAS helped us a great deal. They're terrific.

"This was about the time I went to synagogue for the very first time. I asked the Rabbi, *"Why Nelya? Why does this innocent and fine woman have to suffer when it was I who transgressed? Why does G-d punish her instead of me?"*

"What did the Rabbi say?" a captivated Raya asked compassionately.

"He said that it's an eternal question, as to 'why bad things happen to good people,' and that people have been puzzling over this age-old question for generations, ever since the biblical time of Job. The Rabbi told me that he wasn't a prophet who knows G-d's mind, but that I had to have faith that *He* loves us and knows what is best for us. With the Rabbi's guidance I learned to pray. I couldn't help Nelya as a doctor, so I prayed," Joseph concluded.

"But sadly it didn't help, Joseph. Your prayers went unanswered," Raya commented sympathetically.

"I understand what you're saying, Raya, but I can't agree. My prayers actually helped. Nelya liked the idea of my attending synagogue and praying for her. Sometimes we prayed together near her bed. I sincerely believe that it helped to comfort her. During her last month when most cancer patients are in dreadful agony, it was a peaceful time for Nelya and she accepted the inevitability of death. She implored me to continue to pray for her soul after she was gone.

"She also asked me to promise to see to it that Svetlana received a proper Jewish education. It was Nelya that suggested we start calling Svetlana by her Hebrew name, Orit.

"Nelya died peacefully. Sometimes I think that it was her pre-ordained destiny in this life to lead our family out of that godless country and to bring us here. She completed her mission and then she was gone." Joseph's voice had remained strong and steady all throughout his tale, but there were tears welling in his eyes.

"Joseph, I'm truly sorry for you, but I'm afraid I don't buy the idea that 'He loves us and knows what's best for us.' Death is so final. There's nothing positive or redeeming about the death of a young woman and devoted mother. May I ask what possible good came of your wife's tragic death?"

Joseph thought for a moment about the question Raya had posed, and then he smiled and replied, "My daughter Orit and I became very close. It made us stronger as a family, even in the absence of her mother."

Raya continued looking at Joseph as if still puzzled. "Do you still pray?" she asked.

"Every day, Raya, every single day. Every morning I attend morning prayers and then I learn one new page of the Talmud. I also go to the synagogue for evening classes two or three times a week. There's so much to learn and I still know so very little," Joseph acknowledged.

"What's the most important thing you've learned from your religious studies, Joseph?" Raya wanted to know.

"That you have to love and fear G-d," Joseph replied without hesitation.

"I understand about love, but why fear?" Raya inquired further.

"Back in the Leningrad hospital I was always worried that somebody would unexpectedly come into the room where I entertained those nurses and that Nelya would somehow hear about it. But would I have done any of those things if I had known that I was in the eternal presence of G-d? It's so easy for us to justify any of our actions, especially when we think that no one else will find out.

"Raya, have you noticed that the standards of morality and ethics differ from one country to the next, and evolve from generation to generation? I guess that's to be expected, but there must be some absolute truth, some inalterably fundamental morals governing life on this Earth, don't you think?"

"So where do we find this eternal truth? How is it supposed to be revealed to us?" Raya asked. She was becoming increasingly intrigued by everything that Joseph had to say.

"In the Torah," Joseph responded with conviction. "It's all in the Torah."

Then he fell silent again for a moment until he said, "Raya, we both did things in our past that we aren't especially proud of. We can dwell on them and allow our conscience to tear us apart, or we can learn from our past mistakes and try to be better human beings in the future."

It was time to go. They walked together in silence towards Raya's apartment and when they reached the door, Joseph asked, "May I invite you and the children for Shabbat dinner on Friday evening?"

"Yes, Joseph, you certainly may and that would be very nice. I'm sure Leah would be thrilled to spend Friday evening with Orit. And it wouldn't hurt Ben to spend an evening with his family for a change instead of rushing off to play soccer in the park. We'll come with great pleasure, thank you," Raya responded.

"Wonderful! I'll see you Friday, Raya."

"Until Friday, Joseph."

But Joseph called the next day and they met once-again at the same café. Then on Thursday, upon seeing them enter the café yet again, the waitress brought them tea, even before they had an opportunity to order it. There was so much that Joseph and Raya had to say to each other, so much to discuss.

On Friday after work, Raya went directly to Joseph's place. When she rang the bell, a beautiful *Thumbelina* right out of the fairy tale (at least that was Raya's first impression) opened the door. The young girl was petite, with a mane of dark brown, curly hair framing an elfin face. Raya recalled Joseph's description of his late wife: *"She was such a sweet, pretty, petite girl"*. Those very words described his daughter to a tea. Even so, Orit's large, dark brown, soulful eyes were clearly inherited from her father.

Raya smiled kindly at the girl. "I'm Leah's and Ben's mother, dear."

"Come on in please, Dr. Kushnir. Leah and Ben are already here," Orit said politely, while at the same time her eyes were boring deeply into Raya's own eyes.

The first thing that Raya noticed in the living room was a large, framed portrait of a strikingly beautiful woman. She had the same elfin features as her daughter, and the emerald-green eyes in the portrait appeared to look back to the observer with transparent innocence and trust.

How can he even look at me seriously after being married to someone like her? Raya wondered. For a split second she felt a twinge of inexplicable anger. *How could he have so callously betray the trust of such a woman?* But Raya's musing was cut short when she noticed Joseph approaching and she smiled warmly in greeting.

Everything was in readiness for Shabbat.

"Mom, you're finally here!" Leah exclaimed. "It's almost time to light the candles."

For the second time in her life, Raya lit Shabbat candles. This time, however, no one interrupted her when she was reciting the prayer, following after the lead of the girls.

Ben and Joseph stood quietly nearby, wearing their kippot and observing the women's traditional ceremony.

Raya was somewhat amused at the formally of all four of them, and she was struck by how seriously they were adhering to the rituals. Everyone took their places around the table but didn't immediately sit down. They sang a Hebrew song. Then Joseph placed his hand on Orit's shoulder and blessed her. He handed Raya a prayer book so she could read out the appropriate passage. Raya blessed her son and wished him to be like Ephraim and Menashe (*Who are they?* Raya pondered. *I should remember to ask the children later.*) Then she blessed Leah and wished her to be like Sarah, Rebecca, Rachel, and Leah. *At least I've heard those names before,* she thought.

Joseph mixed the red grape juice with a bit of red wine and poured it into a large silver goblet.

"Mom, after the blessing, remember not to speak until you drink your wine," Leah whispered.

Joseph recited the blessing, poured a bit of the mixture of grape juice and wine into the individual serving cups and took the first ceremonial drink, followed by everyone else.

"Now we have to wash our hands," Leah instructed.

"Oh, but I washed mine just before dinner," Raya replied innocently.

"It's a part of the ritual," Leah explained patiently. "Wash your hands as I do. Then we'll say a blessing together. After that, we won't speak again until we've eaten a little piece of challah."

To Raya's bemusement, even her hands had to be washed in a certain way. There was a special metallic cup with two handles. Each person filled the cup with water and poured some of the water, three times on the right hand, and then similarly on the left hand. After drying their hands and saying the appropriate blessing, everyone responded, "Amen."

Like children playing a game, Raya thought. *What difference does it make if I wash the left hand first or the right?* Nonetheless she dutifully repeated the words of the blessing after Leah and wisely kept her thoughts to herself.

Everyone returned to the dining area and took their seats around the table. Joseph stood and raised the two challahs that beforehand had been set on the table with an ornate cloth covering.

It was at that moment, while Joseph was performing the time-honoured ritual of asking the Lord to bless the bread, that something suddenly rang true for Raya and she felt inexplicably moved, even over-awed.

So that's what this is all about. That's how a family should dine together, honouring the food that they eat, and not just rushing to consume some nourishment before running off to do something else.

There was an aura of peace and contentment around the table and Raya felt overwhelmed by it. For the first time in her life she silently prayed, *"Please G-d, make this family mine; make this man love me and help this girl to accept me. I promise to be a good mother to her."*

Early on Sunday morning, Raya received the anticipated weekly call from Israel. "Miriam," she said, "I don't know what's going on with me! This past week I actually had to force myself to stay focussed and concentrate on my new job. I have such an exciting, interesting project, something that I've been dreaming about, ever since we left Kiev. But all I can think about right now is Joseph. He's definitely not as good-looking as Maxim; he's not very tall and he doesn't have an athletic physique, but I feel so happy and at ease when I'm near him. It's as though I've known him for ages."

Before Miriam even had an opportunity to respond, a male voice teasingly broke out from the phone extension, "My sister's fallen in love! True love at last! It only took her thirty-nine years!"

Two women's voices shot back simultaneously, "David, hang up that phone!"

"Oh well. Misunderstood and unappreciated, like always. But I really would like to meet this Joseph of yours. He must be quite the guy to make you feel this way, Raya." And with that, David hung up his phone extension.

Then Raya continued. "Miriam, I don't know what he really sees in me. His late wife was so beautiful; I've seen her portrait in his home. I think maybe he's just looking for a companion who will be his friend and I'm taking this all out of proportion," Raya said with a touch of melancholy.

"Raya, don't underestimate yourself. He clearly likes you and appreciates your company a great deal, so just take it one day at a time.

The most important thing right now is to win the trust, respect and approval of Orit," Miriam advised her sister. "Your Joseph will never marry anyone that his daughter doesn't endorse."

"I know, Miriam, and I really like that girl. I just want to hug and protect her but I'm just not sure how she'd respond to that," Raya said wistfully.

"Everything will work out, dear sister. You'll see. You just have to keep the faith and be patient, Raya. I'll keep my fingers crossed for you," Miriam proclaimed reassuringly.

Family Matters

R AYA'S PROJECT WAS proving to be significantly more difficult and demanding than she had anticipated. This was the first time she was facing challenges and issues quite unfamiliar to her: project budget and timeline constraints. In her Kiev lab, Raya could concentrate on the pure research aspects, leaving the day-to-day management logistics in the capable hands of Vasily. Now she had to learn how to compromise - how to weigh the need for additional experiments and extra resources against higher cost considerations. Quite often she was leaving work feeling exasperated and practically in despair.

Meanwhile, Joseph's internship was not going as smoothly as he would have hoped either. He soon came to realize that the atmosphere and the culture of Canadian and Russian hospitals were distinctly different. It was not easy for him to adapt to this new environment, to form working relationships with other interns and doctors, to understand the patients' needs and expectations, and to establish an appropriate manner of approaching and communicating with them as a medical practitioner.

And so, it was time of learning and adjustment for both Raya and Joseph and it was their growing friendship that helped them and kept them going throughout this difficult period.

All through that summer, Raya and Joseph managed to find the time to meet one-another almost daily. They discussed their work and daily challenges, and they talked about the children - Ben's school issues, Rita's struggle with two teenage boys, and Leah and Orit's summer activities. They talked about virtually everything except their personal feelings towards each other. They guardedly sought to assure everyone that they were simply good friends who enjoyed one-other's companionship.

It was only during her telephone conversations with Miriam that Raya revealed her true feelings for Joseph and her growing angst to see their relationship progress.

"What should I do, sister? Do you think I should make the first move?" Raya was asking. "And what do you think I should do about Orit? She's always excruciatingly polite with me, but I find her to be as cold as a block of ice! '*Yes, Dr. Kushnir…: No, Dr. Kushnir…*' She steadfastly refuses to refer to me by my given name. Do you think that perhaps I should try to talk to her one-on-one? In that case, what would I say to her to break the ice?

"As for Joseph, I'm not even sure that he's interested in me as a woman. He's never tried to kiss me or anything like that, but sometimes he looks at me in such a way that is difficult to describe, Miriam. There is definitely tenderness and care reflected in his eyes, and seemingly a hunger for intimacy too. I mean it, Miriam; I can feel this hunger and I don't believe it's just my imagination. But why wouldn't he say anything romantic or make some sort of advance towards me?"

"Patience, my dear sister. You just have to have patience. I know very well that this is not exactly your strongest trait, but I wouldn't force the issue if I were you. Give Joseph some time and space.

"Why don't you take Leah and Ben and disappear for several days, at least for a weekend. You know what they say: absence makes the heart grow fonder."

The very next weekend, Raya followed through on Miriam's advice and took the children on the bus to Niagara Falls. On the Thursday prior, she deliberately placed a call to Joseph's home in the daytime while he was at work and left him a short message, apologizing for having to regretfully decline his invitation to spend this week's Shabbat dinner together. She explained that the children wanted to see Niagara Falls and she had promised it to them a long time ago, and that she felt that it was important to devote some family time with them.

It was a splendid weekend. Raya and the children did all the *touristy* things, marvelling at the splendour of The Falls and roaming the streets of the town, taking in all the garish attractions. On Sunday morning they took a bus to the nearby, quaint town of Niagara-on-the-Lake and enjoyed a long, relaxed stroll along the river. Finally, in late afternoon they boarded the bus for the return trip to Toronto.

That evening when the exhausted but contented family returned to their apartment, Raya found a note pasted to the door. *"Please come to my apartment when you get home, all three of you."* The note was signed by Rita.

A baffled Raya and the children looked at one-other, opened the door to set their bags inside the apartment, and then proceeded quickly up to Rita's apartment.

When Rita opened the door they observed Rita's two sons, together with Joseph and Orit, all sitting around the table. There was a large pot of tea and pastries laid out but the food had not been touched. Everyone had a sombre expression about their faces, while Joseph was looking positively nervous.

"What happened?" an alarmed Raya asked, as she walked in and approached the group gathered around Rita's dining table.

"Raya, I wanted to talk to you," Joseph began hesitantly, but he was promptly interrupted by his daughter who took command of the conversation.

"Dad told me that he wanted to marry you and I have agreed that this is a fine idea," Orit proclaimed loud and clear in her melodic voice.

Astounded, Raya sat down on a chair and looked directly at Orit. "Can you tell me, dear, what makes you feel that way?" For some reason it was neither Joseph's proposal of marriage nor the strange circumstances under which it was delivered, but rather this girl's attitude and emotions that took precedence at this moment for Raya.

"Because it's not right for a man of my father's age to continue living unmarried," Orit asserted.

"But how do you really feel about my becoming part of your family, Orit?" Raya probed cautiously.

"I talked to my Rabbi at school and he told me that I shouldn't try to prevent or otherwise interfere with my father's marriage wishes and intentions. The Rabbi said that it's the proper thing for my dad to do. And if he's going to get married anyway, you're the best choice, I suppose. At least I could be with Leah all the time."

"So, I'm something of a necessary evil for you, is that it, Orit?" Raya asked indignantly. She was quite startled by Orit's brusque manner of speaking to her.

"For now," Orit replied crisply, at which point she got up from the table and walked off to another room. Everyone else but Joseph got up too and followed slowly after her. Apparently Ben wanted to say something but his sister dragged him away. And so, Joseph and Raya were left to themselves in Rita's dining room, facing one-another across the table.

"Joseph, this is a preposterous way to propose! How could you...?" But Joseph paid no heed to Raya's indignant reaction. Instead, he wordlessly rose from his chair, came near and fell upon one knee before her. Then he retrieved from his jacket pocket a small, black jewellery box which he snapped open before offering it up to Raya.

Raya stared awe-struck at the glittering diamond ring and was left utterly speechless. She didn't know what to say or what to do in response to this wholly unexpected turn of events.

"Raya, I love you very much and I want you to know that. I fell in love with you from the very first evening we met. I've wanted to tell you about my true feelings all this time but I had to talk to Orit first. I had to be sure that she wouldn't be traumatized by my feelings towards you. We talked about you and our possible future as one family quite a few times. Please forgive Orit for her testy attitude. She's just cautious but she likes you, she really does.

"Raya, I want you to be my wife and mother to my daughter. I want us to be together as one family. I love Leah and Ben and I promise to be good to them... Raya, please say something!"

Raya made a move to sit down beside Joseph on the floor. She took his hand and said, "You're a silly man, Joseph, but I love you too."

A moment later, the rest of the family rejoined the newly-betrothed couple and Rita popped open a bottle of champagne that had been chilled in advance for the occasion.

Raya and Joseph were married just before the High Holidays. They traveled with Leah and Orit to Israel for their honeymoon and an introduction to Raya's family. Because he attended the public school and didn't have any vacation days during the Jewish holidays, Ben remained behind under Rita's care.

Happily, Raya's family unanimously approved of Joseph, although that didn't prevent Vera from seizing an opportunity to give him a hard time. "Do you ever feed this poor child?" she asked, while giving Orit a heartfelt hug.

"During the next two weeks I have to fatten her up a bit," Vera declared. Orit looked imploringly at Leah for support but her friend just shrugged her shoulders. Orit was now in the hands of her grandmother and she would eat, or else!

For many years, Raya had been trying but failing in all her attempts to bring David and Maxim closer together. On the other hand, Joseph and David became almost immediate friends, even before the end of the first day of their visit. They agreed between themselves on almost everything as far as the subject of modern medical science was concerned. Of course they had divergent viewpoints about Israeli politics but that was to be expected. They also discussed religion and countless other subjects. What was most important, they clearly enjoyed each other's company immensely.

Meanwhile, Hannah, Ilan and Malka promised to take the two visiting girls under their wing and introduce them to some of the many splendours of Israel.

The newlywed husband spent most of that first night in Israel on his own. His wife was engrossed in talking with her sister until the wee hours of the morning. There were so many things for them to discuss with one-another.

Miriam brought Raya up-to-date on all her news about her family. Hannah and Ilan were already talking about marriage, even though Hannah was only nineteen and Miriam was of the opinion that the two of them should wait at least for a couple of more years. Malka was not yet interested in boys; she wanted to become a doctor like her father and was studying very hard. Hannah, on the other hand, had no clue what she wanted to do with her life, other than becoming Ilan's wife. Aryeh was the most mischievous boy in the world; he was constantly terrorizing his cousin Jonathan. Lily was expecting a second child.

Vera had organized a club for the 'over-fifty' crowd (actually, it was more like over sixty-five) of immigrants from the Soviet Union. Some of the club's members were former actors, singers and dancers. They were staging nice performances from time to time and Vera seemed to be in charge of everything! Oh yes, and Uncle Phillip's son, Anatoly, was planning to immigrate to Israel with his family in the near future too. On and on it went...

Then it was Raya's turn to recount in considerable detail the events surrounding her life in Canada.

The sisters had talked about all these subjects on the phone and in their letters to each other, but talking with one-another face-to-face made all the difference. Only now they realized how much they missed and still needed each other.

After Rosh Hashanah, David and Miriam drove the newlyweds to a resort at Eilat and left them there for their honeymoon.

For the first time, Raya experienced the real meaning of the expression 'to be pampered'. The hotel was luxurious, the service impeccable, the food delicious, and the people she met in the hotel and in the town were openly friendly.

But the most important thing Joseph and Raya learned during that week of bliss was what it meant to truly belong to one-other, not just in body, but equally-so in mind and soul. They experienced what it meant to share the most intimate of thoughts and desires, and what it meant to become as one in every way.

On one occasion while they were strolling along the beach holding hands, Raya noticed a large military ship stationed not far from shore and they encountered some soldiers patrolling the beach. "It's kind of hard to feel relaxed with the military lurking around you like that," she remarked.

Joseph reflected on that observation for a moment or two and then commented, "Actually, I think the only way the Israeli people *can* relax on the beach is by having a visible military presence nearby."

"Now I realize how strong and determined my family must be in order to live here... how strong all Israelis must be. Until we came to Israel, I simply couldn't imagine how hazardous life could be here," Raya reflected.

"Yes, that's true, but I do like it here very much," Joseph replied.

"Me too. And I would love to live closer to my family, but I'm hardly ready for a second immigration, certainly not yet. There's so much for both of us to do right now in Canada!"

"I have an idea, Raya. You will become a famous scientist and I'll become a famous doctor. And then we'll retire in Israel, together of course."

"It's a deal," Raya agreed, laughing.

A week later when the happy couple returned to Haifa, they found two very enthusiastic girls waiting for them. Leah and Orit had fallen in love with Israel. They couldn't stop telling their parents about all the interesting places they'd been to and all the things they had done. Orit had even gained some weight, evidence that she had completely acceded to the authority of Vera whom she even fondly called *Babushka*. Leah was entranced with the country, its history, and all that it signified for the Jewish people.

David and Miriam were exceedingly happy for their sister. Raya had a fine family and at last her life had become normal!

After their return from Israel, Orit's attitude towards Raya started to change, and thankfully it was evolving for the better. Perhaps she had finally understood and come to accept the fact that Raya would not be disappearing from her life. Maybe it was by way of delayed reaction after the whole-hearted acceptance of her and her father by Raya's family, not to mention Vera's warmth and kindness. But whatever the reason or reasons may have been, Orit's outward resentfulness started to fade and she finally began to informally address her step-mother more warmly and by her given name.

Two months later, Miriam received a frantic call from Canada. "Miriam, I'm in big trouble! You'll never believe what's happened!"

"You're pregnant," was the astonishingly calm response from her sister.

"How did you guess? Do you realize how old I am? What am I going to do now?" Raya was pleading in consternation.

A male voice at the other end of the line piped up, "You're going to start taking vitamins!"

"Oh, David, you're always listening in on our conversations!" Raya chastised. "Please hang up that phone and let me talk in privacy with my own sister, for goodness sake."

David was quick to retort, "Not so fast this time, sister. Have you told Joseph yet?"

"Yes of course I did. And that crazy man started to scream *Mazel Tov*" and ran off to tell the children. The next thing I knew all four of them were dancing around me in jubilation. But later on I found the girls sitting in a corner and whispering to themselves, as if they were trying to console one-another. I sat down beside them and we had a long and honest conversation. Sure, there was some stress and a bit of jealousy that their places in the family would be a bit diminished with the arrival of a new baby, but I think afterwards they were glad that we had that talk. I think it helped them to rationalize that the arrival of this baby would actually solidify their own relationship as true siblings.

"Start taking those vitamins," Miriam repeated with a chuckle.

It was a busy but exceedingly happy time in the lives of Raya and Joseph. Two families were becoming as one, more-so with every passing day. It wasn't always easy but it was decidedly interesting and exciting.

The girls decided that it would be a fine idea to encourage Raya's integration into the Jewish religious community, but their initiative didn't go very smoothly at first.

Not long after Joseph, Raya and the girls had returned to Canada, the family attended synagogue together for the first time. Joseph and Ben sat in the main hall with the men, while Raya, Leah and Orit were upstairs in the women's balcony.

Raya didn't care for the service at all. Her organized and analytical mind anticipated some sort of order in the proceedings, some rhythm to the service, and perhaps even some kind of inspiration.

On the contrary, she perceived nothing less than chaos. She was surrounded by women and some of them, as far as she could tell, had no interest whatsoever in the service. Two ladies who were sitting in the row directly in front of Raya were talking amongst themselves incessantly, and not even in whispered tones. Raya became agitated and eventually moved to another row and the girls trailed after her.

Raya had no idea what she was supposed to do or how she should behave. The majority of the women were much older than her and many of them, even if they weren't chatting, looked totally bored. Meanwhile, down on the main sanctuary level, the men seemed to be fully engaged in the performance of their rituals. They opened the Ark, carefully removed the Torah scrolls, ceremoniously shook each other's hands, and formally announced the name of each member of the congregation who was being called up to read from the Torah.

It was surprising to Raya to see that Leah and Orit where entirely familiar with the order of the service. They knew precisely when to stand up and when to sit down again. They knew all the words of the songs and the prayers, and seemed to be quite at ease and enjoying the service. But it was impossible for Raya to follow along with the pray book that she saw for the first time in her life.

Even when the Rabbi was delivering his sermon, try as she might, Raya couldn't properly hear him. She was sitting too far away, the buzz in the women's section was too loud, and he was speaking too quietly anyway.

After the service, Raya returned home extremely upset. She suggested to her family that perhaps organized religion wasn't her cup of tea and that she would be happy to stay home next Shabbat and make sure that the lunch was ready for them after the morning service.

Ben had no problem concurring with his mother's proposal. Joseph nodded his head in mute agreement but he looked so disappointed that Raya felt rather sorry that she had spoken up. The girls, however, wouldn't hear of Raya's opting out, and so the first serious family debate ensued. It quickly became a full-blown fight, during which Raya stopped mincing words and asserted in no uncertain words that Judaism was a sexist religion, and that she considered herself essentially an atheist in any event.

Ben, who was taking in this lively debate with somewhat detached amusement, eventually spoke up and offered a compromise. "Mom, maybe it's not the religion as such that's the problem; maybe you just didn't feel comfortable in that particular synagogue. Each synagogue is different and conduct their services somewhat differently too. Besides, you might like the women more in another synagogue. Why don't we all do some *shul-hopping*," he suggested. "Then you'll feel better about making a decision, whatever it is."

"What are you saying, Ben?" Raya asked. She didn't understand what it was that Ben was proposing.

"The Yiddish word for synagogue is *shul*. The idea of shul-hopping is to attend a different shul each week until you find the one that suits you best," Ben explained.

"Do you know Sasha from my class, Mom? He's the one that told me the meaning of the word *shul* and what was meant by shul-hopping. His family did that before they eventually decided on the synagogue that they liked the best and now everything is fine," Ben explained.

"But I thought Joseph likes this particular Rabbi," Raya countered. "It wouldn't be fair to him."

"Actually," Joseph chimed in, "my Rabbi recently moved to Israel and I have no strong attachment to this new one. Let's try shul-hopping, as Ben has suggested. Good thinking, Ben! I quite like that idea too."

The girls had no objections to the experiment, and so the next Sabbath the entire family, Raya included, attended the service at a different synagogue. As the weeks went by, the process actually proved to be quite fun for everyone. The family met a lot of interesting new people, and afterwards each week, they discussed the service and compared what aspects they liked or perhaps disliked.

Each Sunday morning, Raya was continuing to call Miriam and the sisters would discuss the events of the prior week. Miriam found Raya's new-found interest in religion simply amusing. As far as Miriam was concerned, her intense sister was taking everything (like always) to an extreme, although she didn't share that particular thought with Raya.

One Saturday morning, the family went to a synagogue where informal education classes were being conducted immediately after the service. Raya and Joseph didn't know one class leader from another so they selected a class that was devoted to a discussion about the excerpt from the Torah that had been recited during that day's service.

The Rabbi that was conducting the class was an excellent speaker and a Torah scholar. All at once, the story that at first seemed to be little more than an amusing fairy tale to Raya, took on a different and much deeper meaning for her. How was it that she hadn't perceived the profound implications underlying in the words from the scripture on her own? She was actually disappointed when the class was over.

"I think we should come here again next Saturday," Raya suggested on their way home. "I'd like to try more classes. Today's class was really quite interesting and I'd like to hear what sort of topics they're discussing in some of the other classes."

A month later, the family decided to become members of that modern-orthodox congregation.

The ironic thing was that no sooner had the rest of the family settled into a routine at their chosen synagogue, than Ben inexplicably lost all further interest in religion and started to look for excuses to avoid attending the service each week. The excitement of the search was over and so, unfortunately, was Ben's passing curiosity.

Raya expressed her concerns to Miriam during one of their weekend conversations. "I worry about Ben. He takes everything about life as some sort of exciting game. Now that the high drama associated with the divorce is over, Ben is back to being Ben. He's always cheerful and smiling but he doesn't take anything the least bit seriously. He likes soccer but not enough to make the effort required to get accepted on a team in some league. He likes skiing too, but he doesn't have Maxim's passion for that sport. And as far as Judaism is concerned, his temporary interest has completely dissipated now. He has absolutely no goals in life and no demonstrable keen interest in anything at all as far as I can tell."

"Oh, Raya, you're worrying far too much!" Miriam replied somewhat impatiently. "What are you so concerned about? The boy's only fourteen; give him time to mature a bit! I'm sure he'll find his way."

Miriam had her own problems. Hannah and Ilan had announced their decision to get married in the summer and the family had no choice but to accede to their wishes. The sisters started discussing and making plans accordingly.

Just when and where the wedding should be held? Raya could hardly afford another trip to Israel with her entire family in tow, but on the other hand she couldn't imagine missing Hannah's wedding. Raya's pregnancy made the planning all the more complicated. The sisters ultimately decided that Hannah and Ilan ought to have their honeymoon in Canada and that there should be two receptions - one in Israel, immediately after the wedding, and then another later on when they came to Canada. The mounting cost of the overseas telephone bills was of concern, yet the sisters were on the phone almost daily discussing a myriad of details concerning the upcoming event.

But then in April, tragedy struck. Ilan was killed during one of the army's border skirmishes with the Palestinians. Hannah's grief was immeasurable. She had known Ilan for almost five years and she was certain that they would be together forever. All of her dreams and plans had been centered on her Ilan. Now her life was shattered and she professed no desire to carry on living. David, Miriam and Vera were keeping a watchful eye on her around the clock, fearful of possible suicidal intentions. The situation with Hannah was *that* serious.

At the beginning of July, Miriam called to Canada and accosted her sister with an unexpected proposition. "Raya, I know that you're going to be having the baby soon, and I realize how busy you are already with three teenage children and with your work. But Hannah is exceedingly depressed and she isn't getting any better. Everything here in Israel reminds her of Ilan. We thought that if she could move to Canada for a year and study at university, this might help her to recover a bit more easily and get on with her life. Of course she'd be living in a university dormitory, but if you could keep an eye on her and allow her come over to visit on the weekends..."

"Miriam, how could you even suggest such a thing?" Raya countered. "Do you really think I'd allow our Hannah to live in a dormitory? She'll live with us. She's family. Don't worry about a thing. I'll take good care of my niece."

Raya gave birth to a baby boy at the end of August. In honour of her stepfather, they named the boy Shimon. Miriam, David, and Hannah hastily made arrangements to travel to Canada in time for Shimon's traditional circumcision ceremony. Two weeks afterwards, Miriam and David left to return to Israel, while Hannah stayed on to begin a new stage of her life in Canada.

It was only a little over a year ago that Raya had thought that the life looming ahead of her would be one of loneliness and tedium, what with children growing up and not really needing her any longer, a worthwhile job being unattainable, and with Maxim lost to another woman.

Raya was anything but lonely now! Her life had never been as hectic as it became after Shimon's birth, now that there were five children at home, a husband who was busy with his medical practice, and coping with the demands of her own highly responsible job – it was all quite the load. She found that this new phase of her life was even more intense than when she had been studying in the Kazan University, working in the lab, and raising two children, all at the same time when they were living in the Soviet Union.

Early the following year, Joseph and Raya carefully calculated their finances and bought their first house. Joseph joked that their mortgage was bigger than the house.

Joseph's mother agreed to baby-sit little Shimon each day so Raya resumed her work when the baby was just four months old.

If truth be known, Raya had always found her mother-in-law to be rather overbearing and sometimes too intrusive. Nonetheless, for the sake of the family, she listened patiently to numerous advices about how to look after the baby. All the while she was silently thanking G-d that Joseph's mother had her own apartment and was always leaving soon after Raya would arrive home from work.

Raya's project was stimulating and demanding and she loved the work, in spite of the pressure of her responsibilities. But even so, her family life was firmly entrenched as her highest priority. She loved Leah and Ben very much, even though when they were young children her university studies and her career had been the central preoccupations in her life. Now Raya's priorities were quite different. Baby Shimon was incredibly precious to her and she was able to enjoy him much more than she had managed with his older siblings. At the same time, it seemed to Raya that she had somehow rekindled a closer relationship with the lives of her older children. She had come to a better appreciation of how much her teenagers still needed their mother, and she was now performing in that role for Orit too. To top it all off, there was the added sense of responsibility that she felt for the well-being of her niece.

Leah and Orit were both still attending the *Bais Yaakov School for Girls,* while Hannah began studies in Business Administration at York University in suburban Toronto. It was not that she cared much about that as a vocation, but at this point in her life she didn't much care about any profession. Business Admin had seemed the easiest to her, so that became her default selection. Without explanation, Hannah also chose to change her name to the English form - Anna.

Miriam and David's decision to send their Hannah, henceforth Anna, to Canada turned out to be an astute one. Slowly but surely she was coming back to life. What apparently helped her most was observing Joseph and Orit. They understood the tragedy of losing a loved one, yet they had survived and moved on with their lives. Time heals.

Despite their age differences, Orit and Leah became Anna's closest friends. Leah was a very strong and determined girl, while the petite Orit was outwardly expressive and compassionate. It seemed that together they were a perfect complement to Anna's character. Ben was simply Ben as usual with his sunny and carefree disposition. He invariably brightened up the room with his presence.

A year later, Anna suggested to Joseph and Raya that she should drop Business Admin and instead apply to the Department of Graphic Design at Ryerson College.

"But you need a portfolio even to be considered for admission," Joseph cautioned her.

"I already have one," Anna promptly replied.

She showed the family a number of her sketches. Ilan in a soldier's uniform; Ilan in the old Jerusalem market; Ilan in Jaffa...

Anna was admitted to Ryerson and Miriam was very pleased and grateful that with the support of Raya and her family, her daughter had found a new purpose in life. "Raya, you saved my baby!" she said tearfully during one of their traditional Sunday morning phone conversations.

"Miriam, don't even give it another thought. I stopped counting a long time ago how many times you saved *my* life," Raya responded.

With the passage of time, the extended family grew even bigger and became more diverse. Rita married a divorced man with two grown children. And then Miriam's cousin, Uncle Philip's daughter Nadia, immigrated to Canada with her husband Ilia and their two children.

Raya had been eagerly anticipating Nadia's arrival but was distinctly disappointed with the newcomers in more ways than one.

Nadia bore no resemblance whatsoever to her father. She was a dark-haired woman with broad, square shoulders, a wide face that was rather mannish, and she had unusually large hands that evidently were used to hard physical labor. Her husband Ilia was a mountain of a man, well-beyond six feet tall, with a stocky build and a protruding beer-belly.

From the first time that they met, Raya and Joseph were taken aback by their new relatives' abrasive manner and their unquenchable and impatient hunger for life's niceties. Raya remembered Philip as an intelligent, compassionate man and was expecting his daughter to exhibit similar traits. But Nadia's rudeness and lack of tact were startling. When she first came to Raya's house, she walked around observing each and every detail and then boldly declared, "This place is way too small. We're going to have a much bigger and more expensive home within a year."

Ilia nodded his head in agreement and said, "This is a capitalistic country, right? We've decided that we aren't going to work for anybody but ourselves. We want to start a business. A year should be more than enough to make sufficient money for a decent house, wouldn't you think?"

"Admirable decision," Joseph muttered. His house had been unceremoniously declared less than adequate, so he took a deep breath before responding cautiously. "I do strongly recommend that you concentrate on learning English first. Take your time and observe as much as you can about Canada and the lifestyle of Canadian people. I wouldn't rush into opening a business prematurely if you want it to be successful."

The newcomers glanced sceptically at one-another, apparently unmoved by Joseph's advice and logic. A week after their arrival, Ilia secured a position as a door-to-door salesman for Electrolux vacuums, and Nadia ploughed all the money that they had brought with them into a network marketing company, *Herbalife*.

Joseph and Raya observed the activities of their new relatives with interest and no small degree of scepticism. They had never witnessed a couple working so hard with so little visible or meaningful result to show for their efforts. Ilia and Nadia were both working twelve-to-fourteen hours a day, knocking on doors, calling everyone they knew, meeting new people, and conducting their sales and marketing presentations.

On one occasion Nadia even made a presentation to Raya and Joseph, urging them to become *Herbalife* distributors under her sponsorship.

"Joseph, you have so many patients. You can sell lots of products and sign-up all of your patients as new distributors. You'll be a rich man in no time at all!"

"I can't do that, Nadia," Joseph replied patiently. "It would be unethical."

"Then how about you, Raya?" Nadia persisted. "From what I understand you became a member of a synagogue so you could help Joseph secure more new patients, but what good are you getting out of it? I'm sure there are a lot of overweight women in your synagogue. Sell them the product, and then when they lose some weight, sign them up!"

"Nadia, I'm not attending synagogue for the sake of any altruistic objectives. I wouldn't even think of insulting my friends by discussing *Herbalife* with them," Raya replied matter-of-factly.

"Then why are you even going there?" Nadia wanted to know. "I can hardly believe that such an intelligent woman as you, a research scientist, could actually fall for those religious fairy tales."

At that point, Joseph and Raya wished for nothing more than to be able to toss that unpleasant and persistent woman out of their house, but for the sake of her father and Miriam they managed to restrain themselves.

"Well then, Raya," the unperturbed Nadia continued, "at least buy the product for yourself. You could do to lose at least twenty to thirty pounds, as I am sure you're well-aware."

Every woman who takes pride in her appearance abhors the idea of being perceived, never mind being bluntly referred to, as *fat*, and Raya was no exception. She had had altogether more than enough. "Nadia, we'd better finish this meeting right now because there's nothing more for us to discuss," she said in a stern, dismissive voice.

"Fine then," Nadia acceded reluctantly, as she got up and headed for the door. Then she stopped, walked back into the room and unceremoniously deposited a package containing several bottles and jars on the table. "Start taking it, Raya. You can pay me for the merchandise later." Then she left the premises without a parting word.

To Raya and Joseph's considerable surprise, Nadia and Ilia's persistence actually started to pay off. He sold a number of vacuum-cleaners and she signed-up quite a few distributors.

But the pace of their progress was much too slow for these impatient entrepreneurs. None of the people in Nadia's network *down-line* shared her enthusiasm or drive, so the royalty money was slow in coming. Meanwhile, Ilia soon grew tired of the brash rejections which more often than not were the outcome of his door-to-door canvassing, and so he decided to find some other, more lucrative pursuit.

He organized a small crew of immigrant workers to whom he paid minimal hourly wages and started to offer handyman services such as household repairs, construction of porches and decks, as well as some landscaping services. No job was too small for Ilia and his team.

Meanwhile, Nadia diversified her endeavours too. She started to prepare homemade pies in substantial quantities which she was selling to local Russian deli shops.

A year later, true to their word, Ilia and Nadia bought a house. In fact, it was actually even smaller than Raya's and in terribly run-down condition, but at least the location was good. With their seemingly unbounded enthusiasm, Ilia and Nadia undertook the renovation and re-modelling of the house.

About this time, Miriam's half-brother, Vladimir, immigrated to Canada with his wife Dina and their newborn daughter.

Vladimir's attitude towards immigration couldn't have been more different than that of his relatives from Sverdlovsk.

"I didn't spend five years of my life studying in university for nothing. I'm an electrical engineer and I'm determined to work as such," he pronounced categorically.

Like all new immigrants, Vladimir and Dina were the beneficiaries of all kinds of advices, whether solicited or not, from neighbours, friends and relatives. Most of these advisors suggested that he should tone down the stated qualifications on the resume he was preparing.

"Don't write *engineer*," they were saying. "Nobody would hire you. Write *technician* instead; that will make finding a job much easier. Gain some Canadian experience and then in a year or two you can change the qualification references on your resume back to engineer, or whatever, if that's what you really want."

Vladimir listened politely to these advices and then proceeded to finalize his resume clearly setting out his education, his experience and his specific qualifications as an electrical engineer.

He attended his first job interview but failed it miserably. "I don't know the standards of their engineering code or their terminology," Vladimir lamented to anyone who would listen.

So, after that initial disappointment, he started to go to the library to study technical references related to his profession. He wasn't at all interested in any temporary job and had absolutely no intention of earning a pittance of a wage by delivering pizza or something of that ilk.

"We're landed immigrants here and Canada has to help support us until we get a job according to our qualifications and skills," Vladimir insisted. He managed to have his entire family accepted for welfare assistance. All the while, he continued to spent at least eight hours a day studying the Canadian electrical codes and standards and didn't seem at all anxious to start looking for any other job while he was busy studying.

The relationship between Nadia and Vladimir soon became tense and outright hostile, and before long Raya and Joseph found themselves caught in the middle of a family feud. "She's a fool!" Vladimir asserted. "She's my cousin and she's older than me but I have no respect for her whatsoever. Back home, Nadia was a teacher and Ilia was a supervisor on large construction projects. Both have a bachelor's degree from their universities. And for what? To construct patio decks or to bake pies?"

Nadia's attitude in turn towards her cousin was even less favourable. "He's a selfish jerk!" she declared. "He doesn't care in the slightest how difficult and demeaning it is for Dina to live on welfare. He could easily make some money to help his family if he made the effort. Ilia even offered Vladimir a job with his work crew, but oh no! Our Vladimir is above getting his hands dirty. What a snob!"

Precisely a year after arriving in Canada, Vladimir did secure a position as an electrical engineer with a large company. When Nadia learned what his starting salary was going to be, she paled with envy.

Not long after that, Nadia and Ilia sold their small, renovated house for a tidy profit and bought a larger one. Again they immediately undertook a major renovation.

It took time for both families to start to recover from the initial period of adjustment and the cultural shock associated with immigration. Nadia had ceased talking about immediate riches. She and Ilia had come to the realization that the road to success in Canada was long and arduous and that instant wealth was a mere *pipe-dream.* Eventually they bought a small apartment building, renovated it and rented out the individual units. At the same time they continued buying, renovating and re-selling more houses.

After studying for more than a year, Nadia obtained her real estate licence. Her attitude had changed too. She had mellowed somewhat and become more tolerant towards others and less envious of their successes.

On one occasion, Vladimir almost lost his prized job after insulting his boss. He was called to the HR Department and was obliged to endure a harsh reprimand, after which he was moved to another department and given a conditional second chance, if only because of his high qualifications. After that experience he became distinctly less arrogant and more thoughtful about his actions and his words, especially at his workplace.

Galina and Philip were no longer counted among the living, but their offspring were all alive and well and they eventually prospered, whether in Israel or in Canada. Nobody communicated with Uncle Nikolai, however, and the whereabouts of his children was unknown.

At the commencement of the Winter Olympics, the entire family gathered together in Raya and Joseph's house. Miriam and David were in Canada for a visit at the time too and everyone was in a fine, celebratory mood.

The television was tuned to the station reporting on the Games, just in time for the opening procession of the athletes.

"Oh, look at ours!" Nadia exclaimed. "I just love their new Olympic outfits! They're parading into the Olympic stadium like true champions."

"Well," Joseph commented, "I hope our team will be more successful this time 'round. In the last Games four years ago, they missed out on several gold medals that I was sure they were going to win."

"Just a second," Vladimir intervened. "Which team are you referring to as *ours?*"

"The Soviet Union team of course," Nadia and Ilia responded in unison.

"The Canada team," Raya and Joseph immediately countered.

Vladimir raised a glass of wine, and as he turned to face Raya and Joseph, he bowed his head respectfully and pronounced, "Congratulations! Your immigration is officially over!"

A New Generation

TIME WAS LITERALLY flying by! Raya had hardly noticed how quickly Ben had grown up. Before she knew it he had graduated from high school and had made it abundantly clear that he had no intention of continuing his education. He wanted to go to work, make some money to gain his independence, and later on to do some travelling with his friends.

Raya was devastated. She'd spent seven long years just trying to gain admission to university herself, and even had to travel far away from home. She had spent long hours for many days, or to be more precise – years, preparing for her entrance exams, whereas the only thing that Ben would have to do was simply to apply to the college of his choice! But he had no desire whatsoever to study any longer. Despite the inevitable fight with his mother, a long talk with his stepfather, and the ridicule of his sisters, Ben would not be moved and instead found himself a job in the Sears department store selling television sets.

The next year, Leah and Orit left to study at the *Jerusalem Seminary for Girls*. To be sure, Raya was a bit worried about how her girls would manage to live on their own so far away from home, but she took some comfort in knowing that they would not be alone. If needed, Miriam and David would always be there to help.

It was a two-year program, and the girls were originally planning to return to Toronto for a couple of months during the summer holidays after finishing their first year. But that summer Malka was getting married and so Raya traveled to Israel with all her family instead.

Miriam was contemplating the strange twists of fate. "I was always worrying that Anna would rush into marriage too early, and I was equally worried that my introverted Malka would never find a suitable husband. Now, Malka is marrying the son of a prominent Israeli lawyer and having a five hundred-guest wedding, while her outgoing older sister isn't even dating anybody these days. Anna will be twenty-five already this year."

"I've tried to encourage her to get out and meet people but she's outright refusing to date anyone," Raya commented.

"Well, at least she has a good profession and seems to be enjoying her life again," Miriam sighed in quiet resignation.

"That's true, thank goodness. She makes decent money and she's independent, so give her time, Miriam. For now you need to concentrate on Malka and her wedding," Raya advised.

The wedding was a lavish and joyous affair. Miriam had spent months organizing every little detail and it paid off handsomely.

After the wedding, Ben, Orit and Leah took off to do some voluntary work in a kibbutz for a few weeks, while Anna was busy catching up with her old friends and Vera was monopolizing young Shimon. And so, the two couples decided they couldn't pass up an opportunity to travel to Cyprus for a short vacation.

It was there on a busy street of Cyprus, not far from the beach, that Raya was startled to hear an old familiar voice. "Raisochka Borisovna!"

She spun around and there he was – her dear old friend and lover, Vasily Andreevich Kovalenko, or rather a notably Americanized version of Vasily. He was casually dressed in Bermuda shorts and wearing a light t-shirt bearing the words '*I love New York*', complemented by a Yankee baseball cap.

He's looking good, Raya thought, *as if the years have hardly touched him. Well, maybe he's gained a few inches around the waist and has several more gray hairs, but he's still the same Vasily.*

Vasily gave her a warm embrace, shook hands with David, and gallantly kissed Miriam's hand. Then he looked inquisitively in Joseph's direction.

"My husband, Dr. Joseph Feldman," Raya announced proudly.

"Good! Finally the woman has come to her senses!" Vasily thrust his hand enthusiastically to Joseph and introduced himself. "Jeff Kovan."

"I beg your pardon?" an astonished Raya asked.

"That's right; I changed my name, Raya. Vasily sounds awkward in English and Basil is downright comical. My wife Rimma suggested *Jeff* and I liked it just fine. Don't you think that *Jeff Kovan* is a much more appropriate name than Vasily Kovalenko for the VP of Operations of a large pharmaceutical company in New Jersey?"

Questions were hurled simultaneously at Vasily from various directions.

"Congratulations! What company are you working for?" David asked.

"I thought you were in California. How did you end up in New Jersey, of all places?" Raya wanted to know.

"California didn't like me and I didn't like California," Vasily-Jeff explained dismissively, "so I've been living and working near Princeton for the past five years."

"I like your pendant. Is that just a decorative piece or ...?" the observant Miriam asked in a polite manner.

Raya in turn glanced at Vasily's neck and was startled to see a large, golden Star of David hanging from an ornate gold chain.

"Rimma bought this for me after my conversion," he explained, evidently enjoying the surprised looks that had suddenly appeared on everyone's faces, especially Raya's.

"I started the conversion process initially for the sake of my family, but I completed it for myself. Different religious observances had become too confusing for the children. One day they would be lighting Hanukkah candles with their mother and the next day decorating a Christmas tree with me. One day it would be Easter bunnies and the next day we would be eating matzos. I feel nothing but sympathy now for the offspring of inter-marriages; celebrating a bit of everything and not knowing what to really believe, so believing in nothing! I decided that I wanted my children to belong to a community and to have the spiritual support of some faith, so I started taking the conversion classes. I actually liked what I heard, so I converted. It's as simple as that."

Knowing him as well as she did, Raya could surmise that there was indeed a deep-seated conviction behind Vasily's outwardly casual tone.

Just then a woman dressed in bright resort garb emerged from the nearest shop with an eight-year-old boy and a younger girl in tow.

"Daddy, look what Mommy bought me!" the girl exclaimed as she ran into Vasily's waiting arms. He happily lifted up and hugged his young daughter.

Remembering Vasily's gorgeous first wife and many good-looking mistresses, Raya would have expected his Rimma to be a strikingly attractive creature. Instead, Raya observed a pleasant but rather plain-looking woman of average height who was as thin as a rake. However, when Rimma smiled at her husband, Raya perceived an incredible warmth and charm about her.

Rimma's smile remained but the warmth faded when Vasily introduced his wife to Raya. Rimma's eyes were sharply focussed and wary when she acknowledged their introduction. "Charmed; nice to meet you, Raya."

Then Rimma turned to her husband, saying, "Jeff, if you remember, we have a previous engagement. We should be going." The firmness of her tone of voice was tempered with just the slightest hint of apology.

Rimma took tight hold of her husband's arm and Vasily hastily wished everyone goodbye and dutifully followed after his wife.

"Oh good grief! Why don't I have any Shakespearean talent?" David exclaimed in mock exasperation when they were beyond earshot. "I could write the perfect play: *The Taming of the Shrew, Part II.*"

Later on, when Raya and Joseph were alone in their hotel room, he commented, "Your Vasily's quite the handsome fellow. You have good taste, Raya."

She batted her large eyes innocently and started to say, "Joseph, what makes you think that ...," then she looked directly into his eyes and changed her tune.

"Fine, you're right. However, he isn't mine. He's Rimma's and I'm happy for both of them. And I'm even more happy that *you* are mine," Raya said. Then she proceeded to prove her point to her husband.

The following day, the sisters and their husbands flew back to Israel. During the flight, Miriam commented, "I'm really quite surprised that Vasily changed his name and that he actually converted too. I wouldn't have expected those kinds of things from him."

"Look who's talking about changing their name, sister! Anyway, Vasily was always an opportunist. He's smart, witty and charming, but a chameleon nevertheless. I suspect he could easily adapt to any environment or any situation if it suited his purposes. Anyway, I'm glad that he's happy. But that's enough about him."

"Good, but you know, I used to be very angry with you for keeping that affair of yours with Vasily a secret for the longest time. I've never held back from telling you anything, Raya," Miriam pouted.

"Really...is that so? And who was it that told Aleksander all about the plan for emigrating before even mentioning it to me?"

"Okay," Miriam sighed. "I guess we're even. But please, from now on let's not have any more secrets between us." She was quiet for a moment and then added, "I miss Aleksander a lot."

"So do I," Raya agreed.

Upon their return to Israel from Cyprus, there was an unexpected and somewhat shocking development awaiting them. Ben announced that he had decided to stay. He explained to his family that he had now come to the realization that if he wanted to have an interesting job and make a decent living, he needed a better education. He had decided that he wanted to study marketing. Apparently, two years of mundane sales experience in Sears had accomplished what Raya and Joseph's rational arguments could not. That aspect of Ben's decision was very much welcomed by Raya.

But when it became clear that he wanted to study at Jerusalem University and live in Israel, Raya became upset and apprehensive. She couldn't imagine living so far away from Ben. And then there was the matter of mandatory army service. Ben would be conscripted into the Israeli army, he might have to become involved in some serious conflict, and worst of all he could be maimed or even be killed! This fear, so familiar to every Israeli mother, took hold of Raya, who reacted with consternation.

"Ben, you could get yourself killed here!" she cried out before realizing that with her adverse reaction she had inadvertently offended all of her family. Both David and Misha had served their time in the army; Malka too. Young Jonathan and Aryeh were already talking about their mandatory future service requirement as something that was not out of the ordinary and they had no apparent reservations about it.

"Oh, that would be dreadful!" Ben responded with biting sarcasm. "To fight in defence of Israel... can you imagine?"

Miriam broke into the escalating dispute between mother and son. "Raya, don't worry. We'll take care of Ben. If he wants to stay, let him stay."

"Mom," Ben pleaded, "let me study here. After I graduate and I've done my army service, I'll come back to Canada. Don't worry; it's only for several years."

A week later, Raya and Joseph were saying their tearful goodbyes, not only to their Israeli family, but also to their two daughters, and to Ben.

The next summer, Orit and Leah returned to Canada after their two years of study in Jerusalem. Orit arrived with a young husband but Leah returned with a broken heart.

When Raya and Orit were alone, Orit related the story to her step-mother. Leah had been introduced to a young man from the Yeshiva. He was an intelligent, good-looking boy from an old rabbinical family. Leah immediately fell in love.

"He was so sweet and he really liked Leah. They looked so happy together," Orit recounted. "Everything was going perfectly until his mother met Leah. She took one look at Leah's blonde hair and blue eyes and admonished her son, saying that she wouldn't tolerate that *shiksa* being a part of her family. Last month the boy promptly married another girl from our class. I'm sure his mother had a hand in that."

"Leah's a devoted and observant Jewish girl!" an outraged Raya exclaimed. "How dare that horrid woman call my Leah a *shiksa*! Well, good! I'm really glad that it didn't work out after all! Leah doesn't need that sort of mama's boy for a husband."

Raya was truly relieved that Leah hadn't gotten married in Israel. After all, the girl was only twenty and Raya wanted her daughter to receive a proper education and to experience a bit more of life before getting married and settling down.

In September, Orit and Leah began attending York University to earn their Bachelor degrees. The following year, Orit gave birth to a baby daughter and took a year off from her studies, while Leah continued her program at the university. The girls remained close, but their lives had diverged along very different paths. Orit became a full-time wife and mother, while Leah decided she wanted to continue on at the university and earn her PhD in Psychology.

Leah was not on Raya's 'worry radar'. She was pleased that her daughter was progressing so well with her higher education and remained steadfast in her opinion that marriage could wait. Raya had no doubt that her beautiful Leah would find a suitable young man when the time was right.

Even to his own surprise, Ben enjoyed his studies, but most of all he loved living in Israel. Raya was fearful, and with good reason, that Ben would not be moving back to Canada any time soon.

With Miriam's daughter living in Canada and Raya's son now living in Israel, the sisters felt a closer bond than ever before, if that was possible. And thanks to the advance of Internet technology, their interaction with one-another became even more frequent and intense.

By now they were e-mailing back and forth almost daily. They wrote about their families and their work and all the exciting events in their busy lives, but the real heroes in both of their correspondence for the next several years were Anna and Ben and the high drama in their lives.

Ben was twenty-two years old when Miriam wrote to Raya:

Ben is hopelessly in love. Her name is Tova. She's a nurse in our hospital, two years older than Ben and she's absolutely gorgeous. You know how my David and your Joseph are always drooling over long-legged Sabra women, right? Well, Tova is just that type.

Her parents came to Israel from Yemen, so her skin is that beautiful tone of coffee-latte. She has dark, curly hair that tumbles down almost to her waist and her eyes are large and dark brown and incredibly beautiful.

Raya, you should see those eyes! Ben met Tova when he was visiting me at work and ever since then he's been finding any number of excuses to visit our hospital almost daily.

Raya was alarmed by this development and sent an immediate response:

I don't care how gorgeous that Tova is and how many great features she possesses. Ben isn't anywhere near ready for marriage. He needs to study two more years in order to graduate and even after that he needs to determine where he wants to live and what he's planning to do with his life, not to mention his army service. Little things like that. Miriam, try to slow it down. They want to date – fine, but no marriage!

Raya was not entirely surprised by Miriam's response.

Slow down our Ben? Do you have any other instructions, dear sister of mine? Stop a hurricane? Perhaps arrange a permanent peace treaty between Israel and our neighbours? The chances of success are probably about the same, if not less. Ben is head over heels in love and what's more, surprisingly or not, the much more level-headed Tova really loves our helter-skelter Ben! Actually, I suspect that she would be a good influence on him; maybe she could even instil some appreciation of reality into his head!

Three months later, Ben called his mother to announce his engagement.

"Ben, what are you going to live on?" Raya asked in earnest. "Are you dropping out of the college? And where are you planning to live? Are you coming back to Canada anytime soon?"

"Mom, we will live here in Israel. We both love it here. Besides, Tova has a large family here and she would never abandon her family.

"I've missed you and Leah and Orit and Shimon, and Joseph too, but I really do love it here. I'll be staying on in Israel, Mom. Please try to understand me! As far as the financial aspect of my life is concerned, you have nothing to worry about. I'm not planning to stop my studies. I want to graduate and Tova agrees with me entirely.

"I have a couple of ideas about how to make some money in the meantime. I think I will make a trip to Taiwan or China and start some import-export business. I also hope to work with some of my friends here to market the new software they've been developing. It has a lot of potential and as you know, hi-tech is a big deal here in Israel."

"What friends are you talking about?" Raya asked faintly.

"I befriended three guys here - Motti, Nathan and Moshe. They are geniuses! I mean it. They've developed software to make online e-mailing much faster, more reliable and more secure. You should see all the new features they've developed! They need someone to market their product and they've asked me to get involved. We're talking about starting a new company. I would be the President and Director of Marketing; Motti – the VP of Research and Development; and Nathan – the VP of Operations."

"And what title will you bestow on your third friend Moshe?" Raya asked, trying not to sound overly sarcastic.

"We haven't decided yet. Moshe doesn't like to get involved in managing anything; he just wants to sit alone and work undisturbed at his computer. He thinks best when he's left to his own devices. But he's a great guy, Mom. All three of them are. So that's why I decided to go to Taiwan when I complete this college year. Hopefully I can make some money in the import-export business I have in mind, and then use this money to finance the start-up of our company. How does it all sound, Mom?"

"Ben, quite frankly it sounds totally unrealistic! Marriage, trip to somewhere in Asia, college, marketing of some unproven software! Please, Ben, come to your senses. You will burn yourself out and probably accomplish nothing! What's more, think of what harm that could do to your marriage."

The long-distance conversation came to a rather abrupt close after that.

Ben and Tova were married in August of 1984 and over three hundred guests attended their wedding. Raya and her family arrived in Israel a week ahead of the grand event, which also happened to be on the same day that the groom-to-be returned from his Taiwan business trip.

Ben had made this trip with Dov, Tova's father. Ben was very proud of his accomplishments. He had organized shipments of a variety of children's toys and reached agreements with several wholesalers in Israel willing to take them into their stock. In addition, while they were still in Taiwan, Ben had helped his future father-in-law, an optometrist, to locate a good contact as a supplier for eye-glass frames. Moreover, Dov and Ben decided to open a new optical store together.

The money that Ben was expecting to receive from the distribution of the toys was to be divided into three portions. Half of the funds would be used for the down-payment on Ben and Tova's new apartment. The other half would be allocated in part to the three *geniuses* to fund continuation of the development of their ground-breaking software, and the remainder as his share of the investment in the optical store.

Raya's head was spinning just listening to all of Ben's seemingly convoluted ideas and plans. He was like a whirlwind, like some unstoppable force of nature. On the plus side, however, Raya's reservations about his marriage dissipated from the moment she met his bride. Sure, at twenty-three years of age, Ben was still rather young to have gotten married, but Raya was reasonably confident, as Miriam had indicated, that the calm and strikingly beautiful Tova ought to be able to keep him on the right track and out of any serious trouble. Hopefully...

Ben was severely disappointed that his father didn't attend his wedding, although Maxim did promise to come for a visit later on during the Christmas holiday season. Maxim had any number of excuses why he couldn't come for the wedding ceremony, but Raya understood very well the real reason behind his reticence. He didn't want to be put in the position of seeing her, along with Miriam and David in that social setting. In a way, she was relieved. It meant less confusion and less tension for all concerned.

Raya was introduced to Motti, Nathan and Moshe (*the M-N-M boys*, as David called them). Motti and Nathan were typical Israeli lads, tall and lanky, a bit too abrupt, and definitely too overconfident for Raya's taste. Moshe was a typical nerd, wearing unfashionable clothes, thick glasses, and with a spaced-out look about him. Raya wasn't overly convinced about the prospects of a great future for their new enterprise but she wisely decided not to interfere. After all, what could she do? Only time would tell if those three boys were as smart as Ben thought they were, or if their software was indeed going to be commercially viable.

A year later, Miriam wrote to Raya:

Congratulations, you're a future grandmother! Tova is almost five months pregnant. Tova and Ben kept it a secret for as long as possible. I suspected it for a while but said nothing to them. Anyway, dear sister, I'm very happy for them. Ben seems to be doing fine too; he spends half the day in Dov's store and the rest of the time he divides between his college studies and the M-N-M boys. Actually, I'm proud of our Benny and I'm sure you must be too.

Raya responded to Miriam immediately:

Oh yes, Tova's pregnancy is wonderful news. Of course it pains me to think that my future grandchild will be so far away from me but there's nothing I can do about that right now.

By the way, I think Anna is finally dating someone. She doesn't say anything to us, but there's been a gentleman calling her almost daily. His name is Ted and they always manage to spend at least an hour on the phone. When I asked Anna who Ted was, she evasively said, "Just a friend." Oh sure, just a friend! Anna is watching the clock nervously every evening, glancing at the phone every five minutes and when it does ring, she blushes, grabs the receiver and disappears into her room.

September 15th, 1985 - Miriam to Raya:

What do you know about this Ted fellow? Ted is certainly not a Jewish name.

September 16th, 1985 – Raya in reply to Miriam:

Not much, actually. They met during some birthday party. Magda, Ted's sister, is working in the same advertising agency as Anna. The agency organized a party for Magda's thirtieth birthday. Anna was one of the organizers. Ted showed up at the end of the party to pick up his sister and that's when he met Anna. It seems everything developed from that chance encounter. I found out that he's working in a bank as a Project Manager in the IT Department. It sounds like he's got a pretty good job. Anna mentioned that he's one year younger than Magda.

September 25th, 1985 - Raya to Miriam:

Those two went out last Sunday. Anna returned home all smiles and with sparkling eyes. In fact, I hadn't seen her looking that happy for years.

September 26th, 1985: Miriam replies to Raya:

I'm glad to hear that Anna is dating at last. After all, it's more than seven years since Ilan's death. It sounds like it might even be serious. However, I'd really like to know more about this mysterious Ted fellow. For some reason, I have long-distance bad vibes about him. Why doesn't Anna tell you or me anything more about him? I asked her during our last conversation on the phone but she just changed the subject. As it turns out, I'm relieved that you convinced her to continue to live with you and to save money for a down payment for her own condo. At least this way you can keep an eye on her for now. Have you seen or met this Ted yet?

October 10th, 1985 – Raya's response to Miriam:

No, I haven't seen him so I certainly haven't met him, but I'm sure those two are seeing a lot of each other. Anna is coming home quite late these days and heading straight to bed without any supper. I have the distinct feeling that she's avoiding me because she doesn't want to answer any of my questions.

October 30th, 1985 - Raya to Miriam:

The affair with Ted is over. You were quite right to be concerned - you and your famous intuition! Anyway, a week ago, a woman called asking to speak to Anna. Anna took the phone, started to listen to what this woman had to say, and became flustered almost immediately. We didn't hear the actual words, of course, but we could all detect the shrill female voice of the caller and the screaming that was coming from the other end of the line.

Anna was trying to defend herself without much success. She was saying, "I'm sorry... I didn't know... I thought... I promise..." Then she hung up the phone and broke into tears. She managed to say to us, "It was Ted's wife. He told me that it was over between them and that they had been separated for more than two years. I didn't know..." Then she ran off to her room and slammed the door. An hour later, she emerged. Her eyes were red and swollen but she had calmed down and the expression of her face was very resolute when she said, "If Ted ever calls again, I'm not home!"

November 1st, 1985 – Miriam replies to Raya:

I knew it; I just knew it! My poor baby! Why can't she meet a nice single Jewish man? Raya, can't you introduce her to somebody? Aren't there any eligible bachelors in your congregation?

November 15th, 1985 - Raya to Miriam:

Anna refuses to meet anyone else. Ted is still calling daily, but Anna 'isn't home'. As far as I know, she hasn't spoken to him even once since the day of that fateful phone call from his wife.

November 30th, 1985 – Raya to Miriam:

It's not over after all, for goodness sake! Ted is back in the picture and it's complicated to say the least. Have you talked to Anna recently?

Anyway, I'll try to describe the events of last Saturday. Even if you hear about any of this from Anna, I want you to know as many details as possible about this whole affair. I will try to explain objectively... at least as objectively as I can under the circumstances. I want you to form your own opinion and let me know what you think.

Here's the story...

Ted Pietchakowski Makes His Appearance

ON THE LAST Saturday of November, Raya and her family returned home from the synagogue and started to prepare for lunch. Orit arrived with her husband and their two children; Rita and her husband joined them as well. Leah and Anna were both at home, so the entire adult contingent of the family was present for this occasion. Shimon was over at his friend's apartment.

Just then, as the family was sitting down around the table and about to start their Shabbat lunch, they heard a knock at the door. There was a tall, lanky gentleman with a bottle of wine in one hand and a bouquet of flowers in the other standing at their doorstep. Raya's first visual impression was that this gentleman was nothing special, certainly not exceptionally handsome. However, he bore a determined, serious expression and was looking outright grim.

Anna got up from the table to approach the doorway and said, "I'm sorry Ted, but we're having lunch. It's a family affair."

Ted responded in a resolute tone of voice. "I know, Anna. That's actually why I came here today. I wanted to be sure that you'd all be at home. I'd like to talk to you and to all your family together, if you wouldn't mind."

Joseph tried to intervene, but Ted said, "Nothing that I'm going to say is untoward or can't be discussed in the presence of your family, sir. You're having a Shabbat lunch and my understanding is that it's a mitzvah to welcome strangers to your table, isn't that so? I've brought you a bottle of wine - it's kosher, of course."

Ted handed the wine bottle to Joseph and presented Raya with the bouquet of freshly-cut flowers. The family was left with no alternative but to invite Ted to join them. He was dreadfully nervous and constantly looking in Anna's direction. She was sitting as stiff as a statue, trying her utmost not to look directly at him, but looking distinctly uncomfortable.

Ted didn't say much during the lunch, just small talk.

Later on, in her e-mail to Miriam, Raya had to admit, *He was acting quite respectfully and didn't seem to be taken aback by any of the blessings, songs, or other traditions.*

Eventually, when the family was having tea, he took the initiative and related his story.

"I met Connie," Ted began, "when I was a freshman at the University of Toronto. We were both studying computer science. Connie was, and frankly still is, a very beautiful woman. Not only that, she was smart, witty, had a great sense of humour, and was easy to get along with. She loved life, was very adventurous, and had great aspirations. She was everything I ever dreamt about for a wife. I proposed at the end of the second academic year and she readily accepted.

"Connie is the only child of a divorced woman. Mary, her mother, is a lovely lady who dedicated her entire life to the upbringing and well-being of her daughter. I liked her right from the start.

"Anyway, my family and Mary approved of our intended marriage without reservation and started preparations for the wedding. We were supposed to be getting married at the end of our third university year. Everything was going great until the winter when Connie started to feel unwell. We thought that it was just stress. You know – the combination of her studies plus preparations for the wedding. I asked her to take things easier and sometimes I helped her with her academic work. Mary insisted that Connie start taking vitamins and supplements but that didn't seem to help. Eventually Connie went to see a doctor. She was diagnosed with MS."

"Oh, no!" Joseph exclaimed.

"Yes," Ted replied, "multiple sclerosis. Connie was even insisting on returning the engagement ring and told me that I didn't owe her anything; she said that I should get on with my life without her."

Ted fell silent for a few moments, seemingly reliving and reflecting upon the horrendous experience he had gone through during that time.

Everyone remained quiet while he collected his thoughts, waiting for him to continue recounting his story.

"I was quite young, very inexperienced, and obviously without the wisdom and maturity to envisage what my life might be like, caring for a spouse afflicted with MS. I was in love and I felt exceptionally noble when I told Connie that I would never leave her and that we must still get married, just as we had planned. My mother was crying but didn't try to dissuade me. Magda, my sister, was supportive, praising my dedication and self-sacrifice in the name of true love. My younger brother, Stan, didn't get involved in any of these family discussions. He was only fifteen at the time.

"My aunt from Montreal was the only one who tried her utmost to discourage me from going through with the marriage. She told me in no uncertain terms that I was a fool; that it was one thing to perform some heroic act or even to die with honour for some noble cause, but it was quite another thing to live one's entire life as a martyr.

"I disregarded her advice. The next summer, Connie and I were wed. Her disease even went into remission. Perhaps that was because of all the treatments she was taking, or maybe it was because of her happiness... hard to say. But the most gratifying part was that she was feeling strong enough to complete her studies and graduate from the University, and then to get a job as a programmer.

"We actually started working on the very same day in similar positions. I was hired by a bank and she started working for an insurance company.

"Her disease suddenly returned some months later, and this time with a renewed vengeance. Connie had to stop working and a couple of years later she was confined to a wheelchair. We tried everything: traditional medicine, herbs, and Chinese medicine – you name it. Nothing helped and Connie's condition was continuing to deteriorate.

"I tried to be a good husband. Believe me, I really tried. I'm not looking to defend myself and I'm certainly not looking for sympathy. My inconveniences were nothing compared to Connie's suffering, but you can imagine it wasn't easy for me either. At a time when my friends were enjoying their lives, I was spending every evening reading to my wife or watching television with her… doing whatever I could to comfort her. There was no going to the clubs, playing pool, or having a beer with my buddies - none of that kind of thing."

"So, of course you started to feel sorry for yourself," Anna interjected harshly, apparently unmoved by Ted's sad story, and seemingly going out of her way to sound as derisive as possible.

"Yes, I did," Ted acknowledged while managing to maintain his equanimity in the face of Anna's snide remark, and then he carried on. "But not being able to even socialise with my friends was hardly the worse of my problems. I was ambitious and I wanted to make a career for myself. I was recognized by the bank for my skills and told that I had good potential for advancement. But in the world of Information Technology 'making a career' is tantamount to spending long hours in the office, often working on the weekends, and keeping up with the rapid pace of changes in technology by studying in the evenings. I always thought about an IT career as a marathon - you stop for a second and before you know it you fall behind everyone else.

"So, those next several years were a period filled with a combination of constant guilt and frustration for me. When I was working late I felt guilty for leaving Connie alone; when I was leaving work at five o'clock to rush home, I felt guilty about short-changing my career. In spite of all that, I did manage to get several promotions.

"Connie's personality had changed, which I suppose is understandable, but more than anything else, it was her attitude towards me that felt hurtful. She wasn't the warm and cheerful girl that I'd fallen in love with anymore. She became moody, short-tempered, and ironically, what was the worst, extremely resentful of my advancing career. With each new promotion that I received our relationship became more and more tense. I had a difficult time understanding why she couldn't be the slightest bit happy for me. But she just couldn't bring herself to do that... She wasn't jealous of some other woman in my life, it wasn't that. I never gave her a reason to be jealous, but..."

"She was jealous of your good health and of your life outside the confines of the house," Leah volunteered.

"Exactly," Ted nodded his head in agreement. "By this time we were frequently getting into fights. Connie hated it when I was coming home late, and it got to the point where I hated coming home at all because I knew what was waiting me - tears and misguided accusations. By this time I was the one who had to prepare the dinners, clean the apartment, and do all the shopping. I always thought that if I was shown some appreciation, some encouragement from her for my efforts, I would have been able to cope with the situation a bit better. But she had become excessively insecure, as though every day she was expecting me to walk out on her. I tried to reassure her that she had nothing to worry about and promised her again and again that I would be her husband for as long as we both shall live."

"But did you really mean it, Ted? Did you still love her?" Anna interjected.

Ted looked directly at Anna for a long while until he eventually replied, "No, Anna, I guess I didn't, but I certainly pitied her. Quite honestly, I was angry that life had dealt us such bad cards. I thought it was grossly unfair that Connie had to endure all that physical and emotional pain; and that she seemingly couldn't trust me; and that all my, well, if you allow me to say so, self-sacrifice was for naught.

"There came a time when I was promoted to the position of Project Manager of a Credit Card application. The development itself was almost completed at the time I was appointed and the team was engaged in testing the system. Part of the software application was purchased from an outside vendor and part was based on in-house system development.

"I didn't realize what a can of worms I had inherited. The previous manager was very laid-back and left the project largely in the hands of the developers. So everyone concentrated on his or her own little piece, but there wasn't any solid integration and end-to-end testing to confirm the integrity of the entire system. Perhaps that's why I was asked to replace him.

"In addition, the documentation provided by the vendor was cursory and incomplete.

"At that time, I had expressed my concerns about the rigid timeline for implementing the new system but I was informed that no delays were going to be tolerated. Frankly, I have my own share of blame. I was proud to have been promoted and didn't want to jeopardise my new position by taking issue with the management. Besides, I was too self-assured of my skills, believing that I could manage through and salvage any unexpected circumstances.

"From another side, I was dealing with the distraction of the challenging situation at home at the same time. To make a long story short, I didn't do a diligent job of assessing the situation and I allowed the implementation to proceed according to the original schedule, in spite of my misgivings.

"I'm sorry I'm taking so much of your time," Ted digressed, "but I'm almost finished.

"On the implementation weekend, I spent the entire Saturday in the office. I was extremely tired but proud of our team's accomplishments up to that point. The critical part of the application had been implemented and successfully executed.

"All that was left to do was the printing of the actual client statements. For that process a special machine would be used to fold and insert each statement into a mailing envelope with a small window. The statement was formatted and folded in such a way that the client name and address would be displayed in the window of the envelope. When I left the office late that evening, I felt confident that things were under control.

"As you might imagine, Connie was not at all happy with my late arrival and had no interest in hearing anything about my hectic day. We went straight to bed, but in the middle of the night there was a phone call. Connie took the phone and said, *"It's for you, Ted. Some woman."*

"It was one of my project leaders, Claudia. She informed me that twenty-five thousand statements had been produced, but every single one of them was printed with the name and address of one of our programmers, Marcel. Apparently, during the testing he realized that there was a provision on the Customer Database for more than one customer address. Each of the address fields was mandatory, but there was no explanation of their relevance in the documentation. Marcel decided that the second address was a superficial one and in order to proceed with the testing, he had 'hard-coded' his own personal data in every client record."

At that point, in spite of Ted's long-winded tale of woe, Orit and Leah started to giggle. In some fashion it seemed humorous to them to hear about twenty-five thousand statements with the very same name and address. Anna, however, was not amused and remained seated stoically throughout the entire narration with a stony face. Ted was frequently glancing nervously in her direction, looking for some modicum of sympathetic reaction, but he still pressed on with his story.

"I had to return to the office in the middle of the night and stay all day Sunday in order to unscramble the mess. When I finally returned home that evening, Mary was there, trying to console her hysterical daughter. I explained what had transpired and then I called Claudia and asked her to speak to Connie, essentially to confirm my story. I was grateful that Claudia did whatever she could but it wasn't easy to comfort Connie and get her to calm down.

"After such a strenuous weekend and having spent more than twenty-four pressure-packed hours in the office, the last thing I needed was such turmoil at home. I remember being extremely frustrated by the whole ordeal and quite angry at Connie for her outlandish suspicions. She had been an IT professional herself and knew perfectly well how stressful the implementation weekends could be.

"Anyway, a week or so after that, things finally settled down and got more or less back to normal.

"Then there was another disaster in the office. We realized that the Customer Database was corrupted. Completely corrupted! It means that each and every record that was updated after the implementation was incorrect in one way or another. It's hard to explain but we had to painstakingly restore the entire Customer Database, and that was more complex than the implementation itself. I spent the next five days in the office – literally non-stop. I ate there and I slept there whenever I could. It wasn't about me or my career, or even my job security any longer; the reputation of the bank was on the line.

"I had called home and explained what was going on. At first Connie seemed sympathetic to my situation, but she eventually became increasingly frustrated to the point where she even refused to pick up the phone. When I eventually showed up at home at the end of that horrendous week, Connie was gone and so were all of her belongings.

"What I found instead was a manila envelope from her lawyer containing a proposed separation agreement. I called Mary; it turned out that Connie was in her house at the time but she refused to speak to me.

"Mary and I arranged to meet and she explained that Connie was feeling extremely insecure; she apparently didn't want a divorce or even an actual separation, but she was insisting that I sign the proposed separation agreement as a security measure. She was fearful that if at some future time I actually walked out on her, then she would have no means to survive. Her mother indicated that Connie was not prepared to talk to me until the agreement was executed. Mary begged me to sign it and then take Connie back home, but I felt that I was being unduly manipulated and I was feeling extremely angry and resentful. After such a difficult time at the office, I was exhausted, both physically and emotionally, and it seemed as though I was being stabbed in the back with this separation agreement issue.

"I have an uncle in Montreal who's a lawyer and so I sent him a copy of the proposed agreement. He urged me not to sign anything but to leave it for him to deal with. To say that the initial agreement was quite unfavourably biased against me would be the understatement of the year. Over the months that followed, there was an ongoing battle between the lawyers and obviously Connie and I were caught in the middle of it. By the time an agreement was finally signed, there was no longer any talk of reconciliation. Regrettably, we had come to actually despise one-other by that point.

"I haven't seen Connie since and that was more than two years ago. We're speaking very rarely. However, Mary unexpectedly called me recently and begged me not to apply for an official divorce - she said that would kill Connie. Even after all that's happened I don't want to cause her any more pain; she's suffering enough with her illness as it is. To this day I haven't applied for a divorce.

"So, that's my story, and thank you for your patience in allowing me to explain. I don't have much to offer. I'm still officially married and I pay fifty percent of my income to my wife for her medical bills and for her support. As a consequence I have no house and very few other worldly possessions. I am not a Jew, and I realize that it's an important consideration for Anna whom I care for deeply. I am certainly not a hero, as life has so clearly proven, but I'm not a villain either. Good Shabbos to all of you. Good Shabbos, Anna."

Having concluded his incredibly distressing tale of woe, Ted rose from the table and quickly saw himself out of the apartment on his own accord, even as everyone else remained speechless and still seated at their places around the table. Shortly after Ted's departure, Anna retreated to her room without speaking a word and remained there all afternoon, isolating herself from the rest of the family.

The Saga Of Ted And Anna Unfolds

R AYA HAD RECOUNTED Ted's story in an e-mail to Miriam as precisely and in as much detail as she could recall and was hardly surprised by the response.

December 1st, 1985 – Miriam replies to Raya:

Raya, you must put a stop to this nonsense! That entire story sounds 'fishy' to me. In any case, Anna doesn't need all those complications. Since that man chose to marry a woman with MS, it's his responsibility to take care of her and he shouldn't be involving my Anna in this affair! I know it sounds very harsh, but I'm the mother after all, and I worry about my child.

If Ted is such a good person, he's not going to divorce his wife (he even said so himself) and it means that Anna would never get married to this guy in any event! What should she and all of us wish for - the passing of an infirm woman just to make this Ted a free man? That would be inhumane and totally counter to everything our religion stands for. We have to celebrate life, even if it is the sad state of affairs as you describe.

Anna is a kind girl and this situation will come to no good – it will only serve to warp her soul! And even if this Ted changes his mind and decides to go ahead with a divorce, then he isn't the caring and devoted person he claims to be after all, and obviously it means that Anna doesn't need any part of him or his problems!

Raya, my dear sister, please explain the facts of life to Anna. It's difficult for me to talk with her rationally from such a distance. She's very emotional as you know; she always thinks with her heart and not with her head. Please, help me to help her in whatever way you think best.

December 3rd, 1985 – Raya responds to Miriam:
Dealing with Anna is easier said than done, Miriam, but I will try my best. I think they went on a date yesterday evening.
December 17th, 1985 - Raya to Miriam:
I just received a phone call from Ben. I have a grandson! I'm thrilled. I'm buying an airline ticket today and I'll see you in a week. I'll be travelling alone this time. Everyone wants to come, naturally, but they all have some commitments. I promised to take lots of pictures. See you soon.
January 15th, 1986 - Raya to Miriam:
It was so wonderful to spend a week with all of you, darling. Little Ronny is perfect! I miss him already. Ben really seems to take to his role as a father quite seriously.

Now, my dear sister, about Anna's situation. Please forgive me but there is nothing more I can do. I talked to her at length. She hugged me and said, "Aunt Raya, I know everything that you're going to say. You and mom are right. Ted is not the match you had envisioned for me. Frankly, I'm terrified of all the implications, but I do love him very much. I'm happy with him and I plan to be with him. I hope you will come to accept my decision."

Miriam, I tried to talk to Anna about the issues with inter-marriages and how the children would ultimately pay the price. I had plenty of examples! But she just smiled indulgently. I'm afraid it's a lost cause.
February 15th, 1986 - Raya to Miriam:
Anna has decided to move in with Ted. There is absolutely nothing I can say or do, other than to help her in any way that I can. She needs all the support that we can give her, whether she realizes it or not.

Over the course of the next three months the sisters continued to correspond with each other frequently. Ben's little Ronny and Anna's new life with Ted were the most frequent topics of discussion in their e-mails.

Anna and Ted seemed to be happy settling into their new life together. They rented a new apartment closer to Raya's neighbourhood and were keeping busy furnishing and decorating it. The only 'fly in the ointment' from Anna's point of view was her shoddy treatment by some members of Ted's family.

Magda, Ted's sister, was making Anna's life in the office quite miserable. In public forums Magda was always civil with her, although at the same time formal and insufferably polite. But Anna overheard a couple of less than complimentary whispered conversations between Magda and other ladies, and she noticed several curious and accusatory glances. People were definitely gossiping about her behind her back.

During office meetings, co-workers started to look at her askance. Even Anna's boss, a man who had always gotten along well with her and had been supportive of her steady rise in the company ranks, had now reverted to speaking to her icily, and even then, only when it was absolutely necessary. As far as her colleagues were concerned, Anna was nothing more than the despicable 'other woman' who had stolen a husband from an invalid, helpless spouse. Anna tried to talk to Magda to clear the air on several occasions but all her attempts were met with the proverbial 'cold shoulder'.

On the bright side, Ted's brother Stan was very congenial with Anna. He introduced her to his own girlfriend, helped Ted and Anna to move into their new apartment, and seemed to be genuinely happy for his brother. Ted's father, on the other hand, never called or visited him, and up until this point had completely avoided meeting Anna.

In May, Anna decided to host a party in honour of Ted's birthday and to invite close family members from both sides. "Ted," she told him, "I want to have some recognition from your father, at least some form of acceptance. I know that we can't be officially married but I don't want to be regarded as just a casual, live-in girlfriend either. If you are truly sincere in your feelings towards me, as I believe you are, then don't keep me insulated from your father any longer."

"Anna, my love, that's certainly not my intent," Ted replied. "It's just that my father is not an easy person to get to know and to get along with. He changed a lot after my mother's death and unfortunately, not for the better. For the last two years he's been living with another woman and claims he wants to marry her.

"Dad's lady-friend and I don't exactly see eye-to-eye; frankly, we can hardly stand one-another. However, you're quite right; sooner or later you have to meet my old man. By all means, let's have that party."

May 20th, 1986 - Raya to Miriam:

We just got back from Ted's birthday party and I'm dying to tell you all about it. Have you talked to Anna about it already? If not, don't call her until you finish reading this e-mail. It's going to be a long one!

I'm sure that the poor girl is as confused and overwhelmed as I am. I'll try to explain as best as I can.

Miriam, I'm so astounded by everything that happened earlier this evening that I don't even know where to begin. Can I scream first? Okay, I've calmed down. Now I can continue.

Do you remember your thirteenth birthday party? That was the time when Aunt Galina invited everyone in order to make peace in the family and encourage us all to be good friends. I'm sure you remember it well; who can ever forget that disastrous evening?

From the very beginning of this party I had a strong feeling of déjà-vu; the same pervasive feeling of enmity, of open hostility, and barely disguised anti-Semitism.

Let me start with the cast of characters. I've changed my opinion about Ted, for the better actually. Now that his expression of hopelessness and dejection isn't etched on his face any longer, he looks quite handsome. I can see what attracted Anna to him. You know, as people say: tall, dark and handsome. Well, he's a bit too skinny for my taste and his hair is too thin, but overall he looks like a pretty fine specimen of a man.

His brother, Stan, is a younger and an even better-looking version of Ted. Stan came to the party on his own; apparently he recently broke off with his girlfriend and didn't seem overly upset about it. He had this amused expression on his face, as if he found the entire evening to be thoroughly entertaining in one way or another.

Magda was accompanied by her husband, a huge man who couldn't care less about Anna or anyone else for that matter, although I must say he was more than enthused about her cooking. What's his name? Hmm...I don't recall. No matter. Anyway, I've never seen anyone who could eat and drink as much as he did! There was lots of hard liquor and wine available and he drank rather more than his fair share, shall we say.

As for Magda, I suppose she's pretty, but in a mundane, undistinguished sort of way. I can see why she would be envious of Anna's strikingly good looks, what with her flaming hair and dark, gorgeous eyes. Magda, on the other hand, has a face that's easy to forget. I don't know... her lips are too thin, her hair is bleached light without looking properly blonde, and her nose is too pointy. In addition to her non-descript appearance, that woman is a bitch as far as I'm concerned. Sorry to use this word, but that's what she is!

Ted's father, Ian, is not bad looking and he's in quite good form, especially for his age. However, he had a permanent scowl on his face and behaved as though he would rather be anyplace else other than at his son's birthday party. He frequently glared at Anna and basically ignored the rest of us. He wouldn't touch any of the food; he just drank non-stop. Not the best dinner companion and I wouldn't wish such a father-in-law on my worst enemy. And Gosya, his live-in girlfriend, is Aleksander's Lisa incarnate. That should give you a pretty good picture. Just imagine Lisa fully made-up and in her fifties. As far as personality is concerned, however, Lisa is a sweetheart compared to this Gosya woman. What a name!

I came to the party with Joseph, Shimon, Leah and Orit (her hubby stayed home with the children). Now that you know the entire cast of characters, let's start from the beginning of the dinner.

Magda's husband, as I mentioned, was eating and drinking as if there was no tomorrow. Ted's father was glaring at Anna. Magda and Gosya sat together and were picking away at the food, while exchanging meaningful glances, giggling from time to time, and frequently whispering confidences to one-another. Stan was observing everything that was going on around the table with an air of detachment and as I was saying, apparent amusement. Ted was constantly casting reproachful glares in the direction of his sister and at Gosya, as though he was ready to strangle the both of them. Through it all Anna was as nervous as hell, as you might imagine. I think you get the picture.

During a lull in the dinner proceedings, Anna rose and proposed a toast, wishing Ted a happy birthday and a lot of happiness and love.

If looks could smite, Anna would be dead by now. Ian slowly got up from his seat, stared angrily at Anna and in response to her toast, directed his wrath at Ted. "I wish you would come to your senses, reconcile with your wife whom you married in the church, and put a stop to all this nonsense. You can't continue living in sin with this slut while your wife is suffering all alone. You swore 'for better or for worse', so you damn-well ought to keep your promise!"

"You have no right to insult my niece like that!" Joseph roared, hastily jumping out of his chair to confront Ian. Miriam, just imagine – I've never seen Joseph that angry!

"I don't know what kind of family would endorse a single girl of their own kin living with a married man!" Ian growled in retort. "Only a desperate and immoral family, that's what! I suppose you must be happy to get rid of that overripe niece of yours, but don't try to push this whore onto my son. He's a Polish man from a good Catholic family and he's never going to marry this Jewess! I will not tolerate Jewish grandchildren. Never! I would rather kill him first!"

We were all totally stunned beyond words. In all my years in Canada I've never experienced such blatant anti-Semitism. To be in the company of this raging Jew-hater was truly unbelievable.

"He's insane," Joseph said, and then he said to me, "Raya, help Anna to pack her belongings. We're leaving right now and Anna is going with us."

"Anna, please wait," Ted pleaded.

"Let her go," Ian insisted. "Don't contaminate our bloodline, Ted."

"Ta-ta-ta, Yankele. If I didn't know any better, I would have thought that it was the son of pan Pilsudski speaking, not a Yankele Modzelewski, son of Avram and Rochelle!" proclaimed a woman who had made a sudden dramatic appearance in the doorway of the apartment during all this commotion.

"Hi, Aunt Dora," Ted said. There was a profound sense of relief in his voice.

"What is **she** doing here?" an agitated Ian asked.

"What do you think, Yankele? I came to wish happy birthday to my favorite nephew, of course."

"Don't you dare to call me by that name! I'm Ian Pietchakowski!"

"And I'm the Princess of Wales!" the woman shot back mockingly.

Turning to face Ted, his father then said, "I did my best to raise you as a good Catholic and to isolate you from that accursed race, but if you prefer living in sin with this Jewish woman instead of your own wife, then all my efforts have been in vain. You are being stupid, Ted - naïve and stupid. I have nothing else to say to you and what's more, I'm having nothing more to do with you. That's it; I'm leaving."

On that note, Ted's father, Gosya, Magda and her husband all made an unceremonious exit from the apartment. What's-his-name was actually quite reluctant to leave and looked back longingly at the table which was still piled high with the variety of delicious food, but Magda dragged him away.

In the meantime we were left sitting at the table like total idiots. You can just imagine the expressions of incredulity on our faces. It must have been very funny in a perverse sort of way, because as soon as the 'guests-of-honor' had disappeared out the door, Stan burst into a loud gale of laughter.

Ted of course was looking downcast after being castigated mercilessly by his father, but he forced a meek smile and said, "I'm so sorry for dad's intolerable behavior. Frankly, I'm not completely surprised; he became impossible after my mother's death. I suspect he wanted to prove something to Gosya with his 'holier-than-thou' performance. In any case, let's forget about him. This is my dear Aunt Dora from Montreal."

Miriam, I can tell you Aunt Dora didn't look as if she was from Montreal, or even originally from Poland; she looked like a typical Jewish woman, straight from the Odessa market or out of the Podol bazaar! Well, she was better dressed naturally, but otherwise… You know the type: wide hips, ample breasts, a large fleshy nose (almost as big as mine), and large full lips. I immediately took a liking to her. Maybe it was because of how she confronted her brother and put him in his place, or possibly it was because of the twinkle I could see in her eyes. She seemed like a cheerful person and I could tell that Ted and Stan both adored her. I believe that if Anna stays with Ted, then Dora, you and I could become very good friends.

I suppose you can guess at least some aspects of their story. Dora and Ian lost their parents in the war and it completely messed up their lives.

Dora told us the background about her family. Her father was a renowned doctor in Warsaw, while her mother ran a small kindergarten. They loved the mountains and spent every year vacationing in Zakopane, a Polish mountain resort town - hiking in the summer and skiing in the winter. They always stayed at the same place: a small hotel belonging to Magda and Stan Pietchakowski. The landlords and their frequent guests became close friends. Then Stan became very ill and needed surgery. The Pietchakowskis traveled to Warsaw for his operation and spent the next two months living with Dora's parents. Dora's father not only performed the surgery but also then personally supervised Stan's post-operative treatment.

During the war the Modzelewski family was herded into the Warsaw ghetto. Somehow the parents still found a way to communicate with their old friends from Zakopane. In the spring of 1942, Magda and Stan came to Warsaw and when they travelled back home, Dora and Ian accompanied them.

Miriam, I don't need to go into the details of that horrifying story. Suffice it to say that the kids had been fortuitously rescued from the ghetto. The Pietchakowskis had children of almost the same age - Bozhena and Ted, so Dora and Ian traveled using their documents.

There in Zakopane, the Modzelewski children chose different life-paths. Dora was waiting for the end of the war, hoping to reunite with her parents and to resume her life in a traditional Jewish family. Even while in hiding she tried to maintain adherence to at least some of the traditions. Magda attempted to convince her to become baptized as a Christian, but obviously that was to no avail.

Ian's life evolved in a totally opposite direction. Even before the war he liked to play with the Polish boys and wanted to fit in, to be accepted as one of them. When the war started and he saw how deeply folks around him despised the Jews, and then when he was forced to live in the ghetto, he began to hate his own people. Dora told us that he felt a deep resentment over the fact he was born a Jew. He didn't have to be convinced to undergo baptism; he actually welcomed the opportunity. He also changed his name from Yaakov to Ian.

The townspeople had not seen the Modzelewski children since 1938 and didn't even recognize Ian. He was presented as a nephew of Stan and lived throughout the occupation much like the rest of the locals, doing his best to maintain a low profile and not to be noticed by the Germans. He attended church every Sunday and helped Magda and Stan with the daily chores. In short, he survived unscathed.

Dora wasn't presented publically to the neighbors; rather, she remained safely hidden in the basement of the house belonging to Magda's mother.

In the summer of 1944, the Pietchakowski's son Ted was caught in a raid conducted by the Nazi's and was killed. He just happened to be in the wrong place at the wrong time. After that incident, Ian became much more than a foster child of Magda and Stan – for all intents and purposes he became their son.

When the war was finally over, Dora's uncle was miraculously able to locate them. He had immigrated to Canada before the war with his wife and three daughters and had established a small business in Montreal. He informed Dora and Ian that their parents had participated in the Warsaw ghetto uprising and had been killed in the spring of 1943. His intent was to take both of his sister's children with him back to Canada, but Ian refused to leave Poland.

So Dora alone accompanied her uncle. In Canada she enjoyed a good life with her uncle's family. She learned French and English while attending the high school. Then she was accepted to a community college and graduated as a paralegal secretary. Dora met her future husband in the law firm where she was working and eventually they had two children. In time she was rewarded with a grandson.

Ian's life after the war in Soviet Poland was not nearly as rosy. The little hotel became the property of the government without compensation and the family consequently suffered great financial hardship. For many years after the war, their Uncle Moshe was sending money and parcels to Poland to assist Ian and his adopted family. It was Magda senior that kept the communication going; Ian didn't bother to write to his relatives.

In 1951, Bozhena and Ian got married. For years Bozhena had been dreaming of emigrating and in 1968 it finally became possible. Dora sent them all the required documents and when they arrived she helped them to get settled. They stayed in Montreal only for a few months before moving to Toronto.

Even in Canada, Ian maintained a strictly arms-length relationship towards his sister and her family. If it had been up to him, his children wouldn't have associated with his Montreal relatives at all and wouldn't have learned anything about their ancestry either.

Nonetheless, Bozhena had quite a different attitude and the children actually did spend a lot of time with their relatives in Montreal. There came a time, however, when Magda junior stopped coming from Toronto and she disassociated herself from that side of the family.

After Bozhena's death and in particular after Ian started to date Gosya, he stopped calling his sister, ceased going to see her, and even discouraged his boys from communicating with their aunt. But Stan and Ted had an altogether different viewpoint in that regard and did their best to keep the family relationship alive.

So, my dear sister, now you know the condensed version of Ted's family history. This Dora woman, his aunt, is a powerhouse. I've never seen anyone like her! She came to Anna and took hold of her hands while looking directly into her eyes and said, "Maidele, you're the answer to my prayers. I was hoping that my brother would return to the religion of his parents; I wanted him to at least stop hating his own people. That, unfortunately, is not meant to be, but thankfully our bloodline will continue all the same. You and Ted will make

many nice Jewish kinderlech together, right? Please don't ever give up on him - he's such a good man. One day I expect to see you and Ted under the chuppah and I will dance with joy at your wedding."

Ted was trying cautiously to slow her down and to curb her unbridled enthusiasm, but Dora had already essentially planned all of Anna and Ted's life for them. Probably it's just as well that she resides in Montreal and there is some distance between Anna and her. I mean, I really do like Dora, but she can only be taken in very small doses at a time!

In any case, Anna is not moving out; she's staying with Ted and she decided to start looking for a new job. And that's all my news for today. Rather more than you might have expected, wouldn't you say?

May 25th, 1986 – Miriam responds to Raya:

That was quite the story! Let it be, sister. I talked to Anna yesterday and in spite of everything, she says that she loves Ted. Of course the entire situation of being with a married man, Connie's disease, and Ian's hostility tarnishes her happiness. It's not easy for her but she's decided to continue living with Ted in spite of it all. Perhaps it's her destiny. I don't know and who can really say?

Raya, I'm very worried about Ben. Dov came over last evening to discuss the situation with David and me. Ben has asked Dov to buy him out. He needs the money for his software business. Dov said that Ben had been neglecting the optical store for the past half-year or so, but he didn't want to make a big issue out of it. Now he has no choice but to act. Dov needs a working partner and Ben doesn't want to be involved with the store any longer. Raya, I'm afraid the money that Dov will give Ben in settlement of his share of business will be frittered away and gone in no time at all, and then what will become of him?"

The Trials And Tribulations Of Businessman Ben

ONE DAY SEVERAL months later, Miriam wrote to Raya:
You wouldn't believe it. Ben made a killing in the commodities market! He made enough money to pay off a nice chunk of his mortgage and to provide ongoing financing for the M-N-M boys' company too. Even so, we are all, especially Tova, still quite concerned about Ben's future. The commodities market is so risky; he could lose it all just as quickly.

Raya in turn wrote back to Miriam:
I had a long conversation with Ben last night. Commodities market indeed! What will he get into next? I told him quite plainly that enough is enough! Enough of his harebrained schemes and risking the family money on the market! Not to mention supporting three so-called business partners who spend all their time playing on the computer. Ben promised to look for a more secure job and not to touch the commodities market again, and to wind down his participation in the software business too. Time will tell.

Scarcely three months after Raya's conversation with Ben, he lost heavily on the commodities market. Ben and Tova had no alternative but to increase their mortgage again, as much as the bank would allow. And in spite of his promise to back out of the business partnership, Ben was still financially supporting his three friends and actively trying to market their software. There was a time when Tova would staunchly defend her husband but it was obvious that it was becoming stressful for her. As the months and years passed, she became more and more distraught over the perpetual instability in their life.

During those next several years, Ben and Tova's lives amounted to a virtual rollercoaster with even greater ups and downs, peaks and valleys. Ben again went to Taiwan, then to China, and made some money in the import-export business; he was dabbling in the market again too – sometimes winning big and other times losing big.

Ben finally succeeded in making an initial sale of the software that his friends had created, but the payback was not as great as he had been hoping for. Nevertheless, Motti and Nathan continued working on an updated, even more miraculous version of the software, and Ben remained convinced that it would lead to an Internet revolution. Meanwhile, Moshe dedicated his time to creating new computer games. Eventually, the boys split their company into two independent entities, but Ben was still marketing the products of both companies.

At long last, when Ronny was already three years old, there was a ray of hope in Ben's complicated business affairs. He sold Moshe's computer games to an international distributor and secured a provision for royalties based on the number of games sold. In addition, he negotiated an advance sales contract for future game releases with the same buyer.

Moshe by now was making decent-enough money from his share of the sale proceeds and the on-going stream of royalties, so he bought an apartment and became engaged. Ben used his share of the earnings from the computer games to once-again reduce his inflated mortgage. The share of royalties that Ben was receiving should have been sufficient to supplement Tova's salary and maintain a decent standard of living for their family, but Motti and Nathan were still struggling and since Ben was still chasing his 'big dream', he continued to divert the larger portion of his income to support their software business.

Two unrelated events then occurred at about the same time: Ben's company was invited by a large Internet provider in the United States to demonstrate their software product, while Tova learned that she was expecting their second child.

Husband and wife had a long and tense family conversation, but in the end, Tova promised to give Ben one more chance and to support him for the next six months. In return, Ben promised not to speculate any more on the market, and if the new version of software that Motti and Nathan had developed was not sold by time the new baby was born, he would find a permanent job and abandon all his business ventures.

From all indications the trip to the United States was highly successful. The American corporation indicated great interest in the latest version of their software product, and undertook to finalize a substantial financial agreement within a matter of weeks.

But day after day passed, and then one month lapsed into the next as Ben and his business associates continued waiting anxiously to receive the anticipated contract. Meanwhile, they were asked to prepare some additional documentation, to create a more robust demo version, and to respond to countless questions. They fulfilled every one of their prospective client's requests and supplied all necessary technical documentation. And yet, the contract still did not materialize and their main client contact was vague about the reasons of delay.

Late one evening when Raya was getting ready to retire for the night, she received a long distance phone call from Israel.

"Tova delivered a baby girl this morning," Miriam announced in a decidedly grim voice.

"But she was only thirty weeks pregnant!" a startled Raya exclaimed. "What happened? Are Tova and the baby okay?"

"It was more like twenty-nine weeks to be precise; and no, they are not okay." Miriam said. "Tova was alone at home when the labor unexpectedly began and just about everything that could go wrong did go wrong. The baby is tiny, even for a premature birth; she weighs less than three pounds and she's very weak. She's in an incubator and attached to a life-support system to maintain her breathing. David is there with her constantly. Raya, if the life of this baby can be saved, I promise you, David will save her.

"Tova lost a lot of blood and now she seems to have some sort of infection too. She's running a high fever. I'm calling from the hospital now. I just stepped out of her room for a few minutes so I could call you."

"Where is Ben for heaven's sake? Why was Tova left alone?" a frantic Raya inquired.

"He's in the States. He, Nathan and Motti were summoned to give an additional demo of their software. They flew three days ago but we don't even know how long they will be away. I suppose they were called on short notice; we didn't even know about it until after they were already gone. What's more, we haven't been able to make contact with Ben as yet."

"Was this trip what caused Tova to be so stressed that it triggered her premature labor?" Raya asked. When no immediate answer was forthcoming, she cried out, "Miriam, what did my good-for-nothing son do this time? Tell me everything, Miriam. I must know the entire story."

"From what I know," Miriam said, "Tova received a call yesterday from Ben's commodities broker. He was demanding additional margin funds; otherwise, he indicated he was going to be forced to close out Ben's position at a substantial loss.

"Tova knew nothing about any of this. She tried to reach Ben on the phone but he wasn't available. Finally she managed to make contact with Nathan and found out that in order to finance this unplanned trip, Ben had made a hasty deal with some loan shark. He signed over the apartment as security and in that way he obtained a sizeable loan quickly and without Tova's signature. All the extra money that Ben didn't need for this trip was invested in the market. Apparently he was told that a particular trade was 'a sure thing' and he had hoped to make enough money to repay the loan quickly without having to say anything about it to Tova.

"Raya, Tova and Ben have lost everything: all the money Ben invested in that 'sure thing' trade and now they are about to lose their apartment. When Tova learned about the deal, she called to those lenders that Ben was dealing with. They were quite an unpleasant bunch; not the kind of people you can negotiate with. Tova was advised in no uncertain terms that the money must be repaid within a month or the apartment had to be vacated.

"The probable loss of the apartment was a terrible blow to Tova, but Ben's betrayal, the fact that he was dealing behind her back, was so much worse.

"Anyway, Tova's mother is right here in the hospital. We don't want to leave Tova alone, so we're going to establish some sort of shift schedule. However, someone needs to take care of Ronny."

"Miriam, I will be in Israel tomorrow. I'll get on the first available flight," Raya assured her sister.

"I hoped that's what you'd say, but what about your work, Raya? Don't you need a few days to arrange for the time off?"

"Joseph will talk to my boss tomorrow. If everything is okay, I'll be able to work remotely, but that's the least of my worries. I'll see you tomorrow, dear sister; and Miriam, please take care of Ben's family! If something were to happen to Tova or the baby... Oh, I just don't know what I would do to that Ben! I've never been so angry with that boy in my entire life!"

"I'll see you tomorrow, Raya. I must go now," Miriam said and rang off the phone.

The next day, Raya emerged from a restricted area of Ben Gurion airport and immediately noticed her younger brother, Misha.

"How is everyone?" Raya asked while embracing him warmly.

"Touch and go, Raya," Misha replied. "David spends as much time with the baby as he possibly can. Tova's mother stayed all night at the hospital but this morning we insisted that she go home and catch at least a few hours of rest. Miriam is running back and forth between the hospital and home to be with Ronny as much as she can. Between Miriam and Lily he's being taken care of adequately, but it's so good that you're here. For now you can stay in Ben's apartment until we find out for certain what the final deadline to vacate is going to be and what's really going on."

"Let's get going, Misha. I want to be in Haifa as soon as possible," Raya said.

Misha glanced at Raya and explained, "We have to wait for the arrival of Ben's flight from New York; it should be here within half-an-hour." Misha sighed and added, "Raya, please try to keep a hold of yourself. I think life has punished the boy quite enough already."

"Ben is not a boy," Raya reacted, clenching and unclenching her fists in transparent anger. "He's a grown man and it's high time he started behaving as such."

But when Raya spotted her son amongst the arriving passengers from the New York, all the harsh words of rebuke that she had been prepared to say immediately dissipated. Ben looked terrible. There was a look of anguish mixed with hope on his face when he asked, "Are they both alive?"

"So far," Misha said crisply. "Let's go."

The drive to Haifa was interminably slow in heavy traffic. Everyone was keeping silent. Time from time Raya would stare at Ben as if she was about to say something, but when she saw how miserable he looked, she refrained from saying anything at all.

When they eventually arrived at the hospital, Misha led them to Tova's room. It was difficult to recognize that this sick woman with the flushed face was actually the beautiful Tova. Ben knelt at the side of the bed, gently took hold of her limp hand and kissed it again and again, before saying, "I'm so sorry, darling. I can't even begin to say how sorry I am. Please get well. I can't be without you. You are my whole life; you, and Ronny, and our baby. Everything else is *'babkes'* and so unimportant.

"I've been such an idiot! I wanted to give you everything and instead I took everything from you. Tova, I'm not asking you for forgiveness because I know that my guilt's beyond that. All that I'm asking right now is to please get well, my darling. Please live Tova, for yourself and for our family," Ben pleaded as he began to sob.

"Her name is Chava," Tova said in a very weak voice.

For a moment Ben didn't realize what Tova was talking about and then he said, "But I thought we wanted to name our girl Shoshanna."

"Chava means life, Ben. I want my Chava to live."

"Of course, sweetheart, of course. Chava it is."

Ben continued whispering words of endearment and apology to Tova. But Miriam and Raya didn't care to listen to that any longer. Tova was apparently still willing to listen to him and that was more than they expected, and in their opinion much more than he deserved.

The sisters stepped out of Tova's room and Miriam led the way to the nursery. When Raya saw the tiny body draped in assorted tubes and wires she began to cry. She felt an enormous wave of love, tenderness and compassion towards her tiny new granddaughter. Raya looked intently at David who was hovering over the baby's incubator and asked him from a distance the unavoidable silent question with her eyes. David could only shrug his shoulders in resignation - he had no ready answer.

For the next month Raya was kept busy taking care of her four-year-old grandson. During this time the abstract love of a long-distance grandmother had been transformed into a very real and deep bond. Little Ronny was such a delightful child: cute, curious, witty and fast... very fast. Raya had to keep an eye on him constantly and she wondered from where he was getting all his unbounded energy. She felt exhausted just watching all his jumping and running about the house.

Ben was spending all his time during the day in the hospital with Tova and only coming home in the evenings, but he always made sure to arrive before Ronny's bedtime. Only now Raya came to understand how deeply Ben really cared about his family. He was an excellent father - thoughtful, patient and loving. If only he would just straighten out his priorities once and for all! In any case, the damage from his speculations and his unrealistic business ventures was done and nothing good could be salvaged from any of that. His family was destitute.

Tova's condition gradually improved and three weeks later she was recovered sufficiently to be discharged from the hospital and brought to Miriam's house. Raya and Ronny had already moved there as well. Meanwhile, Ben was moving his family's furniture and belongings into storage. For now, they would be obliged to stay at Miriam's until he could secure some kind of employment and find a different place to live.

Perhaps it was David's skills, or Miriam's care, or the prayers of the entire family, but gradually the wires and the tubes started being removed from Chava's tiny body. When she was eight weeks old, the overjoyed and immensely relieved parents brought their baby home, or rather to her great-aunt Miriam's house.

When the tiny girl was fed and settled into her crib for the first time, the entire family gathered together around the dining room table. Only Ben was absent. He had disappeared soon after his daughter was brought from the hospital to attend to some errands.

"Where is he this time?" an irritated Raya inquired. "What kind of errands does he have to do today of all days? I hope he's not up to something again!"

"No, I don't think so," Tova volunteered plaintively. "I think he went to see his partners, basically to put them on notice that he would not be working with them any longer.

"On a different subject, Raya, I know that by now you must be anxious to get back home as soon as possible, and we appreciate more than I can say everything that you've done for us, and especially for Ronny. But can you please stay in Israel for just a couple of more days? Ben and I will go to look at some apartments. He's still getting some royalty money from Moshe's games, so that should be enough to tide us over for now. He's looking for a proper job too, so I think we ought to be able to manage the rent. I really want to live in my own place."

"Tova, that's all perfectly understandable but why do you rush?" David asked. "You and the baby have just gotten out of the hospital. You need to relax and take care of Chava. And besides, all that you would be able to rent right now is some small apartment in a poor part of town. Why don't you stay with us until Ben gets a steady job? Then you would know better what you could afford."

"David's right," Miriam chimed in, endorsing her husband's suggestion. "You're most welcome to stay with us. But for the sake of interest, in what area of the city would you be looking?"

"What's wrong with this area?" they unexpectedly heard Ben's upbeat voice as he stepped through the front door. "I would really like to live close to Aunt Miriam and Uncle David. And Tova, I'm sure that you would prefer a comfortable house with a lovely garden instead of some dinky apartment. As a matter of fact, I've heard that Mr. Pritsker's house is on the market. You must know it, Tova. It's the one with a large garden that you were admiring so much a few months ago. Would you like me to arrange a viewing for us tomorrow?"

If Ben had anticipated that Tova or his relatives would become excited or at least be intrigued by his seemingly incongruous statements, he was quite mistaken. The entire family reacted by staring at him with stony faces and expressions of dismay and disappointment.

"What have you been up to this time, Ben?" Raya asked.

"Where did you get more money to throw at the market, Ben?" David inquired.

"Ben, you promised, you promised not to speculate on the market anymore! I don't want to hear about it, even if you won big this time!" Tova exclaimed in utter exasperation.

"Relax, everyone," Ben responded in as urbane a voice as he could muster, as he ceremoniously deposited a large binder of documents on the table. "This isn't anything like what you're all thinking."

Ben sat down near his wife, embraced her gently by the shoulders and said, "We've finally sold the Internet software and it's a big-time deal!

"Here's the firm contract. I know that it was very wrong of me to risk everything but I was desperate. I had to fly to the States to finalize the deal. But when I received a phone call from Aunt Miriam, all of a sudden the contract, the software – it was not important any longer.

"I left right in the middle of the negotiation process and knowing the negotiating skills of Motti and Nathan, or should I say lack thereof, I was almost convinced that our big opportunity was going to be lost. Well, to my complete surprise I was wrong. We have an iron-clad contract and it's even better than I might have hoped for in my wildest dreams."

Ben opened the binder and pointed out some numbers. "This is the selling price for the rights to our software that is to be paid in a lump sum immediately upon delivery of the product."

Tova looked attentively at the contract and began to murmur very softly, "One, two, three..."

"What are you counting, baby?" Ben asked.

"The number of digits," she said in a hushed voice.

"Seven! There are seven whole integers in that number. The boys and I will divide it equally between us, just as we had agreed a long time ago. My share is going to go for the purchase of our dream house. You and the kids will have a comfortable place to live and a beautiful backyard garden for them to play and grow strong and healthy. You and our kids deserve it, Tova. But that isn't even the best part of the deal!"

"It isn't?" Tova asked, as she tried to wrap her mind around this astounding new reality.

"Take a look here. This is the percentage of ongoing royalties that we'll be receiving. And here," Ben paused as he slowly turned the page with a touch of dramatic effect, "here is the most wonderful part of all. Our company will be wholly-owned by Microsoft Corporation but it will still be kept intact as a separate operating entity. We're going to become the Israeli subsidiary of Microsoft, concentrating on other new software development. I will have the title of President of this subsidiary and the boys will retain their own V-P titles too.

"Microsoft wants our company to continue to grow and prosper because the better we do, the better it is for them too as our parent company.

"We have also agreed on a plan of expansion. Within a year I expect to be managing a staff of up to twenty, and in five years our company is projected to grow to between one and two hundred staff – all software developers.

"This is the annual salary I'll be receiving right away and here are the salaries for Motti and Nathan. Microsoft wants them not to have to worry about money or logistics, but instead to concentrate all their energies on creating innovative new software products. I told all of you that they are geniuses!" Ben concluded jubilantly.

Raya's mind was already racing full speed ahead. "It all sound great but you've never managed other people before, Ben! It's one thing to work on your own with a couple of partners, or to run around by yourself trying to sell something; it's quite another thing to be responsible for a large team and for the fortunes of an entire company!"

"So I'll learn! Mom, can you please be happy for me and stop worrying? I've been waiting for this day for more than six years. So now, let's celebrate!"

"Benny, we don't have to go to inspect the Pritsker's house. I've already been inside and I love it. Let's buy it, Benny," Tova said with tears of happiness streaming down her cheeks.

The evening that had started off on such a somber note concluded with multiple toasts in celebration of Ben's good fortune.

Now that her son's circumstances had taken such a spectacular turn for the better, Raya decided that she could safely return home. She felt a sudden urge to be back in Canada, to see Joseph and Shimon and Orit, and also to go for a visit to New York where Leah was attending the graduate program at Columbia University. Raya would miss her Israeli family, of course, but her place was in Canada.

She called Joseph to let him know about all the exciting new developments and to inform him that she would be coming home the following day.

Joseph responded enthusiastically. "I'm so glad for Ben and Tova. That is great news!" But Raya was quite taken aback when he went on to say, "Raya, you know I've missed you terribly; we all have. But can you put off your homecoming for just a few days? Why don't you arrange your ticket to fly in three days?"

"Joseph, I don't understand. What's going on? Why shouldn't I come home tomorrow after being away for so long already? What are you up to there?" a bewildered Raya wanted to know.

"Me? Nothing at all," Joseph said innocently. "I don't want to give away any surprises for you, Raya, so please stick around in Israel for now. I'll see you in three days," Joseph said, and then he abruptly cut off the phone connection.

"He sounded very strange," Raya announced to the entire assembly. "Very strange indeed."

"I'm not sure that I can handle any more surprises," Miriam declared, "but honestly I'm very glad that you'll still be here with us for a few more days."

"Okay, I'll call the airline tomorrow and arrange my ticket for three days from now," Raya said, still shaking her head in bemusement over Joseph's strange behavior on the phone.

The next day was extremely busy for all concerned. What with arranging for purchasing a new house, looking after Chava and Ronny, and discussing the outlook for the expansion of his company with Ben, nobody had time to contemplate any sort of apparently impending surprise. But in the late afternoon, soon after David had arrived home from his work at the hospital, the doorbell rang, and when Miriam opened the door she was greeted unexpectedly by Ted and Anna standing before her.

After the inevitable hugs and kisses had been exchanged, Miriam said, "This is a wonderful surprise and I'm so happy to see both of you. But why didn't you at least phone ahead and let us know that you would be coming?"

"Mom, Dad, and everyone," Anna announced, "Ted and I got married yesterday and we came to spend our honeymoon here in Israel."

"Congratulations," David said, somewhat dryly. "But is it not customary to notify the parents before the event, instead of springing such news on us after the deed is already done?"

"You're quite right, Dr. Kushnir, but please allow me to explain," Ted said respectfully. "Just four days ago we had no plans to get married right away. It all happened quite suddenly. You see, that's when we received an envelope in the mail from Mary, Connie's mother. When I opened it there was no letter, not even a note. Instead, what I found was a copy of Connie's death certificate and a clipping from the local newspaper announcing her death and the arrangements for her funeral. The date of the newspaper was more than a month ago."

The family looked askance at the couple. Miriam's worst fear that Anna's happiness would only materialize at the expense of another woman's life had indeed come to pass.

"My first feeling," Ted continued, "was one of anger; not grief and not even sadness, just anger. After all, I was still her husband, at least in the eyes of the law. I had continued to support Connie financially and I did everything that was requested of me. I never asked her for a divorce, in spite the fact that I knew how awkward it was for Anna to be living with a married man and understanding how much she wanted to have a normal family.

"Connie and I had our history but not all of it was bad; I tried, I really tried to be a good husband to her. I felt that it was so unfair and humiliating that I should find out about her death in such a callous way, and not even be notified of her funeral. I called Mary but she was too devastated by the death of her only daughter to have any kind of useful conversation with me. She just said that it was Connie's wish that I would not be at the funeral.

"After I finally calmed down," Ted continued, "I felt incredibly sorry for Connie and for all the suffering she'd endured. It's hard to explain but I felt guilty for not being with her at the end. Anyway, that phase of my life had clearly drawn to a close.

"The very next morning I asked Anna to marry me. She had waited all this time for me to become a free man and under the circumstances, I couldn't bear the thought of having her wait any longer. It was time to start our new life together as a true couple, so we got married yesterday at the city hall in Toronto. Stan, Joseph, Shimon, Orit and her family were the only ones present. Then we bought our tickets to fly to Israel. We already called my Aunt Dora and Leah from the airport. We weren't in the mood for a big wedding celebration; we just wanted to be married," Ted concluded.

"But…" David started to speak up.

"Oh, let it be," his wife interrupted him. Then Miriam came forward and kissed her daughter and her new son-in-law.

"Ted," she said, "I really do sympathize and I understand the very mixed feelings you've experienced, but now my Anna deserves some sort of proper wedding, over and above that civil ceremony."

Then Miriam turned towards Raya and said, "Now I understand how Mama Vera must have felt when you announced your marriage to Maxim."

"You have me here to help you. We'll have a nice family dinner tomorrow," Raya enthused. "But when I get home I'll be giving Joseph a piece of my mind! How could he attend the wedding ceremony and not even tell me anything about it? Surprise, indeed!"

Two days later, Ted and Anna departed for their honeymoon in Eilat, while Raya said goodbye to her Israeli family and flew back to Canada. David and Miriam had gone to the airport with her and as always when the sisters were separating, there were abundant tears.

"Stop crying," Miriam was saying. "Think about how everything has turned out so well. Tova and Chava are alive and healthy and Ben is a big businessman now so you have to be happy."

"I am happy," Raya asserted. "I'm very happy, but I still hate saying goodbye to you guys. And why are *you* crying, Miriam? Anna is finally properly married and you were so needlessly worried about her! You must be very happy for her now."

David stood by and refrained from saying anything during this parting exchange; he was accustomed to these emotional goodbyes. He was just sorry that his beloved sister was living so far away.

Leah's Marriage

SIX MONTHS PASSED following Raya's trip to Israel and then the sisters reunited again, this time in Toronto. Shimon was celebrating his bar-mitzvah and quite a number of relatives and friends flew from Israel to be with Joseph and Raya on that special day.

Shimon was a skinny lad and rather short for his age, but his oversize feet and long arms gave Raya hope that one day he would grow taller to reconcile with the size of his limbs. His red hair and freckles reminded her of Ben, but his personality couldn't have been more different. He was a thoughtful, serious and compassionate boy, and already single-mindedly determined to become a doctor, following in the tradition of his father and his uncle David.

On the day of Shimon's bar-mitzvah, Raya took a seat in the women's section of the synagogue, surrounded by her relatives and feeling immensely happy and proud. Her Shimon had done a fine job reading publically from the Torah for the first time! Indeed, her youngest son was a boy that any mother could be proud of. Raya looked down at the bimah (a small stage from which the Torah scrolls are read) where Joseph, David, Misha, Ben, Aryeh, and Jonathan were all standing congregated around Shimon. She squeezed Miriam's hand and whispered, "I'm so blessed to have such a wonderful family!"

Then Raya cast her eyes on Leah, who was seated nearby and balancing Orit's new baby boy on her lap.

"Miriam, what should I do about Leah? She's almost twenty-eight and still not even dating! Is she destined to remain a spinster aunt and never to be a mother?"

"Raya, you can't be serious! Leah is gorgeous! What do you mean she's not even dating?" Miriam inquired.

Orit, who had overheard the sisters whispering, interjected, "Auntie Miriam, Bais Yaakov girls don't date casually. They're introduced to proper Jewish boys and then they get married."

"So then why isn't Leah being introduced to anybody?" Miriam pursued the issue.

"After her experience in Israel, Leah wasn't interested in meeting anybody for a long time, and meanwhile all of the eligible boys were already spoken-for. Mama Raya, don't worry about it! As soon as Leah gets her PhD and moves back to Toronto, we'll find a good husband for her. I promise you that in a year or so our dear Leah will be happily married."

Orit's promise actually came to pass and not the least due to her own pro-active intervention.

When it had come time for Leah to defend her dissertation, Raya, Joseph and Shimon drove to New York. Leah's presentation to the university panel was scholarly and highly successful. Her dream had been realized at long last - she had earned a PhD degree in Psychology.

After the presentation, quite a number of attendees came forward to congratulate Leah. Her family stood aside, wishing to be as unobtrusive as possible. When the crowd thinned somewhat, a tall young man stepped forward to introduce himself.

"Congratulations, Dr. Sokolov. I'm very much interested in your work. I received my own PhD just six months ago and it seems that our areas of research are quite complementary. I would welcome the opportunity to discuss some of my own observations and findings with you, that is if you would be interested in arranging to meet."

The young man then extended his arm with the intention of shaking Leah's hand and graciously introduced himself, "Dr. Daniel Meyer."

Leah's heart skipped a beat when she looked closely at this dark-haired, Jewish man who was wearing a tell-tale kippah. She casually glanced at his left hand - no ring! But instead of offering her hand to reciprocate Dr. Meyer's greeting, Leah demurely placed her hands behind her back and said, "They taught us in Bais Yaakov School that it's inappropriate for a Jewish man to exchange handshakes with woman who is a stranger."

Dan's arm promptly dropped to his side and he stuttered in response, "I'm sorry... I didn't realize that...but I still hope you wouldn't mind discussing your research work with me. We could meet in the university library, if that would be convenient for you."

By now Dan was acutely scrutinizing this gorgeous, tall and slim, blue-eyed blonde. He took note of the apparel she was wearing and realized that what he had initially perceived to be an elegant though conservative dress was in fact an outfit entirely suitable for an Orthodox girl: high collar, long sleeves, and an ankle-length skirt of muted colors. His next subtle glance was at Leah's left hand – no ring!

Raya had been observing the scene as it unfolded and decided that it was an opportune moment for her to casually interject herself and her family into the conversation.

"Hi, Leah. Mazel Tov!"

"Oh, there you are, Mama."

"Dr. Meyer, this is my mom, Dr. Raya Kushnir, and my stepfather, Dr. Feldman; and this little brat is my baby brother, Shimon."

"Hey, I'm not so little," Shimon protested mildly. "I already had my bar-mitzvah!"

"How do you do, Reb Shimon," Dan said warmly, but with deliberate seriousness. The phrasing of Leah's introductions had conveyed quite a bit about her background and her upbringing.

"Nice to meet you sir, but I'm doing tired and hungry!" Shimon said in reply. "If I had known that my sister's presentation was going to be so long and boring I'd have stayed at the hotel."

"Anyway, congrats, sis. Can we go to get something to eat now?"

"I know a small and very nice kosher restaurant not far from here," Dan volunteered. May I invite you all to lunch?" he asked.

"Thank you, Dan, that's very kind of you," Leah promptly agreed. "I'm in the mood for some good, greasy, homemade food, now that my presentation is over and done with."

During their lunch, Dan posed the question, "Is everyone in your family a doctor?

"Not everybody, but I'm going to be a doctor for sure," Shimon piped up.

"My mother is a biochemist and my step-father is a medical doctor. My Uncle David is an MD too," Leah added.

"What about your family, Dan?" Joseph asked. "Are you the only proud holder of a PhD degree or are you following in the footsteps of others before you?"

"Well, as a matter of fact my father also has a PhD degree, but he's a Rabbi. My grandfather and his father were Rabbis too. My brothers are all Rabbis and my only sister is married to one as well. It definitely runs in the family."

"So why, if I may ask, didn't you carry on the family tradition?" Raya inquired.

"Actually, that was the plan, but then I decided that it wasn't for me, even though it cost me my engagement," Dan explained with a slight shrug of his shoulders. "My former fiancée was determined to become a Rebbetzin, no matter what."

"I'm so sorry," Leah commented, although she didn't feel the least bit sorry about that.

"Thank you, Leah, but in any event that was a long time ago. She's married to a Rabbi now anyway and has two children," Dan replied.

That evening Leah called Orit. "I'm in trouble! Another Rebbetzin! His mother will take one look at me and that will be the end of it!"

"Leah, did you say his name was Dan Meyer? Do you know his sister's name by any chance?" Orit asked.

"Yes, he mentioned it - Deborah. I think that was it."

"Leah, in that case you know her!" Orit exclaimed.

"I do?" It was Leah's turn to be surprised.

"Don't you remember Deborah Meyer from our class in the seminary? She was always bragging about her brothers. She and I got to know each other quite well so let me give her a call."

"Okay, if you'd like to, but please be careful about what you say. Dan and I only met today. Besides, he isn't particularly interested in me as far as I can tell, just my PhD work," Leah cautioned, before adding, "but I do like him, Orit. I *really* like him."

Two weeks later, Leah was invited for an upcoming Shabbat dinner at the Meyer's residence. As soon as Orit caught wind of that news, she promptly made arrangements to fly to New York to join her old friend Deborah for that occasion.

The dinner was extremely tense for Leah. She was wary of making a bad impression and hesitant to say a word that might somehow be interpreted in the wrong way. She was acutely aware of her *non-Jewish* appearance and the reserved scrutiny of Dan's family during the dinner.

After the Shabbat meal, Orit, Deborah and Dan's mother took their leave from the dining room. Leah remained at the table and had a pleasant, engaging chat with the Rabbi until she eventually excused herself and went to seek out the other ladies. As she approached the kitchen, Leah could hear the discussion that was underway.

"I like Leah very much; she looks like such a nice girl. My son told me about her family and her background. I can tell you quite confidently that he likes her very much. In fact, he's been talking about her virtually non-stop for the past two weeks. I want Dan to get married, of course, and I certainly think that he and Leah would make a very fine couple. The only drawback, as far as I can tell, is that the entire congregation will be thinking that their Rabbi's son has married out of the faith."

"Oh come on, Mom, don't be so narrow-minded. You won't find a more devoted Jewish girl than our Leah," Deborah gently admonished her mother.

"What's the big deal?" Orit asked offhandedly. "After the wedding she'll be wearing a wig anyway. She'll buy a suitable dark wig and that'll be the end of the story. No problem."

"True. Deborah and Orit: you two are in charge of shopping for Leah's wig. Make it medium-brown so as not to contrast too much with her eyes," Dan's mother instructed.

They're already talking about wigs, Leah mused hopefully as she made her delayed entrance into the kitchen, smiling sweetly.

Half-a-year later, Dan and Leah were married in New York City. The entire congregation turned out to see the wedding of the youngest son of their Rabbi. There were numerous guests from Toronto and more than twenty people made the trek from Israel. There was just one unfortunate upset for the bride – for unexplained reasons, her father wasn't able to make it to the ceremony.

The following weekend Raya hosted a luncheon at her house for her Israeli guests and those of their Toronto-based friends and relatives who couldn't be in New York for the wedding event.

Ben had spoken in advance of the occasion with his father on the phone. "Dad, please don't do this to Leah. I know that you may not feel like coming to mom's house and meeting her new husband, but Leah's really anxious to see you. She was very disappointed you didn't make it to the wedding. And you should finally meet your new son-in-law and his parents too. I promise you that mom will not bite Natasha or your girls! No excuses, Dad. We'll be waiting for you."

And so, that weekend Maxim found himself driving toward Raya's house. He struggled with mixed feelings of anticipation and trepidation. His daughters, Katie and Christina, were playing video games in the back seat while he was carrying on a quiet conversation with Natasha.

"Maxim, relax," his wife was urging him.

"I'm perfectly relaxed," he responded, albeit without much conviction.

"No, you're not. I've never seen you quite so uptight. Is it because of me? Maybe I shouldn't be going; I could've stayed at home," Natasha fretted.

"Natasha, you were invited, so don't give it another thought. Besides, this is not about you, it's about me. I haven't seen Raya for fifteen years, give or take. I'm just curious about how she looks now, that's all."

Maxim fell silent for a short while as he continued driving and then he picked up the conversation again. "It's not only that, Natasha. Do you remember when we first met and I told you that I was extremely angry at my wife and that I hated her?"

"Maxim, you can't continue to be angry at somebody for fifteen years, even if it's your ex-wife. Life goes on," Natasha responded.

"I'm not angry anymore. At that time I was angry because I felt that she had manipulated me into emigrating when I really didn't want to do that. My anger, if you can call it that, dissipated a long time ago.

In a way, actually, I'm grateful to Raya for bringing me to Canada because I met you here, darling," Maxim said as he fondly smiled and reached across the seat to gently squeeze the hand of his wife.

"Now I'm blessed with my beautiful girls and I have a lot of good friends, a nice house and a good business. And best of all I have you, sweetheart. I'm such a lucky man. Canada has been kind to me."

"Okay, Maxim, that's all well and good, so why are you even bringing up the subject of that feeling of anger that you yourself admit passed such a long time ago?" a puzzled Natasha asked.

"Well, it's hard to explain, but I'll try. It took me many years to sort it out in my own mind but I finally understood why I was so angry with Raya in those days. I hated not fitting in, pure and simple. I never did fit in with her friends, with her co-workers, with her relatives, or even with my own children. I always felt out of place, you know, like the village idiot who always says something inappropriate at the wrong time," Maxim explained.

"Maxim, just stop it! You're a wonderful man and you don't have to put yourself down like that," Natasha gently admonished him.

"You're right, dear, I don't, and that's actually the point. Now I'm surrounded by family and friends who love me, respect me, and share my interests. Maybe my interests and hobbies are primitive and simple, but I do enjoy them.

"Perhaps now you can understand a bit better why, even after all the time that's passed, I still don't relish the idea of going to Raya's place. I know that we won't fit in and we'll be made to feel like outcasts, at least in some subtle way. I can't explain what it is, Natasha, whether it has to do with education, nationality, religion or social standing – I just don't know. I can't put my finger on it. But I can just visualize people whispering behind my back, *is that Leah's father?*

"Everybody will be smiling politely, even Raya's snobbish brother, but nobody will really care whether we're there or not," Maxim said with bitter resignation.

"Maxim, you seem to be forgetting that Borya and Lena will care," Natasha assured him.

"Do you remember when Borya and Tova came to visit us three years ago? I couldn't even talk to my own daughter-in-law then! I didn't know any Hebrew and she didn't know much English or Russian," Maxim grumbled.

"Natasha, don't get me wrong. I love Borya and Lena. I love them very dearly. It's Ben and Leah whom I have a problem with," he said wryly.

"Wow!" Katie suddenly exclaimed from the back seat. "Look at these giant houses! They're all mansions! Does Lena live near here?"

"These houses are so much bigger and look much more luxurious than ours," Christina agreed.

"Just be happy that you don't have to help clean a house like this. You have enough trouble keeping your own room neat," Natasha admonished. Then she turned to Maxim and asked, "What's the name of their street?"

"It's called Arnold Street and we're already here," Maxim said, parking his car near the street number of Raya's house.

A skinny, red-headed boy in glasses opened the front door.

"May I help you?" he asked politely.

"I'm Lena's father," Maxim said in a relatively composed voice.

"Lena?" the boy asked in a mildly surprised voice. "Ah, you mean Leah."

"Leah!" the boy exclaimed. "Your dad's here!" Then he smiled and said, "Please come on in."

Leah and Ben were already rushing to the door to greet Maxim and his family. Leah kissed and hugged her father and her sisters, offered a peck on the cheek to Natasha, and then commanded, "Shimon, you're responsible to make these two girls welcome guests in our house. Please, take them to meet the other kids."

Ben was already leading Maxim and Natasha towards the living room, where Maxim observed a number of familiar faces: David, Miriam, Misha, Lily, and even the JIAS worker, Inna. It seemed everybody whom he had known in years past was gathered there. And then he spotted her – his first love, his Raya, and Maxim felt his heart beating faster.

Raya has aged considerably. She had never really looked younger than her age but now she looks old enough to be my Natasha's mother, Maxim thought to himself.

Even so, the class, the elegance, and the poise were still very much in evidence. In a more mature way, Raya looked as regal and exotic as she did when they met for the very first time.

"Maxim, I'm so glad that you could come," Raya cheerfully greeted him. "It means so much to Leah and Dan. My G-d, how many years has it been since I've seen you? Fifteen, I think. You look wonderful, Maxim, and much younger than your age, I might add."

"Thank you, Raya. You're looking very well too," Maxim responded, politely bowing his head in acknowledgement.

"You're a liar!" Raya chuckled. "Let's go. I'd like to introduce you to Leah's husband and the in-laws."

After making suitable introductions, Raya invited Natasha to accompany her, leaving Maxim alone with the Rabbi and his wife. Maxim suddenly felt an acute sense of unease. He managed to excuse himself as soon as it was politely feasible and wandered off.

Maxim found Natasha on the patio in the backyard, busily chatting with Leah and Dan. He paused near the sliding door to observe the beautiful landscaping. At the far end of the yard there was a gazebo adorned with flowering vines, and the nearby rose garden exhibited an array of flowers of various shades in full bloom. The in-ground swimming pool was gleaming with its bright blue water in the center of the yard and the surrounding grass-covered area was as neatly groomed as could be found on the green of a golf course. There were a number of trees and ornamental bushes lining the privacy fence along both sides of the property. The backyard landscaping looked absolutely pristine in every respect.

"Do you like my backyard?" Maxim heard Raya calling out to him.

"Wow! We have a much smaller yard and it still takes time for us to maintain it properly. How do you find the time to take such good care of this amazing backyard, Raya?" Maxim asked.

"I don't, actually. We hired a landscape architect to design the yard when we bought this house. Now we have a part-time gardener to maintain it," Raya explained.

"I might have guessed. Still don't like those outdoor activities, eh?" Maxim half-asked with a touch of friendly sarcasm.

"Still don't have time for that kind of thing. I'm as busy as ever with my work and my family," Raya replied.

"Raya," Maxim smiled, "when will you learn to relax a little bit? Do you take time to watch some TV at least?"

"I never liked television; you should know that. So where do you and your family live now, Maxim?" Raya asked, looking to change the subject.

"We're living in Bob Smythe's old house. He retired four years ago and I bought his business and his house at the same time. By the way, he was more than a little upset with me when he learned that we had separated. I was afraid that he might even fire me at the time."

"Well, I'm certainly glad that he didn't do that."

"Raya, are you still angry with me?" Maxim suddenly asked out of the blue.

Raya had to gather her thoughts for a few moments before responding to this wholly unexpected question. "For leaving me... not at all, Maxim. After you left, I was actually more upset with myself than with you. But truthfully, I *am* angry to this day that you've completely detached yourself from the lives of Ben and Leah. You have a great new family and I congratulate you for that, but Ben and Leah are still your children too, Maxim."

"Raya, I hear you but please let me say something. I just hope you will not think of me as an anti-Semite."

"There was a time when you did a pretty good imitation of one," Raya replied with a thin smile.

"Raya, please, you should know better than that. I'm not an anti-Semite and I never was. I have absolutely nothing against Jews. I just didn't want to become one myself," Maxim protested.

"And you didn't want your children to be Jews either," Raya reminded him.

"I was afraid that putting emphasis on their Jewish roots would divide us, that's all. In a way, I was right, wasn't I? I'm not close to Lena and Borya, and that truly saddens me, but I don't think it's entirely my fault," he retorted defensively, in as calm a voice as he could manage.

Raya let Maxim's comment ride, wisely choosing not to create any unwanted tension.

At that moment a young man ventured into the room looking for Raya. "Professor Kushnir," he asked, "do we have more wine?"

"Yes, of course we do. Just look for Shimon; he knows where we keep it," Raya replied offhandedly.

"Professor?" Maxim inquired, after the young man had left.

"I've started teaching at the university recently. I've been offered a long-term tenure and I'm seriously considering it. I like to teach and I especially like the research that they're doing in the university. That nice young man just happens to be one of the students in my class," she explained.

"It sounds great, and I imagine it would be much more to your liking than a full-time job in some commercial firm," Maxim commented.

"You're right about that, but I'm still doing some independent consulting work as well, and I'm not planning to give it up entirely."

"Raya, you will never learn to slow down!"

"I like to be busy," Raya replied.

Looking Maxim straight in the eye and as gently as she could, Raya said, "Maxim, it took me time to understand one simple fact: your children will always need you, no matter how old they are. It doesn't matter where they live, or what languages they speak. They still need you... and that applies equally to both of us."

"Raya, why would a Doctor of Psychology need a simple furniture maker?"

"Because he's her father and because he's a good and caring man. Your children love you, Maxim."

"Thank you, Raya. I appreciate and I'll remember what you've said." Maxim then cautiously asked, "No hard feelings, Raya?"

"No hard feelings, Maxim."

When Maxim was driving home, Natasha commented, "Raya's quite different from what I expected. She seems rather intimidating, somewhat like a stern school teacher."

"She's teaching at the university. You know, Natasha, its only today that I fully realized how wrong Raya and I actually were for each other. I would have always held her back and she would have always been pushing me. I'm such a lucky man to have met you, my love. You're so perfect for me in every way," Maxim gushed and blew a kiss to his wife. Natasha just smiled contentedly.

Maxim remained silent throughout the rest of the drive home. He was engrossed in thinking about Raya's words of advice about his relationship with his grown-up children and about his role in their lives. Did he still have one?

After all the party guests had departed and Raya and Joseph were finally alone, she commented, "Maxim did make one correct observation: I don't know how to relax. I honestly don't even remember when I last sat down to watch a program on the television."

"Raya, you don't care for TV, so that wouldn't relax you anyway, but I quite agree that Maxim has a good point," Joseph replied. "You should start going to the fitness club and we should be taking some long walks together in the fresh air. You spend far too much time near that computer of yours! I do worry about you, Raya, and especially about your blood pressure. You have to take better care of yourself."

"You're absolutely right, Joseph. I'm going to try to start doing some regular exercises," Raya promised. She discreetly observed herself in the mirror. *Gosh,* she thought, *I look pathetic! Worn out and overweight! I really must find time to start going to the gym.*

Joseph came close to Raya, hugged her and whispered in her ear, "I want you to be healthy for our retirement, darling. I want us to spend many more years together, and not to be worrying about patients or conferences. Just the two of us, Raya – just you and me."

"Let's make it the four of us," Raya slightly corrected. "I hope that David and Miriam will always be a part of our retirement years too. But we can't even think about retirement until Shimon finishes university and that day is still quite a way off in the future," Raya contemplated with a touch of resignation.

ℱinaℓ ℛeunion

THE SIXTY-FIFTH BIRTHDAYS of both sisters were looming way too fast for their own liking. In Raya's case it seemed that Leah's wedding and her acceptance of tenure at the university were events that had occurred scarcely yesterday, yet now she was almost ready for retirement.

The watchword was *almost* because there was a big family reunion and birthday celebration planned in Israel that still had to be organized. After the celebration, Joseph and Raya were intending to move to Israel permanently for their retirement. Their house in Toronto was already on the market. David and Miriam had started to e-mail them information about the available condos and villas in the popular resort towns near the Mediterranean Sea.

The idea of a full-scale family reunion originated when Ben decided to celebrate his fortieth birthday in style. Then the family members started to talk about Shimon's upcoming twenty-fifth birthday and the fact that while he had gotten married the previous year, many of his kin still hadn't met his wife. And then there was the consideration that Aryeh's wife had just had a new baby girl, but the Canadian contingent of the family hadn't had an opportunity to see her yet. Last but not least was the fact that the sisters were both turning sixty-five in that same year.

The family consensus was to schedule the celebration on the last weekend of June. The school year would be over and the children would be able to travel. In addition, June was the month when Raya, Ben and Leah were all born. Everyone was making their vacation arrangements at his or her job. They all wanted to be present for the grand event.

Joseph and Raya were put in charge of co-ordinating the purchase of all the necessary airline tickets and were busy trying to determine the exact number of required seats.

"Orit – seven tickets," Joseph was noting down.

"Does she have to take all five of the kids with her?" Raya asked.

"The Israeli grandparents want to see the children. Now then, Meyers – five tickets," Joseph resumed his count.

"Four. You don't need a separate ticket for the baby. Leah was originally thinking to leave the baby in New York, but the Rabbi and Rebbetzin, along with Deborah and her family are all going too. Oh yes, and Anna also needs four tickets."

"That's fine, Raya. I still have to find out if Rita's boys will be going, and if so, how many tickets they would need. They'll likely want at least eight to ten tickets."

"Vladimir – six. Nadia – just two. I don't think her children are going," Raya was saying.

"Maybe we should just charter the entire airplane!" Joseph muttered in exasperation.

"Let's not grumble, Joseph. Just think about all the things that Miriam and David are taking care of! They have to book the hotels, organize the transportation, and decorate the banquet hall, not to mention arranging the catering, and the music and everything else," Raya reminded him.

"But we're staying with the Kushnirs, right?" Joseph wanted to be sure.

"Of course, like always, dear," Raya assured him.

Before long, the big day had arrived and the horde of Canadian family members descended on Israel.

There was the predictable chaos at the airport in Tel Aviv. After all the other newly-arrived guests had been organized and were being driven off to their pre-arranged accommodations, the sisters settled into the back seat of a car being driven by David and which was headed for Haifa.

"I'm sorry to tell you this but you could easily lose twenty pounds," Miriam said rather critically, casting a disapproving glance at Raya. "Actually, at least thirty pounds would be more like it."

"I know that, Miriam!" Raya cheerfully acknowledged. "I've tried dozens of diets and yet somehow I always end up on this side of 'massive'. But now I'm in your hands and I promise to eat and drink only what you recommend to me, Madame Nurse."

"Okay, good. We'll get started with your new diet right after the party," Miriam asserted with a chuckle.

"Hey, sister, quite frankly you aren't looking so great yourself," Raya commented. "Is there anything wrong, Miriam? You look pale and... I don't know, somehow you don't look very healthy."

"Just tired, I suppose. You can't imagine how trying this reunion has been for me. Hundreds of details to consider; all those preparations have left me exhausted. Everyone was trying to help, but still it was just too much and I'm simply worn out. I suppose it's a terrible thing to say but I can't wait until the party is over and done with."

"Even so, I want Joseph to have a look at you," Raya said, looking askance at her sister.

"Okay, but after the reunion. For now, let's just enjoy ourselves," Miriam replied.

The party was a fantastic success. Miriam's hard work paid off and Ben didn't spare any expense. The children made a small concert as was customary back in the Ukraine and apparently the tradition still lived on among the immigrant families. Ronny played on a guitar and eleven-year-old Chava was singing beautifully. She had already grown to look just as lovely as her mother, even at that tender age.

Tova had changed noticeably. She looked confident and relaxed; her new-found wealth definitely agreed with her. Dazzling diamond earrings with a matching necklace adorned her gorgeous and seemingly ageless face. For his part, Ben was looking like a sophisticated business executive in his elegant, tailor-made suit.

Miriam had arranged for a six-piece orchestra. A variety of Hebrew songs were inter-woven with Russian, English, Yiddish, and even Italian popular songs. Raya and Miriam couldn't stay of the dance floor. The celebration lasted 'till the wee hours of the morning.

When Raya awoke the next morning, she felt light-headed and her mouth was dry, so she made her way to the kitchen for a glass of cold water.

Miriam was already there, drinking freshly-brewed coffee. She looked at her sister and said, "Raya, you look like something the cat dragged in."

"Have you seen yourself in the mirror this morning?" Raya retorted mildly.

"Yeah, I know. We ate too much, drank too much, and danced way too much. I think we're getting too old for these parties," Miriam sighed.

"Speak for yourself," Raya said bravely, but she sat down heavily at the table and rested her head on her hands.

"Let's go for a walk while everyone else is still asleep. Just the two of us," Miriam suggested.

"I'd love to. I really need some fresh air," Raya agreed.

The sisters strolled slowly through the streets of Haifa, chatting about the children and the grandchildren, and about Raya's impending move to Israel.

Suddenly, Raya felt that the morning sun had become too hot and oppressive. A sharp stabbing pain started in the area of her heart and was rapidly spreading through her entire chest and back. She stopped walking and began to gasp for air. In complete distress, Raya forgot how she had addressed her sister for the past twenty-seven years and in primal fear she whispered, "Manya, Manechka, help me." Then she collapsed on the sidewalk.

Miriam immediately dropped to her knees and supporting her sister's head in her lap, she screamed in anguish, "Raaaaya!"

She yelled to the several passers-by in the street, "Somebody, please call an ambulance!"

Miriam, with the experienced hands of a nurse, started to minister to Raya, doing everything possible to ease her pain and distress. It was only after the ambulance arrived and the paramedics took charge of Raya that Miriam called home in anguish.

David and Joseph rushed to the hospital as quickly as was humanly possible, but by the time they arrived, Raya was already gone. She was pronounced dead upon arrival at the hospital due to a massive heart attack.

Joseph looked blankly at David and Miriam with uncomprehending eyes - how could this tragedy have happened? He had grieved terribly when Nelya died, but at least he had had time to prepare himself for her passing and the opportunity to say a final goodbye to her. The shocking and sudden death of his beloved Raya, his soul-mate, wrought grief beyond description.

The family that had arrived in Israel to celebrate life stayed in Israel to mourn Raya's passing.

The immediate relatives were still sitting *shiva* (the seven days of Jewish mourning) when one day Miriam suddenly fainted and was rushed to the hospital.

Now it was David's time to look with eyes filled with a mixture of torment and hope at the doctors when they informed him of Miriam's shocking diagnosis – inoperable pancreatic cancer.

For the next three weeks, David, Joseph, and their children kept a constant vigil at Miriam's hospital bedside. Everything known to modern medicine was done, but the cancer had spread like wildfire throughout her body.

Less than a month after Raya's funeral, the family gathered together at the Haifa cemetery yet-again, this time to bid farewell to Miriam. Her dear sister Raya's final resting place was right next to the freshly-dug grave.

The casket was lowered into the ground and everyone gently tossed a handful of dirt onto it, according to custom. After the crying had subsided, Aryeh gently touched his father's shoulder. It was time to go.

But David remained transfixed near the side-by-side graves of his wife and his sister. Suddenly, and with surprising passion, he spoke out.

"I knew that it was going to happen. On the day that Raya passed away, I just knew that Manya was soon going to follow after her. Because on that day, almost sixty years ago, when they joined hands and ran for safety from Babi Yar, they not only joined hands, they joined their lives."

David paused, seemingly to reflect for a moment, and then he continued. "Nothing could ever separate them; not Manya's anti-Semitic father, and not Raya's indifferent husband who could never understand the significance of that bond between them. And not I, the stubborn fool who dragged Manya away, and not even the ocean that sometimes kept them far apart! They were always destined to be a part of each other's lives."

David swayed unsteadily for a second, and then straightened himself. "But you won, sisters! Do you hear me, sisters? You won! When you had the presence of mind and courage to crawl from that wretched pit, from that unspeakable hell, you crawled away from certain death to the dawn of a renewed life! Your enemies sought to kill you but they failed. You won sixty years of life. And what a glorious life you both had. You dreamed and your dreams came true; you fought and you prevailed! You won, my beloved sisters."

David fell silent again for a brief moment and then concluded his heart-felt soliloquy. "There's a saying in the Talmud: *And whoever saves a life, it is considered as if he saved an entire world.* On that day, when your Uncle Misha saved two naked and frightened girls, he saved a world. We are your world, dear ones. Your children and grandchildren, your entire family. All the books that you wrote and all the discoveries that you made, Raya; all the people that you nursed back to health with your gentle hands, Manya. All those who in some way were touched by you are part of your universe too, my beloved sisters. You won!"

David was overwhelmed by his sobbing and could speak no more. Joseph approached and gently touched his arm. Then the two widowers, with their heads bowed in sorrow, walked ever so slowly together towards the cemetery gate. Their families followed in a solemn procession after them.

And the sisters remained lying close beside one-another in the Haifa Cemetery under the blazing hot sun – as much together in death as they had been in life.